DATE DUE

NOV 4 '70			

GAYLORD   PRINTED IN U.S.A.

The
Novel in Letters

Epistolary Fiction in the Early English Novel
1678 - 1740

Edited with an introduction and notes by
NATASCHA WÜRZBACH

UNIVERSITY OF MIAMI PRESS

Coral Gables Florida

First published in 1969
by Routledge and Kegan Paul Ltd
Broadway House, 68–74 Carter Lane
London, E.C.4
Printed in Great Britain
© Routledge and Kegan Paul Ltd, 1969
Library of Congress Catalog Card Number 70-81618
SBN 87024-116-8

To Y.M. and E.W.

Preface

The English novel is usually said to begin with Defoe, although Aphra Behn's *Oroonoko* (1688), or Congreve's *Incognita* (1692) or even Sidney's *Arcadia* (1590) and Nashe's *Unfortunate Traveller* (1594) might also be called novels. Yet a vast gap remains between the Elizabethan narrative – hardly what we would call a "novel" – and the appearance of Defoe. In the span of a hundred years an enormous bulk of light reading was produced and consumed – most of it second and third rate – the very existence of which is often overlooked. Not only can this material tell us a great deal about the development of the novel, but it provides an insight into the seventeenth and early eighteenth centuries by revealing something about contemporary tastes in entertainment and morality. The epistolary tale played an important part in the development of the novel, especially of the psychological narrative. From the great number of epistolary novels and short stories now in the British Museum Library I have chosen a few which I felt are still worth reading and should be brought to light again.

I have printed the texts without alteration except for correcting obvious misprints in the original (emendations which are listed in Corrections to the Text at the end of the volume) and normalising the long "s". There were no hard and fast rules concerning orthography in the seventeenth and early eighteenth centuries, merely tendencies – so that capitalizing, for example, often (but not always) indicates the importance of a word. Names were frequently italicized, functioning as landmarks in the text. On the whole, I feel that with the old spelling something of the flavour of the original is preserved.

My thanks are especially due to Professor Fritz Wölcken for his advice and assistance in my research. Mrs Evelyn Samuel has been of great help to me in copying the texts from the originals in the British Museum. I am most grateful to Mrs Jean Bonheim and Mr John F. Davis for their patient help in revising the English text of the introduction.

NATASCHA WÜRZBACH
University of Munich

Contents

Introduction

For the reader interested in the history of literature, tracing the rise of a new literary genre is a fascinating experience. Much has been said about the development of the novel in the eighteenth century as it takes shape in the works of Defoe, Richardson, Fielding, Sterne, and Smollett. Less attention has been paid to minor fiction, written either during the lifetime of these authors or before. Yet the major novels do not simply appear out of the blue; their way has been prepared for to some extent by smaller writers and hacks who tried out this or that technique, perhaps to make their book more successful, or just for the fun of it – certainly not with the conscious craftsmanship of a Fielding or a Sterne. In fact, many of the minor narrative writers of the late seventeenth and early eighteenth centuries indulged in experiments from which, at a later date, the writer of genius was able to extract hints and suggestions which he then made use of in his own novels. The earlier, minor works, though they went through several editions in their own time, are now largely forgotten, even by students of literature. Nevertheless, if we want to understand the genesis of the novel we have to go back not simply to its birth, but, following the example of *Tristram Shandy*, back to the time when it was begotten.

The epistolary novel, which made up about one fifth of the total of eighteenth-century fiction, provides a useful paradigm of the rise of the novel in general. It is easily distinguished from other kinds of narrative by its form and enables us to examine within confined limits those circumstances which marked the development of the novel as a whole. There are about fifty to a hundred epistolary short stories and novels before Richardson, depending on how one defines the term and the extent to which transitional forms are included. I have chosen nine representative examples spanning a period of roughly seventy years, from 1670 to 1740. The stories are, I think, of more than historical interest.

The letter as a literary convention

Autobiography and diary, dialogue papers and question and answer periodicals, character-writing, manuals and letter collections of all kinds contributed to the development of the epistolary novel. The *letter* itself obviously plays the most important part in the rise of this genre, for in the seventeenth and eighteenth centuries letter-writing became very fashionable and was taken much more seriously than nowadays. Not only was it a means of communication and personal expression, but – through the efforts of such practitioners as Balzac, Voiture, Scarron, and Mme de Sévigné – it had become a recognised literary form with standards of style and wit which English letter-writers from the Duchess of Newcastle to Pope and Lady Montague did their best to equal. Ladies and gentlemen of breeding in the country as well as in town endeavoured to write letters following these models, and a host of manuals assisted them. Letters were carefully written, and read for pleasure and entertainment not only by the recipient but by his friends and relations as well. Publishers like John Dunton and Samuel Briscoe speedily took advantage of the new vogue, and collections of genuine or fictitious letters became favourite reading matter. The form of the letter was so popular that travel books, political and philosophical treatises, satires and essays on various subjects were written in the form of a "Letter from . . . to . . .". It is therefore hardly surprising that fiction too began to make use of this device.

Epistolary fiction has much in common with *genuine* letters describing personal feelings and events. The letter-writing heroes and heroines record their troubles in letters which differ little from non-fictional ones, and of course a succession of letters results in a story. No wonder, then, that it is often difficult to distinguish the first-person epistolary narrative from a genuine correspondence. A third-person narrative usually reveals its fictional nature through the comments on the action and on the characters of the omniscient narrator; but a first-person narrative by its very nature purports to be genuine (one of the reasons for its popularity in the eighteenth century). The narrator, who is also the hero, describes nothing that he himself could not have seen or heard or experienced. The novel has always tried to depict some kind of reality, and in fact the preface to almost every novel of the time contains the claim that the work in question is *not* fictional. Such claims made in support of novels in letter-form manage to sound fairly convincing.

A collection of genuine letters does, however, differ from an epistolary novel in one important respect: no matter how detailed such letters may be, they are never quite self-explanatory. We need a commentary which tells us who the correspondents are, what they are hinting at in this or that passage, which important events indispensable for the understanding of the whole are missing, etc. Such information is usually given in an introduction and in notes, not in the text itself. Unlike a novel a group of genuine letters is not a world complete in itself but still in close connection with reality. In the epistolary novel the letters themselves generally keep us adequately informed about what is going on, and also manage to illuminate the characters of the fictitious correspondents. Of course, as in any novel, we may be temporarily kept in the dark about an issue in order that our attention be captured and our curiosity heightened. Where there are footnotes and a preface by the "editor" (actually, of course, the author), this is simply a device for making the novel seem more like real life: such paraphernalia have little importance for the understanding of the plot. These various devices to make the story seem true should not, however, distract our attention from the fact that the epistolary novel is indeed a novel, and its mimetic nature is revealed to us in its self-contained artificial construction.

Sometimes letters which are in fact genuine strike the reader as highly artificial; such a situation may arise where the writer is dominated by particular stylistic influences. George Farquhar's love-letters to Mrs Centlivre, which were published in a collection of various letters in 1705 under the title of "Seven Passionate Love-Letters written by Celadon to his Mistress", use the language of the heroic drama and the letter of gallantry, an established literary genre:

> Be just therefore, be compassionate: save me from Distraction! Keep me your Slave. Oh, use not a Mark of your Tyranny, but Pity, and lawful Reign. 'Tis great, when 'tis in your Power, not to destroy, to damn and torture. Be like the Heav'n in your Mind, that your Person represents. Come, come, let me swear, protest Ten Thousand Vows and Oaths, enough to melt the most Obdurate Heart. See all my Agonies, hear all my Eloquent Sighs...[1]

Farquhar, though writing to a real person, has fabricated a dramatic situation in which he plays the major rôle: his beloved is seen as the "cruel mistress", a type invented by the troubadours, part of the stock-in-trade of the sonneteers, taken over by the romance and the heroic drama. The poor wretch at her feet is utterly distracted by hopeless passion. He speaks and acts like Celadon and not at all like the Mr Farquhar who would like to have an affair with Mrs Centlivre. The real Mrs Centlivre showed little appreciation for heroic attitude and style. In another letter she compares his sufferings to her own experience of tooth-ache:

> Thousands can judge of mine who have felt it, but scarce one in ten thousand ever really felt what you pretend to; and 'tis as natural for your Sex to write and make Love, as 'tis for ours to be caught by your flattering Baits.[2]

Astraea does not act her part satisfactorily and so destroys the illusion.

It was not uncommon in the literary world and at court to write gallant letters to one's mistress; like disguise and pastoral plays such literary exercises were part of the game of love. Voiture in one of his letters to Mme de Rambouillet plays the rôle of Gustav Adolph, in another he pretends to be an expert on paintings and drawings and encloses some pictures by Callot as a present to her. Dryden, Congreve, John Dennis, Abel Boyer, and Thomas Brown, among others, occasionally wrote letters in which they assumed the part of the heroic lover. Most love-letters of the time, however, were written in a plainer, less pretentious style. Thus even the Earl of Rochester, a famous courtier and rake, wrote fairly natural letters to Elizabeth Barry, showing that it was quite possible to make love without playing the game of gallantry. The artificiality and idealistic vein of the *letter of gallantry* was particularly suited to the romantic epistolary novel, and in fact the heroic language of the seventeenth-century romances and the heroic drama is found in the epistolary novels of Aphra Behn, Mrs Manley, and other writers of the romantic tradition.

The process by which the personal letter of gallantry develops into the epistolary narrative can be followed step by step: the letter-writer, by adopting a rôle, creates a fictitious second self who tends to become a separate figure in an invented story. Gradually the hero of the novel disengages himself, as it were, from the person of the author, and only the first-person form conceals this fact from the reader. The letters of George Farquhar make quite clear how, out of autobiographical letters, a character may evolve who tells his own story. Farquhar, unlike the author of an epistolary novel, obviously didn't intend to deceive anyone; he was simply playing an enjoyable game, and one which was not without aesthetic value. It is one of the rare cases where genuine letters strike us as fictitious not because of any clearly fictional content, but because the author consciously adopts a pose. The next step is for the author to write a first-person novel imagining himself in the rôle of the hero; and, finally, to write a novel in which the characters have little to do with the author himself.

Obviously, there is no hard and fast line between a genuine letter, a *fictitious letter*, and an epistolary narrative. Sometimes it is impossible without external evidence to decide whether a correspondence is genuine or fictitious. In other cases – the *Portuguese Letters* and the *Letters of Captain Ayloffe* for instance – no decision can be arrived at because we know little or nothing about the writers. The history of the epistolary novel abounds in examples of transitional kinds of writing and shows how close is the interplay between fact and fiction. Letter collections, such as *The Works of Monsieur Voiture . . . Containing His Familiar Letters To Gentlemen and Ladies . . . With Three Collections of Letters on Friendship and several other Occasions : Written by John Dryden Esq., William Wycherley, Esq., William Congreve, Esq., Mr Dennis, Mr ——, Mr Tho. Brown, Mr Edward Ward. And Facetious Letters out of Greek, Latin and French. By the late Ingenious Mr Tho. Brown.* London, 1705, contain genuine letters side by side with fictitious ones; moreover, some of the fictitious letters seem quite genuine, whereas genuine letters are revised and touched up to make an interesting story. The letters of Abélard and Héloïse, for instance, underwent a series of changes and adaptations and became something of a novel in the end.[3] Some letters were influenced by literary models; thus Aphra Behn, in writing her love-letters to a certain Lycidus (who cannot be identified with any certainty), was imitating the passionate love-letters of the Portuguese nun. Like Farquhar, she too was playing a rôle, but her rôle was based on a specific literary model, whereas Farquhar made use of the courtly game of love. Many letters written to a particular recipient were penned with future publication in mind. Cicero and Plinius as well as Dryden, Wycherley, Congreve, John Dunton, Tom Brown, Pope, and many others wrote such letters – letters in which more attention was paid to style than would have been normal in a strictly private message. The writer seems to be addressing "my dear Lady XY" but the fact that he secretly imagines a wider audience introduces a note of unreality into his letter; for the intimate tone which would have been appropriate were he *really* addressing Lady XY is discarded, and the lady becomes a mere surrogate for the "gentle reader". The ambiguity of the apostrophes marks one small step along the way separating genuine letters from fiction. The author of such a letter may have wanted to express certain ideas of general interest, to write an essay in the form of a letter. We wonder, for example, what lay behind Lord Chesterfield's letters to his natural son and his godson, although we cannot prove that the writer meant them to be published after his death. In the epistolary novel, as we shall see, the person who is writing the letters addresses not only another character in the novel, but under this disguise may also appeal to the reader.

Models and manuals

A further impetus was given to the letter form as a narrative device by a great number of *manuals* like *The Wit's Academy* (1677), *The Young Secretary's Guide* (1687), and *The Lover's Secretary* (1692). Each manual provides the letter-writer with a number of models dealing with stock situations in life:

> "A Letter written to reclaim Youthful Extravagancies in a Son, &c."
> *(The Young Secretary's Guide*, p. 91)
> "A Letter of Advice from a Mother to her Daughter."
> *(The Secretary's Guide*, p. 32)
> "A Letter to break off a rash Contract in Love-affairs."
> *(The Secretary's Guide*, p. 40)
> "A Letter from a Daughter to her Parents who had married without
> their Consent." *(The Secretary's Guide*, pp. 9–10)

These letters express feelings, intentions, and thoughts in the most general way so that the letters will be widely applicable as models. It is precisely this generality which allows us to recognise that they are indeed fictitious. For example, this one:

A Letter returning Thanks to a Mother.

> Loving Mother,
> I have received the things you expressed in your Letter, and find myself highly bound in general and particular Obligation to return my hearty Thanks, and express the true sense I have of your Care and Tenderness towards me, which makes me wish it in my power to make a larger Acknowledgement; but seeing that Wish cannot bring forth the desired effects, I must humbly beg you to accept of my good Will, and dutiful Affections towards you, together with my Prayers for your Prosperity . . .
>
> *(The Young Secretary's Guide*, p. 19*)*

The individual correspondent was able to adapt such a model for his own purposes simply by inserting a few personal details. The stock situations treated in the manuals also provided material for a story or even a novel. Indeed, the manuals themselves tended to become entertainments in their own right, their instructional purpose taking second place. In Nicholas Breton's *A Poste with a Packet of Mad Letters* (1609) a correspondence between two young people develops to the point where Margerie promises Roger: "on Friday ile meet you at ten of the clock, and bring a peece of bacon in my pocket, to relish a cupe of Ale . . ." (p. 35), and in the end they marry. The professed aim of the author in Charles Gildon's *Post-boy rob'd of his Mail* (1692) was to divert the reader. The transition from model correspondence to epistolary narrative was not a hard one to make: detail needed to be added, the character of the letter-writer depicted more clearly. Richardson's *Pamela* evolved from the model letters which the author composed for a manual called *Letters Written To and For Particular Friends* (1741).

The autobiography

The *autobiography*, like the epistolary novel, tells the story of a person's life, and like the epistolary novel the autobiography is more complete and self-sufficient than a mere collection of letters. Biographies and auto-biographies often include a scattering of letters which may help to convey a vivid picture of the life and times of a person; and, similarly, letters are inserted into the third-person narrative of novels of the seventeenth and eighteenth centuries in order that the fictional events described seem as real, as "documentary", as possible.

Autobiography and epistolary narrative are linked by more than the biographical or pseudo-biographical purpose. They share, in addition, an important narrative technique. A first-person narrator is involved in two time-schemes: the time which operates as the narrator records and comments on his past experiences – what may be called the *narrator's present*; and the time which operated in that past about which the narrator writes – *the narrative past*. The narrator's present may provide, as in the following example, a framework for the events recounted:

> *Faithful Friend!*
> I WROTE you very lately the News of my Captivity, receive now those of my Inlargement, as unexpected, and as unaccountable as the other.[4]

Then the writer starts to look back at events in his past:

> Yesterday Morning, Papa sent for me to Breakfast. I drank tea as usual, without betraying any uneasiness at my Restraint, and when the Things were taken away, my Father told me I might walk in the Garden if I pleased . . .

The use of the narrator's present establishes a link between the reader and those past events which form the chief subject matter of the narrative; the reader is, as it were, present during the actual process of writing, he is taken by the hand to be shown what happened yesterday or some years ago. And in this narrative past into which the reader has been led, the hero (or heroine) disappears as a writer, the process of remembering, reflecting on, and recording past events is forgotten. Both reader and narrator are in the past.

These two narrative levels are obviously closely related, for the person who underwent the adventures is the one who, seated at his desk, now looks back on them, remembers and perhaps relives them. Here we have arrived at an essential difference between autobiography and epistolary narrative: the writer of an autobiography knows the outcome of those past events which he describes, and his view of his own actions is characterised by a certain detachment; he is able to comment critically, to arrive at definite conclusions. The letter-writer, on the other hand, is involved; he usually reports what happened yesterday or the day before, or even a few minutes before he sat down to write the letter. He does not know how things will develop, and his letters reflect the changing moods called forth by the various events he relates; moreover, his absorption in these events of the moment leads to that minute psychological analysis so characteristic of the epistolary novel, and of many genuine letters as well. Richardson was very well aware of the artistic advantages of the letter form, which permits the description of events and emotions while they are still alive to the characters who participated in them:

> That the Letters on both sides are written while the Hearts of the Writers must be supposed wholly engaged in their Subjects: The Events at the Time generally dubious: – So that they abound, not only with critical

Situations; but with what may be called *instantaneous* Descriptions and Reflections; which may be brought home to the Breast of the youthful Reader...[5]

Richardson was and is often reproached for being far too lengthy and circumstantial in his novels. But he argues that it is precisely the wealth of detail found in epistolary narrative that holds our interest in what we are reading:

> The Nature of Familiar Letters, written, as it were, to the *Moment*, while the Heart is agitated by Hopes and Fears, on Events undecided, must plead an Excuse for the Bulk of a Collection of this Kind. Mere Facts and Characters might be comprised in a much smaller Compass: But, would they be equally interesting?[6]

The interplay between the past and the present as experienced by the writer is much closer in the epistolary narrative than it is in the auto-biography; in the epistolary novel the two time-schemes are linked in various ways, as the following example from Richardson's *Clarissa* will make clear. Clarissa's family wish to force her into a marriage with "the despicable Solmes", whereas she would much rather stay single and renounce him to her younger sister. She has only her friend Anne Howe to turn to:

Letter XVI – Miss Clarissa Harlowe to Miss Howe
(Her preceding not at the time received)

Friday, 3 March

O my dear friend, I have a sad conflict! Trial upon trial; conference upon conference! But what law, what ceremony, can give a man a right to a heart which abhors him more than it does any living creature?

I hope my mother will be able to prevail for me. But I will recount all, though I sit up the whole night to do it; for I have a vast deal to write, and will be as minute as you wish me to be.

I concluded my last in a fright. It was occasioned by a conversation that passed between my mother and my aunt, part of which Hannah overheard. I need not give you the particulars; since what I have to relate to you from different conversations that have passed between my mother and me in the space of a very few hours will include them all. I will begin then.

I went down this morning when breakfast was ready with a very un-easy heart, from what Hannah had informed me of yesterday afternoon; wishing for an opportunity, however, to appeal to my mother, in hopes to engage her interest in my behalf, and purposing to try to find one when she retired to her own apartment after breakfast: but, unluckily, there was the odious Solmes sitting asquat between my mother and sister, with so much assurance in his looks! but you know, my dear, that those who love not cannot do anything to please us.

Had the wretch kept his seat, it might have been well enough: but the bent and broad-shouldered creature must needs rise and stalk towards a chair; which was just by that which was set for me.

I removed it to a distance, as if to make way to my own: And down I sat, abruptly I believe; what I had heard all in my head.

But this was not enough to daunt him. The man is very confident, he is a very bold, staring man! Indeed, my dear, the man is very confident.

He took the removed chair and drew it so near mine, squatting in it with his ugly weight, that he pressed upon my hoop. I was so offended (all I had heard, as I said, in my head) that I removed to another chair. I own I had too little command of myself. It gave my brother and sister too much advantage. I dare say they took it. But I did it involuntarily, I think. I could not help it. I knew not what I did.

I saw that my father was excessively displeased. When angry, no man's countenance ever shows it so much as my father's. Clarissa Harlowe! said he with a big voice – and there he stopped. Sir! said I, trembling and curtsying (for I had not then sat down again): and put my chair nearer the wretch, and sat down – my face, as I could feel, all in a glow.

Make tea, child, said my kind mamma: sit by me, love, and make tea.[6a]

Clarissa's letter starts off in much the same way as did numerous narrative letters of the time: a person obviously immersed in a sea of trouble sits down to open her heart to a confidante. Even the memory of what she has so recently experienced arouses in the writer thoughts and emotions that in turn place her vividly before the reader. Naturally enough, she goes on to announce that she is going to "recount all" in great detail, just as Fielding and Sterne are wont to do at the beginning of a new chapter. The "self-conscious narrator"[7] who comments on the style, discusses the story, apologises for digressions, etc., is very common in seventeenth- and eighteenth-century literature. Though tempted to regard his remarks as interruptions, the reader knows that in fact the narrator is part and parcel of the story; the self-conscious narrator is simply one side of the narrator – a side frequently used in developing that part of the novel which deals with the narrator's invention and recording of a story. In a letter, of course, it is altogether natural for the writer to comment on the process of writing.

When Clarissa has promised to be "as minute as you wish me to be", she briefly refers to the letter before ("I concluded my last in a fright") but remains more concerned with the present process of writing until she finally decides: "I will begin then". Now, moving back into the narrative past, she reports events and feelings "of this morning", and arrives at the conclusion "that those we love not cannot do anything to please us". This reflection moves us back into the narrator's present, for the context makes clear that Clarissa neither thought nor said this when she was actually in the room with Solmes. It is often difficult to decide whether Clarissa's more general reflections originate in the past or at the moment of writing: thus her observation, "When angry, no man's countenance ever shows it so much as my father's", pinpoints a characteristic of her father which applies at any time, not just on the particular occasion Clarissa is describing. When, however, Clarissa writes "But you know my dear, that those we love not cannot do anything to please us", the apostrophe to her friend makes the observation appear spontaneous, and, indeed, an apostrophe usually alerts us to the fact that the writer is no longer in the past but directly addressing the recipient.

When Clarissa describes Solmes as a "wretch", "bent and broad-shouldered", "stalking" towards a chair, and later on "squatting", "with his ugly weight", we hardly know whether we are dealing with observations made in the narrative past or judgements added at the time of writing; present feelings colour the experience of the past, to the extent that it is almost impossible to decide which of the two approaches is involved – though the narrative past does in this case retain a slight edge. Later on, when Clarissa has to admit "I had too little command of myself" and "I knew not what I did" the two levels are again blended: the writer is summing up part of her story and at the same time pronouncing a judgement on herself. This time, however, the stress is on the narrator's present, for the summing up is performed by the writer at the time that she records her experiences.

The focus of the narrative now moves back and we see Clarissa sitting at some distance from Solmes. What we have here is not so very different from what we might find in any first-person novel – except that in the epistolary narrative we are reminded from time to time of our letter-writing narrator. When Clarissa in the middle of reporting her encounter with the odious Solmes cries out "The man is a very confident, he is a very bold, staring man!" the intrusion of her emotions is clearly indicated by the use of the present tense; her outburst of indignation belongs to the moment when she is telling Miss Howe about what happened; only then in the privacy of her room is she able to give expression to her emotions.

To sum up: the narrative level operative at any particular moment is indicated in various ways: the apostrophe, and the present tense plus the use of the first-person form reveal that the writer is expressing present thoughts; we can usually recognise a fusion of the two levels where the narrator, instead of simply reporting past events, chooses to telescope them; moreover, any report showing the influence of more recent reflection will probably signal the same fusion of the two levels; and a general statement can usually be assigned to both levels, or to neither. The overall effect is that of oscillation between the two levels of narration. Things are constantly being remembered and set down, the past is repeatedly evoked and relived in the present. In this process it is not so much the action itself which takes the central place in the narrative as the writer's reaction to it, the mood which it evokes. The epistolary novel offers its readers writing of the most subjective kind; the attitudes and feelings of the writer are constantly revealed in his narrative. Nowhere else in eighteenth-century fiction are character and plot so interdependent as in the epistolary narrative.

To see how different the epistolary novel is from a strictly autobiographical narrative we need only imagine what would have resulted if Pamela had written down her adventures *after* her marriage to Squire B. Pamela's hopes and fears, plans and disappointments, the close interplay between what she is thinking and feeling and what has just happened or is going to happen next – all those things which continue to make the book readable today would be missing. Put more positively, the epistolary technique may be used to add suspense to the plot and a greater psychological subtlety to the character.

There are, of course, many epistolary novels which seem more like autobiography because the possibilities residing in an interplay between past events and present feelings have not been made use of. Marivaux's *Vie de Marianne* (1731–41)[8] and Tom Brown's *The Adventures of Lindamira* (1702) are epistolary novels of this kind. In other epistolary novels and short stories it is difficult to decide whether the structure is primarily autobiographical or epistolary. In *A Letter from Mrs Jane Jones*, for example, the events of some years before are reviewed by the narrator from her standpoint at the time of writing. Her feelings and opinions, however, seem to have been so entirely shaped by what has happened to her that she seems to be writing about the unsettled affairs of a few days ago. And in a way her affairs are still unsettled: for her purpose in relating these past adventures to her friend is to convince that friend of the unfortunate results these adventures have had, and moreover to persuade her to join the narrator in leaving England for a better life abroad. The strong effect of the past upon her finds expression in the degree to which her memories are coloured by her feelings at the time of writing. Thus despite the distance separating narrative past and narrator's present in this piece, which would seem to suggest an autobiographical approach, the story proceeds with epistolary immediacy. We see that it is not the actual length of time between the narrator's present and the narrative past which determines the narrative structure of a story, but the degree of imaginative involvement of the narrator in the events she relates and the manner in which the two levels of narration are connected and interwoven.

Mrs Manley's *Letter from a Lady to a Lady* is a report of events covering seven years, and once again a real epistolary novel. The narrator does not know whether her lover, Mr Worthy, will forsake her or be faithful; under the pressure of her present situation she views her earlier years with both resignation and despair, and her remarks and apostrophes to her friend Clorinda evidence the extent of her concern with the past; she cannot lay claim to the calm serenity of an autobiographical narrator. The *Lover's Week*, on the other hand, is a first-person narrative which, in spite of occasional attempts to gain immediacy through remarks such as "I'll leave you to judge the Surprise I was in", keeps almost entirely to the narrative past – though the good-humoured and cheerful tone used by the narrator suggests that the events she describes must have led to a pleasant conclusion.

The extent to which autobiography actually influenced the rise of the epistolary novel is a matter about which we can only conjecture. Autobiographical writings of all kinds had been much in vogue since the Renaissance, and similarities both in matter and structure between the two genres make it probable that the autobiography gave a strong impetus to the development of the epistolary novel. Some writers – for example, Scarron, Marivaux, Tom Brown, and John Dunton – wrote both autobiographies and epistolary novels. Some fictional autobiographies use the letter form to frame their narrative, as for example in the autobiography of a famous pirate assigned to Defoe: *The King of Pirates: Being an Account of the Famous Enterprises of Captain Avery . . . In Two Letters from himself . . .* (1720). Other kinds of popular light fiction of the time containing autobiographical elements like the *Spies* and *Letters of Travel* also made use of the letter form.

In one instance we *are* able to observe how autobiography became letter fiction – in the *Letter to the Editor* of a periodical. Originally such letters related a decisive event or a train of events in a person's life which then served as a text for the editor to draw his moral and instruct his readers on how to behave in human society. Gradually genuine (including letters worked over by an editor) were replaced by invented ones – epistolary autobiography gave way to epistolary fiction. These letters, describing real-life situations such as that of a young woman forsaken by her lover and expecting a baby, were often written as though the writer were in the midst of her quandary, and are proper epistolary short stories. Letters to the Editor of this kind, whether genuine or fictitious, were quite popular at the end of the seventeenth century and in the first part of the eighteenth century and, judging from the circulation figures for periodicals like *The Athenian Mercury*, *The Tatler*, and *The Spectator*, they were widely read. *A Letter from Jane Jones* and Mrs Manley's *Letter from a Lady to a Lady* were obviously influenced by the fictitious Letters to the Editor, and differ from them only in length.

Diaries and journals

Apart from the autobiography, the literary form which most resembles the epistolary narrative is the *diary*. Moreover, the diary resembles the epistolary narrative in reporting day-to-day events and intimate thought, as the autobiography does not. The gap in time between the past happenings and the diarist's recording of them is much smaller than in the case of the autobiography, and as in a series of letters the diary is full of expectations and apprehensions, the writer's mood changing from one entry to the next according to the experience and impressions of the moment. Clarissa's letters resemble diary entries in that she faithfully puts down everything that occurs to her, her thoughts and feelings. The detailed day-to-day report, found in rudimentary form in the *Portuguese Letters* and fully developed in *The Double Captive* and in some passages of *The Polite Correspondence*, is even more characteristic of epistolary fiction than of genuine correspondence, especially at a time when the postal service was not so well organised as today so that people were less in the habit of writing frequently to one another than of making entries in their diaries. The detailed, personal, involved nature of the epistolary novel would seem therefore to owe more to the diary than to genuine letters.

The main difference between the diary and the epistolary narrative lies in the fact that the diary is a soliloquy and the letter is something of a dialogue. The diarist does not address himself to anybody; he writes only for himself, possibly even in some code or shorthand, as Pepys did. Of course a diarist might expect his family to read his records after his death, or might even be secretly addressing himself to a wider audience as some letter-writers did. But there are few instances of a diarist addressing himself *expressis verbis* to a certain person. The factual diary, such as the medical diary, the farmer's or the traveller's diary, never contains addresses to a particular person. But the diarist who describes his own personal experiences, his distresses or joys, sometimes cannot help addressing himself to another person. Elizabeth Freke breaks through the soliloquy of her diary in the entry of 2 August 1707, to address all mankind:

> . . . where he Ruined me In my Estate there, by falling all my Rents, & gave Away Twelve hundred Pounds Arrears from me, & brought me over Nothing butt himselfe. Let me be A Warning to Trust Friends.[9]

Mary Woodforde, worrying about her son at school who was involved in a pupils' revolt, suddenly turns to God for help:

> Some of them did submit, amongst which Cousin John Woodforde, and if the others do not, they must be expelled. God I beseech thee subdue their stubborn hearts, and give them grace to repent and accept of their punishment due to their fault, and let them not run on to ruin, for Christ's sake.[10]

The religious diaries of the time are full of apostrophes to God. The recording of one's own thought and experience establishes an atmosphere of intimacy which conjures up the need for someone to confide in. For this reason the letter addressed to somebody else proved an admirable vehicle for intimate thought. Moreover, the analysis of feeling, which in the later novel assumed an importance that it had never had in earlier fictional works, was simplified by allowing characters to describe to somebody else their hopes and fears, joys and disappointments, rather than by having these sentiments conveyed in a more complicated manner through a third-person narrator. Diaries and letters provided ideal models for the earlier novelists and thus they contributed to the development of characterisation in fiction.

Development of dialogue

A letter correspondence is like a *dialogue* in which, since the partners are separated and unable to reply immediately or ask questions, individual contributions are longer, more carefully worked out, more concerned with persuading the recipient and forestalling his objections. The letter-writer, then, is always conscious of talking to somebody else – even where his style attempts to recreate the spontaneity of spoken language through "a kind of diligent negligence".[11] The manuals of the time recommend the letter-writer to be "plain and familiar", to present his subject matter not in the form of a treatise but rather to show the mind in action, one thought leading to the next. This associative technique of writing, in which the story is repeatedly interrupted by the emotions of the writer, introduces yet another conversational element into the letter. In actual fact, letter-writing has often been regarded as a substitute for personal conversation. The Duchess of Newcastle says in Letter I of her *CCXI Sociable Letters* (1664):

MADAM,
You were pleas'd to desire, that, since we cannot converse Personally, we should converse by Letters, so as if we were speaking to each other, discussing our Opinions, discovering our Designs, asking and giving each other Advice, also telling the several Accidents, and several Imployments of our home-affairs, and what visits we receive, or entertainments we make..." (p. 1).

Turning now to the question of the influence of dialogue on epistolary fiction, it is apparent that the transitional forms often reveal a close connection between the two forms. Philosophical and satirical dialogues of the type found in Lucian's *Dialogues of the Dead* appeared in the form of an imaginary correspondence; Tom Brown's *Letters from the Dead to the Living, By Mr Tho. Brown, Capt. Ayloff,* ... (1702) is an example of such a mixed form. In a correspondence called *The Female War* (1697) by John Dunton, men and women of varied character and standing discuss the vices and follies of the other sex. Some of the letters sound very much like parts of a spoken dialogue, others develop into short stories where the dialogue element is less evident. There are also epistolary novels like Mary Davys' *Familiar Letters Betwixt a Gentleman and a Lady* (1725), which are more like letter dialogues, and where the discussion of such matters as politics and religion, love and friendship, almost seems to replace the normal function of the novel – to tell, at some length, a story.

The new and increasingly popular periodicals at the end of the seventeenth century made wide use of the dialogue-form; the periodicals devoted to two opponents, usually Whig and Tory, discussed political topics. Such journals developed into *question-and-answer periodicals* in which the reader was given the opportunity to ask all sorts of questions; for example:

Whether 'tis lawful for a Man to beat his Wife?
Ans. The affirmative would be very disobliging to that Sex, without adding any more to it, therefore we ought to be as cautious and tender as may be in asserting such an ill natur'd Position. We allow a Wife to be naturaliz'd into, and *part of her Husband*, and yet nature sometimes wars against part of itself . . . Now if a man may thus cruelly treat himself, and be an Accesary to his own Torture, he may legally chastise his Wife, who is no nearer to him than to himself . . .[12]

Soon the queries become more personal, as in the following example:

I am sometimes in company with honest young women and *kiss 'em in a Frolick, as other's use to do. Qu. Whether it is a sin or no?*
Ans. There's a Civil Kiss, and an Uncivil. If the first, sure there's no hurt in 'em; if the latter, be your own Judge; for that's a great deal more than looking upon a Woman.[13]

In the course of time the question became more detailed, the writer told more of his thoughts and emotions, went further in characterising himself, so that a full-fledged epistolary story emerged. Right from the start many of the queries in question-and-answer periodicals were invented, and later on the editor himself usually made up the stories supposedly submitted by his readers. The Letter to the Editor proved particularly suitable for accounts of personal conflict: the coercion of a young girl into undesired marriage, or her unhappy passion for a young man without fortune; the difficulties borne by a younger brother or the sufferings of an honest girl at the hands of a rake. The moral bent of the periodicals (a reaction against Restoration licence) gradually took shape in these Letters to the Editor; they became increasingly concerned with questions of conduct, mirroring the rise of the upper bourgeoisie long before this social phenomenon was pictured in the epistolary novel. Defoe's *Little Review* (1705), *The Tatler* (1709–11), and *The Spectator* (1711–12), Steele's *The Lover* (1714) and Ambrose Philip's *The Free-Thinker* (1718–21) contributed much to the propagation of the principles of right living, and not a little to the development of the epistolary novel.

The epistolary short story of the Letter to the Editor type still reveals the *query* as its germ. The action is usually concentrated on one problem which comes to a crisis and ends either happily or tragically. Stories like the *Account of a Lady's Adventures* and *A Letter from Mrs Jane Jones* follow in the steps of the Letter to the Editor to the extent that they revolve around one central concern and retain the concise form of their predecessors. They move away from the romantic story with its endless series of love-adventures towards a pattern resembling the Italian novelette, which was known to the seventeenth-century English reader through translations and imitations. Eliza Haywood's epistolary stories in *The Female Spectator* (1744–46) mark the final stage in the development which started with the queries in question-and-answer periodicals and ended with the epistolary novelette. *The Female Spectator* contains a few pieces entitled "Letters to the Editor" displaying decidedly epistolary technique and bearing the usual claim to authenticity.

The epistolary novel has been described as "dramatic" because of its dialogue structure and the absence of an uninvolved narrator who presides over the story. This statement, however, needs modification. The correspondents tell their own stories to each other at great length, whereas characters in a play usually participate in spoken dialogue consisting of short speeches and replies. More important, the letter-writer tells a story belonging to the past, however near this past may be, whereas the people in a drama are acting out their story – except for the odd passage of expository report. In other words, the epistolary narrative, like any narrative develops on two planes, however closely connected they may be, whereas the drama has only one dimension. Drama normally provides neither a narrator to recall past events, nor an intermediary figure between the actors and the audience to explain and to interpret. In the epistolary novel the letter-writer has this function, and the dialogue element may be regarded as a narrative device to make the presentation of the actual story more vivid. The dialogue partners, because they correspond rather than converse, behave more like narrators, even like self-conscious narrators, than like people on a stage. And indeed, what we have called the narrator's present in nothing but the narrator's plane of the third-person novel transferred to the first-person novel, only with the particularly close connection to the narrative past that is characteristic of the epistolary novel. When Fielding interrupts his narration in order to digress on the process of writing a novel and to appeal to the reader's understanding and reason, action stands still and we have to wait for his "now we return to Squire Western's house . . ." to hear more about Tom Jones and Sophia. When, however, Pamela prefaces her report of the latest news with comments on her situation as letter-writer, the story is actually continuing because Pamela's thoughts, expressed in the narrator's present, are a reaction to her present situation and part of the narrative:

> O My Dearest Father and Mother,
> Let me write and bewail my miserable hard fate, though I have no hope that what I write can be conveyed to you. I have now nothing to do but write, and weep, and pray! But yet, what can I hope for, when I seem to be devoted as a victim to the will of a wicked violator of all the laws of God and man ?[14]

The narrator of an epistolary story is of course identical with the writer of the letters, and so is able to render past events immediate by making us see them through his eyes; the switching over from one plane of narration to the other is thus easily, sometimes almost imperceptibly, performed.

The rôle of the "reader"
To whom is the letter-writer-narrator addressing his story ? The fictitious letter is supposed to be a private message to a fictitious person, but the author of an epistolary story knows very well that the correspondence will be read by a larger audience and may well have asked himself what effect particular phrases and events will have on the reader. When Jane Jones writes her friend Arabella:

> You may guess, my dear *Arabella*, how irksome such a Confinement with such a man . . . must be to a Woman of my free and unconfin'd Manner of Thinking (see below p. 58).

she is drawing attention to a character-trait in herself which is made clear not only to Arabella but to the reader as well. And when Eliza writes to Florimond,

> You will think when you have read this, that some ill Spirits have been lately abroad in *Suffolk*, and breath'd into its Inhabitants a Spirit of Discord and Confusion
> *(The Polite Correspondence*, Letter XII, see below p. 167).

the "you" seems almost to embrace the reader, who will probably be of the same opinion. In Mrs Manley's epistolary story the Lady shortens her report by saying:

> should I dwell on every Circumstance, the Conversation must tire you . . . (see below p. 42).

Like any narrator trying to catch the reader's interest, the letter-writer announces what he is going to relate next or apologises for being too circumstantial, and whether or not the narrator is also the letter-writer, the effect upon the reader is the same. For, under the disguise of the letter-writer the narrator is addressing himself to the reader, who can identify himself with the recipient. In this way the narrator can appeal to the reader without the slightest breach of illusion in the narrative. The apostrophe to the recipient becomes ambiguous, as in the case of genuine letters secretly designed for publication. Similarly the *news letter*, originally addressed to a particular person whom the correspondent served, was later copied or even printed and became accessible to a wider audience.

It is difficult to prove exactly when the addressing of the recipient becomes ambiguous, applying additionally to the reader. There are instances where the author clearly betrays his presence behind the fictional letter-writer, for example when Clarissa writes to Anne Howe:

> I will give you the substance of this communicated conversation after I have made a brief introductory observation or two; which however I hardly need to make to you who are so well acquainted with us all, did not the series or thread of the story require it.[15]

Clarissa, in telling Anne what she already knows, but what the reader ought to know as well, allows the author's concern with writing a novel to show through the pretence of Clarissa writing to her friend.

Not all addresses to the recipient also apply to the reader of the epistolary story. In love-letters like those of the Portuguese nun it is impossible to imagine that the apostrophes to the recipient are also meant for the reader. Indeed, as soon as the recipient is individualised and endowed with particular qualities, as soon as he is shown to have a special relation to the letter-writer, he begins to play a part in the novel; the reader can no longer suppose that he too is being addressed.

That a device designed to catch the reader's attention should have been adopted by the writers of epistolary fiction need not surprise us, for the relationship between narrator and reader was an important one in the eighteenth-century novel. The confidants who play no part in the plot or only an unimportant one (like Pamela's parents, Anne Howe, or Squire Bramble's doctor) thus fulfil an important function; remaining rather pale as characters, they nevertheless allow the author to direct apostrophes to the reader.

It is important to note that the relationship between author and reader is not a real one, for the author cannot tell who will actually be reading his book. Conversations between the narrator and the gentle reader belong entirely to the fictitious world of the novel. The technique of addressing somebody called the "reader" or "Arabella" (the recipient of the letter) has certain aesthetic effects upon the actual reader, but the appeal is not, like a telephone call, meant for him personally. The novel is an art form with its own laws.

We all know from experience that a letter bears the imprint of the writer's personality. His style, his way of describing things, his manner of recording thoughts and emotions at the moment they occur, reflect his qualities and idiosyncrasies. The letter-writer reveals himself indirectly, often without meaning to. The fictitious letter and the epistolary narrative try to imitate the characterising quality of the genuine letter: Jane Jones appears as an ironic and disillusioned woman in her letters; Emilia displays common sense and humour; and the *Portuguese Letters* are so stamped with the personality of the passionate nun that they created a fashion which influenced letter-writing for half a century.

Characterisation

The epistolary novel is, generally speaking, more a novel of character than a novel of action, because the action is usually filtered through the personality of the writer. As E. M. Forster pointed out, "people" and "story" are the basic ingredients of the novel. The novel, in its earliest days, consisted entirely of story; the way was paved for the novel of character by the collections of *characters* inspired by Theophrastus: Bishop Hall's *Characters of Vertues and Vices* (1608), Sir Thomas Overbury's *Witty Characters* (1614), Nicholas Breton's *The Good and the Badde* (1616), and John Earle's *Micro-cosmographie* (1628) were widely read throughout the seventeenth century; many of these characters appeared in letter collections and epistolary stories in the late seventeenth and eighteenth centuries. John Earle's "Discontented Man", for example, turns up in Charles Gildon's letter collection, *The Post-boy robb'd of his Mail* (1692), although the passage has undergone considerable changes:

A Discontented Man.
Is one that is faln out with the world, and will be reuenged on himself. Fortune ha's deny'd him in something, and hee now takes pet, and will be miserable in spite. The roote of his disease is a selfe-humouring pride, and an accustom'd tendernesse, not to bee crost in his fancy: and the occasions commonly one of these three: a hard Father, a peeuish Wench, or his ambition thwarted. He considered not the nature of the world till he felt it, and all blowes fall on him heauier because they light not first on his expectation (No. 6).

From a surly Misanthrope, *who speaks ill of all Mankind, and of every thing;* 'twas directed thus, To Mr. Hawkes *at* Mr. Smith's *House near* Rye, Kent.

Dick,

I Writ to thee last Post to get all things in order against my coming down, that I might have some ease at home, who have met with none here in this damn'd Town, which is so thwack'd with Follies, that 'tis enough to make one out of love with Mankind. I can't stir along the Streets but I meet with a hundred things that give me a great deal of disturbance; here one recommends this Book to me to read, tho' the Sott never read farther than the Title Page, praising it upon trust, because a Block-head of his own acquaintance is the Author; . . . I meet with one, and he pulls his Hat off to me to the ground, tho' I never saw him but once in a coffee-house, and then he only asked me what it was a clock, another Cries he's my humble Servant, when I'm sure the Rogue wou'd not lend me six pence . . . Thus I'm plagued if I stir out, and at my Lodging I have nothing to do but to Eat, Sleep, and Read, the first I want the Stomack to, because I want my Country Recreation to divert me and to prepare my Appetite; the second the rattling, and perpetuel hurry of the Town deny me; and the third is almost as bad for I'm oblig'd to read nothing but Latin, so that if I were to stay here long, I shou'd forget my Mother Tongue . . . (pp. 23–24).

The stock figure of the misanthrope is depicted as stranded in a little town where everything seems to turn against him. The fact that he recounts his own adventures strengthens our sense of his individuality, and the story itself actually develops out of his personality. Other stock types placed in a fictional setting similarly develop into individual characters, as for example the "coquette" or "whore" who is frequently to be encountered in eighteenth-century fiction. Captain Ayloffe is reminiscent of the coarse, swaggering, but good-natured soldier frequently to be met with in character-writing. The "younger brother", the "rake", the "innocent maiden" and other types abound in eighteenth-century fiction. The numerous examples of transitional forms illustrate the long and laborious way from a character in one of the character collections to characterisation in a full-fledged novel.

The narrative tradition

So far we have been considering such non-fictional sources of the epistolary novel as autobiography and diary, letter collections, manuals, character-writing and question-and-answer periodicals – more or less subliterary forms of writing which were read by contemporary readers for information, instruction, and entertainment. To us, their value is more documentary than aesthetic; nevertheless epistolary fiction is, as we have seen, rooted in these practical writings. It is, of course, very difficult and indeed unnecessary to draw a hard and fast line between writings with a practical and immediate purpose and those works whose aesthetic values guarantee them a more lasting validity. Literature arises to no small extent on the basis of subliterary forms; the ideas and techniques developed by more primitive writers are the stepping-stones for the literary genius. Thus literature should not be viewed simply as a series of awe-inspiring landmarks, but as a never-ceasing process of experimentation and development.

Another important source of the epistolary novel is the narrative tradition itself. Seventeenth-century fiction is commonly divided into the realistic literature of roguery and the idealistic love-stories of the *romance*. The first is of practically no importance for the development of the epistolary narrative. In the romance, love is the principal subject; hence the attempts at psychological analysis, which, however, are frequently somewhat less than subtle: "'Tis impossible to describe what Philander felt at that moment...." The feelings and emotions of the characters are most successfully conveyed in such romantic works through the agency of the letter, and indeed, as soon as the letter appeared in the romantic third-person narrative, its main function was to recount inward action. In romances like Mme Scudéry's *Mathilde* (1667) and Roger Boyle's *Parthenissa* (1654-69) the interspersed letters make up perhaps five per cent of the narrative. At first they were nothing more than emotional highlights in the story, in the same way as were songs, poems, and set speeches. Gradually the number of letters increased and began to play a part in the action. As the only means of communication between separated lovers, they carry important messages, are intercepted or even forged, and therefore determine the course of events. The *Scandalous Chronicle* (a scandalous love-story based on actual cases in the style of the heroic romance) and imitations of the Italian *novella* also began to make use of the letter.

The main problem of integrating the letter into a third-person narrative was to introduce action into the letters, to combine narrator's present, with its psychological, emotional tendencies, and narrative past. Thus in *The Constant Lovers*, the correspondence between the separated lovers (forming about one fifth of the narrative) is devoted not only to psychological analysis but also to some extent to the reporting of events. The reactions of Alexis and Sylvia to the trials they have undergone involve us in the narrative past, and quite often they repeat briefly what we already know from the narrative text. But the author apparently does not dare to complete the process by putting all the narrative past into the letters themselves.

There are numerous examples of this transitional type of epistolary novel where the letters take up between five and thirty per cent of the whole; but I have not found a single case where the bulk of the novel consisted of correspondence; this is disappointing, for I should have liked to show how the third-person narrative with juxtaposed letters grew into the epistolary novel proper. In fact, though the narrative with interspersed letters had a great influence upon the rise of epistolary narrative, no direct connection between them seems to exist.

The same cannot be said of the *Lettres Portugaises* (1667), for the *Portuguese Letters*, regarded as the earliest example of the sentimentalism that was to flourish in the works of Richardson, Sterne, and Goldsmith, exercised a decided influence on the epistolary novel. These enormously popular letters describe the thoughts and emotions of a young girl who begins to realise that her first lover has forsaken her. They have a ring of actuality, for they are written almost exclusively in the narrator's present. Imitations followed quickly. *The Seven Portuguese Letters; Being a Second Part to the Five Love-Letters from a Nun to a Cavalier* (1681) includes something of a narrative past: the lover in this work (unlike the lover in the *Five Portuguese Letters*) is present in the town where the nun is writing her letters to him, so that meetings take place between letters, and the reaction of the writer to what has happened can then play a part in the letters:

> Without any flourish upon the matter you must needs pardon me if I tell you that the Lady you were with yester-evening was not at all handsome, and she danced after such an aukward and unbecoming manner, that I protest the sight gave me a very great disturbance ... (p. 13).

Her jealous reproaches are not groundless, as we learn in the course of the letter. On another occasion the nun tries to revenge herself on him by flirting with the Duke of Almeyde at a dinner party:

> I looked upon him with the most soft and passionate regards I could for my life throughout the whole repast, and which I am fully persuaded you would but take notice of; and every now and then I was whispering one silly thing or other in his Ear, which you perhaps, might imagine to be some notable business, and wonder too how I had the assurance to do so; and yet for all this I could not for my soul make you in the least change your Countenance. Ungrateful Man! Cruel Creature! ... (p. 36).

The use of narrative past in close connection with narrator's present not only adds a new dimension, but gives the narrative a plasticity which is missing in the *Five Portuguese Letters*. Subsequent authors of epistolary fiction were very much concerned with the development of this particular aspect of the epistolary novel. Some of them injected more action into the correspondence simply by inserting passages of third-person narrative between the letters, as for example in *The Gentleman Apothecary* (1670) and *A Sunday Adventure, or, Walk to Hackney* (1683). Others really tried to develop a narrative on two levels, as in *The Double Captive*, Aphra Behn's *Love Letters Between a Noble-Man and his Sister* and *The Polite Correspondence*. Yet it is worth emphasising that the sentimental analysis of the

Portuguese Letters provided the strongest single impetus to the rise of the epistolary narrative.

The narrative possibilities of the epistolary novel were further increased by introducing a greater number of correspondents; thus the narrow and possibly faulty view of the single letter-writer could be corrected by adding the reports of others. Naturally some of the correspondents would know more about the course of events than others who were to be the victims of an intrigue; Clarissa, for example, never sees any of the letters in which Lovelace reveals his plans to Belford. The fact that a particular person can write letters to a number of different recipients (as in *Captain Ayloffe's Letters*) provides rich opportunities for characterisation, for the writer can adjust his letter to the recipient. The use of various letter-writers and recipients in the epistolary novel introduces into the novel for the first time the complexities associated with "point-of-view" technique: instead of accepting (because we have no other choice) the observations of an omniscient narrator, we are presented with a series of subjective views which we must co-ordinate and judge for ourselves. Literary critics from Henry James to W. C. Booth have not been of one mind concerning the merits of a narrative device which demands a high degree of attention and intelligence on the part of the reader, and in the case of the epistolary novel there is always the danger of complicating the plot and confusing the reader by too large a number of correspondents.

In discussing the rise of the epistolary novel I have chosen to concentrate on structural considerations, since such an approach seems to me the most fruitful. But of course other factors played their part in the development of the novel – in particular the social and economic conditions of the time; to readers interested in following the effect of contemporary conditions on the early novel, I would recommend Robert Adams Day's recently published book, *Told in Letters. Epistolary Fiction Before Richardson*. Mr Day points out that the £2 to £6 which a novelist could expect for his labours (as compared to about ten guineas for a longer poem or £50 to £100 for a play) encouraged hasty work and negligence in matters of style and composition. Book prices, however, were high, so that novels were purchased by the well-to-do, who might, then, pass them on to their servants. Most people relied on the relatively cheap periodicals for a supply of novels and stories. Mr Day describes the reading public for fiction as follows:

It probably excluded the poor, the learned, or the intellectual, the religious, and the commercial "lower middle class". (There is no question that other members of the *economic* "lower middle class", such as the very numerous group of upper servants, were readers of popular fiction.) It included many members of the nobility and gentry, the bourgeois rich, the young, and the fashionable; and although the tastes of women may have dominated its choices in fiction, it also included many men (p. 77).

The novel at the end of the seventeenth and the beginning of the eighteenth century had not emerged from the shadow cast by the dubious respectability of its predecessors, the romance and the scandalous chronicle; moreover, Puritan morality branded any kind of fiction as a sinful lie – hence the universal attempt on the part of authors of novels to convince their readers that what they were about to read was the truth. That the stories themselves contained a great deal of incredible coincidence and characterisation did not matter; the author's assurance (and, in epistolary novels, the inclusion of actual "documents") permitted the reader to follow with a quiet conscience the "true" story of "people like you and me". The additional claim found in the prefaces and advertisements (and documented in Mr Day's book) that the novel in question presented "passion, sentiments, and feelings" reflected an increasing public demand for a depiction of the emotions, and shows that long before Richardson and Sterne the tendency towards sentimentalism was making itself felt in English literature.

I would not wish to give the impression that the epistolary novel developed gradually and continuously from its primitive beginnings to the full-fledged novel. For although the seventeenth century produced several respectable epistolary works, a number of eighteenth-century novelists used the letter form without attempting to make use of its advantages. The quality of an epistolary novel depends in the last analysis not on the current stage in the development of narrative technique (though the author may receive stimulation and ideas from what is going on in the literature of his own day), but on the individual talent of the writer, on his own stature as a novelist.

We have observed in the rise of the epistolary novel the gradual transition from the literature of facts and historic reality to the fictitious, that is to say imaginary, world of the novel – something essentially different from the world of reality. Any attempt to draw a hard and fast line between what is a literary work and what belongs to the world of reality, to set up, in other words, a definition of the novel, would seem to be doomed to failure. Yet a distinction can be drawn, and one which is less a matter of whether a narrative is historically true or not than of whether its structure reflects the specifically literary intention of the author. Formal qualities such as self-sufficiency of the plot, the stylistic disguise assumed by the author, the way he forms and organises his thought, the way he makes use of the apostrophe to appeal to a wider audience or takes over stock motives from other stories, determine whether a work is fictitious enough to be considered a work of fiction. It is, then, the literary device, the artistic form in which the ideas are served up, that alerts us to the fact that what we have before us is a work of fiction.

I hope to have made clear that the epistolary novel, although possessing its own particular merits and limitations, has, *mutatis mutandis*, much in common with other kinds of narration. The technique of narration on two levels, questions of immediacy and point-of-view, and the relationship between narrator and reader are matters of concern in first-person and third-person novels as well. The epistolary novel, with roots in the realm of "practical" writing as well as in traditional fiction, proved especially suitable for psychological analysis, so that this aspect of story-telling developed considerably during the course of the eighteenth century. Towards the end of the eighteenth century the epistolary novel was replaced by other literary forms and never again regained its former importance; nevertheless, Fanny Burney and Jane Austen wrote epistolary novels and short stories before they found other means of expressing what they wished to say. The introduction into the novel of psychological analysis and point-of-view technique, as well as the attainment of a high degree of dramatic immediacy, are achievements of the eighteenth-century novel, and particularly of the epistolary novel. These are qualities which have remained important elements of story-telling ever since.

NOTES

1 *The Works of Monsieur Voiture . . . Containing His Familiar Letters To Gentlemen and Ladies . . . With Three Collections of Letters on Friendship and several other Occasions: Written by John Dryden, Esq., William Wycherley, Esq., William Congreve . . . And Facetious Letters out of Greek, Latin and French. By the late Ingenious Mr Tho. Brown.* London, 1705, vol. II, p. 58.

2 *The Complete Works of George Farquhar*, ed. by Charles Stonehill. London, 1930, vol. II, p. 243.

3 Cf. Charlotte Charrier, *Héloïse dans l'histoire et dans la légende*. Paris, 1933.

4 Cf. *The Polite Correspondence*, Letter XV, Eliza to Florimond, see below p. 171.

5 *Clarissa, Or, The History of a Young Lady Comprehending the most Important Concerns of her Private Life. . . .* London, 1748, vol. I, p. v.

6 Preface to *The History of Sir Charles Grandison. . . .* London, 1754, vol. I, p. vi.

6a *Everyman's Library No. 882*, London, 1932, pp. 67–68.

7 W. C. Booth, "The Self-Conscious Narrator in Comic Fiction before *Tristram Shandy*". *PMLA*, LXVII, 2, March 1952, pp. 163–85.

8 Translated into English 1736–42.

9 *Mrs Elizabeth Freke. Her Diary 1671 to 1714.* Ed. Mary Carbery, Cork, 1913, p. 72.

10 *Woodforde Papers and Diaries.* Ed. Dorothy Heighes Woodforde, London, 1932, p. 15.

11 W. H. Irving, *The Providence of Wit in the English Letter Writers*. Durham, North Carolina, 1955, p. 10.

12 *The Athenian Mercury*, March 17th, 1690/91 (vol. I, No. 1) Quest. 6.

13 *The Athenian Mercury*, November 24th, 1694 (vol. 15, No. 24) Quest. 1.

14 *Everyman's Library No. 683*, London, 1955, p. 82.

15 *Everyman's Library No. 882*, London, 1932, p. 53 (vol. I, Letter XIII).

Five Love-Letters
from a Nun to a Cavalier

Done out of French into English
by Roger L'Estrange
London, 1678

Five Love-Letters
from a Nun to a Cavalier

The authorship of *Les Lettres Portugaises* (1669) – allegedly a translation from the Portuguese – is still a mystery to literary scholars. The Portuguese original is not extant and it is quite possible that it never existed, especially since it was a common device to introduce fictitious letters and memoirs as translations from a foreign language in order to support their claim to veracity. Yet if the five love-letters of the forsaken nun to her lover, who was an officer in the French army and reputed to be the Count of Chamilly, were just invented, they are extraordinarily convincing. Until the late nineteenth century their authenticity was scarcely questioned and scholars even succeeded in finding a nun to whom they ascribed the authorship, one Mariana d'Alcoforado of the *convento da Conceião de Beja*, who in 1709 became abbess of the convent and died in 1723 at the age of eighty-seven. Rilke, who translated the letters from French into German, regarded the nun as one of the great lovers in human history. F. C. Green, however, is strongly convinced that the letters are fictitious and produces much evidence to support his opinion:[1] Lavergne de Guilleragues, French ambassador to Turkey, may be the author, if he is identical with the Guilleraques cited in the *Registre des privilèges accordés aux auteurs et libraires* of 1668. Yet another commentator, Raymond Mortimer, is inclined to believe in Mariana d'Alcoforado.[2] Were we to judge the authenticity of the *Portuguese Letters* only by examining the letters themselves, their immediacy of passion would lead us to think them genuine, whereas their highly rhetorical style points to the conscious shaping of an author.

Whether genuine or fictitious, the *Portuguese Letters* were a great success in their time and exerted considerable influence upon the fiction of the seventeenth and early eighteenth centuries. In 1678 they were translated into English by Sir Roger L'Estrange and by the time that *Pamela* appeared in 1740 they had run into their tenth edition. Continuations and innumerable imitations followed their appearance. To write "à la portugaise" became a literary vogue and the seduced and forsaken nun, or at any rate the mourning, forsaken, letter-writing lover, developed into a stock fictional figure. It is surprising that a story – if it can be called that – consisting almost entirely of emotions should become so popular at a time when fiction was mainly concerned with outward action, with duels and wars, intrigue and mistaken identity, elopements, travel adventure and the like. Obviously the reading public was ready for the emerging age of sensibility.

The recipient of the five letters, who is the unfaithful lover, of course knows about the unhappy love affair; the forsaken lover is therefore able for the most part to dispense with descriptions of the past and concentrate on what is going on within herself. Her feelings change from passionate love to just as passionate reproach, from pride in her unique passion to profound unhappiness, and so on. At times she is strongly repetitive – a realistic touch which adds to our consciousness of her emotional state. The letters move from an optimistic belief in her lover's return, through jealous suspicion, passionate protest against her fate, disillusion, to final despair; this shift of attitude provides a framework for the author's minute sentimental analysis, and is in a sense a substitute for a story, psychological events replacing outward adventures.

Sir Roger L'Estrange's translation, which appears here, provided a stylistic and linguistic model for all the later imitations. More natural and unpretentious than the original French text, its impact is greater. A modern translation (1956) by Lucy Norton resorts to the language of the Augustan Age in an attempt to imitate the classical French style. The result is a formal and rather stilted version that has little to do with the passionate document perused by seventeenth-century English readers. Even in Sir Roger's translation the language is highly rhetorical, but it is a rhetoric which was to become typical of sentimental literature. Exclamations, enumerations and repetitions, rhetorical questions and hyperbole were used in a context of sensibility and served to express passion rather than rational thought. A new vocabulary of tenderness developed, and words like "hope", "fear", "pain", "torment", "joy", "delight", "heart", "soul", "sigh", "tears", "sensible", and "feel" were used more frequently, replacing metaphors centering on captivity in love, suffering under love's tyranny, Cupid's enchantments, etc. In the *Portuguese Letters* we recognise an attempt at emotional realism within the bounds of the linguistic possibilities of the time. A detailed examination of a psychological process such as that attempted in these letters called for new narrative skills, and in the work of subsequent novelists we can follow the gradual emergence of the necessary techniques. The *Portuguese Letters*, like the religious diary and the spiritual autobiography, contributed much to the rise of psychological analysis in literature, and helped to initiate that cult of feeling so prominent in the eighteenth century.

NOTES

[1] F. C. Green, "Who was the author of the 'Lettres Portugaises'?", *MLR*, XXI, 1926, pp. 159–67.
[2] Cf. his introduction to the recent translation by Lucy Norton (1956).

THE FIRST LETTER

OH my Inconsiderate, Improvident, and most unfortunate Love; and those Treacherous Hopes that have betray'd both Thee, and Me! The Passion that I design'd for the Blessing of my Life, is become the Torment of it: A Torment, as prodigious as the Cruelty of his Absence that causes it. Bless mee! But must this Absence last for ever? This Hellish Absence, that Sorrow it self wants words to express? Am I then never to see those Eyes again, that have so often exchang'd Love with Mine, and Charm'd my very soul with Extacy, and Delight? Those Eyes that were ten thousand worlds to mee, and all that I desir'd; the only comfortable Light of Mine, which, since I understood the Resolution of your Insupportable Departure, have Serv'd mee but to weep withall, and to Lament the sad Approach of my Inevitable fate. And yet in this Extremity I cannot, me-thinks but have some Tenderness, even for the Misfortunes that are of your Creating. My Life was vow'd to you the first time I saw you: and since you would not accept of it as a Present, I am Content to make it a sacrifice. A Thousand times a day I send my Sighs to hunt you out: and what Return for all my Passionate Disquiets, but the good Counsel of my Cross fortune? that whispers me at every turn; Ah wretched *Mariane*! Why do'st thou flatter, and Consume thy self in the vain pursuit of a Creature never to be Recover'd? Hee's gone, hee's gone; Irrevocably gone; h'as past the seas to fly thee. Hee's now in *France*; dissolv'd in pleasures; and thinks no more of thee, or what thou suffer'st for his false sake, then if he had never known any such woman. But hold: Y'ave more of Honour in you then to do so ill a thing; and so have I, then to believe it, especially of a Person that I'm so much concern'd to justify. *Forget me?* 'Tis Impossible. My Case is bad enough at best, without the Aggravation of vain suppositions. No, no: The Care and Pains you took to make me think you lov'd me, and then the Joyes that That Care gave Me, must never be forgotten: and Should I love you less this Moment, then[1] when I lov'd you most, (in Confidence that you lov'd me so too) I were Ungratefull. 'Tis an Unnatural, and a strange thing methinks, that the Remembrance of those blessed hours should be now so terrible to me; and that those delights that were so ravishing in the Enjoyment, should become so bitter in the Reflection. Your last Letter gave me Such a Passion of the heart, as if it would have forc'd its way thorough[2] my Breast, and follow'd you. It laid me three hours sensless: I wish it had been *dead*; for I had dy'd of Love. But I reviv'd: and to what End? only to die again, and lose that Life for you, which you your Self did not think worth the saving. Beside that there's no Rest for me, while you're Away, but in the grave.

This fit was follow'd with other Ill Accidents which I shall never be without, till I see you: In the mean while, I bear them yet without repining, because they came from you. But with your Leave: Is this the Recompense that you intend me? Is this your way of treating those that love you? Yet 'tis no Matter, for (do what you will) I am resolv'd to be firm to you to my last gasp; and never to see the Eyes of any other Mortal. And I dare assure you that it will not be the worse for you neither, if you never set your heart upon any other woman: for certainly a Passion under the degree of mine, will never content you: You may find more Beauty perhaps elsewhere (tho' the time was when you found no fault with mine) but you shall never meet with so true a heart; and all the rest is nothing.

Let me entreat you not to stuff your Letters with things Unprofitable, and Impertinent to our Affair: and you may save your self the trouble too of desiring me to THINK of you. Why 'tis Impossible for me to forget you: and I must not forget the hope you gave me neither, of your Return, and of spending some part of your time here with us in *Portugal*. Alas! And why not your whole Life rather? If I could but find any way to deliver my self from this unlucky Cloyster, I should hardly stand gaping here for the performance of your Promise: but in defiance of all opposition, put my self upon the March, Search you out, follow you, and love you throughout the whole world. It is not that I please my self with this Project as a thing feasible; or that I would so much as entertain any hope of Comfort; (tho' in the very delusion I might find pleasure) but as it is my Lot to be miserable, I will be only sensible of that which is my Doom. And yet after all this, I cannot deny but upon this Opportunity of writing to you which my Brother has given me I was surpriz'd with some faint Glimmerings of Delight, that yielded me a temporary Respite to the horrour of my despair. Tell me I conjure you; what was it that made you so sollicitous to entangle me, when you knew you were to leave me? And why so bloudily bent to make me Unhappy? why could you not let me alone at quiet in my Cloyster as you found me? Did I ever do you any Injury?

But I must ask your Pardon; for I lay nothing to your Charge. I am not in condition to meditate a Revenge: and I can only complain of the Rigour of my Perverse fortune. When she has parted our Bodies, she has done her worst, and left us nothing more to fear: Our hearts are Inseparable; for those whom Love has United are never to be divided. As you tender my soul let me hear often from you. I have a Right me-thinks to the Knowledg both of your Heart, and of your fortune; and to your Care to inform me of it too. But *what ever you do, be sure to come; and above all things in the world, to let me see you. Adieu.* And yet I cannot quitt this Paper yet. Oh that I could but convey my self in the Place on't! Mad fool that I am, to talk at this Rate of a thing that I my self know to be Impossible! *Adieu.* For I can go no farther. *Adieu.* Do but Love me for ever, and I care not what I endure.

THE SECOND LETTER

There is so great a difference betwixt the Love I write, and That which I feel, that if you measure the One by the Other, I have undone my self. Oh how happy were I if you could but judg of my Passion by the violence of your own! But That I perceive is not to be the Rule betwixt you, and me. Give me leave however to tell you with an honest freedom, that tho' you cannot love me, you do very ill yet to treat me at this Barbarous Rate: It puts me out of my Wits to see my self forgotten; and iti s as little for your Credit perhaps, as it is for my Quiet. Or if I may not say that you are Unjust, it is yet the most Reasonable thing in the World to let me tell you that I am Miserable: I foresaw what it would come to, upon the very Instant of your Resolution to leave me. Weak Woman that I was! to expect, (after this) that you should have more Honour, and Integrity then other Men, because I had unquestionably deserv'd it from you, by a transcendent degree of Affection above the Love of Other Women. No, no; Your Levity, and Aversion have overrul'd your Gratitude, and Justice; You are my Enemy by Inclination: whereas only the Kindness of your Disposition can Oblige me. Nay your Love it self, if it were barely grounded upon my Loving of you, could never make me happy. But so far am I even from that Pretence, that in six Moneths I have not receiv'd one sillable from you; Which I must impute to the blind fondness of my own Passion, for I should otherwise have forseen that my Comforts were to be but Temporary, and my Love Everlasting. For Why should I think that you would ever content your self to spend your Whole Life in *Portugal*; and relinquish your Country, and your fortune, only to think of me? Alas! my sorrows are Inconsolable, and the very Remembrance of my past Enjoyments makes up a great part of my present pain. But must all my hopes be blasted then, and fruitless? Why may not I yet live to see you again within these Walls and with all those Transports of Extacy, and Satisfaction, as heretofore? But how I fool my self! for I find now that the Passion, which on my side, took up all the faculties of my soul, and Body, was only excited on your part by some loose Pleasures, and that they were to live and die together. It should have been my Business, even in the Nick of those Critical, and Blessed Minutes, to have Reasoned my self into the Moderation of so Charming, and deadly an Excess; and to have told my self before-hand, the fate which I now suffer. But my Thoughts were too much taken up with You to consider my self; So that I was not in Condition to attend the Care of my Repose, or to bethink my self of what might poison it, and disappoint me in the full Emprovement of the most Ardent Instances of your Affection. I was too much pleas'd with you, to think of parting with you, and yet you may remember that I have told you now and then by fits, that you would be the Ruin of me. But those Phancies were soon dispers'd; and I was glad to

7

yield them up too; and to give up my self to the Enchantments of your false Oaths, and Protestations. I see very well the Remedy of all my Misfortunes, and that I should quickly be at Ease if I could leave Loving you. But Alas! That were a Remedy worse then the disease. No, no: I'le rather endure any thing then forget you. Nor could I if I would. 'Tis a thing that did never so much as enter into my Thought. But is not your Condition now the worse of the two? Is it not better to endure what I now suffer, then to enjoy Your faint satisfactions among your French Mistresses? I am so far from Envying your Indifference, that I pitty it. I defie you to forget me absolutely: and I am deceiv'd if I have not taken such a Course with you, that you shall never be perfectly happy without me. Nay perhaps I am at this Instant the less miserable of the two; in regard that I am the more employ'd. They have lately made me doorkeeper here in this Convent. All the people that talk to me think me mad; for I answer them I know not what; And certainly the rest of the Convent must be as mad as I, they would never else have thought me Capable of any Trust. How do I envy the good Fortune of poor *Emanuel*, and *Francisco*! Why cannot I be with you perpetually as they are? tho in your Livery too? I should follow you as Close without dispute, and serve you at least as faithfully; for there is nothing in this World that I so much desire as to see you; But however, let me entreat you to think of me; and I shall Content my self with a bare place in your Memory. And yet I cannot tell neither, whether I should or no: for I know very well that when I saw you every day I should hardly have satisfy'd my self within these Bounds. But you have taught me since, that whatsoever you will have me do, I must do. In the *Interim*, I do not at all repent of my Passion for you; Nay, I am well enough satisfi'd that you have seduc'd me; and your Absence it self tho' never so rigorous, and perhaps Eternal, does not at all lessen the vigour of my Love: which I will avow to the Whole world, for I make no secret on't. I have done many things irregularly 'tis true; and against the Common Rules of good Manners: and not without taking some Glory in them neither, because they were done for your sake. My honour, and Religion are brought only to serve the Turn of my Love, and to carry me on to my lives end, in the Passionate Continuance of the Affection I have begun. I do not write this, to draw a Letter from you; wherefore never force your self for the Matter: for I will receive nothing at your hands; no not so much as any Mark of your Affection, unless it comes of its own accord, and in a Manner, whether you Will or No. If it may give you any satisfaction, to save your self the trouble of Writing, it shall give me some likewise, to excuse the unkindness of it; for I am wonderfully enclin'd to pass over all your faults. A *French* Officer, that had the Charity this morning to hold me at least three hours in a discourse of you, tells me that *France* has made a Peace. If it be so; Why cannot you bestow a visit upon me, and take me away with you? But 'tis more then I deserve, and it must be as you please; for my Love does not at all depend upon your Manner of treating me. Since you went away I have not had one Minutes Health, nor any sort of Pleasure, but in the Accents of your Name, which I call upon a Thousand times a day. Some of my Companions that understand the deplorable Ruin you have brought upon me, are so good as to entertain me many times concerning you. I keep as Close to my Chamber as is possible; which is the dearer to me even for the many Visits you have made me there. Your Picture I have perpetually before me, and I Love it more then my hearts bloud. The very Counterfeit gives me some Comfort: But oh the Horrours too! When I consider that the Original, for ought I know, is lost for ever. But why should it be possible, even to be possible, that I may never see you more? Have you forsaken me then for ever? It turns my Brain to think on't. Poor *Mariane*! But my Spirits fail me, and I shall scarce out-live this Letter? – Mercy – Farwel, Farwel.

THE THIRD LETTER

What shall become of me? Or what will you advise me to do? How strangely am I dissapointed, in all my Expectations! Where are the Letters from you? the Long and Kind Letters that I look'd for by every Post? To keep me alive in the hopes of Seeing you again; and in the Confidence of your faith, and Justice; to settle me in some tolerable state of Repose, without being abandon'd to any insupportable Extream? I had once cast my Thoughts upon some Idle Projects of endeavouring my own Cure, in Case I could but once assure my self that I was totally forgotten. The distance you were at; Certain Impulses of Devotion; the fear of utterly destroying the Remainder of my Imperfect health, by so many restless Nights, and Cares; the Improbability of your return; The Coldness of your Passion, and the Formality of your last *Adieu's*; Your Weak, and frivolous pretences for your departure: These, with a thousand other Considerations, (of more weight, then profit) did all concurre to encourage me in my design, if I should find it necessary; In fine; having only my single self to encounter I could not doubt of the success, nor could it enter into my Apprehension what I feel at this day. Alas! how wretched is my Condition, that am not allow'd so much as to divide these sorrows with you, of which you your self are the Cause? You are the Offender, and I am to bear the Punishment of your Crime. It strikes me to the very heart, for fear you, that are now so insensible of my Torments, were never much affected with our mutual delights. Yes, yes; 'Tis now a Clear Case that your whole Address to me was only an Artificial disguise. You betray'd me as often as you told me, how over-joy'd you were that you had got me alone: and your Passions, and Transports were only the Effects of my own Importunities. Yours

9

was a deliberate design to fool me; your business was to make a Conquest, not a friend; and to triumph over my Heart, without ever engaging or hazzarding your own. Are not you very Unhappy now, and (at least) Ill-natur'd, if not ill-bred, only to make this wretched use of so Superlative a friendship? Who would have thought it possible that such a Love as mine, should not have made you happy? 'Tis for your sake alone if I am troubl'd for the Infinite delights that you have lost, and might as easily have enjoy'd, had you but thought them worth the while. Ah! If you did but understand them aright, you would find a great difference betwixt the Pleasure of Obliging me, and that of Abusing me; and betwixt the Charming felicities of Loving violently, and of being so belov'd. I do not know either what I am, or what I do, or what I would be at. I am torn to pieces by a Thousand contrary Motions, and in a Condition deplorable beyond imagination. I love you to death, and so tenderly too that I dare hardly wish your heart in the same condition with mine. I should destroy my self, or die with Grief, could I believe your nights and Thoughts, as restless as I find Mine; your Life as Anxious and disturb'd; your Eyes still flowing and all things and people Odious to you. Alas! I am hardly able to bear up under my own Misfortunes; how should I then Support the Weight of yours; which would be a Thousand times more grievous to me? And yet all this While I cannot bring my self to advise you, not to Think of me. And to deal freely with you, there is not any thing in *France* that you take pleasure in, or that comes near your heart, but I'm most furiously jealous of it. I do not know what 'tis I write for. Perhaps you'l pitty me; but what good will that pitty do me? I'le none on't. Oh how I hate my self when I consider what I have forfeited to oblige you! I have blasted my Reputation; I have lost my Parents; I have expos'd my self to the Lawes of my Country against Persons of my Profession; and finally, to your Ingratitude, the worst of my Misfortunes. But why do I pretend to a Remorse, when at this Instant, I should be glad with all my Soul, if I had run ten thousand greater hazzards for your dear Sake? and for the danger of my Life and Honour; the very thought on't is a kind of doleful Pleasure to me, and all's no more then the delivery of whats your own, and what I hold most Pretious, into your Disposition; And I do not know how all these risques could have been better Imploy'd. Upon the Whole matter, every thing despleases me, my Love, my Misfortune; and alas! I cannot perswade my self that I am well us'd even by You. And yet I Live, (false as I am) and take as much pains to preserve my life, as to lose it. Why do I not die of shame then, and shew you the despair of my Heart, as well as of my Letters? If I had lov'd you so much as I have told you a thousand times I did, I had been in my Grave long ere this. But I have deluded you, and the Cause of Complaint is now on your side. Alas! why did you not tell me of it? Did I not see you go away? Am I not out of all hopes of ever seeing you again? And am I yet alive? I have betray'd you, and I beg your pardon. But do not grant it though; Treat me as severely as you will: Tell me that my Passion is Weak, and Irresolute. Make your self yet harder to be pleas'd. Write me word that you would have me die for you. Do it, I conjure you; and assist me in the Work of surmounting the Infirmity of my Sex; and that I may put an end to all my fruitless deliberations, by an effectual despair. A Tragical Conclusion would undoubtedly bring me often into your thoughts, and make my Memory dear to you. And who knows how you might be Affected, with the Bravery of so Glorious a death? A death Incomparably to be preferr'd before the Life that you have left me. Farwel then; and *I wish I had never seen the Eyes of you.* But my heart Contradicts my Pen; for I feel, in the very moment that I write it, that I would rather chuse to Love you in any state of Misery, then agree to the bare Supposition that I had never Seen you. Wherefore since you do not think fit, to mend my fortune, I shall chearfully submit to the worst on't. *Adieu*; but first promise me, that if I die of grief, you will have some Tenderness for my Ashes: Or at least that the Generosity of my Passion shall put you out of Love with all other things. This Consolation shall satisfie me, that if you must never be mine, I may be secur'd that you shall never be Anothers. You cannot be so Inhumane sure, as to make a mean use of my most Affectionate despairs, and to recommend your self to any other Woman, by shewing the Power you have had upon me. Once more, *Adieu*. My Letters are long, and I fear troublesom; but I hope you'l forgive them, and dispense with the fooleries of a Sot of your own making. *Adieu*. Me-thinks I run over and over too often with the story of my most deplorable Condition: Give me leave now to thank you from the Bottom of my heart for the Miseries you have brought upon me, and to detest the Tranquillity I liv'd in before I knew you. My Passion is greater every Moment than other. *Adieu*. Oh what a World of things have I to tell you!

THE FOURTH LETTER

Your Lieutenant tells me that you were forc'd by foul Weather to put in upon the Coast of *Algarve*. I am afraid the Sea does not agree with you; and my Fears for your Misfortunes make me almost to forget my own. Can you imagin your Lieutenant to be more concern'd in what befals you, than I am? If not, How comes he to be so well inform'd, and not one sillable to me? If you could never find the means of writing to me since you went, I am very Unhappy; but I am more so, if you could have written, and would not. But what should a body expect from so much Ingratitude, and Injustice? And yet it would break my heart, if heaven should punish you upon any account of mine. For I had much rather gratifie my Kindness, than my Revenge. There can be nothing clearer, than that you neither

Love me, nor Care what becomes of me; and yet am I so foolish, as to follow the Dictate of a blind, and besotted Passion, in oposition to the Counsels of a demonstrative Reason. This Coldness of yours, when you and I were first acquainted, would have sav'd me many a sorrowful Thought. But where's the Woman, that in my Place, would have done otherwise than I did? Who would ever have question'd the Truth of so pressing and Artificial an Importunity? We cannot easily bring our selves to suspect the Faith of those we Love. I know very well, that a slender Excuse will serve your Turn; and I'le be so kind as to save you even the Labour of That too, by telling you, that I can never consent to conclude you guilty, but in order to the infinite Pleasure I shall take to acquit you, in perswading my self that you are Innocent. It was the Assiduity of your Conversation that refin'd me; your Passion that inflam'd me; Your good Humour that Charm'd me; your Oaths, and Vows that confirm'd me; but 'twas my own precipitate Inclination that seduc'd me; and what's the Issue of these fair, and promising Beginnings, but Sighs, Tears, Disquiets, nay, and the worst of Deaths too, without either Hope, or Remedy. The Delights of my Love, I must confess, have been strangely surprizing; but follow'd with Miseries not to be express'd; (as whatever comes from you works upon me in Extreams.) If I had either obstinately oppos'd your Address; or done any thing to put you out of humour, or make you jealous, with a design to draw you on: If I had gon any crafty, artificial wayes to work with you; or but so much as check'd my early, and my growing Inclinations to comply with you, (tho' it would have been to no purpose at all) you might have had some Colour then to make use of your Power, and deal with me accordingly. But so far was I from opposing your Passion, that I prevented it; for I had a kindness for your Person, before you ever told me any thing of your Love; and you had no sooner declar'd it, but with all the joy imaginable I receiv'd it, and gave my self up wholly to that Inclination. You had at that time your Eyes in your Head, tho' I was Blind. Why would you let me go on then to make my self the miserable Creature which now I am? Why would you train me on to all those Extravagances which to a person of your Indifference must needs have been very Importune? You knew well enough that you were not to be always in *Portugal*; Why must I then be singl'd out from all the rest, to be made thus Unfortunate? In this Country without dispute you might have found out handsomer Women than my self, that would have serv'd your turn every jot as well, (to your course purpose) and that would have been true to you as far as they could have seen you, without breaking their hearts for you, when you were gon: and such as you might have forsaken at last, whithout either Falsness, or Cruelty: Do you call this the Tenderness of a Lover, or the Persecution of a Tyrant? And 'tis but destroying of your own neither. You are just as easie, I find, to believe ill of me, as I have always been to think better of you than you have deserv'd. Had you but lov'd me half so well as I do you, you would never have parted with me upon so easie Terms. I should have master'd greater Difficulties, and never have up-braided you with the Obligation neither. Your Reasons, 'tis true, were very feeble, but if they had been the strongest imaginable, it had been all one to me: for nothing but death it self could ever have torn me from you. Your Return into *France* was nothing in the World but a Pretext of your own contriving. *There was a Vessel* (you said) *that was thither bound.* And why could not you let that Vessel take her Course? *Your Relations sent for you away.* You are no stranger sure to the Persecution, that for your sake, I have suffer'd from mine. *Your Honour* (forsooth) *engag'd you to forsake me.* Why did you not think of that scruple, when you deluded me to the loss of mine? *Well! but you must go back to serve your Prince.* His Majesty, I presume, would have excus'd you in that point; for I cannot learn that he has any need of your Service. But, Alas! I should have been too happy, if you and I might have liv'd, and dy'd together. This only Comfort I have in the bitterness of our deadly separation, that I was never false to you; and that for the whole World I would not have my Conscience tainted with so black a Crime. But can you then, that know the Integrity of my Soul, and the Tenderness that I have for you; can you (I say) find in your heart to abandon me for ever, and expose me to the Terrours that attend my wretched Condition? Never so much as to think of me again, but only when you are to sacrifice me to a new Passion. My Love, you see, has distracted me; and yet I make no complaint at all of the violence of it: for I am so wonted to Persecutions, that I have discover'd a kind of pleasure in them, which I would not live without, and which I enjoy, while I love you, in the middle of a thousand afflictions. The most grievous part of my Calamity, is the hatred, and disgust that you have given me for all other things: My Friends, my Kindred, the Convent it self is grown intollerable to me; and whatsoever I am oblig'd either to see, or to do, is become odious. I am grown so jealous of my Passion, that methinks all my Actions, and all my Dutys ought to have some regard to you. Nay, every moment that is not employ'd upon your service, my Conscience checks me for it, either as misbestow'd, or cast away. My Heart is full of Love, and Hatred; and, Alas! what should I do without it? should I survive this restlessness of thought, to lead a Life of more tranquility, and ease, such an Emptiness, and such an Insensibility could never consist. Every Creature takes Notice how strangely I am chang'd in my Humour, my Manners, and in my Person. My Mother takes me to task about it: One while she speaks me fair, and then she chides me, and asks me what I ail. I do not well know what answers I have made her; but I Phancy that I have told her all. The most severe, even of the Religious themselves, take pity of me, and bear with my Condition. The whole World is touch'd with my Misfortunes;

your single self excepted, as wholy unconcern'd: Either you are not pleas'd to write at all; or else your Letters are so cold; so stuff'd with Repetitions; the Paper not half full, and your Constraint so grosly disguis'd, that one may see with half an Eye the pain you are in till they are over. *Dona Brites* would not let me be quiet the other day, till she had got me out of my Chamber, on to the Balcon that looks (you know) toward *Mertola*: she did it to oblige me, and I follow'd her: But the very sight of the Place struck me with so terrible an Impression, that it set me a Crying the whole day after. Upon this, she took me back again, and I threw my self upon my Bed, where I pass'd a thousand Reflections upon the despairs of my Recovery. I am the worse I find for that which people do to relieve me; and the Remedies they offer me do but serve to aggravate my Miseries. Many a time have I seen you pass by from this Balcon; (and the sight pleas'd me but too well) and there was I that fatal day, when I first found my self strook with this unhappy Passion. Methought you look'd as if you had a mind to oblige me, even before you knew me; and your Eye was more upon me than the rest of the Company. And when you made a stop, I fool'd my self to think that it was meant to me too, that I might take a fuller view of you, and see how every thing became you. Upon giving your Horse the spur (I remember) my heart was at my mouth for fear of an untoward leap you put him upon. In fine; I could not but secretly concern my self in all your Actions; and as you were no longer indifferent to me, so I took several things to my self also from you; and as done in my favour. I need not tell you the sequel of Matters (not that I care who knows it) nor would I willingly write the whole Story, lest I should make you thought more culpable (if possible) than in Effect (perhaps) you are. Beside that it might furnish your Vanity with subject of reproach, by shewing that all my Labours, and Endeavours to make sure of you, could not yet keep you from forsaking me. But what a fool am I, in thinking to work more upon your Ingratitude, with Letters, and Invectives, than ever I could with my Infinite Love, and the liberty that attended it! No, No: I am too sure of my ill Fortune, and you are too unjust to make me doubt of it; and since I find my self deserted, what mischief is there in Nature which I am not to fear? But are your Charms only to work upon me? Why may not other Women look upon you with my Eyes? I should be well enough content perhaps to find more of my Sex (in some degree) of my Opinion; and that all the Ladyes of *France* had an esteem for you, provided that none of them either doted upon you, or pleas'd you: This is a most ridiculous, and an impossible Proposition. But there's no danger (I may speak it upon sad Experience) of your troubling your head long with any one thing; and you will forget me easily enough, without the help of being forc'd to't by a new Passion. So infinitely do I love you, that (since I am to lose you) I could e'en wish that you had had some fairer colour for't. It is true, that I would have made me more miserable; but you should have less to answer for then. You'l stay in *France*, I perceive, in perfect Freedom, and perhaps not much to your Satisfaction; The Incommodities of a long Voyage; some Punctilioes of good Manners; and the fear of not returning Love for Love, may perchance keep you there. Oh, you may safely trust me in this Case: Let me but only see you now and then, and know that we are both of us in the same Country, it shall content me. But why do I flatter my self? Who knows but that the Rigour and Severity of some other Woman may come to prevail upon you more than all my Favours? Tho' I cannot believe you yet to be a Person that will be wrought upon by ill usage.

Before you come to engage in any powerful Passion, let me entreat you to bethink your self of the Excess of my Sorrows; the Uncertainty of my Purposes; the Distraction of my Thoughts; the Extravagance of my Letters; the Trusts I have repos'd in you; my Despairs, my Wishes, and my Jealousies. Alas! I am affraid that you are about to make your self unfortunate. Take warning, I beg of you, by my Example, and make some Use to your self of the Miseries that I endure for you. I remember you told me in Confidence, (and in great Earnest too) some five, or six Months ago, that you had once a Passion for a *French* Lady. If she be any Obstacle to your Return, deal frankly with me, and put me out of my Pain. It will be a kind of Mercy to me, if the faint hope which yet Supports me, must never take effect, even to lose my Life, and that together. Pray'e send me her picture, and Some of her Letters, and write me all she says. I shall find Something there undoubtedly that will make me either better, or worse. In the Condition that I am, I cannot long continue; and any Change whatsoever must be to my Advantage. I should take it kindly if you would send me your Brothers, and your Sisters pictures too. Whatsoever is dear to you must be so to me; and I am a very faithful Servant to any thing that is related to you: and it cannot be otherwise: For you have left me no power at all to dispose of my self. Sometimes me-thinks I could Submit even to attend upon the Woman that you Love. So low am I brought by your Scorns, and ill Usage, that I dare not so much as say to my self, *Methinks I might be allow'd to be jealous, without displeasing you.* Nay, I chide my self as the most mistaken Creature in the World to blame you: and I am many times convinc'd that I ought not to importune you as I do, with those passages, and thoughts which you are pleas'd to disown.

The Officer that waits for this Letter grows a little Impatient: I had once resolv'd to keep it clear from any possibility of giving you Offence. But it is broken out into Extravagances, and 'tis time to put an end to't. But Alas! I have not the heart to give it over. When I write to you, me-thinks I speak to you: and our Letters bring us nearer together. The first shall be neither So long, nor So troublesome. But you may venutre to open it, and read it upon the assurance that I now give you. I am not to entertain you, I know, with a Passion that displeases you, and you shall hear no more on't. It is now a year within a few days, that I have deliver'd my self wholy up to you, without any Reserve. Your Love I took to be both Warm, and Sincere: And I could never have thought you would have been so weary of my favours, as to take a Voyage of five hundred leagues; and run the Hazzards of Rocks, and Pirates, only to avoid them. This is a Treatment that certainly I never deserv'd at any mans hands. You can call to mind my Shame, my Confusion, and my Disorders. But you have forgotten the Obligations you had to Love me even in despite of your Aversion. The Officer calls upon me now the fourth time for my Letter. He will go away without it, he Says; and presses me, as if he were running away from another Mistress. Farwell. You had not half the difficulty to leave me (tho' perhaps for ever) which I have, only to part with this Letter. But *Adieu*. There are a thousand tender names that I could call you now. But I dare not deliver my self up to the freedom of Writing my thoughts. You are a thousand times dearer to me than my Life, and a thousand times more than I imagine too. Never was any thing So barbarous, and so much belov'd. I must needs tell you once again, that *you do not write to me*. But I am now going to begin afresh, and *the Officer will be gone*. Well, and what matters it? Let him go. 'Tis not so much for your sake that I write, as my own; for my Business is only to divert, and entertain my self: Beside that the very Length of this Letter will make you afraid on't: And you'le never read it thorough neither. What Have I done to draw all these Miseries upon me? And why should you of all others be the poisener of my peace, and blast the Comfort of my Life? Why was I not born in some other Country? forgive me, and farwell. See but to what a Miserable point I am reduc'd, when I dare not so much as intreat you to Love me. *Adieu*.

THE FIFTH LETTER

You will find, I hope, by the different Ayre and stile of this Letter, from all my former, that I have chang'd my Thoughts too; and you are to take this for an Eternal farwell; for I am now at length perfectly convinc'd, that since I have Irrecoverably lost your Love, I can no longer justify my own. Whatsoever I had of Yours shall be sent you by the first Opportunity: There shall be no more writing in the Case; No, not so much as your Name upon the Pacquett. *Dona Brites* is a Person whom I can trust as my own soul, and whom I have entrusted (as you know very well) Unfortunate Wretch that I am! in Confidences of another Quality betwixt you and me. I have left it to her Care to see your Picture and your Bracelets dispatch'd away to you, (those once beloved Pledges of your Kindness) and only in due time to assure me that you have receiv'd them. Would you believe me now, if I should swear to you, that within these five days, I have been at least fifty times upon the very point of Burning the One, and of Tearing the Other into a Million of Pieces? But, You have found me too easy a fool, to think me Capable of so Generous an Indignation. If I could but vex you a little in the story of my Misfortunes; it would be some sort of Abatement me-thinks to the Cruelty of them. Those Bawbles (I must confess, both to Your shame, and Mine) went nearer my heart than I am willing to tell you, and when it came to the Pinch of parting with them, I found it the hardest thing in the World to go thorough with it: So Mortal a Tenderness had I for any thing of Yours, even at that Instant when you your self seem'd to me the most Indifferent thing in Nature: But there's no resisting the force of Necessity and Reason. This Resolution has cost me Many, and Many a Tear; A thousand, and a thousand Agonies, and Distractions, more than you can imagine; and more, Undoubtedly, than you shall ever hear of from me. *Dona Brites* (I say) has them in Charge; upon Condition, never to name them to Me again; No, not so much as to give me a sight of them, though I should beg for't upon my Knees; but, in fine, to hasten them away, without one Syllable to Me of their Going.

If it had not been for this Trial to get the Mastery of my Passion, I should never have understood the force of it; and if I could have foreseen the Pains, and the hazzards of the Encounter, I am afraid that I should never have ventur'd upon the Attempt: for I am verily perswaded that I could much better have Supported your Ingratitude it self, though never so foul, and Odious than the Deadly, Deadly Thought of this Irrevocable Separation. And it is not your Person neither that is so dear to me, but the Dignity of my unalterable Affection. My soul is strangely devided; Your falseness makes me abhor you, and yet at the same time my Love, my Obstinate, and Invincible Love, will not consent to part with you.

What a Blessing were it to me now, if I were but endu'd with the Common Quality of other Women, and only Proud enough to despise you? Alas! Your Contempt I have born already: Nay, had it been your Hatred, or the most Raging Jealousie; All this, compar'd with your Indifference, had been a Mercy to me. By the Impertinent Professions, and the most Ridiculous Civilities of your Last Letter, I find that all mine are Come to your hand; and that you have read them over too: but as unconcern'd, as if you forsooth had no Interest at all in the Matter. Sot that I am, to lie thus at the Mercy of an Insensible, and Ungrateful Creature; and to be as much afflicted now at the Certainty of the Arrival of those Papers, as I was before, for fear of their Miscarriage! What have I to do with your telling me the *truth of things*? Who desir'd to know it? Or the *sincerity* you talk of; a thing you never practis'd toward me, but to my Mischief. Why could you not let me alone in my Ignorance? Who bad you Write? Miserable Woman that I am! Me-thinks after so much pains taken already to delude me to my Ruin, you might have streyn'd one point more, in this

Extremity, to deceive me to my Advantage, without pretending to excuse your self. 'Tis too late to tell you that I have cast away many a Tender Thought upon the Worst of Men; the most Oblig'd, and the most Unthankful. Let if suffice that I know you now as well as if I were in the heart of you. The only favour that I have now to desire from you, after so many done for you, is This: (and I hope you will not refuse it me) Write no more to me; and remember that I have conjur'd you never to do it. Do all that is Possible for you to do, (if ever you had any Love for me) to make me absolutely forget you. For Alas! I dare not trust my self in any sort of Correspondence with you. The least hint in the World of any kind Reflection upon the reading of this Letter, would perchance expose me to a Relapse; and then the taking of me at my Word, on the other side, would most certainly transport me into an Extravagance of Choler, and Despair. So that in my Opinion it will be your best course not to meddle at all with Me, or my Affairs: for which way so ever you go to work, it must inevitably bring a great disorder upon both. I have no Curiosity to know the success of this Letter: Me-thinks the Sorrows you have brought upon me already, might abundantly content you (even if your Design were never so malicious) without disturbing me in my Preparations for my future Peace. Do but leave me in my Uncertainty, and I will not yet despair, in time, of arriving at some degree of Quiet. This I dare promise you, that I shall never hate you; for I am too great an Enemy to Violent Resolutions ever to go about it. Who knows but I may yet live to find a truer friend than I have lost? But Alas! What signifies any mans Love to me, if I cannot Love him? Why should his Passion work more upon my heart, than mine could upon Yours? I have found by sad Experience, that the first Motions of Love, which we are more properly said to Feel, than to Understand, are never to be forgotten: That our souls are perpetually Intent upon the Idol which we our selves have made: That the first Wounds, and the first Images are never to be cur'd, or defac'd: That all the Passions that pretend to succour us either by Diversion, or Satisfaction, are but so many vain Promises of bringing us to our Wits again, which, if once lost, are never to be recover'd: And that all the Pleasures that we pursue, (many times without any desire of finding them) amount to no more, than to convince us, that nothing is so dear to us as the Remembrance of our Sorrows. Why must you pitch upon Mee, for the subject of an Imperfect, and Tormenting Inclination; which I can neither Relinquish with Temper, nor Preserve with Honour? The dismal Consequences of an Impetuous Love, which is not Mutual? And why is it that by a Conspiracy of Blind Affection, and Inexorable fate, we are still condemn'd to Love where we are Despis'd, and to hate where we are Belov'd?

But what if I could flatter my self with the Hope of diverting my Miseries by any other Engagement? I am so sensible of my own Condition, that I should make a very great scruple of Using any other Mortal as you have treated me: and though I am not Conscious of my Obligation to spare you, yet if it were in my Power to take my Revenge upon you, by changing you for any other, (a thing very Unlikely) I could never agree to the gratifying of my Passion that way.

I am now telling my self in your behalf, that it is not reasonable to expect, that the simplicity of a Religious should confine the Inclinations of a Cavalier. And yet methinks, if a body might be allow'd to reason upon the Actions of Love, a man should rather fix upon a Mistress in a Convent than any where else. For they have nothing there to hinder them from being perpetually Intent upon their Passion: Whereas in the World, there are a thousand fooleries, and Amusements, that either take up their Thoughts intirely, or at least divert them. And what Pleasure is it (or rather how great a Torment, if a body be not Stupid) for a man to see the Woman that he loves, in a Continual Hurry of Delights; taken up with Ceremony, and Visits; no discourses but of Balls, Dresses, Walks etc. Which must needs expose him every hour to fresh jealousies? Who can secure himself that Women are not better Satisfied with these Entertainments than they ought to be? even to the Disgusting of their own Husbands? How can any man pretend to Love, who without examining Particulars, contentedly believes what's told him, and looks upon his Mistress under all these Circumstances with Confidence, and Quiet? It is not that I am now Arguing my self into a Title to your Kindness, for this is not a way to do my business: especially after the Trial of a much more probable Method, and to as little purpose. No, no: I know my Destiny too Well, and there's no strugling with it. My Whole Life is to be miserable. It was so, when I saw you every day; When we were together, for fear of your Infidelity; and at a distance, because I could not endure you out of my sight: My heart ak'd every time you came into the Convent; and my very life was at stake when you were in the Army: It put me out of all Patience to consider that neither my Person, nor Condition were Worthy of you: I was afraid that your Pretensions to me might turn to your Damage: I could not Love you enough me thought: I liv'd in dayly Apprehension of some Mischief or other from my Parents: So that upon the Whole Matter my Case was not much better at that time then it is at present. Nay had you but given me the least Proof of your Affection since you left *Portugal*, I should most certainly have made my Escape, and follow'd you in a disguise. And what would have become of me then, after the loss of my honour, and my friends to see my self abandon'd in *France*? What a Confusion should I have been in? What a plunge should I have been at? What an Infamy should I have brought upon my family, which I do assure you, since I left loving of you, is very dear to me. Take Notice I pray'e, that in Cold thoughts I am very Sensible that I might have been much more Miserable than I am; and that once in my Life I have talk'd Reason to you: but whether my Moderation pleases you, or not; and what Opinion soever you entertain of me, I beseech you keep it to your self. I have desir'd you already, and I do now re-conjure you, never to Write to me again.

Methinks you should sometimes reflect upon the Injuries you have done me; and upon your Ingratitude to the most Generous Obligations in Nature. I have Lov'd you to the degree of Madness; and to the Contempt of all other things, and Mortals. You have not dealt with me like a Man of honour. Nothing but a Natural Aversion could have kept you even from adoring me. Never was any Woman bewitch'd upon So easy terms. What did you ever do that might entitle you to my favour? What did you ever Lose, or but so much as hazzard for my Sake? Have you not entertain'd your self with a thousand other delights? No, not so much as a Sett at Tennis, or a Hunting-Match, that you would ever forbear upon any Accompt of Mine. Were you not still the first that went to the Army, and the last that came back again? Were you ever the more Careful of Your Person there, because I begg'd it of you, as the greatest Blessing of my Soul? Did you ever so much as offer at the Establishment of your fortune in *Portugal*? A place where you were so much esteem'd. But one single Letter of your Brothers hurry'd you away, without so much as a moments time to consider of it: and I am certainly inform'd too, that you were never in better humour in your Whole Life, than upon that Voyage. You your self cannot deny, but that I have reason to hate you above all men Living; and yet, in Effect, I may thank my Self; for I have drawn all these Calamities upon my own head. I dealt to openly, and plainly with you at first: I gave you my heart too soon. It is not Love alone that begets Love; there must be Skill, and Address; for it is Artifice, and not Passion, that creates Affection. Your first design was to make me Love you, and there was not any thing in the World which you would not then have done, to compass that End: Nay rather than fail, I am perswaded you would have lov'd Me too, if you had judg'd it necessary. But you found out easier ways to do your Business, and so thought it better to let the Love alone. Perfidious Man! Can you ever think to carry off this Affront, without being call'd to an Accompt for't? If ever you Set foot in *Portugal* again; I do declare it to you, that I'le deliver you up to the Revenge of my Parents. It is along time that I have now liv'd in a kind of Licentious Idolatry, And the Conscience of it strikes me with horrour, and an Insupportable Remorse; I am Confounded with Shame of What I have done for your Sake; and I have no longer (alas!) the Passion that kept the foulness of it from my Sight. Shall this tormented heart of Mine never find ease? Ah barbarous Man! When shall I see the End of this Oppression? And yet after all this I cannot find in my heart to wish you any Sort of harm; Nay in my Conscience I could be yet well enough content to see you happy: which as the Case stands, is utterly Impossible.

Within a While, you may yet perhaps receive another Letter from me, to shew you that I have outliv'd all your Outrages, and Philosophiz'd my self into a state of Repose. Oh what a Pleasure will it be to me, when I shall be able to tell you of Your Ingratitude, and Treacheries, without being any longer concern'd at them my Self! When I shall be able to discourse of you with Scorn; When I shall have forgotten all my Griefs, and Pleasures, and not so much as think of your Self, but when I have a mind to't.

That you have had the better of me, 'tis true; for I have Lov'd you to the very Loss of my Reason: But it is no less true that you have not much cause to be proud on't. Alas I was young, and Credulous: Cloyster'd up from a Child; and only Wonted to a rude, and disagreeable sort of People. I never knew what belong'd to fine Words, and Flatteries, till (most unfortunately) I came acquainted with you: And all the Charmes, and Beauties you so often told me of, I only looked upon as the Obliging Mistakes of your Civility, and Bounty. You had a good Character in the World; I heard every body Speak well of you: and to all this, you made it your Business to engage me; but you have now (I thank you for't) brought me to my self again, and not without great need of your Assistance. Your two last Letters I am resolv'd to keep, and to read them over oftener than ever I did any of the former, for fear of a Relapse. You may well afford them, I am sure, at the Price that they have cost me. Oh how happy might I have been, if you would but have given me Leave to Love you for ever! I know very well that betwixt my Indignation, and your Infidelity, my present thoughts are in great Disorder. But remember what I tell you: I am not yet out of hope of a more peaceable Condition, which I will either Compass, or take some other Course with my self; which I presume, you will be well enough content to hear of. But I will never have any thing more to do with you. I am a fool for saying the Same things over, and over again so often. I must leave you, and not so much as think of you. Now do I begin to Phansie that I shall not write to you again for all This; for what Necesity is there that I must be telling of you at every turn how my Pulse beats?

NOTES
[1] Here as elsewhere the old spelling "then" is used instead of "than".
[2] Here as elsewhere the old form "thorough" is used instead of "through".

Captain Ayloffe's Letters

(Letter I to Letter XIV by Captain Ayloffe in: *Letters of Wit, Politicks and Morality* . . . *Also Select Letters of Gallantry* . . . *To which is added a large Collection of Original Letters of Love and Friendship. Written by several Gentlemen and Ladies; particularly* . . . *Capt. Ayloffe;* . . . London, 1701, pp. 310-30).

Captain Ayloffe's Letters

The fourteen letters attributed to Captain Ayloffe appeared in 1701 in Abel Boyer's letter collection of *Letters of Wit, Politicks and Morality*. . . . Once again, we do not know whether they are genuine or fictitious letters. John Ayloffe was executed in connection with the Rye House Plot in 1685, and it is quite possible that his letters were revised and touched up for publication. However, the use of fictitious names, the subtle narrative technique of the letters, the essay-like passages in the letters to his friend and the fact that the recipients reflected in the letters are types rather than individuals, make it unlikely that these are the untouched letters of Captain Ayloffe, printed sixteen years after his death. They may even be altogether fictitious, for it was not uncommon to attribute letters of gallantry and love to some well-known person in order to make them seem authentic. Certainly Captain Ayloffe's letters provide a good example of the difficulties of distinguishing fiction from non-fiction at that time.

What makes the correspondence especially interesting is the way in which the style of each letter is suited to the recipient. There is a remarkable difference in mood and attitude between the letters to his intimate friend and those to his mistresses, and the letters to his mistresses vary from case to case: "unkind" and "lovely" Melanissa seems to have been indifferent from the very beginning although pretending to some affection; "charming Aurelia" has conquered him against his will and better judgement; and "cruel Amarantha" serves to intensify his hatred and contempt for all womankind – an emotion which also finds expression in his letters to his friend Dick, whom he warns of the dangers of forming a tie with one of the perfidious sex. Captain Ayloffe's reflective letters to his friend serve as a natural counterpoint to his letters to his mistresses; moreover they shed a special light on the gallantry in his love-letters, showing that it is not to be taken too seriously. The preponderance of general reflection in the letters to Dick is typical of the "letter to a friend" – a type frequently found in the miscellaneous letter collections like those of Abel Boyer and Tom Brown – and forerunner of the essay. Fiction lends itself to essay-like digressions, for the narrator often reflects on subjects far removed from the actual story.

Whereas the language in the letters to his friend is fairly informal, in the love-letters the style of the letter of gallantry predominates. The stock motives and metaphors of gallant love (the cruel unfeeling lady who scorns her lover, the conquering power of her eyes and his own state of imprisonment, his position as her vassal, etc.) make up the bulk of what he has to say. The *Portuguese Letters*, in contrast, seem very individual indeed. But taking Captain Ayloffe's letters as a whole, behind the conventional metaphors and phrases we detect the beginning of the revolt against the gallant game of love, for this sort of love is both ridiculed and rejected. The love-letters may seem conventional, but read in the light of the letters to Dick we cannot ignore their implicit irony.

LETTER I

Captain Ayloffe to Mr.———

Honest Dick,

That *Mariana* should at first reject your Vows, is no ways surprizing to me; and that she should alter her mind too, is not impossible, unless her Heart is prepossest in favour of some other *Swain.* The commencements of Love are alike in all Persons; but the several Humours in Men, make 'em take such differing Methods in declaring it. No two gamesters ever play a set at chess alike; yet both play what they think best. Women are obliged by their Sex (as we have made it) to sustain the Charge, and not to give it, which is an Imposition I utterly declaim against; for by this means we rob the fair sex of the greatest Pleasure of Life, and increase our own Misery. Since we cannot hinder 'em from Loving, why should we injoyn 'em Silence?[1] The raging Flames of our Inclination are not like those of a Candle, which go out of themselves if they have not vent; this immaterial Fire is more active and devouring for being confin'd; and though these Passions be never so impetuous, 'tis my Opinion, they are conceiv'd the first instant such Parties meet; and if not then, they are never to be kindled by any subsequent Endeavours. Alas! we cannot like, or loath at Will; there is something in our own Soul, which too violently opposes such unreasonable Attempts: Not but that Conversation may improve the growing Kindness; and Time shew us Charms in their Mind, which were not to be discern'd by the common Opticks. We know not at first what it is, and when we have discover'd the Power of *Cupid*'s Dart, we are almost undone. I fear you may look upon this as a Heterodox Opinion in Matters of Love; but had I more leisure, and more room, I would engage to convince you of its Verity.

Adieu.

LETTER II

The same to the same

Well, *Dick*, you have a design then to ruin me, or make me give my self the Lye some time or other, when we are together; for if this Letter is ever seen by your Sister, God knows what may be the Event: For some Women are Jilts, others are foolish, yet all designing at bottom; and she that now appears so mighty Coy, and Nice, may peradventure do it only to make you the more eager.

Faintly she struggles to avoid a Kiss,
Only to make us fonder of the Bliss :
But if the baffled Swain, perchance give o're,
She'll poorly sue for what she scorn'd before.

Women are like Commanders in small Garrisons, reject the *Carte Blanche*, and pretend to maintain to the last Man; but when your Approaches are made, and the Batteries play smartly upon 'em; they'l hang out the Flag, and that Town is not far from Surrendring, which begins to Parley. This we know, but Women don't think we do: However, 'tis a most incontestable Truth, that Women love the Sacrifice, though they care not for the Priest. Vanity and Pride make up two thirds of their Composition; so that Flattery, with a seeming Fidelity, will prevail much with the severest of 'em all. They expect some Courtship, least their sudden yielding should disgust the Lover. The difficulty of obtaining always enhances the Pleasure of Possessing; and a cheap Woman is the most despicable thing upon Earth. If you really like your Mistress, you will think her worth some Pains, and some Services. The Chase may be pleasant, though we take not the Game. Some Lovers are for Coursing, and either kill, or loose in a short time; but the prudentest Men are for Hunting; the Exercise is not so violent, but is more durable, and the deep mouth'd Hound rarely misses at the long run.

LETTER III

The same to Melanissa

Too unkind Melanissa,

I Was not a little concern'd at your unkind proceeding last Night; nay, I am sure you would have repented your Cruelty, if you could see what tormenting Thoughts it has occasion'd in me ever since. But why should I desire to examine a Heart wherein I may possibly find only the fainter Embers of an expiring Affection? perhaps nothing but Infidelity? Well, I confess I stand indebted to you for this Mystery, and perceive it was an act of Charity, (as you thought) to conceal from me the littleness of your Love, or the coldness of your indifference; for too sudden a discovery of either, might have had such fatal Consequences, as your own self (how unkind soever you resolv'd to be) would not willingly should happen. Why, were you not this insensible Creature the first Minute I saw you, my Heart had then regulated its Motions by yours, and I had not been undone? But you kindly receiv'd my first Addresses, and gave me leave, not only to love you, but to tell you so too: Now you have blown the kindling Flame into a rapid and all-consuming Fire, you run from it, as if you fear'd it might make some Impression on your Heart. The increase of my Passion has occasion'd a Wane in yours; and because you know I can't possibly love you more, you think you may not love me at all. These are killing Reflections, (cruel *Melanissa*) yet I can't forbear 'em; since not to think upon your Unkindness, were to forget how much I lov'd you, and to how little purpose I have a thousand times renew'd those solemn Vows of being inviolably, and eternally Thine.

LETTER IV

The same to the same

Lovely Melanissa,

I should willingly confess my self in the wrong, but such an Action would be an Injury to my Love; and where either my Tenderness, or Fidelity are concern'd, I cannot, will not receed; nay, I were unworthy of your Affection, if I offer'd at any thing that might seem to lessen my own, How readily your self propos'd an eternal Separation? And by one cruel Resolution would have dash'd the Joys of an inviolable Passion, which otherwise could not have concluded but with the extreamest Moment of my Life? How could you exhibit so desperate a Remedy, to so indearing a Malady; or how could you think it possible for me to take it? I am so nice in these Points, that it would be much more intolerable to me to be suspected of a Crime, than to see you actually commit one. I am more jealous of my own Heart than of yours, and could sooner pardon you an Infidelity, than that you should think me capable of one – But the Consciousness of my own Integrity and Passion shall constitute that Felicity you seem not very solicitous of. My love is so dear to me, that I should offend it, if I let you doubt of its Violence, or Verity. But how can you doubt of it, when, notwithstanding all your Injustice, and all your Unkindness, I continue still to adore you with the same Fervency as ever.

LETTER V

The same to the same

Unjust Melanissa,

HAD I foreseen your Indifference, or that coldness at least, wherewith you Love, my Heart, alas! had not been left yours: For my Passion ows its Birth not more to your Beauty, than a violent necessity of Inclination, I could not withstand the Dear, the powerful Flames, and though I have suffer'd all the Torments, and Miseries, of an unhappy Lover, yet I cannot repent of my Passion. No, it is charming to me, for your sake, and I hug the Chain, because it was of your Imposing. How great would my Felicity be, if with a reciprocal Ardour you crown'd my Love; Since, alas, I am not without some Satisfaction how cruelly soever you triumph over me? Oh, (insensible Creature) assure your self that Indifference is more prejudicial to the Person that shews it, than those against whom it is design'd. But you know not how to Love, I would not change the Transports of my Passion for the lazy Tranquillity of your Heart. The Soul can feel no Joys but those of Love, and the excess of the Passion, determines the excess of the Pleasure. True Love is impetuous, eager in its Desires, and violent in its Possessions, and can never be judg'd of advantageously, but by its rapid irregularity. There is no moderation either in its Joy, or Grief, equally furious when crown'd, as when disappointed; and as jealous as it is tender. Alas! not one of these convincing Symptoms appear in you, and it is only out of Charity to the violence of my Passion that you would seem to make it some sort of Return. Oh! Love has too many Eyes to be long impos'd upon, and knows too well the nature of its own tender Motions to be deluded by a fictitious Flame.

LETTER VI

The same to a Friend

Was it not an unpardonable Error in the Ancients, to feign *Cupid* either a Boy, or the Son of *Venus*? The celerity of his Progression, when once a pleasing Object has wounded a tender Heart, argues more the Vigour of an adult Person, than the infirmer Wadlings of a blind Child; and we see frequently (not to say always) that the Pleasures of his long reputed Mother, prove her rather a fatal Parricide than an indulgent Parent. The greatest Favours *Phillis* can confer, owe the most of their Joys and Transports to the Affection of the Person who receives 'em; and were there not an unaccountable Charm in Vanity: we should hardly be constant, tho' Women were as true as they could be kind. If any thing destroys Love, it is Fruition; Despair does not determine our dislike of the Object; but the desire of succeeding some where invites us to discontinue the fruitless Expectations, and baffl'd Hopes, and use the same Endeavours to be happy in some other place. Not, but if Men would ingenuously declare the Truth, they, most of 'em, would confess that they wish'd they had met with the compliance of the latter, in the Person of the former, presupposing that they really lov'd, for there is no Account to be made of those transient Inclinations, which expire almost as soon as conceiv'd, and never subsist longer than the Nymph is present. If the rigours of our Customs had not impos'd so severe Laws on the fair sex, we should not always be so unfortunate in our Amours, or so frequently Shipwrackt in Matrimony. But, Sir, since the Woman must be content, when her too cautious and covetous Parents command, no wonder that Marriage is a Misery, by so much the more intolerable, as it is for Life. Some People have had no longer time to learn each others Humours and Dispositions than the Taylor had to make their Cloaths; and when at the Altar, have vow'd Love, Honour and Obedience to one they were the least acquainted with of the whole Congregation; and knew no more of each other, than that their Parents had agreed together. What Harmony can you expect when there is but one String in Tune? Had Women the liberty equally with us of declaring their Affections, it would facilitate some People's Felicity, and prevent others[2] a vain and tedious, nay, expensive Courtship. This you are as sensible of, as that I am,

Sir, your most obliged Servant,

LETTER VII

The same to the Charming Aurelia

THE Influences of your conquering Eyes have been so fatal, that Lovers are now become no Novelties to you, each hour informs you of more than one Victory, and you look no where but at the expence of a Heart. Why should this sort of sacrifice offend my *Aurelia*, when Importunity pleases even Heaven it self? If you will not regard my Passion, pitty at least my Pain. The Severity of the Law was never extended so far, but the most notorious Criminals were allow'd to sigh upon the most deserved Rack: And since Love has made me suffer so much more than I can express, though not than you merit; forgive *Aurelia*, forgive the Presumption of this Declaration. 'Tis some Satisfaction to me, that you know my Love, but it would be a greater, if you believ'd its Violence. *Aurelia's* Kindness alone must, or can remedy those intolerable Pangs her own Beauties cause. That loving a Person so divinely Fair, should occasion so much Misery to a faithful Heart, is what I can't comprehend, though I too fatally experienc'd it. Accept the pious Incense of your adoring Slave, then your Goodness will be little inferiour to your Charms, though both of 'em are to the Sincerety and Passion wherewith I am inviolably yours.

LETTER VIII

The same to the same

Dearest Delight of my bleeding Heart.

THE Torments of Uncertainty are more insupportable for the time than those of Disdain. Whatsoever you resolv'd should be my inevitable Fate, it would have alleviated its Horrors, to have been pronounc'd by your inchanting Lips. Is it then possible, cruel *Aurelia*, that there should be so little Mercy where there is so much Beauty, and that you should be in every thing Divine; but your Heart, when you should chiefly be so? Well, I see, that he who loves, must prepare to suffer, and that Courage and Patience are as necessary Ingredients in a Lover, as Tenderness and Fidelity. Do the Miseries of your Adorers add any thing to the Lustre of your Triumph? If not, why are you more transported with the Horrors of their Despair, and the height of their Misery, than sollicitous of making them happy? That Beauty should thus delight in Blood, and the brightest of the fair Sex, smile to see a tender faithful Lover gasping at her Feet; is less natural than Ice in *June*, and Thunder in *January*. But if my anguish can advance your Felicity, I am ready to undergo any thing, my dearest *Aurelia* shall inflict; and would tear my very heart out, if it could shrink at any pain that would procure you one easie moment. My Obedience shall shew my Love, tho at the expence of my Life; and I dare be wretched to express how inviolably I am

Yours.

LETTER IX

The same to the same

Charming Aurelia,

To have yielded, even at first sight, was more an Argument of the mighty Power of *Aurelia*'s Charms, than of baseness and timidity in her adoring Vassal. If the violence of a tender Passion, which despair it self cannot lessen, can meet with nothing but disdain, Heaven has no Justice, or no Power. Yet tho your mortal Hatred were equal to my faithful Love, I would not alter my Affection. You injure your self while you question my Passion, and me if you question my Integrity. Ah! could *Aurelia* see these gaping Wounds her Eyes have made in *Strephon*'s Heart, cruel as you are, you could not longer doubt the fatal Truth. My Martyrdom speaks my Love, and your very Scorn is less insupportable than your thinking I but dissemble. Nothing ever ingag'd my Thoughts till I saw the charming *Aurelia*, and nothing now can dispossess her of an absolute Empire over my Soul. When I conversed with others, 'twas without Assiduity or Consequence, and I preserv'd my Liberty in a crowd of Fair ones. As yet I repent not that I've lost it; nor will I wholly despair, tho you assur'd me there was no hopes, Since you were at the pains to write me that News, I hope in time you may come to change your Style.

Adieu.

LETTER X

The same to Mr.——

Sir,

To Answer your last Question, I must propose another, which is this; since there is nothing more pleasing or surprizing than Beauty, more diverting than Wit, and more desirable than Gold, whence proceeds it that many celebrated young Ladies have reapt no other Fruit from 'em, than the vainer hopes of being Great, or well Marry'd at least? Nay, have languish'd under that tedious Expectation, till 30 Years had put a fatal Period

31

to the Lustre of their charms; yet during so considerable a space of time as they were Marriageable, they never met with one tolerable Advantageous offer? This misfortune has not only befallen those whose Beauty alone was their Patrimony, but it has not seldom too attended Women of great Estates; tho some of them are patient of the bitter Reflection, have taken off the shameful Reproach of being Old Maids, by a most incongruous (not to say scandalous) Marriage. Noblemen have Wedded their Menial Servants, and Countessess little better than their Footmen. Some love no body but themselves, and others love every body but their own Wives. There is a hidden Spring that gives a Motion to all sublunary Things: what it is we can't comprehend, Providence it may be, but Chance it cannot possibly be: 'Tis too regular not to be order'd, tho how we cannot tell: Some Marry whom once they had an Aversion to; and others again hate in a little time those they marry'd only for Love. What should, partly, be always, and sometimes is the bond of Affection, proves as often its Dissolution.

Since then neither Beauty, Wit, nor Wealth, can get some Women Husbands, you ought not to wonder why the Negative of either has met with happy Matches. There is one standard, or everlasting Reason for all our Actions. That *Strephon* should have impos'd upon *Aurelia*'s credulity, and with a feign'd Passion insinuated himself into her Favour, (I will not say, he has created a real one in the lovely Maid, tho 'tis not impossible,) has nothing in it that astonishes me. For as he loves no body in Truth, he might much more easily effect this. But, believe me, he had found it very difficult to have succeeded in this pretended Amour, had he at the same time had a real, violent affection to conceal: For some words or actions before we are aware, often will drop forth, and betray the counterfeited Flame. No man ever lov'd but he shew'd it; and if his Friends do not find out the Person as well as the Passion, 'tis because they do not often see 'em together. Some men I have known, who have endeavour'd to be in Love, and could never effect it; they have hunted after a Mistress, and could never find a Chain they could put on, they are necessitated to be free; for amongst all they converse with, they meet with none they can love.

Adieu.

LETTER XI

The same, to the cruel Amarantha

That you should reproach me thus with Inconstancy! I think Injustice; tho that I have chang'd I protest is true. Her Beauty vindicates the Action, but perhaps she is less Inhumane too. Were it not an unheard of price of Madness in me, to have persisted in my Adoration, to an inexorable Divinity; when with fewer sacrifices, and less Incense, I could obtain the same Blessing from another? That you had vaster Empires to dispose of, I'll readily allow; but what was that to your humble Suppliant, who could never obtain the least considerable Employment under you? We never pray but when we want something; and if we are devout enough to return Thanks for the kind Collation of one benefit, 'tis out of hopes of more. Fear first taught man to carry Oblations to the angry Gods, and if they had not equally apprehended their Displeasure and stood in need of their Mercy, *their Altars had been without Smoak, and their Priests without Employment.* In the crowd of your Adorers, too unkind *Amarantha,* you took no notice of me; the mounting Clouds of various Incense, hindred you from distinguishing my pious Hands that offer'd their part. I went to a less frequented Temple, and met with the felicity I had so long pray'd for, in vain, at yours. What can oblige me to an eternal Obedience, nay even a Vassalage to a Prince, who is so far from protecting me, that he persecutes me, and invidiously forbids me to accept of that happiness from another's Hands, which he obstinately refuses me from his own? I could have been constant in my Love, but not in dispair; that part of Passive Obedience I cannot digest. Too severe a usage damp'd the Loyalty of more than one Kingdom; and he that might have continu'd an Emperour at home, is now a Mendicant abroad. You might have had a faithful Subject in me, if you had not tyrannized; and by the continuance of your Cruelty, given me a fatal Assurance, that there was nothing to be got from you but Frowns. I am happy enough at present, and peradventure might have been much more so, if you had pleased. And this I think Triumph enough for you, to compensate the loss of a Lover, you esteemed not enough, since you treated him so barbarously.

Adieu.

LETTER XII
The same to Mr.──
On the Vanity of Intrigues

Sir,

You must pardon my Vanity, if I am not a little pleas'd that my Letter gave you any Satisfaction; not that I have so much as to imagine it merited that advantageous Character you were so indulgent as to give of it. Indeed I could not well expect less from a Person of your Civility, nor more from the kindest Friend. As for the rest, I can say but little: I am sorry it is so; yet dare not be certain, that if any kinder Stars had ever favour'd me with an Intrigue worth relating, I should not have augmented the Number of those ungenerous Men, I so much abhor at present. I confess it is no Virtue to be Innocent, when there is no Temptation to Sin; and perhaps I owe all mine to a certain insensibility of Temper, and not to choice. I can safely say, that since I writ Man, I never lov'd two days together; nor was ever a

Woman so dear to me, but for one kiss more than she allow'd, I should have sacrific'd her to the next I Visited. After some Conversation, I found, I will not say (a Defect in them) but a disappointment to me, which made me endeavour to find that satisfaction in the whole Sex, which I had so long and so vainly sought in the Individuals. Not that I would justifie this Levity at all, but it was a powerful Byass of Nature, which secured my Tranquility by the frequency of my Change; and the short livedness of my Love. You your self, Sir, are not unsensible that we court them only for our own ends; and were there not a probability of succeeding, we should soon give over the troublesom pursuit. However, with all our precautions, 'tis we for the generality that are made the Properties. Some, I know, have boasted of their happy Triumphs over Virgin Modesty, and would not be convinc'd of the contrary, till the one found his Mistress in three Months deliver'd of a fine Child, and the other in twice as many days was forc'd to confess her Maidenhead was a C——p. There is a secret satisfaction in divulging a Favour of this nature; but its origin is nothing but Vanity and Self Conceit. It seems an injury to our merit to conceal its Power; and if we did not proclaim 'em, others would not know our Conquests: Tho to a considering Man there's not much to brag of, in the having met with a Woman who yielded to his Sollicitations, his Passion, his Perseverance, and his Presents; nay, perchance, besides all these, had an Eye to the gratifying one other humour more, I shall forbear to set down.

The World is so full of Censure, the Men of vain Glory, the Women of Malice and Curiosity, that no Intrigue can be long manag'd in privacy, and the Gallant has hardly received two considerable Favours from his Mistress, but every body knows it. A *Mountford*, a *Goodman*, and a G—*aine*, have distinguish'd three Women of Quality; and they were as well known by those Men, as by the Names of their Husbands. Those things will be so sometimes.

Adieu.

LETTER XIII

The same to Mr. —— to dissuade him from Marriage

Honest Dick,

I Have not only heard of, but born a part in some of your Frolicks; yet never observ'd any so extravagant, as gave me reason to apprehend you would be so mad to *Marry*. Sure, the Devil is in Thee or Her, for without Fascination, this miracle could not be wrought. To be very sick of Love, is no wonder, but that can't last long: the raging Feaver must pass or kill; your Fate is soon determined; a few days brings it to its Crisis, and is it not better dying quietly in your own sheet, than in a whining Wive's Arms? You can never live in Charity with her ten days together, unless you are a stricter Christian than I take you to be, or think possible for one of nineteen to be. Experience, dear bought Experience, has convinc'd you, that the difference between Women consists more in our capricious Humours and the Sense of variety, than any intrinsic Goodness. The Novelty may please, 'tis true, but after the first Night's Enjoyment, a Wife is eternally the same; the Ruin of your Estate, and the disquiet of your bed. If she live three years with you, she'l spend more than her Fortune in Cloaths alone; abstracting from all those vast and unavoidable Expences that attend a married Life. If she bring you any Children, these are so many fresh additions to your Misfortunes, creating Torments if they live, and grief if they Die. Which of thy Sins, *Dick*, has been so black in it self, or so heinous in its Circumstances; so frequently repeated, or so long unrepented of, as to deserve so heavy, so lasting a Punishment? You that could never Love a Woman above a Week, and chang'd your Mistresses faster than they did their Lodgings; how, alas! do you think it possible for you not to be miserable under this Confinement? As a Friend, I forwarn you, and assure you, that you would give five times her Estate within the Year, to be at liberty again. Alas! *Dick*, this is not a humour that Ten Guineas will Bail you out of; but what is the greatest mischief 'twill last all your Life. The knowing that we can't alter our condition, is, I believe, a more sensible Affliction, than all the others that make it anxious to us.

A Husband is the most insipid Character of all Mankind, never pleasing, and as seldom pleas'd. Tormented in his own Person, and more feelingly in that of his Children, who are continually whipt and beaten by the Wife, to be revenged of his unkindness or to provoke his Anger. Be sober once in thy Life, and renounce the Thought of so fatal, so unpardonable a Distraction. Why will you affect drinking out of a Horn, when you have so much and so good Plate? You had best shew this to your fair Charmer, and demonstrate the Power of her Eyes, by resisting so wholsom and seasonable Advice. If you think fit do so: I had rather lose her good Will, than shew my own Integrity to you, and would refuse your Friendship, if I might not express my own.

LETTER XIV

The same to the same

Honest Dick,

WHY all these fond Addresses to a Woman, who can't be kind unless she is Criminal? Why so hot in your Attacks, so close in your Siege, so pressing with your Batteries, when you can't carry the Town without Injustice, as well as Cruelty? Not that I take upon me to vindicate that unreasonable Custom which circumscribes our Pleasures; but your having so tamely submitted to it, makes the very Tyranny of the Law obligatory to you. What is there more in her you desire, than is in her you enjoy, unless the one is your own, the other cannot be so? He that wishes, wants, is most certain; but that possession should render you poor, is a Paradox I can't resolve. I know it is the most considerable Blemish upon Mankind, the first Fruits of our Parents Transgression, that Reason it self should not be able to withstand the furious Instigation of Lubricity, and that we should rashly and foolishly hazard the Tranquility of our whole Lives, for the Pleasures of one Tumultuous Moment; which how prone soever Nature is to, she does not enjoy without the confusion of a Blush: but what is very worthy your Reflection, the Law it self which makes it no longer Sinful, is not powerful enough to make it not Shameful at some times, or in many places. 'Tis a hardship upon Humanity, to stand by a River, to be Thirsting, and yet prohibited Drinking: Such a desire is a misery of deprav'd Nature, and all of us feel sometimes those softer Motions, which we would willingly gratifie at (almost) any rate; but they being for the most part involuntary in their Beginning, and like so many Surprizes upon us, we easily forgive 'em in every body. Now you make it your business, and seek danger, which you might shun without difficulty; and this I take the liberty to reprehend you for. I thought the World had long since taught you what was the utmost value of a Woman. But your deluded Imagination furnishes you with strange Ideas of late, and Experience that improves other Men's Understandings has only perverted yours. Men as wise as both of us, have said, that *every Woman is the same* (and our selves have found, that when Desire is pressing, and such an object at hand, there is seldom room left for Niceties, all having that conveniency about them, which we stand immediately in need of. Now to expect and seek for more, is a Distemper of the Mind, and a Dishonour to the Man. What would lessen much of the Esteem we for the generality have for the Sex, is, that all the Advantages possible, cannot long retain our eagerest Affections; and the most perfect Beauty that ever adorn'd a Female Face, never alone insur'd the Fidelity of any Man, against the Allurements of Variety. The satisfaction those tender Commerces afford, are never long-lived, and loathing succeeds to a fated Desire: a few years, or a fit of Sickness, destroys all those Charms, and if they are not cropt in their Bloom, they quickly fade of themselves; and she whom Pride kept chast at seventeen, if not marry'd, will be contemn'd at thirty. You have ty'd up your hands, *Dick*, and by a spontaneous Act, renounc'd that dear Freedom we Batchelors may sometimes indulge our selves. 'Tis the misery of our Condition, to stand in need of Physick, but to make it our Food is a Folly that Wants an Epithet.

Farewel.

NOTES
[1] Enjoin them to silence.
[2] Save others.

From a Lady to a Lady

*being an Account of her own Adventures
and Loss of her Lovers*

(Letter XXXIII in: *Court Intrigues, in a Collection of Original Letters,
from the Island of the New Atlantis, &c. By the Author of those Memoirs.*
London, 1711, pp. 171–99).

From a Lady to a Lady

Most of the novels of Mary de la Rivière Manley consist of political and social gossip and few of them are more than historically interesting for modern readers. *The Account of the Adventures of a Lady*, however, is not as scandalous as one might expect considering the author and the title. The heroine is not simply a coquette, but a woman who, though harshly treated by fate, is capable of genuine love and self-denial. Mrs Manley's *The Adventures of Rivella* (1714) – commonly regarded as an autobiographical novel – tells a similar story about a similar character. Its heroine Rivella, like the heroine of *The Account of the Adventures of a Lady*, persuades her lover Cleander (presumably the son of the Duchess of Cleveland with whom Mrs Manley is said to have had an affair) to marry a rich widow rather than to lead the miserable life which marriage to herself would entail. *Rivella* is a third-person novel, and the heroine's renunciation is related in a brief and straightforward fashion. In the letter *From a Lady to a Lady* the young woman herself depicts in some detail her attempts to forget her first lover, hiding neither her secret desires nor her errors from the intimate friend she is writing to. She cannot resist the temptation to revenge her own sufferings by making other men suffer an unrequited love for her. Inevitably, however, she herself becomes emotionally involved – this time with the shy and inhibited Mr Worthy. Here again all the phases of the rising passion on both sides are convincingly rendered. The care with which Mrs Manley motivates her characters and interprets their actions goes far beyond anything we find in most of her other fiction. Not only the heroine but also the lover, young Worthy, reveal an ambiguity of character which deserves to be called realistic. Modest and shy at the outset, the young man develops into an enthusiastic and apparently honest lover who, however, weakly succumbs to the pressures exerted by his intriguing family to abandon his new love. As so often in epistolary short stories, the eventual outcome of the affair is left somewhat indefinite, increasing our sense of having read an account of events recorded as they occur. The title of the book and some hints towards the end suggest an unhappy ending. The lady's bias towards religion and mysticism illustrates a new tendency in eighteenth-century prose and letter-writing. Piety and renunciation of the world in favour of a spiritual life come to be regarded as desirable attitudes for young ladies. Letters and diaries seem to have been especially favoured media for religious sentimentalism (see, for instance, Mrs Rowe's *Letters Moral and Entertaining* and *Friendship in Death in Twenty Letters from the Dead to the Living* 1729). Following in the wake of these narrative-didactic prose writings came Richardson's *Clarissa*.

The psychological acuity and budding realism evident in Mrs Manley's epistolary story was altogether lacking in the idealistic romances of the time, where constant lovers endure innumerable trials without the slightest wavering. And although this story contains various stock motives of romance (the discovery of the heroine with a secret lover, the mutual misunderstandings due to separation and intrigue), the domestic background is not ignored. The heroine, a widow without fortune, cannot be accepted by her lover's family. Worthy's brother has the same trouble with his beloved; and the first engagement of the letter-writer miscarried because her lover had been ruined by a law-suit, so that he had to marry a wealthy widow. The lovers are separated not by shipwreck and slavery but by financial difficulties and domestic intrigue. Moreover, in addition to its realism and psychological insight, the novel can boast of a moral approach altogether lacking in the scandal-mongering chronicles so favoured by Mrs Manley. As in the romance and the tale of scandal, love is the principal subject of the story, but some attention is paid to probability, previously much neglected; it was, with the advent of Fielding and others, to become one of the main concerns of the novel.

YES my Dear, my ever-valu'd Friend, you shall here know all that my poor tortur'd Soul has suffer'd, in these long cruel three Years separation. Have I one spark of Joy remaining in my Soul? Your Letter brought it forth; and tho' dead to Hope, and lost to Happiness, or ev'n wish of Happiness, I find still a pleasure in being esteem'd by you. Oh *Clorinda!* in other Loves there is no Constancy; even Friendship to me is but insipid; fit only to amuse a Soul unfeeling a more exalted Heat. Had our Sex been different, I fear, my Dear, by this, we had forgot to Love; or perhaps have learnt to Hate: Tho' that's a Passion so Foreign to my Mind, that, as yet, I am Ignorant of what it means. My Soul rebounds not at an Injury; engross'd by softer Passions, it has no room to entertain so rough a Guest.

You ask me the meaning of that melancholy Strain, that runs through all my Letters; and conjure me to explain my self with Friendship. You will remember me, that when we parted, I was envy'd by most, and by all thought happy. 'Tis true, I had not suffer'd Shipwreck then, but since. Oh, what have I not endur'd! Will you have patience to hear a three years Anguish? 'Tis all dark, a melancholy Gloom; my gayer Genius is fled and lost in its Shades: I'm the Reverse of what I was; no more the Pleasure of the World; the Delight of Conversation; no more *belov'd*, yet still *loving*. Is there a Misery beyond this? Is there a Rack in Nature I have not felt? May I not well complain? But to give you in particular my Misfortunes: You left me in the possession of a Heart worthy mine; but the World and Interest divided us: An Eminent Law-Suit ruin'd my Lover's Fortune, in which part of mine was involv'd, and left him no hopes of repairing it, but by a Wife more Rich than I cou'd be. The coming *Term* was to take him in Execution for a Sum too mighty for him to struggle with. This was kept a Secret from me, for fear of my Disquiets. At length, finding him excessive melancholy and dejected, beyond what I cou'd ever have suspected from his Fortitude of Soul, he told me his Misfortunes, that he was undone; but his own Sorrows were inconsiderable to him in comparison of mine. He was indeed by Promise, by Vows and Inclination my Husband: But shou'd I call him to the performance, we both were lost, and must expect to languish out the rest of his life in Prison, oppress'd with Misery and Wants: That such a Lady had been offer'd him for a Wife, considerable in her Fortune, and so destitute of Charms, that it could not give me the least Suspicion, that Inconstancy had any part in what was his only Refuge, the last Plank that could preserve him from Shipwreck. I took Time to weigh and examine the Truth of what he said; but was soon convinced of his ill Circumstances, and could not suffer my Heart to hesitate a moment on what it should do, to save him; the Thoughts were death to me, that for my sake, he should live poor, contemn'd, and wretched; I concluded, that tho' (like other Men) he might prove ungrateful, 'twas a more tolerable Evil, than having him (through my means) unfortunate. Let all, who have not generous Souls (as I suppose they will) condemn me for what they may call Weakness: But sure *Clorinda* does better know how to value so unpresidented a Sacrifice. I gave up all my Happiness to his Interest, and by Permission saw him three Weeks after marry'd. Indeed, Misfortunes in prospect are only guess'd at; they are not to be describ'd till felt, tho' I had prepar'd my self for all that could be expected of Sufferings; yet when once I began to feel the real Load, I sunk under 'em; since He was safe and happy, no matter what became of Me; neither Honour nor Policy would permit his Visits, for his Engagements with me had been no secret; his Lady would soon have heard of 'em, and consequently have had her own and his Pleasure poison'd that way. Besides, I was resolved to put an end to a Flame, that could not now burn with Innocence: I gave my self up to the Diversions of the World, Visits, Cards, Plays, all that ought to divert the Mind; my Love was to suffer a violent Death, since it would not resign to a natural; but in vain, it withstood the Efforts of Reason; Diversions, Duty; it mock'd all my Endeavours, and augmenting by Resistance, threw me into a violent Illness, out of which, I did not, but after much danger, recover; the Pain was at my Heart, which the Physicians had no Cure for. Then it was, my *Clorinda*, that, with the rest of the World, you heard the Report of my death; and truly I was so near it, that it was the work of ten Months, before I could stand alone, or under my own hand give you to know I was not yet so happy as to be Nothing. They remov'd me into the Country, to try their last Experiment, the change of Air. By the Time of my return back to *London*, almost two Years had pass'd since that fatal Marriage, My Heart still engag'd, still tortur'd by a Love, which I could not perswade my self to be Criminal, because I once had a Right and Title to his Love; though when I consider'd my self had releas'd all Pretences, I doubly blamed my Heart for persevering; but Love is Power too mighty for us to controul. I saw my Murderer, and my old Wounds bleed afresh at the fatal Sight; he complained of his own want of Happiness, and Secretly pleas'd my Heart by finding, if his Grief were less, his Satisfaction was not more. How insignificant a Relief is this? How is it, that a Power so mighty as Love, can be serv'd, and find its account in Trifles? He complain'd, that Marriage had not answer'd his End; for though it sav'd him from impending Ruin, in his Law-Suit, and discharg'd his Execution; yet many other of his Debts being unpaid, gave him much uneasiness. That his Lady, like a right Widow, had secur'd the greatest part of her Fortune to her own use; their Humours were extreamly different, and he had little Hopes of prevailing on hers, because he wanted the first Principles, that should give his their aggreeable Motion; she lov'd Flattery, as most Ladies do, and he was not Master of it; he had almost said of Kindness too: In short, he was too dangerous for my Conversation; his Eyes had still the same Beauty, his Words their usual Softness, and I think a certain melancholy Air heightned all his Charms; should I dwell on every Circumstance, the Conversation must tire you; in a word, I tore my self from these Enchantments, and forbid my Heart such Criminal Delights: Yet my Torment pursu'd me wheresoever I fled; I had once more recourse to the Country, and went by Recommendation to Board in *Bristol*, at a Gentleman's House, who, with his Family, were all Strangers to me. A Cronick Distemper, which my Melancholy had contracted, could only expect its Cure from change of Air. The Family I was receiv'd into, consisted of an old well natur'd Gentleman, govern'd by his spleenetick Wife, who had as much Cunning, as Nature alone could give her; and had her Education been good, her Wit might have been more considerable. They had formerly merchandiz'd, but being pretty easy in the World, had lately left off. A Brother of hers liv'd in the Family, who had been bred up with them in their Way; he appear'd to me as a Person well made, and hansome, but perfectly unfashion'd, having had no Conversation, but Business; who declin'd Women's Company, and rarely ever spoke among the Men; he seldom eat at home, and I believe I was near seven Months in the House with him, before we had any Conversation, tho' you know me easy of Access, and pleas'd with Company; my Business was to seek Diversion which my ill Health had made perfectly necessary to me. An ugly unmarried Maid of Thirty (a Sister of theirs) brought up the Rear of this goodly Family; and here, in reading, and conversing with some of the Town who visited Mrs. *Woudbe* (which you must know is my Landlady's Name) I pass'd a considerable Time; the Poison still at my Heart, daily wasting by a consuming hopeless Fire, what would I not have done for my Cure? How was I alone, of all human kind, plagu'd with a never dying Passion? I had read indeed, that Inconstancy was counted the greatest Weakness of the weakest Sex, but here I imagin'd it would have been meritorious, for there can be no Appeal from Marriage; that certainly ought to destroy all precedent Inclinations, and they must be unpardonable, who preserve theirs after it.

At length another Brother (the Squire of Mrs. *Woudbe*'s Family) came upon a Visit to *Bristol*; he dress'd at the Ladies, had seen some of the World, was half bred, as to Gallantry, and about that pitch in Understanding; but good Natur'd, and a very honest Gentleman; what his Brother wanted in Tongue, he supply'd; and 'twas not his falt if Conversation languish'd; his kind Endeavours would relieve it, though sometimes at the Expence of his Reputation, as to Wit. (For 'tis very hard for great Talkers always to escape Impertinence.) Mr. *Peregrine Worthy* was his Name; he quickly told me, that his Heart had been mortgag'd above these two Years, to a young Lady passionately fond of him; but he was one, whom her Father would not permit her to marry, because his Estate did not answer the Fortune he could give her. He was not so young as his Brother by six Years, nor so well shaped, but more polish'd; and it came into my Head, by a malicious Diversion, to make him in Love with me, notwithstanding his Engagement: It seem'd intolerable, that any other Woman should be a quiet Possessor of the Heart she lov'd, whilst I was so unhappy to be depriv'd of what I had adored. The general ill Opinion I had of all Mens Constancy, made me conclude I should have no great trouble in conquering *Peregrine*'s; I look'd not at the Consequence, nor had debated with my self what to do with that Toy, his Heart, or that Lumber, his Person, were they once made an Offering to me. What I wanted was present Amusement; for, as Poisons are said to expel Poisons, I would with all my Heart have lov'd any Thing, to put out of my mind the Phantom that haunted me. But this was not the Diamond that was to cut mine; for tho' we enter'd into a Commerce of Galantry, and after his departure writ Letters as mutually tender, as if we had been really touch'd; I suppose we both remain'd unwounded by each other. All I know of my side is, that my former Passion found not the least abatement; and therefore 'tis easy to conclude, a new one did not succeed. At length young *Worthy* fell so ill, that his Life was for some time in danger. Mrs. *Woudbe* had Business [that] call'd her to *London*; after she was gone, I debated with my self, whether I should be so ill-natur'd, to let a Brother of the Family, where I was, die, and never give him a Visit. I knew he did not love Company, and least of all, Ladies; but my good Manners and good Nature over-ruling, I resolved to my Duty, though it should prove unacceptable. I came to his Bed-side, and had a much civiler Reception than I expected; the heighth of his Distemper, as I then supposed, had master'd his Native Roughness. I found him in a violent

Fever; and having too lately had an expensive Experience of what Physicians could do, I was able to advise him in many things proper for the Recovery of his Health. Had Mrs. *Woudbe* been there I should not have attempted it, for she has that Quality peculiar to her self, to believe none besides her self knowing in any thing; and that she is ignorant of nothing. Mrs. *Abigal* the Surly, her Sister, of Thirty, (dull, and heavy in Make, as well as Understanding) was his chief Nurse. I had Compassion for him, in the ill hands he was in, and therefore failed not to be often with him, which he seem'd to receive very civilly; His Fever abated, but his Temper being melancholy, the Distemper had so seiz'd his Spirits, that I found it must be a powerful Diversion of the Mind, that could be able to throw it thence; but whence it should proceed I could not guess, to a Man wholly free from Vice or Passions; I found his Understanding very good, what he did speak, proper, and well imagin'd; and I doubted not but he would shew us he had Wit enough, could he once dispence with Custom and Modesty, that had hitherto kept him silent. We read to him Books of Wit and Gallantry; I found he had a true Taste of things, and could commend in the right place; thus a sort of Satisfaction succeeded Compassion, and I felt my self better pleased in his Company, than I imagin'd I could have been. We grew acquainted; his Conversation became free and genteel; we chanced to talk of *Love*, he protested he never knew what the least Spark of it meant; and my Judgment was, he never would, not considering that Nature makes nothing in vain; however, a defect of Constitution might happen. I talk'd of the *Language of the Eyes*; he innocently protested, he knew not what I meant by that; neither could he imagine: Nay, was more and more confounded, when I told him *Lovers Eyes could talk*; he assured me he never minded the difference of Glances, he thought all Eyes had the same Looks, tho' not the same Colour. This was wonderful, I thought, from one who had himself the finest I ever saw; and a very bad encouragement for me, if I had had the least design upon his Heart tho' in jest, as before, with his Brother. He liked my Company, or my Library, or both, so well, that after he was up and dress'd, he never was from us. I suited him with the gay part of reading, being properest to remove his Melancholy. We chanced one day to light upon *Brown*'s Translation of *Fontenel*'s and *Aristaenetus*'s[1] Letters; he seem'd mightily pleas'd with 'em; there was one from a Lady, who permits a Lover all but the last Favour, and gives him leave to touch her Breast, to kiss her Eyes, her Mouth, and squeeze her with her Stays off; he could not imagine what Pleasure could be taken in that. Not long after, we were returning with Mistress *Abigal* late from a Visit out of Town, where we had been merrily entertain'd, and had all three, contrary to Custom, drank enough to elevate us. *Bacchus* is counted a Friend to Love; after putting me into the Coach, young *Worthy* staid not for Compliments, with Mrs. *Abigal*, but threw himself with a Gaiety (wholly new to him) on the Seat by me; 'twas dark; tho' the surly Maid was our Opposite, in the Humour we were all in, it pass'd for Raillery: He pretended to make the Lady's Experiment of squeezing, since he found I had only a Morning-Wastecoat on, thence he attempted to kiss my Cheek, then my Lips; and if I'm not mistaken, could no longer wonder where the Pleasure was of *That*. After we came home, we continued the Frolick, sitting upon Mrs. *Abigal*'s Bed; he sighed after ever Kiss, no ill Omen of a Heart touch'd with Pleasure. I may truly protest to you, that for Nine successive Years, that I had been tormented with an unintermitting Passion, this was the only Moment that I first found it suspended. I confess, I was then lost to any Thoughts but the present; there his Eyes first gave, and knew the distinction of Looks; he could no longer boast of Ignorance, they had a Softness wholly new; so full of sparkling Fire, so Tender, nay, so Passionate, that I catched the Distemper into mine, and look'd on his with an uncommon Pleasure; you may perhaps too nicely blame me for giving into those Delights, but I was suddenly betray'd by one, from whom I never expected any danger, and therefore could not arm my self against it. I was also charm'd, with thinking my self the first that gave him Wishes, that gave him Desire, and Joy; that Heart, that formerly insensible Heart, seem'd no longer so to me. I was pleas'd to encourage a Pleasure that destroy'd my former Pain, and I found young *Worthy* had in an hour done more towards my Cure than all my own whole two Years endeavours. Mrs. *Abigal* thought our Conversation something too Tender; the Wine working out in ill Nature with her, as in Kindness with us; she was impertinent enough to have offended us, had she been worth it. After this, when he found me alone, he would sometimes pretend to the Pleasure of a Kiss, but never declar'd himself; so that I believed my self mistaken, when I reckon'd upon my Conquest. He took occasion to be always with me; we read, we walk'd, we eat together, but still not a word of Love; he became unimaginably improv'd like *Cymon* for *Iphigenia*, in the Fable; he dress'd, he discours'd, he no longer avoided the Ladies Company. All the World wondr'd at the Change; he became genteel as any Body, and appear'd with as good an Air; I told you at first, that he was perfectly well-shap'd; to me, they attributed these Improvements, calling him my Scholar; my Pain was inverted from *London* to the Country. I would have given all the World to hear his Mouth confirm, what his Eyes so often told me. What Laws? What Manners? What Customs have our Sex? How must we be Tantaliz'd? How Tortur'd? Why was it not permitted to search his Heart? Why not to ask him, if yet he knew whether there was a Deity call'd *Love*? Our perpetual Opportunities, our long Converse, might have well excus'd it; but Modesty over-rul'd even Curiosity and Vanity: I was forced to suffer in Uncertainty and Silence. Thus a whole Year run on since that Moment he first began to make an Impression upon my Heart. At length, amidst the pleasing Liberty of un-number'd Kisses, he brought out (with doubting Modesty) that transporting word, *I love you*. I could have swore that till that minute, I never knew, what Joy, what Pleasure was; I could not stay for Reflection, I could not speak; I more than spoke; I hug'd him in an extatick manner, more Charming, more Intelligible than a Thousand words. You have known, my dear *Clorinda*, the Force of Love; wonder not then, that thus, in me, he exerted his Tyrannick Sway; or think the Person I've describ'd, because lower than my self in Rank, unworthy of my Heart; his was by Inclination Noble, and *Dryden*, who so well knew the Passions, tells us.

> *Love either finds Equality, or maks it ;*
> *Like Death he knows no diffrence in degrees,*
> *But plains and levels all.*

After that he would perhaps have no longer scrupled to speak his Passion, but our Opportunities of being alone were few; what was now no Secret to me, was long since, by his Actions, suspected by the Family. Mrs. *Woudbe* and Mrs. *Abigal*, were our perpetual Companions; nay, we had an additional Spy, a Friend of Mrs. *Woudbe*'s, that was received there upon some Misfortunes of her Husband. This was a Damsel, that pretended to Airs and Charms; would ogle my Lover, and (whether by their desires, or her own Inclinations) attempted to have made a diversion of his Kindness. She offer'd at so many Advances, that my jealous Eyes called 'em unpardonable. However, her Charms were no way dangerous, and I believe I need have given my self no pain that way. This Creature won upon my easy Nature by her Assiduities; and she us'd often to rally at Mrs. *Woudbe*'s fears for her Brother. Thus were we interupted in the full Course of our Amour; and 'twas impossible to speak without being over-heard, one or both of the Sisters were perpetually upon the hearken. It was not so when any other Company was with me, for I had a ridiculous Pretender or two out of the Town, which had not my Heart been engag'd, might perhaps have serv'd me to laugh at. But I was ever uneasy, as well as *Worthy*, out of each others Company; and tho' we could only steal a Glance, or sometimes a Touch of the Hand, Fancy improv'd our Pleasures, and made them greater than any other Satisfaction out of our selves! My first Fires were in their full force, the Object only changed by an invisible Transmutation. I lov'd to the heighth of all my former disorder, but it was with a more pleasing Pain, a secret Satisfaction, in having made a Conquest over that hitherto inexorable Virgin Heart!

I conceive their F e a r s were, least young *Worthy* should marry me; I was a Widow with an incumber'd Jointure, and his Affairs requir'd a Wife with a Fortune in ready Money. However, our Intelligence had proceeded no farther than the word *Love*; and it seems to me, that he had not form'd (no more than my self) any designs towards the possession of what he lov'd.

Mrs. *Woudbe*, and Mrs. *Marwoud*, (the Name of the other Lady) were invited to an Entertainment in the Town, that was like to hold till late! Mrs. *Abigal* was diverted another way, so that I was left alone; the old Husband being abroad upon his Occasions, Young *Worthy*, Ignorant of their Designs, (for they kept it from us) was likewise from Home: The Weather was hot, I undress my self to loose Night-Gown, and *Marcilles* Petticoat, and laid me down after Dinner upon the Bed to sleep. Young *Worthy* returned by instinct, or the Whispers of his good Genius, as he calls it; and hearing all were gone out, came as usual to my Chamber; I cast my Eyes to the Door as it open'd, and saw him with so elevated a joy, that scarce gave him time to shut it after him. For running to me as I lay, he threw himself upon my Mouth, and Eyes, and so transportedly kiss'd me, that I cou'd no longer doubt but his modesty was giving place to his Desires; when hearing some body come up the Stairs, (which answer'd exactly to my Chamber) I broke from his Arms, and opening the Door, was ready to swoon at the Sight of Mrs. *Woudbe*, return'd very Ill, or pretendedly so: She wou'd have gone in but I shut it after me, and directed her into the Dining-Room. She ask'd me who I had with me, I told her (in utmost Confusion) a Gentleman; She said why don't you then, Madam, go to him? So I must, answer'd I. And returning, shut the Door to after me but the Key was left on the outside. Young *Worthy* saw my Disorder, and the guilty Air which yet I cou'd not recover: I told him tho' we were never so Innocent, all Appearances were against us. My Undress, the *Dishabilie* of the Bed, the Door shut upon us, and my refusal to let her enter: So that happen what wou'd, for his Sake, I was resolved his Sister shou'd not see him, who most diligently kept Centry in the Dining-Room, to watch who shou'd come out. I ran the Hazard and Scandal of being suspected with any other rather than being confirm'd with him! She goes down to the Servants, to enquire who was with me, they tell her none but her Brother, who was come into two Moments before her. She return'd again to her Post in the Dining-Room, having not so far lost her respect to attempt my Chamber Door; tho' as I told you the Key was on the outside. I was at my Wits end for my Invention, and wou'd have him get out of my Dressing-room-Window upon the Leads, that answer'd to a Window in another part of the House, and which by chance was then open; from whence he might descend the back Stairs, and possibly get off unseen. He objected some Men that were working in the next Neighbours Yard: I told him in a Case like that something must be hazarded. And therefore removing with Expedition, the Glass and Toylet, that was spread upon a Table under that Window, he shot in a Moment from one to the other, and good Fortune favouring him, got down the Stairs, and through the House without any of their People seeing him! This was a Lucky Conveyance, successful Legerdemain. And I recovering my Fright, cou'd not chuse but laugh at the sick Lady upon

Duty; she stir'd not from her Post, (I wonder how her Patience cou'd hold from Interrupting us;) till after three Hours, (I calling for Candles) She ask'd the Servant who brought 'em, Who was with me? And she answering no body: You must imagine what she cou'd think. She had set one Centry at the Street Door, which how they escaped seeing *Worthy* go out I can't imagine, her self had been upon the watch above; I had told her there was a Gentleman in the Chamber with me; one Maid says 'tis her Brother, and soon after another tells her there was no body there. My apparent Confusion, and Dishabilie: All these were what confounded even her Cunning. I believe till that Minute, she suspected not that her Brother had discover'd to me his Love, but the Appearances were now Strong; and she imagin'd us to be really Criminal. Why should I of a sudden be so undrest? Why shut up alone with her Brother, where she was refus'd entrance? Why so confus'd? These were indeed circumstantial Evidences: But what could I have said had she enter'd, and found us as at first? It would certainly have condemn'd us; and getting him off so was all that was left for us to do, as making the best of a bad Market. 'Twas at worst a moot point whether he was with me or no. Politick Mrs. *Woudbe* said nothing to her Brother or me, but kept close, as well as *Abigal*, to their watch. We had not time to speak together for above a Week after. One Night he put a Paper into my Hand, which I have transcrib'd, because your Curiosity may be oblig'd by reading a first Love-Letter without Art or Ornament, the Effects only of what that Passion could dictate; for it seem'd to me 'twas to get the better of his Modesty, that could not (had we had Opportunity) so freely permit him to explain himself.

THE FIRST LETTER[2]

Expressing the Desire of a young Lover under Constraint.

"TELL me (my Dear Inspiring Mistress,) how shall I express the Tender Passion of my Love? Instruct your willing Scholar, and give Directions, by what means I may obtain an uncontroul'd access to your Dear Person, without the Apprehension of dispiriting Fear. The Genius's that haunt your Chamber, prevent the Pleasure of your private Conversation, and puts me into insupportabel Pain to suppress the Appearance of the glowing Flames of Love raging in my Breast.

If you wou'd preserve my Life, you must suddenly find out some way how uninterupted I may freely taste the sweets of Love! 'Tis not in the Power of humane Nature unprov'd, to conceive the inestimable Pleasures of powerful Love! a Pleasure so great, and so transporting, that 'tis inexpressible! My Thoughts too eagerly press upon another, and strive which shall tell you first, how much I Love. To describe your Bright Charms, is too great an Attempt for my weak Genius; I dare only say, I feel the Effect, in Extacy and Rapture! I doubt not but your Goodness will excuse and pardon all defects of Nature; especially when you've my Heart, a Sacrifice for all.

Oh Inconstancy; but why that thought? What need have I to fear? Have not I receiv'd marks of special Favour? But 'tis a Woman: Yet the best of all her Sex; all Truth, and Goodness! Ah but humane Nature (in all things) Love changes; the highest Tides produce the lowest Ebbs. Remember, *Fair One*, who taught me first to Love; who brought me into this Lab'rinth: Will you now desert me? Will you now leave me to be lost, inevitably? tell me truly: Or if I'm lost tell me not at all I'm past recovery, 'tis not in the power of Time, the coolest Thoughts of Reason, nothing less than Death, can unfix my Love grounded upon so firm an Esteem, rivetted immoveable within my Heart, I faint – Give me Life: Let me live, and live to love you."

To tell you the Pleasure this Letter gave me, wou'd too much confirm you in the Opinion of my Weakness. The next day (being *Sunday*) Mrs. *Marwoud* went with me to Church, as I was kneeling, I cou'd not forbear taking out the Paper to read it; I thought her at her Devotions, and never minded her squint over my Shoulders: Whence she gain'd the first part of the Letter, which confirm'd her Opinion (from the Sight of the Character) whence it came. My Lover, for a Night or two after staid in my Chamber, later by half an Hour than the rest; the Door was open, and we cou'd not speak so low, but we were over heard. Those precious Moments! those delightful Embraces! those piercing Kisses, never to be recall'd! all was at the Mercy of Mrs. *Woudbe*, who by hearkning, gave her self a Confirmation to her Fears. And the Second Night met him at his own Chamber-Door (as he came from me) with millions of Reproaches; I knew nothing of what was past till the next Night he put this Second Letter into my Hand.

THE SECOND LETTER

Excusing himself from being any more alone.

"'TIS impossible to express the Concern with which I write to you upon this unpleasant Subject? We were over-heard (if not seen) last Night, by my married Sister; she receiv'd me at the head of the Stairs, shut my Chamber-Door, and began to open.[3]

I was not so much surpris'd as I thought I shou'd have been, upon such an Occasion? she said, she cou'd not believe what she had been told, had not her own Ears convinc'd her as to the Truth of it! she recounted to me many particular Passages, especially that, when you (in so much Confusion) thrust her out of the Room, when you had only a Night-Gown on, and [I was] in the Chamber with you.

I answer'd, That she had given her self a great deal of Trouble, to little purpose: I did not suppose but she'd a truer Opinion of Both; that indeed I lik'd to be with you, because you were improving and delightful Company, but no farther; and that a jealous Listner hearing imperfectly some Words, and not others, turn'd all to the Subject they were apprehensive of, or suspected. If the Talk was never so remote, nothing more uncertain when the sound of Words cannot be distinguish'd; I urg'd my own Innocence, so we parted, and appeas'd her pretty well upon the promise never to be alone with you again, since it gave her so much Uneasiness. Lest you shou'd be ignorant of what has past, I thought it proper this way to acquaint you with it, that you might not judge untruly of my Neglect. The hazard is at present too great for me to break my Promise, therefore if you have (and I can't think otherwise) a real value for me you won't desire it. Believe me, I shall ever have a sincere Love and Esteem for you, you are the same (or more) to me, than ever. Tell me your Thoughts in a Letter, and suddenly, for I'm impatient till I hear from you."

Pride, and Indignation seiz'd me, at the reading of this, in a Stile so different from the former. What his Dependance upon his Sister in point of Interest was, I cou'd not tell; but I thought (be it never so great) he made too large a Sacrifice to it, and such as Love could never forgive him; that I was discover'd, and my Honour wrongfully suspected, was not half my Concern. Tho' that must needs sensibly affect a Soul haughty like mine, and who wou'd rather meet Death than Shame. I gave him my answer next Morning, wherein I complain'd of the weakness of that Love, which cou'd not stand one Assault, the rest you may conclude by his Reply.

THE THIRD LETTER

In Vindication of his doubted Love.

"What have I wrote that you interpret so much to my Disadvantage, I am surpriz'd at your Answer. You take my Meaning quite contrary to my Intentions; don't believe I can renounce and forsake you, in whom I have first my chiefest Happiness! I can't express the Tenderness of my Affections for you! believe me, you shall never find the Fervency of my Love turn'd into Coolness, or my Sincerity into Flattery; nor my Soul guilty of an Ingratitude. If you have any Love for me, don't perplex your self, for that gives me great Uneasiness; nor imagine I can have one unkind Thought for you, I love you most dearly well indeed: Time will produce it, and convince you of the Truth of all I say, when Opportunity permits me to show how much, how unalterably I am yours.

I shou'd not have given you these Letters at length, but only to beg your Judgment of my Lover's Sincerity; he was some time before this about departing from us, upon his own Business, with stupid Mrs. *Abigal* for his House-keeper: I conceive Mrs. *Woudbe* was of use to him (she governing her Husband) in point of Stock, or Partnership, that made him so cautious of disobliging her. She Closeted him the next day, employing Three Hours in railing at me, with the most prodigious absurd Abuses, that Envy, or

Malice, or the Devil himself cou'd invent. Who does not know the power of an ill Tongue upon weak Minds? He ought to have consider'd it, that Interest and Revenge dictated to them; and have, with Fortitude and Justice, withstood any Impression they wou'd have made upon him. I believe indeed he was proof to a great part of it, till industriously Mrs. *Marwoud* (owing me a good Turn, for preventing her a Conquest she had a desire to) told him, I was a Lady only seeking my Diversions, and in whom *Vanity* so much prevail'd, as to expose his Letter to her, and then repeated part of what she had cunningly read over my Shoulder: He persisted in his denial, that he had never writ to me any, but when next we met, I found his Eyes declin'd me; and no longer animated by those bewitching, softning Glances, that Sweetned all the Cruelties of Fortune, and which Love of me first taught; I pursu'd 'em, but they were lost to me; I found time to ask the Cause of the Change. He answer'd, I had expos'd his Letter, 'twas what he cou'd not account to himself for; and therefore must begin to practise a difficult Care upon his Heart, since I did but laugh at him. I had not leasure to answer, but upon Paper endeavour'd to convince him how the Matter hap'ned: This gave me more pain than I can express. If they cou'd succeed in such common Arts, of making a misunderstanding between us, 'twas in vain for me to expect the prospect of any Happiness. I suffer'd more real anguish by his false displeasure than I can describe. My Letter wrought so far upon him, that at the next Meeting I found the kindling Fire returning to his Eyes; and when, upon the first opportunity, he caught me in his Arms to kiss me, I felt the same Ease, the same Release from Pain, as a Wretch took from the Rack; or from that more exquisite Torture, the Rack of Nature; the Ease a Woman feels, releas'd from *Mother-pains*: He said he had in vain strove for his Cure; the more he strove, the harder it was to conquer. But my *Clorinda*, I found how dear I was like to pay for that Letter which had so transported me: Oh! *Why must the Extremity of Pleasure, produce the Extremity of Pain?* I found his Mind daily shaken, ev'n from its Foundation. He never wou'd believe, but that I had exposed his Letter. And all that cou'd be said, was, That he endeavour'd to forgive it me. But 'twas a Weakness he did not think I cou'd have been guilty of: And if on the Side of Love I lost no ground with him, I suffer'd much and wrongfully in his Esteem; besides, the Pain I had been in, taught him the Power he had over me, and which upon all occasions he too much exerted; perplexing me as he pleas'd; taking delight in the alternate Pains and Pleasure, that he cou'd raise in me, and which I can't forgive him; for this was all done by snatches: For since the first discovery, I had never had so much as one quarter of an hours time to talk the matter over with him. Thus stands the present State of our Amour; he is gone to his own House, distant from ours: These three long tedious Days and Nights I have liv'd, and liv'd without one Sight of him. Tell me sincerely, my

Clorinda, (thou infallible Judge of Hearts) What dost thou believe of his? Cou'd I but find my self in earnest slighted, Pride and Disdain in my haughty Soul must cure me: For tho' I so long against my Will persisted constant to my first Engagements, it was, because our Separation was the work of cruel *Fortune*, in which *Unkindness* had not any part. 'Twill be vain to expect my Cure from *Reason*, for that points to *Mutual Love*, as the greatest Good. I am not (my *Clorinda*) born to Happiness; when young betray'd, and married where I cou'd never affect: You know the next, how my first dear Inclinations were cross'd; see if I have any better hopes of this: *Fortune* cruelly is against me; I can't hope not to be happy: Oh, restore me then by your wise Counsels, to that bless'd State of *Indefferency*; Extinguish in me, if it be possible, these eternal Sparks of *Love*, or teach me to transfer it to a brighter, a more whorthy Object; improve this Humane, to a Love Divine: Let me there only fix my *Eternal* Hopes of unfading Joys, of Pleasures unknowing a decay, where (without Reproach) it will be meritorious to excel in Fondness; there only where excess of Passion, gives (without Remorse) excess of Pleasure, free from those allays attending Transitory Joys; Oh! aid me here to fix my Hopes, my Happiness, without End, and without Change, as I am yours.

NOTES

[1] Cf. Thomas Brown (ed.), *The Works of Monsieur Voiture ... With a Collection of Letters on Friendship and several other Occasions ...* London, 1705. The reference to this book reveals that collections of genuine and fictitious letters of gallantry were popular light reading. Fontenelle's letters served as a model for many English imitations. Aristaenetus wrote narrative letters in Greek in the fifth century A.D., which were translated into English by Tho. Brown in 1705 and by Bernard Lintot in 1715. Both Fontenelle's and Aristaenetus's letters were included in Tho. Brown's letter collection together with examples of his own efforts.

[2] In the original text the interspersed letters are printed in italics. In order to differentiate them here I have put them in quotation marks.

[3] *began to open:* obsolete expression for 'to explain herself', 'to express her opinion on the matter'.

A Letter from Mrs. Jane Jones

alias Jenny Diver,* In Drury-Lane, to Mrs Arabella B———wl———s, Near Wine-Office Court, Fleetstreet. Interspers'd With Reflections, Humorous and Moral, Pious and Political. London, 1737

---

*Jenny Diver is one of the prostitutes at Mrs Coaxer's establishment in Gay's *Beggar's Opera* (1728), II, iv.

A Letter from Mrs. Jane Jones

Jane Jones is a character akin to Moll Flanders and Fanny Hill, or, to go still further back, to some of the types in the *Conney Catching Tracts*. The "editor" of the "Letter from Mrs Jane Jones" tells us in his preface how this letter came into his hands. Arabella, the addressee, apparently had not followed her friend's advice to earn her living in a more honourable way and had "dy'd a few Days ago at Mother ... 's in ... Square", where a small cabinet with her papers was purchased by the editor. He tried to find out who Jane Jones – also known under the name of Jenny Diver – actually was, and where she had lived. She is described to him as a woman of noble birth on her father's side, of admirable wit and great beauty, but of mixed fortune. He searches all the haunts of Drury but finds her shutters closed and the house to let. Some of her sisterhood inform him that she is said to have left the country and turned Papist.

Of course, like the letter itself, this "editor's" introduction is a complete fiction. There is no trace of a historical Jane Jones. The author uses the common device of mysterious documents discovered among a dead person's effects to lend his tale an air of veracity, and his use of the letter-form supports his claim to authenticity. Smollett uses a similar trick in *Humphrey Clinker*, where the letters have come into the editor's hands from a rather mysterious source.

The story of Jane Jones represents the limit of realistic portraiture in eighteenth-century fiction. The young lady, drawn into the whirlpool of life at an early age, is not altogether to blame for her subsequent fall. Her story is the usual one, certainly at some point drawn from life before it gradually became a stock motif of narrative literature: an innocent young girl has her first love-affair with a rich young gentleman; at first he seems wonderful, but he speedily forsakes her, so that the bewildered girl is thrown upon the help of another "kind gentleman". The stages of her eventful life are well motivated and linked together. After the second disappointment she begins to lose confidence and no longer cares much what happens to her. Following a period of happiness with a man of quality and social standing whom she loves come years of despair and want; through the evil influence of another woman she sinks to the level of a common prostitute. At the time of her letter to Arabella she is about to leave England in order to retire to a monastery in France. Although the alleged purpose of the letter is to save her friend and younger colleague from the kind of experience she herself has had, it becomes obvious in the end that Jane Jones is not prepared to make any considerable change in her way of life in France. "A new Climate, and a different scene" will make all the difference and provide new chances. There is hidden irony here, as well as in her hope for "a very aggreeable Reception in the House he recommends me to". Without quite knowing it herself, she reveals her secret wishes: what she expects is not monastic solitude. She is going to France, as she makes clear in the last passage of the letter, in quest of fresh adventures. In the process of writing, her fancy leads her away from her original intention of saving her friend from a fate such as she herself has experienced. The change of mood from bitter irony and disillusionment to hectic gaiety and desperate hope makes the letter both lively and convincing as a study of character.

The didactic purpose of *A Letter from Mrs Jane Jones* lies not in her own admonitory reflexions but in the author's depiction of the heroine as a woman who has sunk to the lowest depths, who is at the mercy of her own and other people's vices, hopelessly entangled in the cruel interplay of character and destiny. The author knows more about her, understands her better than she does herself. That she will end miserably and that Arabella will not follow her advice is clear. Jane Jones is meant to be a warning and the "editor" of the epistolary story – presumably the author – calls it "an Epistle more valuable, in my Opinion, than all Cicero's": "The Treasure I now put into thy Hands, if of a mixt Kind. But in it thou wilt discover great Knowledge of Human Nature; and such Traces of Observation, as plainly bespeak Mrs Diver to have kept the best of Company, and to have been no idle Spectator of the World". There is no conversion at the end as in *Moll Flanders*, and no marriage and happy ending as in *Fanny Hill*. Only Jane Jones's confidence in her own charms survives. In her digression on Roman Catholic belief she sharply rejects the consolation of mystic raptures, seeing them as a mere outlet for unsatisfied dreams and desires. In this way she attacks that particular eighteenth-century religious sentimentalism found in epistles, diaries, and novels of the time.

---

3 October 1736

Dear Bell,

It is some Time since I had the Pleasure of your agreeable Conversation. Indeed, of late I have been in so unhappy a Situation, that I could as little wish you to favour it with your Company, as I could bring my self to be tolerably easy in it. And this Uneasiness I have found increase so strongly upon me within these few Days since the Gin-Act's[1] taking Place, that I find a Life, attended with the Inconveniences ours is continually subject to, is not to be borne, without the Assistance of Liquor, to animate our Spirits, and dissipate our Thought. This wretched State of ours I have long felt in a slighter Manner; but now perceive it so intolerable, that I have Thoughts of leaving the Kingdom, and retiring to a *religious House* beyond Sea; where Father B– – – –, (who now, I hear, favours you with his Company, and who wants to be rid of me,) promises I shall be admitted suitably to the imaginary Title I formerly bore; and for which he engages to procure me *proper Testimonials.* I am now 35, having lived much longer than most of my Profession; my first Acquaintance, both Men and Women, being long since gone off. My *Natural Mother* dy'd before I had any Knowledge of her; nor was I much sensible of the good Lady who took care of me in my Infancy. From about my tenth Year Mrs. *Needham,* (to whom you owe your Education, tho' much later,) directed my Behaviour, and gave me Instructions for her future Purposes; and this only Comfort I have in my Reflections, that I never had the Opportunity of being rescued from her Designs, nor the least Sentiment that they were improper, till they were impossible to be prevented. After this, what has been my Condition? Shall I review it? – Dear *Arabella*! what are Men! shall I describe them to you; or do you already think of them as I do? I will however, as you are so much younger, and have not yet *been Common-Hackney'd in the Ways of Men,* just give you a Sketch of some of the Occurrences of the many Years I have been subjected to their Pleasure.

The Noble Lord who first possess'd me, tho' a Man of Genius, and whom I could have lov'd for the Agreeableness of his Person, (with which, I own, I was soon charm'd,) had scarce enjoy'd me, when I was treated by him with a Coolness I had till then no Sentiment of; and in less than three Weeks after he had taken me from Mrs. *Needham*'s, he left me in the Lodgings he had provided for me in *King-street, Covent-Garden.* He had the Humanity indeed, not to leave me entirely destitute; but his Fortune and Extravagancies were such, that I never saw more of his Money than 30 Guineas, which he sent me with his Farewel letter. Thus was I in Lodgings of two Guineas a Week, a Maid and a Black, left with this small Pittance, without a Friend in the World: For Mrs. *Needham,* to whom I would have return'd, would not so much as suffer me to enter her Doors.

I was just leaving these Lodgings, having turn'd off my Black, and about to dismiss my Maid, when one Evening, taking the Air in the Garden, a Gentleman, famed for his Humanity and his Writings, seeing me disconsolate, join'd Company with me; and was not long, before he had artfully got from me my unhappy Story. He ask'd my Lodgings; which I having told him, he desir'd he might have the Liberty to drink a Dish of Tea with me on the Morrow; and taking me by the Hand at parting, slipt a Bank Note of 20 *l.* into it. I was so confounded at this Generosity in an entire Stranger, that I could only acknowledge it by my Confusion: Which he perceiving, immediately withdrew. I had the Pleasure of seeing him the next Morning, according to his Appointment: Which was the greater Favour, as it was a Circumstance he was always too regardless of; and nothing could have made him so punctual at that Time, but the compassionate Sentiments I always discover'd him to have for the Unfortunate. You may be sure, I was not a little happy in such an Acquaintance; so much Wit! such an agreeable Turn of Conversation! the Pleasure of being favour'd by a Man, beloved by Women, and esteem'd and honour'd by every Man of Sense. Dear *Arabella*, the Remembrance is Transport, as his Loss made me quite inconsolable: For I lost him long before his Death; tho' I was often favour'd with his Bounty.

Upon finding myself forsaken, I was at first almost distracted, and soon totally regardless of myself and Conduct: And, like one abandon'd, car'd not who had my Person, while my dear, inconstant, witty, generous K————t alone possess'd my Mind; till after a Succession of Wretches, between whom I perceiv'd no Difference, I found myself constantly visited, (tho' my Lodgings were then much below what I had ever before been reduc'd to,) by One, who I have observed since was far from being the only one of his Character among the Sex. He was admitted to all my Favours; which he was no sooner in Possession of, than he exerted the Tyrant, instead of the Lover. I was kept poor; always suspected; and dared not to stir out without Permission. I had yielded at first to this, being in infinite Perplexity about my lost Favourite, and indifferent what became of me; and when I at last found this Condition intolerable, and would have freed myself, it was then impossible. Every Attempt for Liberty, was fresh Ground for Suspicion and ill Usage; and tho' I was maintain'd, it was barely a Maintenance, and that literally in a Prison. This insupportable Jealously of his, as I afterwards discover'd, proceeded from his having acquir'd, and maintain'd in his Writings, the Character of the *Just*, the *Chaste*, and the *Good*, (without which Epithets he was seldom mention'd,) and of which he was too tenacious to be agreeable to one in our Way of Life: For who should this be, but the most intimate Friend of my Favourite. But, sure never, never were two Men of such different Dispositions join'd together under that Denomination; I remember, he once downright quarrel'd with me, because, upon the Mention of his Friend's Name, I sigh'd, and told him, I was one of his *Band of Pensioners*. You may guess, my dear *Arabella*, how irksome such a Confinement with such a Man (tho' possess'd of the most sprightly Genius, the most natural Turn of Humour in Conversation, and the most inexhaustible Fund of polite Learning,) must be to a Woman of my free and unconfin'd Manner of Thinking. However his Marriage soon deliver'd me from my disagreeable Keeper; and Chance threw me into the Arms of the famous Col. C————s. He had view'd me by Accident one Morning dressing at my Window, with my Hair dishevel'd; and the natural Bloom, and the Delicacy and Tenderness of my Features, rais'd in him a Passion to be better acquainted with them. To this End he had bribed my Maid a few Weeks before the Marriage of my last Gallant; and she took her Opportunity to communicate and forward his Purpose soon after. He was so much a Brute, that tho' he was at first very liberal; yet I soon took so great a Disgust to him, that I had no Means of making my Situation tolerable, but by Drinking; into which indeed my late Keeper had initiated me, as it was privately his Practice; and which at this Time, I fell into too inordinately. But I cannot sincerely repent of it at this Time, as it was the Occasion of my Colonel's leaving me; for tho' he was so much a Brute himself, he could not bear to see me so; and upon that took such an Antipathy, that he soon left me, as my Beauty was inclining to do, by the Practice of strong Liquors.

But from this I was happily recover'd by a Gentleman, whose Memory is yet dear to me. It was the witty, the gay, the polite J—— C——s, Esq; I caught him by a Conversation at the Masquerade. He was so struck with my Prattle, that tho' he was then in a very important Post, and was press'd with a publick Misfortune, which was too soon after his Death, [2] his chief Felicity, as he often told me, and I could easily discover, was with me. How often has he been lost to his high Station, and his most intimate Friends, to toy and chat with his Darling *Jenny*! for such he always consider'd me. He entertain'd so high an Opinion of my Understanding, that, contrary to the general Maxims of the World, he favour'd me with his inmost Sentiments, and all his Thoughts were open'd to my View. In this he was never betray'd. I esteem'd his Compliment to my good Sense and Confidence in my Discretion, infinitely beyond the finest Things that could be said or thought of my Person; nor could any Art or Violence ever have extorted from me what he at any Time intrusted: It was an Honour not to be rated too high, to be the Confident of a Man of his distinguished Abilities. But he had too great a Spirit, to be indifferent to strong Injuries; and such were the Circumstances of the Times, that popular Clamour, added to a private Distress, threw him into a Fever, of which he dy'd in a few Days. You know, Dear *Arabella*, what a Character is given him by the finest Genius now living. I who knew and loved him well, feel the Truth of each Part of the Description – But I must endeavour to forget him.

During this Time, I lived in all the Splendour of a Woman of Fortune, My Dress and Equipage were suited to such a Character; and a Chair was always attending my Commands. But all the outward Ornaments of which our Sex are too fond, were unattended to by me, farther than to render myself more agreeable to the kind Bestower: My Happiness resulted from the Esteem of such a Man; and I never once thought of the Prudence of a Reserve, till his Death, shew'd me the Want of it. For as his Illness was sudden, and I had not Opportunity of seeing him, I was deprived at once of the dear Man I loved, and all the Means of my Support.

I continued in a retired Way for some Months, and lived by converting what was most valuable into ready Money; when I grew acquainted with the afterwards famous *Charlotte* M———r. She was wild and witty, and of an extravagent Taste. Her Beauty was then in its Prime; and as her good Nature was her great Foible, she conceived a Friendship for me, that brought on the most disagreeable Part of my Life. She could not bear my retired Manner, as she called it; but would force me into the World. There was now no Medium in my Fortunes. She led me from one Set of her Acquaintance to another, till I had lost all Sense of Reserve; and was at last, through Necessity and Inattention, as profligate as herself: Not omitting often to frequent the publick Streets. What a Wild of Distress and Irregularity does this Scene open to my View! What Creatures are the general Herd of Mankind! Bad as I was now grown, I could not have supported myself under this State of Ignominy and Subjection, had I not destroy'd all Reflection by strong Liquors. To be the Instrument of Pleasure to Drunkards, Fools and Idiots, to the lowest Baseness, Ingratitude, and Brutality; to be subject to weak and wanton Humour, and to be ill treated for all Endeavours to be agreeable: It is a State, greatly to be pitied, and devoutly to be shun'd.

Dear *Arabella*! 'tis the Thought of this unhappy Condition of the poor Creatures about Town, that drew this Epistle from me. I knew it in its worst Shape; and cannot but pity those who are in it, as I would guard all I had the least Regard to from falling into it. You have hitherto pretty well escaped it; shun the very Possibility of it. Mrs. ———, with whom you now live, as I hear you have done since the Death of Sir C———s B———s, has too selfish a Character, not to expose you to Usage you are yet a Stranger to; and I must own to you, I was extremely sorry you were got into her House. Retire with me, my Dear, into a Land unknown; and prevent, by a timely Escape, all the Evils I have pass'd thro'; if you are not destroy'd long before you come to my Age. You, when you lived with a Character and Reputation, favour'd me with your Friendship and Assistance, in the lowest State of my Prostitution; as you said you discover'd in me something worthy a better Fate: Let me repay those Obligations, by guarding you from the same distressful Circumstances. Consider, there are few Men like some I have named to you, and your late Sir *Charles*, who continued your Friend for Years. Such good Fortune is not to be expected twice; at least by living with Mrs. ——— you are not in the Way of meeting with it. Think of me, my Dear, as one you always profess'd an Esteem for, reflecting on the Ways of Life I have pass'd thro'; and let my Experience prevent your ever making such unhappy Reflections. My Thoughts are now cool, and free from all the intoxicating Powers I have been long inured to; and should you fly to them for Aid in your future Distress, you will find them too ineffectual to prevent the painful Result of your good Sense.[3]

I am now within a few Days of leaving the Kingdom, but not entirely on a Religious Account: For tho' I have convers'd much with Father B———, who has labour'd my Conversion to the *Roman Catholick* Church, with a Zeal as if he thought thereby to extinguish all his Sins, yet he has not reconciled me to any of the *Absurdities* of that Religion. Indeed, I must do him the Justice to own, he never attempted it: And I am so far from charging any thing of that Kind to his Account, that I question much if he himself believes them. This Opinion is founded on the slight Manner in which he has always in Conversation treated *Protestant Mysteries*; some of which he never fail'd to equal to any in his Church. His real Sentiments I take to be in Favour of Deism: Of which he always spoke with great Respect; at the same Time he acknowledged his own Conduct as contrary to *natural* as[4] *revealed Religion*. For this Reason, he said, he could not but wish, tho', he own'd, he could not hope, that the Absolutions of Holy Church would be effectual to extirpate all Offences: But of these Things he avoided Converse with every one, and said, he dared not permit himself often to think of them. He assures me, I shall find a very agreeable Reception in the House he recommends me to, and meet every Thing suitable to a Person of Condition. What had I to do, but to accept this offer, with the greatest Readiness? I have seen Life for these 20 Years past in all its Variety; and there is nothing now to invite my Stay. A new Climate, and a different Scene, may yield something entertaining; but the main Point, as I have told you, is a Subsistence. To obtain which, were it in my Power, I would not chuse to go over the same Track I have already trod. But, alas! that is impossible, were it my Will! All my boasted Beauty is now no more, and I have only the varying Remains of the agreeable Face which once was so engaging.

I consider the Difficulty, my Dear, of spending Time in such a Recluse State. Tho' I have much natural Tenderness, yet, I believe, I shall not readily fall into the Joys of a *Mystick*, and feel the Raptures that attend the heated *Pietist*. Such a Disposition might have been form'd in me, when I ran from Mrs. *Needham* with Earl ——; but my Passions are now too much allay'd and too settled, to turn them to such a Purpose; and I must freely own to you, that were this less practicable from Nature, my Judgment, ever since I have thought upon this Subject, has greatly disapprov'd this spiritualiz'd Wantonness. Shall I tell you the Occasion? When my dear Favourite Mr. C———dy'd, and left me in the Condition I have mention'd; a venerable Clergyman who lodged over-against me, I suppose perceiving me disconsolate, came to visit me; and as he consider'd me an unhappy Woman, who had lost a good Friend and near Relation, (for I put on Mourning for his Death,) he endeavour'd to turn my Thoughts from the Pleasures of This World, by acquainting me, as he said, with those of Another. He furnish'd me with several religious Books to this End; *Meditations* and *Ejaculations*, full of elevated Rapture and passionate Affection. My young Mind was soon caught with the new Transport which my pious Instructor had initiated me into; till, from a heated Contemplation of invisible and inconceivable Objects, the Scale was easily turn'd, and I found myself, as I mention'd before, engag'd in the most dissolute Course that I ever knew: And I am fully persuaded, my Dear, that the heating my Imagination in that unreasonable Manner, without informing my Judgment, only render'd me more capable of my former Flame, and of worse and baser Methods to support it. I recollect now, my Dear *Arabella*, (and with greater Uneasiness than I do any Part of my Conduct,) that it was in this Interval I acquir'd by my Dexterity in the basest, meanest Arts in the World, the Nick-Name of *Jenny Diver*, by which I was deservedly made infamous ever after.

Well, this is past and cannot be recall'd; nor, I fear, forgotten. Another Country, other Customs, other Scenes of Gallantry, may put other Thoughts into my Head. You think this is not talking like a *Recluse*. – Come, I will lay my whole Heart before you. I am not without Hopes of making a Captive in *France*, that will surprize the whole World. While I was at *Paris* one Summer with my dear *Witty*, *Gay* and *Polite*, I contracted a Friendship with Madamoiselle ———, whom the C–d–i M———r, I hear now visits. To her am I now really going. Beauty, my Dear, is but of short Date here in *England*; yet a *British* Face of 35, with a little *Art*, will make as good a *French* 18, as any in *Paris*, If, with all the Charms I am Mistress of; with Gentility, Wit, Ease of Conversation, and my Remains of Beauty, (which I flatter myself, when properly aided, will appear not of the smallest,) I can but make a Conquest of that *Great Man*, and be an *English* R———t of the *F———ch Affairs*; then – But whither does my Fancy lead me? I will have done. But be assured, whatever Station I am in, I shall always be, my dearest *Arabella*,

Most Affectionately Yours,
J. JONES.

Postscript

BEFORE I leave the Kingdom, I shall send you all my Manuscripts; as I know you are a Girl of good Sense, and capable of perfecting what I have left unfinished. You'll see, I had gone a good way in a Scheme for incorporating the Women of our Profession, and had laid down some Rules for their better Management. There are a few Political Pamphlets, half finish'd; Love Songs, without the last Stanza; and a new Design, just enter'd upon, of *Dialogues* between some worthless Living Characters, whom Imagination was to place in the Shades. What an inexhaustible Fund, is here for such a Genius as yours to work on. – How many Authors has my necessitous Muse at Times created! Both Patriots and Courtiers have father'd my Prose, and great Ladies taken the Credit of my Poetical Pieces. The Epistle to Lady *B. G.* burn, when you have read it; but use the others in any Way most to your Advantage. Once more Farewel.

NOTES

[1] *Gin Act:* In the early eighteenth century mortality and crime among the poor were increased by the new taste for gin. The distillers of gin paid so small a duty that the very poorest customers could afford the liquor sold at unlicensed dram-shops. By 1733 there were 6,000–7,000 of these dram-shops in London alone and between five to seven million gallons of spirits were distilled. In 1736 drastic measures were taken by Sir Joseph Jekyll in order to reduce the consumption of gin: a heavy tax of £1 per gallon was imposed by the so-called Gin Act.

[2] Meaning: this misfortune very soon afterwards caused his death.

[3] *Prevent* may be used here in the obsolete sense of 'outdo', 'surpass' or simply 'anticipate'. *Result:* 'impulse', 'prompting' (obsolete). *Good sense:* 'insight', 'realisation'. The meaning of this sentence is: You will never be able to drown the awareness of your condition in liquor.

[4] Should be '... to *natural* as to *revealed* ...'.

The Lover's Week

---

*or, the Six Days Adventures
of Philander and Amaryllis.
Written by a Young Lady.*
London, 1718

The Lover's Week

Amaryllis is a young lady of charm and wit, quick at repartee and not lacking in self-irony. She is capable of analysing her feelings with a certain sense of humour, as her comment of the arrival of her lover's messenger makes clear: "as I judged by my own impatience, [it] would not be long before he came". She manages her chaperoning aunt very adequately, and she manages to regard her lover with a certain critical reserve. She is, however, too much in love herself to act as wisely as her intelligence recommends, so that Philander, a young nobleman, succeeds in half kidnapping her without having to use force. He simply leads her into a situation where it becomes ever more difficult and finally impossible to return to the house of her aunt. Her descent into this embarrassing situation happens not altogether against her will, and at the end of six days she consents to stay with him at his country estate. Not the slightest touch of tragedy mars this pleasant tale – indeed the ending depicts the lovers in an idyllic state of happiness. Occasionally the lovers quarrel: Philander is blamed for his little tricks or for not being gallant enough. But on the whole little happens, and scenes depicting the pleasant recreations of the lovers are not at all infrequent. *The Lover's Week* (by 'M. H') is one of the few exclusively comic epistolary novels, and may be regarded as idyllic counterpart to *Clarissa*.

A continuation of this novel appeared in the following year (1719) under the title of *The Female Deserters*. Here Emelia's letters serve only as a framework for various stories about other ladies who, like herself, have left their relations in order to enjoy themselves with the young gentlemen of their hearts in a country retreat. Far from the town they lead a life of entertainment and rural pleasures. Action and dramatic movement, which usually bring the epistolary structure to life, are almost completely lacking here. In fact the first part, *The Lover's Week*, exhibits the calmness of the autobiographical point-of-view rather than the excitement of epistolary narrative, despite a good number of apostrophes and the small space of time between the past events and the moment of Amaryllis's remembering and writing them down. Although some passages are dramatic enough to be put into the narrator's present, on the whole *The Lover's Week* is a typical example of a hybrid between autobiographical narrative and epistolary story.

The FIRST DAY

IT was my Luck to wait on the Lady *D*––; who, after Dinner was over, obliged me to go with her to Mr. *Russel*'s the Painter's in the *Piazza* in

Covent-Garden, to look on some Pictures, and to have her own finish'd, which he was about. Whilst my Lady and he was busy, I diverted myself with looking out of Window; and hapned to see coming along a handsome Gilt Chariot, with a Noble Equipage. There was in it a young Nobleman, accompanied by a Divine. They seemed indeed both of them to look very earnestly up at the Window where I stood whilst the Chariot drove by. But as, you know, I am not very vain, I thought no farther of them; but went from the Window to see what my Lady and the Painter were doing: When immediately one of Mr. *Russel*'s Servants came up, and told him, That there was a Divine and another Gentleman, who desired to speak with him. He beg'd they would walk up, as being very busy, just finishing my Lady's Picture, it being the last time of her Sitting. The Servant had no sooner carry'd down the Message, but they came up; but what was the reason of it, I am not able to account for. I was in so great a Consternation when they came into the Room, that I much feared it would be taken notice of by my Lady, who, as I thought, observ'd me very much. I felt myself change colour several times, therefore removed to the farther end of the Room, to prevent its being taken notice of by others. My Surprize, however, was not so great, but that I saw the moment this young Nobleman enter'd the Room, his Eyes were fixed on me; for tho' he talked of the Pictures, they still followed me to whatever part of the Room I moved; and, as I thought, told me in a most obliging manner, that we must have a farther Conversation, as it has since proved. My Lady having sat her time, after admiring several Pieces of Painting of Mr. *Russel*'s, asked me, If we should be going? I told her I waited her motion, as having come there purely to oblige her Ladyship. I must indeed own, I could with a great deal of Satisfaction have stay'd; for when I quitted the Room, I left methought my Heart behind me.

Mr. *Russel* handed my Lady to the Coach, whilst the young Nobleman was no less officious in waiting on me. He stood and look'd after the Coach as far as he could see it, then sent a trusty Servant that he had, to watch it, charging him not to return till he had found where I lived; for he understood by our Discourse, that I did not live with the Lady with whom I was. I went home with my Lady. After some Discourse about her Picture, I took my leave, and went home to my Aunt's: Where, after giving my Lady's Service, and answering her a thousand impertinent Questions and Jealousies, (which you know are natural in old Maids, who always hate any Gallantry should pass between others, and are for the generality as censorious and ill-natur'd, as can be, because they are neglected) I went to undress, and indeed must own could not for my Life get this young Nobleman out of my Head by all the Art I was Mistress of. I went into my Closet to read, thinking to try what that would do, but all in vain; it was impossible to remove so pleasing an Idea. At length the Watchman came, Past Twelve a-Clock; at which time I went to Bed; where the God of Sleep took place of the God of Love, and lulled me into a very quiet Repose till the next Morning Ten a-Clock, when I rose, having forgot the Adventure of the foregoing Day.

The SECOND DAY

I Was no sooner up, and drinking my Tea, than the Footman call'd my Maid, and told her, that a Servant had brought a Letter for me; which he gave her, and bid her acquaint me, that he stay'd for an Answer. When she brought it up to me, I was very angry with her, as believing it came from the Duke of *A*--, whose Letters I had absolutely order'd them not to trouble me with. When my Passion was a little over, my Maid assur'd me it was not his Man, nor any other whose Livery she had seen at the House before: I therefore order'd her to reach me the Letter, which I had thrown by without so much as looking on the Direction. I open'd it, and casting my Eye at the Bottom, found it signed *Philander*. I was then more in amaze to think who it came from, than before; when upon Recollection, and giving myself time to read it, I found it came from the Gentleman I had seen the Day before at Mr. *Russel*'s. It was full of Love and Gallantry, which again reviv'd those Thoughts in me, that I imagin'd a Night's Rest had quite extinguish'd. His Writing, I thought, not only shew'd him an accomplish'd Gentleman, but withal discover'd a more than ordinary Passion for me. He pressed for an Answer, and that I would let him know when and where he should wait on me, or if he should see me at my own home; tho' he added, he had been inform'd my Aunt kept so strict a Watch over me, that he could not think that Place any ways proper, as seeing he should have no opportunity to declare that Passion which was so violent, and which, if I would not take pity of, would inevitably cost him his Life. He told me, to add to the Charms of my Person, he had heard much of my Conversation, and as my Sense would carry me above all the little Reflections of the unthinking part of my Sex, (whose Wit for the generality reaches no higher than *Tea-Table*-Chat) beg'd me to lay by the little Scruples that might seem at first to keep me from it, and favour him with an Answer. Indeed, I a little consider'd at first, if it would be Prudence in me to comply with his Request; but at length Love (as it generally does) outwent Consideration (I doubt not but you'll here blame my too easy complying: But, my dear *Emilia*, you know it is not in our Powers to act against our Inclinations, I am sure at least it never was in mine, not being Mistress of those little Arts that, in my opinion, are too much used by our Sex:) But to return to my Story; I writ him word, If he had a mind to see me, and would wait on the Dutchess of *M*--, who had sent my Aunt word she would visit her that Afternoon, it would be a means to introduce him into the Family without Suspicion. I sent the Servant away with this Answer:

Which I thought Encouragement enough for the first time; and make no doubt but you will think me too free, but beg you to be as favourable as you can in your Censure. After I had again perused the Letter, which every time I looked on it appeared with fresh Beauties, I called my Maid, and order'd her to get things ready for my Dressing. I charg'd her to take a particular care to put all my Trifles on exact, being resolved to make what addition to my Person I could by Dress, not doubting but my new Lover would take that Method of seeing me; not that I had any real Design farther on him than the rest of the Sex, tho' it has since proved otherwise.

Dinner being ready, the Footman came to let me know my Aunt waited for me at Table: The old Gentlewoman took particular Notice of me, and told me she never saw me look so well in her Life. *Amaryllis*, says she, If the D. of *A*— (whose Addresses she favour'd) was to see you to Day, in spite of all your Repulses and Denials, it would be impossible for him to recover his Heart, which she much fear'd I had but too fast, unless I would use it better. Without any addition to my Charms, I desired her not to talk to me of a Man that was my Aversion, tho' no doubt he might deserve much finer Women than myself. She at last grew pretty warm: *Amaryllis*, says she, I would not have you so vain of your Beauties, in slighting so fine a Gentleman as the Duke of *A*—. For, added she, I was as fine a Woman as your Ladyship at your Years, and had as many Lovers; but, out of an affected Coyness, slighted them as you do. She vexed me so much with her Talk, that I could not help making her this ill-natur'd Answer; I suppose your Ladyship has often repented your Coyness, being forced thro' your own Folly to live a Maid ever since, and I much fear will die so. She perceived by my Answer, that I was out of humour, so drop'd the Discourse. My Aunt's Compliment, however, did not a little please me, as knowing there must be something extraordinary when she vouchsaf'd to take notice of it.

After Dinner was over, we went to play a Game at Picquet; at which Diversion we had not been long, before the Dutchess of *M*—'s Coach stop'd at the Gate. Her Grace was attended by my *Philander*, (for so I shall call him in the remaining part of my Story:) It is impossible for me to describe, or you to imagine, the different Motions of my Heart, that I found at his near Approach, which Confusion I saw doubled in him; for when he saluted me, he trembled, but had only opportunity to whisper to me, How could you be so barbarous as not to give me a better Opportunity of speaking to you? Our long being together, I was afraid would be taken notice of by the Dutchess and my Aunt, so we broke off our Conversation for that time, and joined with the Company.

After drinking Tea, my Aunt (who you know is a great Lover of Play) proposed Cards, which was readily agreed to by the Company: It was my Aunt's Luck to have *Philander* for her Partner, (at which she seem'd not a little pleased) whether thro' Chance or Design, I can't tell; but Fortune ran hard against them, and the Dutchess and I won each of us near threescore Pieces: It grew near Four a-Clock in the Morning, at which time her Grace thought fit to be going home.

Whilst the Dutchess was taking her leave of my Aunt, *Philander* obtained a Promise of me to meet him the next Day; but their Compliments being over, he had only time to tell me, He would send the same Servant that he had sent to me before, to let me know where we should meet: So, with pressing me once more to be as good as my Word, we parted for that Night.

My Aunt, who, notwithstanding her being engag'd with the Dutchess, took a particular Notice of *Philander*'s and my talking together: After very severely reprimanding me for a Levity in my Carriage, which she was pleased to say I was too guilty of at all times, she told me with a very grave Air; *Amaryllis*, I would not have you rely too much on your Charms, nor let the Flatteries of Men give you any Vanity; whose Words are little to be regarded, they not knowing their own Minds an Hour together, but vary in their Opinions as any fresh Objects offer: Therefore, my dear Niece, have a care of their deluding Speeches, which if you too readily believe, you will, alas! insensibly be drawn into those Snares which you'll too late repent, and wish yourself out of, I thanked her for her kind Advice; but told her, That I could not imagine what her Discourse aim'd at, since I knew of no Body that had laid any Snare for me. She smiled, and said, I am not so blind, but I saw the Motions of the young Nobleman's Eyes, that where-ever you moved, they follow'd you, and that he minded you a great deal more than he did his Cards. I was quite out of Patience at her Talk, therefore would fain have bid her Good-night two or three times; but she, as if she had been in Love with *Philander* herself, (as by the way, I believe a very small Perswasion would have made her) kept me chatting tell between Five and Six; at which time I took my Leave of her, (tho' against her Will:) I undress'd, and went to Bed, I can't say to rest, for really I had not one Wink of Sleep, but was disturbed by various Thoughts till Day-break.

The THIRD DAY

VERY early the next Morning my Maid came into my Chamber to make a Fire, and get things in order for my Rising. She told me the Duke of *A--*'s Footman had been there, and brought a Parcel, and a fine Nosegay of Orange-Flowers, (which he knew I was very fond of, and would, indeed, have been very acceptable had they come from any other Person;) but that she, according to my Order, refusing to take them, the Man said, He would leave them in the Hall, not daring to carry them back to his Lord: Therefore she took them, and brought them up into my Dressing-room. I chid her for medling with it, and bid her, since she busied herself so much with what I order'd her not, (tho' I believe she was very well paid for it by the Duke) to take care, that if the same Servant should come that was here yesterday, to let none of the Family see him, if she could help it, besides herself: So I dismiss'd her for the present from any farther Attendance upon me to wait for this Messenger of Love; who, as I judged by my own Impatience, would not be long before he came. She had not been gone out of my Chamber ten Minutes by my Watch, before she return'd, and brought me the wish'd for Billet: In which there was a thousand fresh Repetitions of his Fidelity, in so natural and moving a manner, as shew'd no Design or Artifice. He writ with the Complaisance of a Lover, and Sincerity of a Friend: And in a most humble and obliging manner beg'd me to meet him that Evening at Six a-Clock: He said, He hop'd I would not use, for an Evasion of coming, the vain, idle Scruples, Of what would the World say of me? for he was sure (by the little Conversation he had with me) I had a Soul above caring what the ill-natur'd part of the World should say of me; and he well knew I was Mistress of Wit enough to silence any impertinent People who should dare to call my Conduct in question: So that, in short, by putting off Doubts, and answering them himself, he left nothing for me to object against. He let me know farther, That on my complying with his Request, his Life depended. I therefore call'd for Pen and Ink, and writ him word, That he should certainly meet me according to his Desire.

I know you will again reflect on me for so sudden a Compliance with his Request: But, dear *Emilia*, consider, my Word was already past; neither would it have suited with my open free Temper, to have let any one suffer a moment's Pain, that I could ease them of, out of a little affected Coyness of my Sex; much less would I let my dear *Philander* be uneasy for so foolish a thing as a Promise of meeting him, since I must own he grew every moment more dear to me than other: And, in short, I could think of nothing but him, and every Thought added fresh Charms to his Person.

I passed the Remainder of the Morning in perusing his dear Letter; which every time I read, I found fresh cause to admire. I thought the Day long, and wished for the appointed Hour, as much as he afterwards told me he did. I had promised my *Philander* to come to him, but how to get out, my Aunt having a great many Visiters that Afternoon, could not tell; therefore believ'd it would be not only an Affront to leave the Company, but that my Aunt would oppose it with all the Authority she was Mistress of: At length, after having fretted above an Hour, and fresh Company continuing to come in, being quite out of Humour, not knowing what to do, and seeing no Likelihood of my Release, I slip'd out of the Room, and went up into my Chamber to consider what was to be done; for resolv'd I was to meet my dear *Philander*, according to my Promise. I had not been long in my Room before this lucky Thought came into my Head; That I would go down, and make my Excuse to the Company, and say, That my Lady *Betty* had sent to beg to speak with me immediately, for that she was much worse than she ever had been. This Project, I thought, would take with my Aunt, who I knew had a particular value for that Lady, and knew she had been ill. In order, therefore, to put my Design in execution, I call'd my Maid, and bid her give me my Fan and Hood: When coming down Stairs, I met my Aunt, who seem'd surpriz'd at my going out, and said, Madam, I think, if you had no value for me, you ought for your own sake not to go out, and leave the Ladies, who to be sure would think you very ill bred. I beg'd her Excuse for it, and told her, I was very sorry for the Occasion, as, I believ'd, she would be when she heard it; and farther assur'd her, that nothing should have oblig'd me to have quitted such good Company, but the melancholy Message I had receiv'd from the Lady *Betty* — who was a Lady I knew she had an uncommon respect for. She seem'd mightily concern'd at what I told her; and instead of any longer reprimanding me, pressed me to make what haste I could to her, saying, She would excuse me to the Company. Thus, I had so far gained my point, when another unlucky Difficulty arose: My Aunt, that I might make the more haste, told me, She would not have me stay for the Horses being put to the Coach, but would oblige me to take her Chair. I thank'd her for her kind Offer, but would fain have excused it, and told her I would take a Hackney-Chair, not knowing how long I might stay, and perhaps her Ladyship might want her Own: But all these Excuses would not do; for she, out of her great Civility, would oblige me to make use of her's at last. Through her over Complaisance, I was forced to accept of it, fearing if I any longer deny'd it, she would suspect I had some Design.

I went into the Chair, with great Uneasiness, not knowing how to contrive to get rid of my Attendants; therefore I order'd the Chair-men to carry me to my Milliner's in *Pell-Mell*, having some Business there. As soon as I arriv'd at the Place, I alighted, and order'd my Footman to go to the Dutchess of *M*—'s, and give my Service, and enquire after her Health. By this means I got rid of one of the Servants, whom I look'd upon at that time as so many Spies: I order'd the Chair home, and bid them come at Nine a-Clock for me to the Lord — in the Square; with whom I did really design to be at that time, had not the more agreeable Company of my *Philander* kept me from him.

As soon as I found they were gone out of sight, and that I was free, I had a Hackney-Chair call'd; which I went into, and order'd the Men to carry me to the — in *Covent-Garden*, that being the Place appointed for our meeting. I was no sooner brought into the Street, but *Philander*'s Man, who was placed by his Master's Order to wait my coming, spy'd me. He went immediately, and acquainted his Lord of my near approach; when he, all in Transport, and without Thought, ran himself into the Street to meet me. Which Action I could not help condemning him for: I thought it shew'd more of Love than Consideration: He walked by the Chair till it came to the House, and caus'd it to be carry'd to the foot of the Stairs, where he took me out, and led me up to a noble Room that was put in exact order for my Reception. There was a Book lying on the Table, which taking up, on examination, I found to be the famous Mrs. *Behn*'s Novels, with which I perceive'd my *Philander* had been diverting himself till I came. He seem'd all Transport at the Obligation I had done him in being as good as my Word, though he could not help telling me, He was afraid (when he look'd on his Watch, and saw it Seven a-Clock) that some Female Scruples would have hindred his Happiness, and notwithstanding my Promise prevented me from coming. I could not help answering a little warmly to what he said; and in a violent Rage told him, I was sorry I was so mistaken in him as I found I was, having thought *Philander* a Person of so discerning a Judgment, that he might easily see I meant all I said; nor did I much question but that he was so still, and what he said was but what I too well deserv'd, a very just Reflection on my too easy complying with his Request, not that I would have him once dare to use my Name in a disrespectful manner; to compleat his Triumph over my Folly, and to add Trophies to his Vanity: I let him know he was the only Man that ever had obtain'd a quarter of an Hour's Discourse with me in private. After having said this, I catch'd up my Fan and Gloves, and had certainly gone away without either Coach or Chair, had not Colonel *P*—— luckily prevented me, who was come that moment into the Room, and was a particular Friend of his. He saw by *Philander*'s Looks (who all this time remained unmoveable) that something had hapned which cruelly disorder'd him; and being himself no Stranger to Affairs of that kind, believ'd it was some little Love Quarrel between us: He therefore, with a great deal of good Manners, perswaded me to sit down: After some small Refusal, I did so, more in compliance to his Request, than any Desire I had to be reconciled to the ungrateful *Philander*, for so at that time I thought him, though I over and over chid myself for yielding so soon to his Request, and represented my own Follies to myself in the worst Colours I possibly could.

Philander all this while stood like a thing unmoveable; but at length a little recovering himself, he, I suppose, gave some Signal to the Colonel, for immediately with the greatest Respect imaginable he quitted the Room. *Philander* no sooner found we were alone, and that there was no Body to interrupt him, but he threw himself at my Feet, and offering me his drawn Sword, beg'd that I would sheath it in his Breast, since I harbour'd so barbarous a Thought of him as to believe he could be guilty of upbraiding the generous Action I had done in saving his Life; for without my Presence Life would be but a Burden to him, and Death would be more welcome than my Frowns: Therefore the better to convince me of his Innocence, he made a thousand Protestations, that what he said was with no design to

74

affront me; and with Tears beg'd me, as he was sure I was all Goodness, to pardon those foolish Expressions of his uttered entirely without the least thought of offending.

You know my Temper to be pretty resolute; so that with all the Rhetorick I was Mistress of, I could not perswade my stubborn Heart to a Reconcilement; tho' Love pleaded strongly on his side, yet Anger for a time prevail'd; till at length turning my Eyes towards him, (which I had not done all this while) and seeing him still at my Feet, I said, That Posture did not become him, therefore desired him to rise, for it would be easier for me to see him sit than kneel. He obstinately refused to stir, and protested he would continue for ever in that Posture, if I would not give him my Pardon: So that I was obliged to be seemingly reconciled to him for fear any one should come into the Room, and find him in that Posture, (though indeed I could not heartily forgive him.) We were no sooner set, but I told him, I resented his letting the Colonel come into the Room, (believing it was by his Appointment:) and told him, I could not help thinking he did it with a design to expose a Person, that by too ready a Condescension to his Request, had in reality laid herself open to his greatest Censure; and that he had now made me thoroughly sensible of my own Folly.

He heard me out with the greatest Impatience imaginable, when he assured me, He knew nothing of the Colonel's coming, nor could he imagine how he knew he was there. His offering to deny it, though it really was so, as he afterwards convinced me, put me in so great a Passion, that silenc'd him for a few minutes; but being resolv'd to clear himself from a Fault which I so unjustly taxed him with, he step'd to the Stairs Head, and call'd his Man, and enquir'd of him, how Colonel *P——* came to know of his being there? He told him, as he was waiting below according to his Lordship's Order, the Colonel came by, and seeing him, ask'd if his Lord was there, and in what Room he was? At this *Philander* interrupted him, saying, What was the Reason you did not come and acquaint me of his being below, without letting him come into the Room? To which the Fellow reply'd, He was coming up to let his Lordship know, but the Colonel follow'd him so close that he got to the Door by that time he had open'd it; so that seeing him come in, he went down Stairs again.

After having receiv'd this Account from his Servant, he came to me with a thousand repeated Protestations, and assured me he was no ways guilty of that Crime: And at the same time told me I might be entirely easy, for he could pawn his Life that my Reputation was as safe with the Colonel as with himself, he being a Man of the nicest Honour. At length Female Weakness prevail'd, and he pretty well reconciled me.

Supper being order'd to be got ready, I began to enquire what it was a-Clock: For looking on my own Watch, I found it did not go, though by what Accident it stop'd, I can't tell: I therefore ask'd *Philander*, What

Hour it was? He readily answer'd me, It wanted a quarter of Eight by his, (having set his Watch back:) I really believ'd him, not suspecting he had taken that Method to deceive me, and Time you know passes away quick in Company one likes, which I must own to you, I did that of *Philander*'s. At length Supper came up, every thing after a most exact manner, there being neither Care nor Cost spar'd upon this occasion. Whilst we were at Supper, the Watchman came, Past Twelve a-Clock, which not a little startled me, (I'll leave you to judge the Surprize I was in, tho' it is not so easily to be imagin'd by any Person as myself:) In short, I could not believe I was awake, till hearkening again, I was fully confirm'd it was but too true. I sat, though with a great deal of Uneasiness, till Supper was over: What to do, or what Excuse to make to my Aunt, I could not tell, not in the least doubting but the Chair had been at my Lord –– waiting for me, as I order'd they should; but hearing I had never been there, as I said, and not knowing where to look for me, I made no longer doubt but they had returned home, and sufficiently alarm'd my Aunt, and all the Family: After all, reflecting seriously on all these Circumstances, I could not tell what to say or do, when strait an Excuse came into my Head, which I believe would have past well enough had I gone immediately: But to let you see how Fortune favour'd *Philander*'s Designs, (which, as I have since been inform'd by himself, were all laid) desiring a Chair might be fetch'd for me to go home, which I was fully resolv'd on, notwithstanding all the Arguments *Philander* used to persuade me to the contrary; just as the Chair was come, the Footman brought up word, that the Duke of *A*––, and two or three more Men of Quality, were that Instant come in, and that it would be impossible for me to go without being seen by them, (they being in a Room we were oblig'd to pass through:) What to do I could not tell, for if they should see me, I well knew the Duke, who had often intreated me to favour him with my Company abroad, and as often been refus'd it, would gladly lay hold of so fair an Opportunity as this to expose me, without paying any respect either to my Character, or the Passion he had so long professed for me, and would sacrifice to his Resentment my Reputation, as well as perhaps the Life of my dear *Philander*, who I was sensible would not hear that call'd in question on his account, without defending it even with his Blood.

Thus reflecting in my Thoughts, I resolved of two Evils, to chuse the least, as hoping I might find some way to make things easy; whilst I only trusted my Honour with *Philander*, who, by all the tender Words and Actions that could possibly be express'd, strove to convince me that it should be the whole Business of his Life to oblige me. I therefore consider'd, that *Philander* had it already in his power to say what he pleas'd of me; not that after what he had promis'd, I in the least suspected he would ever say any thing to my Prejudice: Whereas I knew, should I run the risk of the Duke's seeing me, I could expect nothing but the blackest Calumnies that a slighted exasperated Lover could invent. I knew him to be of a proud haughty Temper, and one that could not brook any Affront easily, therefore was the more afraid of being liable to his Resentment, which I knew would not terminate without the loss of one or both their Lives, as well as my Reputation.

He kept me Prisoner till one a-Clock; when, late as it was, I would have gone home, had not *Philander* persuaded me to the contrary, by using those Arguments which I thought very just: So that at length I yielded myself entirely to his Protection for that Night; and received a thousand Vows from him, that I should be as safe with him as if I were at home in my Aunt's House: He added, to make me the more easy, this friendly Advice, saying, Had you not better return to Morrow Morning, when you may have forty Excuses for your Stay, As that you were at Play or Dancing all Night? and not to go home at this unseasonable Hour, without any Body to wait on you, it being altogether improper for me to go along with you. He added, to what he had already said, That my going home so late would cause a greater Suspicion than if I staid till Morning; and by that means perhaps I might have so strict a Guard set over me, that it would be impossible for him either to see me, or hear from me; so, with earnest Intreaties, beg'd of me that I would not do any thing that might occasion so cruel a Separation, which would inevitably cost him his Life, it being altogether impossible for him to live without me.

Considering all his Arguments, I fully resolv'd to resign myself to his Protection for that Night, however, with a design of returning home the next Morning early: He beg'd me to be easy, for he would carry me where I should be very safe. A Coach was call'd, and *Philander* dismiss'd his Man for that Night, resolving to be perfectly *incog*. He directed the Coach himself, but where I knew not. As we went along, I seemed to be a little uneasy; which he perceiving, took me by the Hand, and said, My dear *Amaryllis*, what makes you tremble, and be so uneasy, since you may assure yourself that you are with the Man who esteems you above all things on Earth, and rather than you should come to any Harm, would freely lose that Life which I value for no other Purpose but to serve you?

This obliging Speech, which I thought was spoke with so much Sincerity, gave me fresh Courage. I was going to make him an Answer, but was prevented by the Coach stopping at the Place where we were to lodge for that Night. When the Coachman knock'd at the Door, a Maid-Servant immediately open'd it; who immediately bid the Fellow open his Door, as if she knew we were come to stay. When I came in, I looked round me, and saw it was a good handsome House. I was presently conducted by *Philander* up Stairs (attended by the Maid) into a very neat Bed-Chamber. *Philander* order'd a Fire to be light. Whilst she was doing of it, he in a very obliging manner again repeated many Expressions of Love; adding, He was sorry he could not entertain me in a Place more suitable to my Birth and Merit; but the best the Place afforded, was and should be entirely at my Command, as himself and Fortune were also: He then order'd the Maid to bring up a Bottle of *Cyprus* Wine, which he, unknown to me, had brought with him from the Place where we sup'd, and it was the best I ever tasted. When the Maid came up, she ask'd me, If I pleas'd to bathe? By this I found I was at a *Bagnio*,[1] which I was before ignorant of. I seemed, notwithstanding the many Assurances I had received from *Philander* of my Safety, to retain a fresh Uneasiness: Which he perceiving, said, Fear nothing, my Angel, you are as safe as if you were in the Royal Palace of *St. James*'s, with all the Guards about you; for, my Life, you may be assur'd, I would not bring that Treasure into any danger, which I more fear losing than Misers do their hoarded Gold. Being pretty well satisfied, I then order'd the Maid to prepare a Bath, and let me know when it was ready. She had not been gone out of the Room above half an Hour, before she return'd according to my Order, to acquaint me that the Bath was ready, and that she had got all things fit for my Bathing; therefore I took my leave of *Philander* for a while, thinking he would have bathed too: But instead of allowing himself that time, he employ'd himself in seeing my Chamber prepar'd after the best manner against I came up, fearing that if he should trust to the People, they would not take that Care to put every thing in the exact Order he would have it.

When I returned from Bathing, *Philander* met me on the top of the Stairs, and led me into the Room where I was to lodge that Night. There was a very good Fire, and some White-Wine mulled with Eggs: We drank it; after which we sat and talked a little time, when I ask'd him, If there were any care taken for preparing a Room for him, and if he had ordered a Fire in his Chamber? He thank'd me for my kind Care of him, and assured me he had ordered every thing to be done that was necessary. He, as I suppose, thought by my enquiring after his Chamber, that I was sleepy, therefore call'd the Maid to wait on me to Bed. When she came, he in a very respectful manner wish'd me a good Repose; and after imprinting Ten thousand Kisses on my Hand, he took his leave of me, as I thought, for that Night. When he quitted the Room, he gave such a Sigh as if not only his Heart, but Life remained with me.

After I was in Bed, I order'd the Maid to lock the Door, and take the Key out, and not to disturb me till Ten a-Clock in the Morning, if I did not call her before. I bid her give my Service to the Gentleman, and tell him I wish'd him a good Night: So being lock'd in secure, as I thought, I turn'd with a design to sleep, but could not for my life: I hearkned if I could hear *Philander* stir, but could not; therefore concluded him at rest, but was mistaken, he being gone, as he afterwards told me, to bathe himself. I had not been in Bed above three quarters of an Hour, before I heard my Chamber-door open; however, a little recovering myself from my Surprize, I turn'd to see what should be the reason of it: When, to my great Astonishment, I saw *Philander* standing close by the Bed-side, (there being a Light in the Chimney.) I ask'd him, What was the occasion of his coming into my Chamber at that unseasonable Hour? but could get no answer from him; so that I began to be more surprized than before, believing it to be a Spirit that stood before me, not that I am very apt to be frighted: However, again importuning him to tell me what was the occasion of his being there, and not yet obtaining any answer, I scream'd out, and had certainly alarm'd the whole House, had not *Philander* thrown himself on the Bed; and after having pressed my Hand, spoke. What he said, was with the greatest fear of disobliging me that could be; when getting off the Bed, he kneeled by the side of it, and beg'd me I would pardon a Presumption which nothing but his violent Passion could have made him guilty of, it being impossible for him to leave the Place where I was, therefore intreated me that I would at least suffer him to sit in my Room till Morning, not daring to leave so sacred a Treasure unguarded. With these and the like Expressions of Love, he at length talked me to sleep. As soon as he found I was fast, he came to Bed, where he lay till Morning.

You'll say perhaps, that *Philander* broke his Word, and you'll wonder how I could forgive him: Indeed, I own it was a little hard for me to do so; but when I consider'd it was Love, which generally hurries us on without Consideration, that made him guilty of it, I at length excused him, though not without sufficiently upbraiding him of ungenerously betraying me into a Fault which my Innocence and too good Opinion of him, had led me into.

It was then too late to say or do any thing, he having me entirely in his power, and by all the moving Expressions that could be uttered, gave me fresh Assurances of his Fidelity.

The FOURTH DAY

THE next Day, according to his Order, the Maid came up to see if we wanted any thing: For my part I was so ashamed and confused when she entred the Room, that I could not look at her, though I found she had been of my *Philander*'s Party, and was privy to his coming into my Chamber. He order'd her to light a Fire, and get us some *Bohea-Tea*.[2] When she was gone out of the Room, I fell to upbraiding him afresh in a most violent manner; saying, O cruel *Philander*, how could you by so base a Breach of your Word, betray me to a Crime that will not only be a continual Torment to my own Thoughts, but make me ashamed to the World! and what should I say or do to reconcile my Aunt to my lying from home all Night, it being a thing I never did before without her knowing where I was? Thus did I in a Confusion of Thought, and almost dying, with Shame perplex myself for my too lately committed Folly; when my dear *Philander* beg'd me to be easy, and told me, that he would freely sacrifice his Life and Fortune to me; and that if I could be so content, he would quit all the Honours of the Court, to pass the remaining part of his Life with me in an agreeable Solitude: He beg'd me not to talk nor think of home; but to compleat the generous Trust I had already reposed in his Breast, and resolve to pass the rest of my Days with him: He ask'd my Pardon for coming so abruptly into my Chamber, and own'd it was a Fault; but hoped my Goodness would excuse it, the future Happiness of his Life entirely depending on his possessing of me; therefore feared, should he let this Opportunity slip, Fortune would never throw the like in his way: So once more he intreated me to pardon an Indiscretion which was purely the Effect of Love.

I had answer'd him, but the Maid came in with the Tea, which prevented me: after we had drank it, we got up and consulted what was to be done, it being very near Two a-Clock; and at so late an Hour, it was impossible for me to think of returning home, therefore I resolved to follow what Rules my *Philander* laid down; which were, that we should take each of us a Coach, and he would go home and hear what was said by the Noblemen that came to his Lodgings, supposing there might have been a pretty many, (who he doubted not would all pass their different Censures on his lying out;) he having the greatest Levee of any Nobleman that belongs to the Court, occasion'd partly from his being well belov'd, and partly in respect to the many Posts of Honour which he enjoys. He beg'd me to meet him at Colonel *P*--'s Lodgings at Four a-Clock, where we would consult what was to be done that he might, uninterrupted, enjoy that Treasure in which he seemed to place all his Felicity.

I made some scruple at first of going to the Colonel's Lodgings, as being a perfect Stranger to him, having never in my Life seen him till the last Night, and that in such Confusion, that I could no ways go where he was without being introduced. *Philander* soon put an end to my Scruples, by telling me he would be at the Colonel's Lodgings to receive me; or if he was not, he would send him word of my coming, who he knew would be glad of any Opportunity to shew his Readiness to serve him: And farther added, My dear Life, you may be assured the Colonel is a Man of Worth and Honour, or I would not intrust him with a Secret on which the future Happiness of my Life depends; besides, as you are a nice Distinguisher of Sense and good Breeding, I am sure you will like the Conversation of the Colonel, he being a perfect Master of both.

After he had in this manner removed my Scruples, I promised I would come to the Colonel's Lodgings: So after a thousand fresh Repetitions of his constant Love, which he failed not to give me as often as he found

Opportunity, we parted for that time, though when my *Philander* went from me, he seemed like one that had left the whole Comfort of his Life, and looked as far as ever he could after my Coach, which I order'd to drive to a poor Woman's House, who was a Pensioner to my Aunt, to see if by that means I could hear any thing of the Affairs of our Family, and if she had heard of my Desertion, and what was said of it. She was much surprized and overjoyed to see me at her House, but did not in the least suspect what was the Occasion of my coming there. I ask'd her, if she had been at our House that Morning? She told me, no; but that she believ'd my Aunt's Woman, or some of the Servants, would be with her presently. I told her, if any of them should come whilst I was there, I would not have her take any notice she had seen me. Whilst we were talking, Somebody knocked at the Door; which proved to be as she expected, my Aunt's Woman, who was come to bring some Charity Money to the poor old Woman, it being what she, by my Aunt's Orders, did twice a Week. After she had returned her Thanks, she, as I suppose it was her usual Way, ask'd how her good Lady did? I heard the Woman answer her, That her Lady was very ill, and almost distracted, and all the Family was in the greatest confusion imaginable, which was occasioned by the Absence of their young Lady, her Lady's Niece, who had been gone from home ever since the Day before; and by all the Enquiry that could be made, they could hear nothing of her.

Whatever Inclinations I had before to return home, they immediately vanish'd on my hearing that my Stay abroad for one Night, had, thro' my Aunt's Indiscretion, been so blaz'd abroad, that should I again appear in publick, there would not be wanting a few of the ill-natur'd part of the World, who would be throwing Reflections. My Heart aked for fear the old Woman, in hopes of a Reward, should tell I was in her House: But that Fear was soon set aside by my hearing her say, I'll warrant the young Lady has stol'n a Wedding. After their Chat was over, my Aunt's Woman went away, and the good old Woman came in to wish me Joy, no longer doubting but it was as she imagin'd. I again charg'd her never to own she had seen me; and the more to deter her from divulging this Secret, I told her she would for ever lose my Aunt's Favour, should it ever come to her Ears that I was concealed in her House, when her Woman was there: Therefore to bribe her to Secresy, I gave her a couple of Guineas.

After trifling away an Hour or two with her, I order'd a Coach to be call'd, and went directly to the Colonel's Lodgings, where I expected to meet my *Philander*. There was a Servant waiting at the Door; of whom I enquired if his Master was at home: He told me he was, and conducted me into a very handsome Apartment; then went to acquaint his Master (who as I suppose was in his Dressing-room) that there was a Lady to speak with him. I, who expected my *Philander* was there waiting my coming, was so surpriz'd when I saw the Colonel come into the Room where I was, without

Philander, that I could not immediately call together my scattered Senses, to return the Civilities he shew'd me: Which he, I believe, perceiving, said, Madam, my Lord has sent a Note to me, wherein he orders me to beg your Ladyship's Pardon for his not waiting on you here to the Minute of his Appointment; but, contrary to his Inclination, he was unluckily prevented by the D. of *B* — — coming to pay him a Visit just as he was stepping into his Chariot, so he was oblig'd to return with him, and is afraid he shall be detained at least half an Hour.

I was a little out of Humour at this Accident, but would not shew it to the Colonel, who entertained me in a very handsome manner, as being one that he supposed *Philander* had a value for, which was enough to gain any Person a particular respect from him, for whom he profess'd the most singular Friendship, tho' at the same time said it was impossible that he, or any other, should lay so just a value on him as he merited. In this, and such like Discourse, we pass'd the time till my dear *Philander* came, who had altered his Dress since I parted from him, and appeared in his new Garb, as well as sprightly Carriage, a perfect Bridegroom: Whatever Charms had but faintly appeared to me before, now shone out in full Light; and, in short, I thought him the compleatest Gentleman I had ever seen. After the first Compliments were over, and we had drank a Glass or two of Wine, the Colonel (with a great deal of good Manners,) withdrew, and left us to ourselves. When we were alone, I could not help shewing my Resentment to *Philander* for making me wait; telling him, I too plainly saw that by giving him a Power over me, he had lost all Respect, though I would not have him believe my not daring to return home, should any ways lay me liable to the least Slight or Affront from him, since I would rather retire into some foreign Land, and pass the Remainder of my Days amongst Strangers, who could not reproach me of my Follies, than bear the least seeming Neglect from him.

Whilst I was speaking in this manner to him, his Eyes were fixed on mine; at length, after having heard all I had to say, he thus began, My dear *Amaryllis*, how can you be so barbarous to harbour a Thought, that my not being here to wait for you (as I own I ought to have been) was out of any Slight or Disrespect to you: So far was I from any such Design, that I thought each Minute an Age till I was with you, and almost cursed my unlucky Fate that threw the Duke of *B* — — in my way to retard my coming to that dear Company which every Moment discovers something new and desirable. After he had thoroughly convinc'd me, that his Stay was occasion'd by Force and not Design, and by that means appeased my Anger, *Philander* told me, if I thought it proper, he would make the Colonel privy to our Amour; For, said he, my Dear, it will be convenient for us to have a faithful Friend, that if Business of Necessity should detain me from you, he would go between us, and make things easy.

Philander having given me these convincing Reasons, why the Colonel should make the third Person in our Intrigue, and again assured me of his Honour, I yielded to his being made acquainted with it. By the time we had done talking, the Colonel came into the Room; but thinking we were still busy in Discourse, he offer'd to retreat, when my *Philander* desir'd we might have his Company: So he sat down, and after several Professions of Friendship between them, *Philander* said to him, Sir, I am now going to let you see how great an Opinion I have of your Honour as well as Friendship, and am fully satisfy'd that you'll not disappoint me in the good Opinion I have of both. The Colonel returned him Thanks for his kind Thought, and beg'd him to lay his Commands, that by that means he might have the opportunity of shewing how ready he would be to serve him, though with the hazard of his Life. *Philander* embracing him in a Friendly manner, said, I will put you on nothing that shall any ways endanger either your Life or Fortune, though what I am going to tell you concerns my Life as well as Happiness: So to keep you no longer in suspence, you are to know that this Lady has blessed me with a Promise to pass the rest of her Life with me; but being afraid of being discover'd, we don't know what to do for a Lodging till Tomorrow, it being too late for us to quit *London* to Night; nor can she go till she has some Necessaries, having nothing but what Cloaths she has on her Back; nor was it possible to get any of my things from home without being discover'd, which I was resolv'd not to be if I could possibly avoid it.

After my *Philander* has ended his Discourse, the Colonel told him, he was the happiest Man in the World; and added, that notwithstanding his great Merit, he could not imagine how he came by the Possession of so fine a Lady.

Philander told him, that he must own he had gained me by clandestine Means; but said, you know, Stratagems are allowable in Love as well as War: And dear Friend, added he, you shall have the Particular of this Adventure when we are settled. The Colonel perceiving we were both uneasy till we were fixed in a Lodging, therefore propos'd a Place where, he said, he was sure I might be as private as I could wish, for that there would be no Questions ask'd on his account, (I suppose, by the way, he had tried the Place on some such occasion before;) and that all things might be done with the greater Privacy, he called his Man, and ordered him to go to Mrs. — and bid her come to him. When he was gone, the Colonel said to me, Madam, this Place I am recommending you to, I own is not fit for you, were you to continue; but the only Motive that induces me to perswade you to it, is, that I know the Woman to be a very honest Person, and one that I can trust.

Whilst we were talking, the Footman returned, and with him the Woman: I liked her very well; she look'd like a good Motherly Dame. The

Colonel bid her sit down, but she absolutely refused it, saying, It was her place to stand in his Presence. He ask'd her, If her first Floor was let? She told him, she had a Cousin that lay in it; but to oblige him, or any Friend of his, she would part from any Lodger at an Hour's Warning, (by this I found he had a very great Influence over her.) He told her, He would not have her put herself, or any Person, to an Inconvenience; but if she could make any shift with her Relation for a Day or two, it would be for her Advantage: She told the Colonel that the Rooms should be got ready.

I gave Orders to have a Fire made, and that my Linnen should be well aired; so dismissed her, to prepare the Lodging fit for my Reception. The Colonel provided a very pretty Supper, but order'd none of his Servants should attend, but that one who saw me when I came. After Supper was over, and we had chatted an Hour or two, I asked my *Philander*, if we should be going? The Colonel offered to wait on us to our Lodging; which we at first refused, as being unwilling to take him from home, but at length he prevailed, on consideration that he was acquainted in the House.

When we came there, every thing was in very decent Order, and the Woman of the House seemed very assiduous to oblige us. The Colonel staid with us, and drank a Bottle, (we having sent a Hamper of Wine, and other Necessaries before us;) but it being Twelve a-Clock, he took his leave, with a Promise to come and drink Tea with us the next Morning: Upon which I ordered the Maid to get the Equipage ready, and call us by Ten a-Clock.

The FIFTH DAY

THE next Morning, at the appointed Hour, the Maid came into our Apartment; and after enquiring how we had rested, and if we liked our Lodging, (which was better than I expected, being a very good Bed and fine Linnen) she made us a Fire, and we got up, I having a great deal of Business to do to prepare myself for our intended Journey the next Day, it being altogether improper for me to continue in Town, where it was impossible I should remain undiscovered without the Punishment of always keeping within Doors.

We had not been long up before the Colonel came, when we drank Tea; after which I dismissed *Philander*, whose Affairs call'd him to Court, and took my leave of the Colonel till Eight a-Clock in the Evening, that I might be the better at liberty to discourse my Milliner, Mercer, and Mantua-Maker:[3] All which People I was oblig'd to have come home to me, not daring to stir out for fear of being seen. I passed this Day among my Trades People, in giving Orders for things that I wanted, till Eight a-Clock; when my dear *Philander*, and his faithful Friend the Colonel, returned. After the Compliment of a Salute was over, my *Philander*, who had been all Day in care for me, enquired what I had got for my Dinner. I told him I had provided what I liked, which was only a Veal Sweet-bread. He seemed concerned that I should have had nothing else; therefore propos'd that I would go out to Supper, saying, It would divert me after my Day's Fatigue within Doors; and farther said, I need not be under any concern for fear of being seen, it being perfectly dark: I therefore consented, and a Coach was called. We went to *Brawne's*, thinking that to be the securest Place, where neither of us could be known, as being at a considerable distance from the end of the Town we usually frequented. There was a very handsome Supper bespoke: Whilst it was getting ready, *Philander* told the Colonel, that he desired him to carry me the next Day to a small Country-Seat that he had about twelve Miles out of Town. You know, *Philemon*, he said, for so he then called him,[4] (intending to make him an Intimate in our Correspondence) the Place I speak of is most agreeably situated, and I verily believe my dear *Amaryllis* will be of my Mind; therefore if you will sometimes give us your agreeably Company, I think we shall pass the Remainder of our Lives in an agreeable Solitude, if my Angel can be so contented: For my part, I am resolved, as soon as good Manners will permit, to quit all publick Places, having now arriv'd to the greatest height of my Ambition, being in possession of my dear *Amaryllis*, which Happiness I esteem more than possessing the Imperial Diadem.

By this time Supper came up, which put a stop to any farther Discourse of that kind: The Waiter being in the Room, we talk'd of nothing but indifferent things till Supper was over, when *Philander*, who watched every Look of mine, said to me, Methinks, my dear *Amaryllis*, you are uneasy, I hope it is not from any thing I have said or done; for could I think that any Action or Word of mine, should in the least disturb you, it would make me the most unhappy Man upon Earth. I assured him, he had not said or done any thing to disoblige me; but told him at the same time, though I must own that he was the most agreeable Man on Earth to me, as I had shewn by my quitting all the World for him, yet he must forgive a few Female Reflections at present, which in a small time would be over; for I assur'd him that it was my Resolution, as I had left all I held dear in the World to go along with him, and even sacrificed my Reputation to his Desires, to lead the Remainder of my Life with him in what solitary Place he should appoint.

Philemon interrupted *Philander*, (who was going to make me an Answer) saying, Madam, the Place which *Philander* talks of retiring to, believe me, is no remote Desart, but an agreeable Retreat for Lovers; it is placed on a rising Hill, though not high enough to make it bleak, nor so low but you may see beneath it a pleasant Vale, enamel'd o'er with various Flowers of Nature's planting, which make a sweet and agreeable Prospect; nor is it so lonely, to make it melancholy, it being within a Mile and a half of a Market-Town, that in a quarter of an Hour's driving you may be as publick as you can wish; and, in short, is the most commodiously situated that can be imagin'd, having Gardens, Orchards and Fish-Ponds, with every thing that can conduce to make a Seat agreeable: I could give you a large Account of the Place, having a beautiful Idea of it in my Mind; but will not forestal your Thoughts with what is not in my power to paint to its full Perfection.

It growing late, I propos'd going home, which was readily agreed to by the amorous *Philander*, whose very Motions seem'd to be governed entirely by my Will. *Philemon*, according to his youthful good Manners, would needs wait on us home, where he staid the drinking of one Bottle of Wine then took his leave of us for that Night, with a Promise to wait on us the next Morning, in order to accompany us three or four Miles on our Journey, Business at that time preventing him to go through; which we were very desirous of. When *Philemon* was gone, the Woman of the House shewed me what things my Milliner, and other Folks, (that I set to Work before I went out) had brought home. After looking on them, and chatting a little, I order'd her to come betimes in to our Chamber, having a great deal of Business to do in the Morning before we set out on our Journey: So taking our leave of the good Woman, we went to Bed without any thing remarkable happening that Night.

The SIXTH DAY

IN the Morning at Nine a-Clock, the Maid came and light a Fire, and I got up, and sent to the Work-Folks to bring me what more things they had done, that they might be packed up. By that time the Equipage was got ready for Breakfast, *Philemon*, according to his Promise, came: He brought with him half a dozen Flasks of the finest Citron Water, that in my Life I ever tasted; and beg'd me to accept of them, saying, it would be very agreeable in our travelling. After we had Breakfasted, and put all things in order for our Journey, my Dear, says *Philander*, I have, for our better quitting the Town privately, order'd my Chariot to wait two or three Miles off till we come; we will go in a Hackney-Coach, which may bring *Philemon* back, since we cannot be so happy as to enjoy his Company the remaining Part of our Journey. I approv'd of his Contrivance very well, and desir'd we might be going. We satisfy'd the good Woman for the Trouble we had given her; and I order'd, that whatever should be left with her, to lay it by till I sent for it: So we took leave of *London*, and set forward on our Journey. It was very pleasant travelling, being the finest Day that has been seen this Spring. We in a short time arriv'd at the Place where our own Chariot and Equipage waited our coming; being willing to enjoy *Philemon*'s Company as long as we could, we staid there and din'd. When we had chatted an Hour or two, we took our leaves of *Philemon*, though not without some Regret to be deprived of his most friendly and agreeable Conversation: However, we were oblig'd to submit to it, he having some Business of the greatest consequence; which, he said, he feared would keep him in Town a

Week or ten Days; but as soon as that is over, says he, I shall with Joy embrace the first Opportunity to kiss your Hands, and in the time of my Absence beg to hear from you as often as Opportunity will permit.

After *Philander* had assured him he would miss no Opportunity of writing to him, and desired he would oblige us in the same manner by sending us what News he thought worth our hearing, and what was said of his Absence from Court; after *Philemon* saluted me, he embraced *Philander*, and with fresh Repetitions of Friendship between them, we parted. *Philander* and I proceeded on our Journey, and *Philemon* returned to *London*.

After a pleasant Hour's Travelling, we arrived at the Place: As soon as we were come into the House, and my dear *Philander* had welcomed me to it in the most obliging manner that could be, he took me by the Hand, and led me to view it all over, that I might the better see which Apartment I would fix on to be our Lodging. After I had seen all the Rooms, (which were very neatly furnished, and every thing in so exact order it might have entertained a Princess) he carried me into the Garden, which was nicely kept. At the upper-end of it was a fine Banqueting-house, paved with Marble: It stood on a Mount, and had a very fine Prospect. When we came to it, *Philander* ask'd me to sit down. We were no sooner seated, but *Philander* took up my Hand, and kissing it, said, Now, my dear *Amaryllis*, I esteem myself the happiest Man living, having in my Possession the only Woman on Earth that could make me compleatly blessed, and that in so quiet and private a Retreat, that I may uninterrupted enjoy the Blessing without the busy prying or malicious Censures of the World: As for the House, I could wish it was better for the Entertainment of my Angel; but for my own part, since she is pleas'd to grace it with her Presence, I prefer this small Cottage before the glittering Court, and must say with the Philosopher, This Place, this Spot of Earth whereon you stand, is more to me than the vast Plains of my Great Fathers Ancestors.

After he had said this, he pressed me to tell him how I liked the Place; for, says he, if my dear Angel can confine herself to this Retirement, I will, as soon as I can, divest myself of all the noisy Impertinences that attend Popularity, and in this agreeable Retreat from the Flatteries of the Court, pass the remainder of my Days with the only Person in the World, whose Conversation can be always agreeably charming, as well in old Age as Youth, should we be blessed to enjoy it together, the Beauties of your Mind being no ways inferiour to those of your Person; which Charms I must only in Silence admire, as well for fear your Modesty should tax me with being guilty of Flattery, as because it is out of my power to give them the due Praises they merit.

When he had made an end of talking, I found he was silent in expectation of my Answer; I therefore said to him, *Philander*, that you are the most agreeable Person in the World to me, I believe I need not now tell you;

my indiscreet leaving all things in this World that ought to be esteemed valuable, and exposing myself to the malicious Censures of the intermedling Part of my Sex, have, I believe, sufficiently convinced you of the Truth of it; therefore as to my being contented with the Place, there is no room for my finding fault with it, it far surpassing my Expectation, notwithstanding the beautiful Description *Philemon* gave of it: But were it as mean as those rural Cottages inhabited by the meanest Shepherd, yet, blest with my dear *Philander's* Company, I should esteem myself more happy than in the greatest Splendor that could be invented.

Philander having received this Assurance of my Love from me, seemed to be very well pleased; and the Evening growing cold, we returned in a Doors:[5] After giving Orders for Supper, *Philander* retired to his Closet to write a Letter to *Philemon*, giving him the Satisfaction of our safe Arrival at our Journey's end; and by his retiring, gave me an Opportunity of sending you this exact Account of my Six Days Adventures, which will, I doubt not, meet with your severe Censure: for I fancy I already hear you blaming my Folly, and too ready Compliance.

Thus, my dear *Emilia*, I have, without Reserve, made you acquainted with every thing just as it hapned, without adding any thing to make my Story more diverting to you, or concealing any thing that may deserve your Blame; therefore I beg you'll use the Indulgence of a Friend in this Case, and consider that I have acted the most prudent, as well as generous Part in what I have done; for though I have exposed myself to the Censure of the World, I have this Satisfaction, that it is for the Man I like; and on the other hand, had I taken my Aunt's Advice, and married the Duke of *A——*, whom I could never have loved, I had not only made myself unhappy, but by my Indifference to him, should have given him, and all the World, reason to have been very free with my Character, and should have undergone the Scandal without having the Satisfaction.

I know you to be a Lady of that good Sense, that you will not be too severe in your Judgment; nor need I bid you suspend your Censure till you see my *Philander*, of whose Person I would here give you some Account, did I not fear you would believe me guilty of Partiality, whilst I know it is not in my power to give so bright a Description of his Perfections as they deserve; therefore shall rather chuse to pass that by, which an ill Description will sully the Beauties of, and leave him wholly for yourself to find out his Charms when you see him. I beg you to enquire what is said of my sudden Departure: I am obliged to leave off here, being prevented from relating a thousand things I had to say, by a Neighbouring Gentleman, who hearing of *Philander's* Arrival, is come to pay him a Visit, and sup with us. He has presented me with a Copy of Verses, lately written by Mr. *Prior* on the Lady *Katherine Hyde*; which I think very well worthy your reading, as well for the Beauty of the Poem, as the Subject it is writ on. She is a Lady

for whom I know you have a particular Value as well as myself; and all the
World, who has the Honour to know her, must have an Esteem for her:
I have therefore, for your Entertainment, transcrib'd them.

I

THUS *Kitty*, beautiful and young,
And wild as Colt untam'd;
Bespoke the Fair from whom she sprung,
With little Rage inflam'd.

II

Inflam'd with Rage at sad Restraint,
Which wise *Mamma* ordain'd;
And sorely vex'd to play the Saint,
Whilst Wit and Beauty reign'd.

III

Shall I thumb Holy Books, confin'd
With *Abigails* forsaken!
Kitty's for other Things design'd,
Or I am much mistaken.

IV

Must Lady *Jenny* frisk about,
And Visit with her Cozens?
At Balls must *She* make all the Rout,
And bring home Hearts by Dozens?

V

What Beauties has *She*, more than I?
What hidden Charms to boast,
That all Mankind for her should die,
Whilst I am scarce a Toast?

VI

Dearest *Mamma*, for once let me,
Unchain'd, my Fortune try;
I'll have my *Earl* as well as *She*,
Or know the Reason why.

VII

I'll soon with *Jenny*'s Pride quit score,
And make her Lovers fall;
They'll grieve I was not loos'd before,
She, I was loos'd at all.

VIII

Fondness prevail'd, *Mamma* gave way;
Kitty, at Heart's Desire,
Obtains the Chariot for a Day,
And set the World on Fire.

FINIS

NOTES

[1] *Bagnio :* denoting both a bathing house and a brothel.
[2] *Bohea-tea :* An adaptation of Wu-i; the Wu-i hills are in the north of Fuhkien (China) from where black tea first came to England. It was applied to black tea in general but also denoted tea of the first quality.
[3] *Mantua-maker :* 'mantua' is a corruption of 'manteau'; mantua-maker denotes 'dress-maker' in general.
[4] The original text runs: 'You know, said *Philemon*, for so he then called him, . . .' which must be a printer's error: Philander is speaking and addresses Colonel P for the first time by his Christian name.
[5] *In a doors :* also 'in at doors'; obsolete form for 'indoors'.

The Double Captive,
or Chains upon Chains

Containing the Amorous Poems and Letters of A Young Gentleman, one of the Preston Prisoners[1] in Newgate. Occasioned by his falling in Love with a Scotch Lady, who came to visit his Friend. To which is added The Execution Dream, Or the Unlucky Disappointment. With a Preface to the Ladies. And an Introductory Novel. London, 1718

The Double Captive,
or Chains upon Chains

The Double Captive combines – as a literary detective might deduce from the title – the tradition of gallantry with a realistic treatment of background reminiscent of the literature of roguery. *The Double Captive, or Chains upon Chains*, is an account of a Newgate prisoner's daydreams: the man (who is in prison for political reasons, as we learn later) tries, with varying success, to escape his actual surroundings by immersing himself in a romantic and imaginary love affair. In his dreams the young lady – actually the visitor of a fellow prisoner – saves his life; in fact, his future looks bleak, for he bears the double chains of the prisoner and the lover. In his letters the prisoner repeatedly plays with the conceit of the double fetters, and, indeed, it may be symptomatic of the transitional state of the novel at the beginning of the eighteenth century that the traditional metaphor of the lover imprisoned by the queen of his heart (as used in the hero's letters of gallantry) takes on a new reality in that the letter-writer is actually in prison.

The narrative is full of realistic detail. The prisoners make their rounds in the press-yard, the drunken jailor interrupts the sensitive prisoner in his dreams, and we learn the details of an execution. The use of such slang words as 'jack Ketch', 'Cart's Tail', and 'within Amb's Ace' establishes an underworld atmosphere in curious contrast to the idealistic love theme. The author's style fluctuates between rough and vulgar diction when referring to prison and execution and a more gallant vein in the addresses to his lady.

The prisoner in double chains lives in constant dread of his execution. His letters reflect his mood of the moment, changing from letter to letter according to circumstances. Sentimental analysis is combined with description of environment and outward events. These letters, which use the epistolary technique to good advantage, are, however, only part of a book which also contains a collection of doggerel verse supposedly written by the same love-sick prisoner, and a few love letters in the manner of a model letter. These, in conjunction with the vein of gallantry in the letters themselves, show a certain indebtedness to the manual and conduct book. There is also a prefatory "Novel" in which the prisoner relates how he came to meet the beautiful Scotch lady 'after a Twelvemonths Confinement in a loathsome Prison' and what turbulent feelings her glances aroused in him, how well she behaved and how sweetly she talked in her Scottish accent. This dramatic little story has, as we might expect, a happy ending.

Letters to the Fair Galatea

Madam,

I Presume these Lines will be very surprizing to you: To find your self accosted with a passionate Declaration from one, – – – who scarce seems to be in a state of Life; yet such is my Fate, that notwithstanding I am loaded with Chains, in the very Condition you saw and pitied me, (which Compassion, by an unaccountable Fatality, has made my former Fetters much more insupportable,) I am forced to acquaint you, that my Affection's too big to be concealed: Therefore Madam, I humbly implore your Pardon, and beg you would excuse my Presumption, in discovering a Passion from a Person truly unhappy, who has a greater probability of being Wedded to a Halter, than your dearest Self.

> *I am, Madam,*
> *with the deepest Affection,*
> *your unfortunate Admirer,*
> *Amoretto.*

My dearest Life,

I AM, this Minute, alarm'd with the fatal News, that to Morrow I shall be no more; but must pay my last Debt to Nature, with some of my Fellow Prisoners. And yet, notwithstanding the near Approaches of Death, (that, methinks, I feel his Icy Hand upon my Youthful Shoulders,) I cannot forbear stealing a Thought on you; and do by these assure you, that I shall, at the last Minute, offer up a Prayer for your Felicity; and humbly intreat, in return, you will do the same kind Christian Office for me, and not forget how inviolably I am,

> *Your most constant and sincere*
> *Dying, yet still Obedient, &c.*

Dearest Madam,

THE Report of my Suffering proves groundless; yet will be inevitably fatal to two of my unfortunate Companions. There were Nineteen of us labour'd under the same melancholy Apprehensions, and every one thought he should be the Man; so that each Person retired by himself, and prepared for the last Hour; and, like Men in a Ship-wreck, every one took care for his own Preservation. Nothing but Supplications and Pray'rs, pious Ejaculations, unfeigned Intercessions for Mercy from our great Creator, could be heard till after one a-Clock in the Morning; when the Dead-Warrant came for Mr. *Paul* a Clergyman, and Mr. *Hall* of *Otterburne*,[2] formerly a Justice of the Peace; I cannot forbear relating to you, the different Impressions the fear of Death and Eternity, as well as the Reprieve had on each desponding Person. One Gentleman had so fixed his

Mind upon, and so well prepared himself for his Departure, that when he heard of his Reprieve, he seemed to be uneasie at the Disappointment, and sighing, said, he could never have a better Opportunity of Dying. On the contrary, others were so elated with Joy, that they couldn't, in some time, recover their former Deportment, but had an alternate succession of Sorrow and Delectation. But one Old *Dundee* Soldier, who was very busie on the Common-prayer-Book, as soon as he found he had escaped the Danger, laid aside the Book, takes up a Pack of Cards, and with a grave and unconcerned Look, as if nothing had happened, says, come, Major (to his Chum) let's have a Game at Ombre for a Bottle. For my part, I retained very dismal Sentiments within my self; being not only unwilling to be cut off in the prime of my Youth from the World, but also from,

> *Madam,*
> *Your*
> *Dear Self, &c.*

Dearest Life,

Yesterday my Mother made me a Visit, and has been informed by some of my Comrades, that I am Melancholy, and in an ill State of Health, which made her very uneasy and inquisitive after the Occasion, resolving, at the same time, to send me a Physician. To prevent this, I made a generous Confession, and told her, you, and only you must be my Doctor. She, with Maternal Indulgence, promised me assistance in my Cure, as far as her Estate would go; and designs to take an Opportunity from my Indisposition, to get me into the Messenger's Custody. If this Favour can be obtained, I hope to have the happiness of seeing you, and demonstrating how far I am, with the sincerest Attachment,

> *Madam,*
> *Your most Devoted, &c.*

Dear Madam,

By the proper Application of a little Gold, I have shaked off my Iron Chains. If I could be so happy to have the like Courtesy from you; could the Pains of my invisible Fetters be softened, by receiving some Marks of Lenity and Condescention, my Confinement would become less troublesome, and nothing a greater pleasure to me, than giving constant and repeated Assurances, of the unalterable Affection I bear you, and that I am inviolably,

> *Madam,*
> *Your most obsequious and*
> *devoted humble Servant.*

Madam,

Having some Hopes of Mercy from a Prince, to whom my Life and Fortune is become forfeit; I cannot neglect this Opportunity of making you a Tender of a Heart that has so narrowly escaped the Flames of the Executioner; but still suffers under the scorching Pains of a much different Nature, an ardent Passion for your charming Self. But alas! when I consider the loss of my Estate, that necessary Ingredient to sweeten the Comforts of human Life, without which, an Amorous Application meets with a cold Reception; my Wishes are all frustrated, and the Rays of your Clemency, which at a distance seem'd to shine on me, are converted to an augmentation of my Misfortunes, and bring to my Mind these following Lines I have somewhere read, I think 'tis in the Ingenious Mr. *Cowley*,[3] *viz.*

> "*A mighty Pain to Love it is,*
> *A greater Pain that Pain to miss,*
> *But of all Pains, the greatest Pain*
> *It is to Love, but Love in vain.*"

This, Madam, I fear, is the unhappy Case of,

Yours, &c.

Dearest Madam,

LET me beg your Patience, whilst I give you an Instance or two, how I spend the major part of my Time. When my Bed-fellow is gone down to take a Turn in the Press-yard, or divert himself at Cards, with any of his Neighbouring Prisoners, I instantly betake my self to my old Companion, the Bed, and immediately the charming Idea of your Lovely self is represented to my Imagination. Sometimes we take a Walk together in the Park, from thence to the Play. Another time to *Kensington* Gardens, in whose pleasant Walks I breath a thousand Passionate Expressions. Sometimes I am a Hero Conquering Kingdoms, and Restoring Injured Princes to their Rights; they in Return, heap vast Honours, Wealth, and Titles on me, and all are laid at the Feet of my lovely fair Enchantress. Sometimes my deluded Fancy turns the Tables upon me in your Favour, and tells me that your generous Soul is above Wealth, and the loss of my Estate is a Trifle; that true Love surmounts all Indigencies; that your Fortune, with prudent Management, is sufficient to make us happy, and supply us with the common Necessaries of Life; and that all Superfluity is only troublesome. These, Madam, are the delightful Amusements of Sun-shine and clear Weather; But on the Dark and Lonesome Days of Fogs and Rain, I am Huff'd and Slighted for my Presumptuous Insolence, in molesting you with my impertinent Letters; am re-minded of my near Affinity to the Gallows; that *Jack Ketch* must be my Executor and Administrator, that *Paul Lorrain*[4] refuses to give me Absolution, unless I make him

Heir to my New Suit of Black in which I received Sentence; and the Hangman Swears and Threatens how indecently he will Butcher me in the Dissection, besides making me hang an Hour naked in the sight of the gazing Multitude, before he'll cut me down, if I pretend to give the Ghostly Father his Fees.

This is the hopeful Way I stand between the 'Squire[5] and the Parson. Sometimes the Sun unexpectedly breaks out upon me, and I do my self the pleasure to believe you are come to make me a Visit, and tell me, you are sorry at my deplorable Misfortunes; wish it was in your Power to redress them; that if I could but obtain a Pardon for Life only, you desired no more; advise me to make Interest to the two *Turks*, or some other great Person at Court. But upon the unlucky interposition of the least Cloud, my Fancy discovers you receiving the Addresses of some Powerful Rival, whom you Smilingly permit to kiss your Hand; then all the Tortures of a *Spanish* Inquisition are but a Flea-bite to what I undergo; and leaping off the Bed, to Sacrifice my Rival to my just Resentment, I beat all the Skin off my Shins with my Shackles; by which Means I am brought to my Senses, and made to know I am not behind *Montague*-House.[6]

I begin now to think, it is time to make Interest for a *Habeas Corpus*, to remove me to *Bedlam*. And accordingly, as any of these different Sentiments has accosted me, they have produced the foregoing diversity of Subjects I have Poetized upon.

Thus, Madam, innumerable Reflections of this kind employ the greatest Part of my Confinement; while my fellow-Sufferers are at a loss to know my Distemper; and I think it not convenient to acquaint them, that none but your dear Self can give Relief to your Afflicted, and almost Heart-broken Slave.

I am firmly perswaded, Madam, that a just Survey of my Sufferings, will excite in you the most generous Compassion for,

> *Your most Obsequious*
> *and Devoted*
> *Humble Servant, &c;.*

The Execution Dream: or, the Unlucky Disappointment

Madam,

HAVING been more than usually perplexed with Dreams last Night, (notwithstanding I went Supperless to Bed) and those Nocturnal Delusions having somewhat Peculiar in them, relating to your self, have made such a strong Impression in my Memory, that I cannot omit giving you the trouble of a Relation.

I Dream't I was lying on the Bed, in the Afternoon, according to custom, running over in my Mind the Perfections of your Dear Self, and pleasing my Fancy with the Notions of those Felicities, I am never like to enjoy; when I thought the Keeper rush'd hastily into my Room, without any Ceremony, and calling me by my Name, told me, Orders were come that I must prepare for Death; bidding me be speedy in my Preparations, for the Sledge and Sheriffs Officers were without ready to receive me. This sudden and unexpected News put me into such a Confusion, that I could not presently recover my former Senses. Methought, I was exceeding desirous, and strenuously importun'd my Keeper, to permit me time to write a few Lines to a Dear Friend, meaning your Lovely Self.

He told me roughly, that if I was not expeditious in dressing my self, I must be hang'd in my Night-Gown, for the Hour was come, and the Sheriffs Officers would not wait. However, what with good Words, and a Note I gave him upon my Mother for a few Guineas, I prevail'd on him to let me write a Letter, which I inclos'd my Ring, and desir'd a Friend to convey it to you. Then I put on clean Linnen, and drest my self in a Suit of Black, that was made up against my Tryal. My Chamber, by this time, being full of sorrowful Spectators, who knew not how soon they might be call'd to undergo the same Fate. I went behind the Bed, and offer'd up my fervent Prayers for a Remission of my Sins; and Notice being given me to prepare, methought I came down Stairs into the Press-yard, with a serene and undisturbed Countenance, where a Crowd of my Fellow-Prisoners made a Lane for me; and as I past by them gave me their mournful and last Embraces, offering up their Petitions for my Salvation. When I was brought into the Street, innumerable Spectators were gathered together to satisfie their Curiosity; the major part of them seem'd to commiserate and bewail my approaching Sufferings; the Women pitying my Youth, and the Men my deplorable Circumstances in general. I thought, as I was drag'd up *Holbourn*, a tall lean, long visag'd, swarthy, full-ey'd Fellow, with a short tye Wigg, that did not cover his Ears, would often thrust his fanatical Countenance between the Constables Shoulders, as they walkt on the side of the Sledge, and with a malicious Snear whisper'd to me, *Traytor, Traytor*; *Rebel, Rebel*. This was the Game he was at, every time there was a stop. At last, one of the Midnight Commanders, who I believe was no well-wisher to the *Calves-head Tribe*[7], gave this Son of King-killing Principles such a push of the Guts with the End of his Staff of Authority, that one would have thought, if he had not been a Case-hardn'd *Antimonarchical Sinner*, it would have beat all the *Schismatical* Wind out of his Body. But on the contrary, as soon as his *seditious* Bellows had drawn in a little *factious* Wind, he accosts my Champion with 'Go ye Jacobite Rascal, you're one of his Gang, I shall see you in his place in a short time.' By this the industrious Rabble smelt out my *Oliverian* Chapman, and crying out a *Pick-pocket*, a *Pick-*

pocket, hurried him away to the next Horsepond; which caused such a desertion of my Followers, that we proceeded with much less trouble, and interruption.

At length (I thought) we arrived at the fatal Tree, wher I was removed from the Sledge I came in, and was conducted to a Cart: Having mounted it, and looking round me, I was surprized at the vast multitude of Spectators. A *Scotch Highlander*, that was never out of his own Country, would have thought all the People in the World were come to see him make his Exit. I Dreamt, that near to the Gallows, many Hackney Coaches were drawn up, whose insides were empty, but the top, and Coach-box was loaded with Swearing, Blust'ring, Blaspheming, Cockaded Sparks, whose Swords were ready drawn, and often gave a flash, and a volley of Oaths to any soft-hearted Christian that pity'd my Misfortune. Methought, altho' my Dissolution was so near, I could not forbear observing, how Ungenerous, Dishonourable, and Unchristian a Practice it was, for Men of Figure, Officers of Note, (for such, by their Garb, they seem'd to be) not only to misuse the pitying tender-hearted Spectators, who in Compassion to my Youth and Suffering, let drop a Tear, or breath'd a sorrowful Expression; but to cast malicious Smiles and Flouts on me, as if they Gloried in my Death.

I thought, sure these can't be the *British* Sons of *Mars*; in Foreign Countries so renown'd for Arms, and valu'd for their great and unparallell'd Humanity. These can't be the Race of *Old England*'s antient Stock; that after they have o'recome their Foe, alleviate his Misfortunes with all the kindest and endearing Acts of Friendship.

No; these must be the Off-spring of a Mungril-breed, Begot in *Forty-One*;[8] the Sons of *Weavers*, *Shoemakers*, and *Taylors*, whose Parents ill-got Wealth, and *Puritanical* Professions of Allegiance have brought them Places near the Crown, the better, when time shall serve, to lop the Head that wears it.

These are Puny, Scandalous, No-Principle Professors, that have the same Notion of a God, that they have of their King, and would, (if it was in their Power) Annihilate him, upon the least distaste given to their Capricious Humour. I say, such surely these must be; for no other Men would thus insult their expiring Fellow-Creature.

Whilst I was involv'd in these thoughts, the Spiritual Physician ascended the Cart, in Order to Administer the last part of his Ministerial Function; who after joining in some Prayers, singing a penitential Psalm, and giving me some pious Exhortations left me to my private Devotions, which I dreamt were very fervent, and sincere. The Axe and Knives lay ready to separate my Quarters, the Fire was pil'd to burn my Entrails, Heart, *&c.* and the Cart just drawing from under me, when a tumultuous and undistinguished Noise throughout the Crowd was heard, which stopt their further Proceedings. Putting up my Cap, that was pull'd over my Eyes, methoughts I saw you, my Charming Fair, more Dear to me than Life, at a distance, labouring thro' the Multitude with a Paper in your Hand, Crying, a *Pardon*, a *Pardon*, which was instantly resounded by thousands of People; upon this the Cockade Gentlemen (I dreamt) sneakt off, biting their Nails, and cursing the Disappointment; whilst the assiduous Crowd us'd their utmost Skill and Endeavours, to clear you a Passage to the Under-Sheriff; who receiving the Paper, methought, without attending what he should say, you was lifted into the Cart; where, with a modest and discomposed Look, you Congratulated me on my *Pardon*. At the same time the Sheriff seconded you, telling me, His Majesty had been Graciously pleas'd to Grant it, provided the young Lady would undertake to bring and deliver it her self; which was perform'd, and I was at Liberty. This occasion'd, a universal Joy and Shouting all over the Place, which rang with nothing but loud Acclamations of, *Long Live the King*; every Person Extolling His Great Clemency and Mercy: Nay, *Jack Ketch* himself Congratulated me upon it, and told me he heartily rejoyc'd at my narrow Escape; but by the scratching his Head, and some other shrewd Tokens of Discontent, he gave me great Reason to question his Veracity, and to suspect, he thought himself bilkt of a Suit of Cloaths, and other Appurtenances; but after I had assur'd him, I would make him a double amends for the Loss he sustain'd on account of my Habiliments, I must do the Squire that Justice, to believe, that he was glad in good Earnest.

After this, I thought we went into a Coach, and were conducted thro' the Streets with the Exultations of innumerable Spectators; while I lost no Time in paying you all, all the Marks of Esteem and Gratitude expressible, for such an unprecedented piece of Goodness, and Generosity: But was interrupted by the Coach's stopping at a Noble Structure, when you conducted me to the Inside, which was embellisht with fine Paintings, and all other rich Conveniences, and Curiosities, which you, with Eyes cast down, and modest Blush, told me, I might command: This additional Favour prompted me to supplicate you, with all the endearing Terms imaginable, to crown my Felicity with your charming self; which, I at last dreamt, you was pleas'd to consent to: Nay, Madam, to enhance my Joys, methoughts, the Priest was performing the Sacred Rites, tying the *Gordian* Knot, which none but Death could separate.

Oh Surprizing Dream! Charming Delusion! never to be Eras'd from my Memory! How transported was I, to be brought from the Brink of Eternity, and the most shameful and ignominious Death, to the appearance of the greatest Beatitude this Terrestrial World could afford me? When, on a sudden, I was awaken'd by a thundring and beating at my Door; nor could I persuade my self it was true, 'till my Bed-fellow, and the repeated Noise, confirm'd it: Immediately I began to fear the first Part of my Dream was come to pass; but, upon opening the Door, found there was nothing in't; only the Keeper was got drunk, with a File of Musqueteers to attend him; and said, my Companion had affronted him; and he did not know but that we had a mind to make our Escapes; so he double-iron'd us, and put us into the Condemn'd Hold; where I can do nothing else but meditate on the Night's Entertainment; and ask Pardon for the Trouble I may have given you, in this nocturnal Adventure.

Dear Madam,

These Lines may acquaint you, that, by the Application of Friends, I am got out of the Condemn'd Hold; and I can much easier forget the Keeper's barbarous and unprovok'd Usage, than the latter Part of that delicious Dream. Had the sottish Rascal put off his Visit, while he drank the other Bottle; by that time I might have seen the Frolick out; (for I remember the Parson had just done his Business) I would have compounded with the guzzling Brute, to have lain a Month in Irons double chain'd, and been oblig'd to keep him drunk all the time at my own Expence, into the Bargain: But to be frighted, and brought so near hanging, that nothing but the Cart's Tail[9] parted us; and afterwards within Ambs Ace[10] of the Fruition of your Dear and Charming Person ––– This, Madam, was insupportable, and can never be forgot by, *Madam, &c.*

Dearest Madam,

I AM in dayly Expectation of being Partaker of the Benefit of an Act of Grace; and begin to think *Paul Lorain*'s Visits too long, and troublesome: And what further adds to the good News; my Mother, who has a competent Estate, has assur'd me of the Benefit of it; which, with frugal Management, is sufficient to make us tolerably easy. And as, my Dearest, you did not totally neglect my Addresses in the worst of Circumstances; I do my self the Pleasure to believe, this will not be unacceptable News to you, from

Your Constant Admirer, &c.
Amoretto.

Pray take the Notice of the following Verses in *Cowley*.

> "*For these few Hours of Life allotted me,*
> *Give me, Great God, but Bread and Liberty:*
> *I'll ask no more; if more thou'rt pleas'd to give,*
> *I'll thankfully the Over-plus recieve:*
> *If beyond this to me bee'nt freely sent;*
> *I'll thank for that, and go away content.*"[11]

FINIS

NOTES

1. *Preston Prisoner:* During the Jacobite rebellion of 1715 Preston (Lancashire) was taken by the rebels and remained in their hands from 9 November till 14 November, when General Thomas Forster surrendered to the crown. We can assume that the "double captive" was one of the prisoners made then.

2. *Mr Hall of Otterburne:* I have not been able to identify this person; he may be fictitious. Otterburne is a place in Northumberland.

3. The poem is slightly altered: Cowley's poem runs like this:

> A mighty Pain to Love it is,
> And 'tis a pain that pain to miss,
> But of all Pains, the greatest Pain
> It is to love, but Love in vain.
> (From: *Miscellanies*, VII, Gold).

4. *Paul Lorraine* was appointed ordinary of Newgate in 1698 and died in 1719. He compiled the official accounts of the dying speeches of criminals condemned to capital punishment. Besides publishing several sermons, he brought out a little book called *The Dying Man's Assistant* (1702).

5. *Squire* denotes the worldly power, particularly referring to the hangman, and *Parson* the ecclesiastical.

6. *Montague-House:* The house of the Montague family on the site of the present British Museum in Bloomsbury, which at that time was a high-class residential area. 'Behind Montague-House' may be an allusion to a fashionable housing area in contrast to our prisoner's present state.

7. *Calves-head Tribe:* an abusive slang word, which also contained a veiled political reference: "Calves Head Club. A club instituted by the Independents and Presbyterians, to commemorate the decapitation of King Charles I. Their chief fare was calves heads; and they drank their wine and ale out of calves' sculls." (*A Classical Dictionary of the Vulgar Tongue By Captain Francis Grose*. Edited with a Biographical and Critical Sketch and an Extensive Commentary by Eric Partridge, London, 1963, p. 67).

8. *Begot in Forty-One:* Possibly an allusion to the year 1641 in which the resistance against the House of Stuart took definite shape and the Catholic revolt broke out in Ireland.

9. *Cart's Tail:* an illusion to a punishment described in Captain Grose's Dictionary: "persons guilty of petty larceny are frequently sentenced to be tied to the tail of a cart, and whipped by the common executioner, for a certain distance: the degree of severity in the execution is left to the discretion of the executioner, who, it is said, has cats of nine tails of all prices" (p. 72).

10. *Within Ambs Ace:* "nearly, very near". (From ambs-ace, the double ace, the lowest throw at dice, known much more widely, after about 1800, as the deuce; Captain Grose, p. 16).

11. From "Several Discourses by way of Essays, in Verse and Prose." I. *Of Liberty*. Slightly altered: l.1 "these" instead of "the"; l.3 "ask" instead of "beg".

The Constant Lovers

The Amours and Adventures of
Alexis and Sylvia

[Part II, pp. 97–248] From: *The Constant Lovers: Being an Entertaining History of the Amours and Adventures of Solenus and Perrigonia, Alexis and Sylvia, etc.* London, 1731

The Constant Lovers

John Littleton Costeker's tale of Alexis and Sylvia is a heroic romance with some of the characteristics of the epistolary novel: a rudimentary domestic background and a certain amount of psychological realism. The conventional story of the constant lovers who have to undergo a series of adventures and trials until they become united is not only concentrated on a single couple but cut down to two scenes of actions; it is thus much shorter than the gigantic prose works of La Calprenède, Mme de Scudéry, and their imitators in England, and in the interest of readability, I have made further cuts. About one fifth of the original text consists of the passionate and excited letters exchanged between Alexis and Sylvia. These letters often repeat what we already know from the narrative because the lovers report their adventures and feelings to each other, and in particular their emotional reactions to outer events. Whereas the third-person narrator frequently finds it "impossible to describe" the emotions of his characters, the correspondents themselves are sometimes able to express more of what they are feeling, and indeed, a rather primitive form of psychological analysis is the main function of the letters. But the epistolary sections convey too little of the plot to be independent of the third-person narrative; moreover, it is the connecting narrative which provides the reader with most of the detail as well as with an overall view of the events.

The heroine of the novel, Sylvia, is at first rather reserved towards her suitor, Alexis, but finally loses her heart to him. Sylvia, however, like Clarissa, is forced by her father to meet a series of odious suitors (the scene with Furfante is not unlike that which Clarissa describes in Letter XVI), and then sent to her father's estate in the country where Caspus, an enterprising beau foreshadowing Lovelace, tries to kidnap her, using, like Lovelace, a second key to the garden. We need not suppose that Richardson knew John Costeker's novel; he could have picked up stock motives and character types such as these almost anywhere in the fiction of the seventeenth and early eighteenth century. Richardson used these conventional elements as the starting point for a new kind of novel in which the ultrasensitive heroine records both events and emotions in hitherto unimagined detail; but Sylvia is still a child of the romance, recording set-speeches rather than introspective psychological analysis.

The language and imagery of *The Constant Lovers* are still highly indebted to the heroic romance. Love appears as a fatal power under the tyranny of Cupid; the lover becomes a captive of his divine lady, whose cruelty pierces his heart; her eyes have wounded him and only her favour can provide the remedy. Once the lady has succumbed, loyalty and constancy are the qualities which should govern the lover's conduct. This lofty view of love finds appropriate expression in an exaggerated rhetoric: the metamorphosis caused by love must be "sudden", a passion "bursts out into a flame", Alexis awaits an answer to his letter "with the greatest impatience", and kisses her picture a hundred times. In letters and conversations they address one another with many exclamatory Ahs! and Ohs! – a dramatic device favoured by the narrator ("Oh! how she was struck!") as well as by the letter-writers themselves ("Oh! Madam, how happy should I be . . ."). The less dramatic descriptive epithets are equally elevated and unindividual: Sylvia is "Lovely", "beauteous", "charming", and "unchangeable", and Alexis "most faithful" and "ever constant". This style was destined to lose its popularity in the course of the eighteenth century, but some of its elements, were taken over – in tempered form and couched in a different vocabulary – by the novel of sentiment.

IN the County of *Kent*, in one of the best Situations in *England*, lived a Gentleman, of whom we shall speak under the Name of *Antimus*. He married a Lady of a good Family, and had four Sons and one Daughter, whereof *Alexis* was the third; he was from his minority a seeker and lover of Learning: at fifteen years of age he was removed from *Canterbury* to *London*, to improve and perfect his Studies, where he, in the space of three years, by an unwearied and indefatigable Industry, attain'd to the knowledge of all the Qualifications requisite for a young Gentleman to begin the World; such as, writing several fine Hands, Arithmetick both vulgar and decimal, *Latin*, *Greek*, *French*, *Italian*, Musick, Geography, Geometry, Chronology, History, Philosophy both natural and moral, Dancing, Fencing and Riding: in short, he excell'd in most of these to perfection.

IT was not difficult, or possible, but that one who was endued with so many Perfections, joined to an affable and courteous Temper, should be insensible to Love! No, no, he was gay, complaisant, free, and obliging to all; he was fair, genteel, and well-shaped: in short, no Man was better made for Love's Enjoyments than he.

BEING once invited to a Ball with other young Gentlemen, amongst the Ladies he cast his Eye upon one of an excellent Wit, beautiful, fine-shaped, genteel: in short, an Emblem of Beauty. Our young Lover (for so we may now call him) immediately perceived the effect of her Charms; he trembled, sweat, was faint, and had all the Symptoms of one in *Cupid*'s Decoy: the more he gaz'd, the more he admir'd; and was every moment finding out new Perfections to feed his Fewel. The young Lady, on the other hand, (whom we shall call *Sylvia*,) who was only Daughter to a Gentleman, (whom we must name *Bracchus*,) was as much smitten with *Alexis* as it was possible for him to be with her; never in all her life did she think she had seen any one so agreeable: various were the Thoughts at that time which filled the Minds of *Alexis* and *Sylvia*.

'TIS impossible to describe the Troubles of their Minds, both being under an uncertainty, and dubious of the cause and event of their Passions; so that neither of them could attribute so sudden a Metamorphosis to any thing but Love: but, as that, like hidden Embers, will, for a while, lie conceal'd, but then bursts out into a flame; so did it happen to *Alexis*. Often did he try to check the Emotions of so powerful a Passion, but in vain; at last, he was forced to yield himself up a voluntary Captive: however, he resolved to make the best on't. Accordingly, embolden'd by the justness of his Passion, and the hopes that *Sylvia* would not be insensible, he, with the utmost diligence, sought for an opportunity of acquainting her with his Passion; and, as nothing was more agreeable to her, you may easily imagine it was not very difficult to be accomplish'd: in short, he begg'd she would honour him so far as to dance with him, which she with little repugnance did. After the Dance was ended, *Alexis* led *Sylvia* to her seat; but, there being no opportunity, he only with a low Bow and a Smile, that sufficiently shew'd the pleasure he had receiv'd, took his leave, and retired to the other side of the Room. The Ball being ended, *Alexis*, who was impatient for a lucky minute, begg'd leave to accompany *Sylvia* to her House; which she, after a few modest Excuses, permitted. There was in the Coach with them an old Lady, who was Aunt to *Sylvia*; so that *Alexis*, to his great disappointment, was balked of his Design: they soon arrived at *Sylvia*'s Habitation, when *Alexis* alighted out of the Coach, and first handed out the old Lady, and then *Sylvia*, who, taking hold of her Hand, he press'd it with a Kiss, that sufficiently shew'd the Excess of his Passion; and, after *les Compliments ordinaires*, took his leave.

'TIS impossible to express the different Agitations which filled the Mind of *Alexis*; often did he blame his Forwardness in encouraging a Passion, which he too plainly saw would be the loss of his Health, if not his Life: sure, never had any one such a Night harrass'd with continual Perplexities; and, after all, was obliged to comply with *Virgil*,

Omnia vincit Amor, & nos cedamus Amori.

Love prevailed over Reason, so that he studied nothing so much as a more happy opportunity. *Sylvia*, in the mean time, was not less perplex'd with the Thoughts she had entertain'd of him: there was a long combat between Love and Reason, but, at last, it was given in favour of *Alexis*. *Sylvia*, as is usual in such cases, thought the Advice of a Friend would bring her some Comfort; and accordingly unburthen'd her mind to a female Confidante, who promis'd her Secrecy and Fidelity: but she dearly paid for her Levity, in trusting a Woman with a Secret, as you shall know in the Sequel.

As People in love have many Inventions, it was not long before *Alexis* found one to see *Sylvia*. He, by a little Assiduity, soon learned, by one of her Servants, the Church she us'd; where he, to be sure, never miss'd an opportunity of seeing her: he had not gone often, before she, with no small surprise, perceived her Lover; Oh! how she was struck! In short, as all of us are apt to favour our Inclinations, so did she; for she thought nothing but a natural instinct could have brought him there so opportunely to her Wishes: nor was it, indeed, a less pleasure to him. *Alexis*, pleas'd with the hopes of Success, was fully determined to run all Hazards to accomplish his Desire. One day, as he was musing by himself, he took Pen, Ink, and Paper, and wrote the following Letter.

To SYLVIA

Madam,

'Twas with the greatest Regret that the other Night I met with so great a Disappointment when I had the honour of waiting on you home, by that Lady's being with you, of declaring how great a Wound I have received from your Eyes: sure, nothing, dear Madam, could ever have rais'd so great a Passion in my Breast but your Beauty! never was any thing equal to my Surprise! to see united in one Person so many excellent Perfections, as are undoubtedly, to be found in no other than the beauteous *Sylvia*; had I been less happy than to have talk'd, and danc'd with you, I should certainly have taken you for a Divinity. Oh! Madam, I want *Ovid*'s Softness to express my Passion! Hyperboles are entirely unnecessary to draw the lineaments of a true Passion, which is only founded on Justice, Honour and Virtue. I can't think that so beautiful a Form as yours can be guilty of Ingratitude, when you consider my Passion on this foundation: on the contrary, I believe you to be endued with more Goodness and Generosity than any of your Sex could ever boast of. Were you but sensible of the Pains I suffer, I am sure you'd pity them. Oh! hear me with an equal Ear when I lay my Bosom open to your Eyes; 'tis you I love, you I adore, and on you alone are all my Thoughts employ'd. Your Beauty has vanquish'd all my Endeavours, I can no longer dispute the Victory; all I desire is a return of Love; if you grant me that, I live replete with Happiness; if not, then must I immediately perish. I commit myself entirely to your Generosity. Adieu, my Soul! the support of my Life.

ALEXIS

As *Alexis* was generally very successful, he was not less fortunate in this; for he had scarce finish'd his Letter, but, looking out of the Window, he very opportunely saw the same Servant passing by, who before had given him some intelligence of *Sylvia*. *Alexis* called out to him, who being come, You already know (said he) how great an esteem I have for your Lady and at this time I stand in need of your Service; which, if you'll perform faithfully and secretly, you shall not find me ungrateful. *Simo* (for so was the

Servant called) thinking sometimes to bite at a golden Bait, promised him the utmost of his Endeavours: so, giving him the Letter, with a strict Charge to deliver it to *Sylvia*, and a Present for himself, dismiss'd him full of Expectation, or rather Hopes, that it would meet with the desired Success.

SIMO coming home, executed his Commission with the utmost Integrity; for, meeting *Sylvia*, Madam, (says he) the humblest of your Servants has done me this Honour, (giving her the Letter;) which she had no sooner taken, but she tore it in a thousand pieces, saying, Will there never be an end to that Villain's Impertinence? supposing it had been a Letter from *Caspus*, a Gentleman who had very much solicited to be her humble Servant, a rich, but ugly Man: in short, she flew out of the Room, leaving *Simo* to bite his Thumbs at his Disappointment.

HOWEVER, he resolved to put the best face on't; and, as he conjectur'd, it might be of advantage to him to continue in *Alexis*'s Favour, resolved to tell him a plausible Story. *Sylvia*, after her Passion was a little abated, return'd to the Room, took up all the pieces of the Letter, and replaced them the best she could; Oh! Gods! how was she astonish'd when she saw 'twas not from *Caspus*, but *Alexis*: how often did she accuse her Rashness and headstrong Passion? This Letter only served to add fewel to her fire; but, however, she was willing to dissemble a little, as will appear by this Letter,

To ALEXIS

Sir,

I MUST confess ingenuously, that you seem to pick me out as the only Person worthy your Ridicule, and one who delights in Flattery: I am not so ignorant of my own Merit, but I can distinguish between that and Reality. I presume you take me for one whose Credulity is easily impos'd on; but I do assure you, that if you persist in your pretended Amour, you must expect to meet with abundance of Obstacles, and the utmost Resolution of opposing your Design.

SYLVIA

THIS Letter she gave to *Ancilla* her Maid, with a particular Charge to find out *Alexis*, and give it him; which she endeavoured to do, but could not 'till the next Evening, by reason of his being gone to welcome *Antimus*, who was come to settle in *London*, to his new Habitation. *Simo*, whose Care it was to be the first with *Alexis*, the next Morning found him, and addressed him after this manner: Sir, (said he) I have obey'd your Commands to a tittle, *Sylvia* took your Letter with a Smile, that flatter'd me you was not disagreeable to her. I thank you, my faithful *Simo*, said he, and will never be unmindful of your Service; so dismiss'd him, and retir'd to his Chamber to meditate on the happy Success of his Love. Oh! (says he to himself) how happy am I, to succeed so well in my first essay! Sure, nothing can compare to thee, my adorable *Sylvia*! But then recollecting on the possibility there might be of *Simo*'s flattering him for the sake of Gain, struck a damp to all his Pleasure. Whilst he was thus agitated between Hope and Fear, he heard a low Voice in the Street, which seemed to call *Alexis*. It being then pretty dark, he look'd out of a Window, and could just perceive something under it; which calling again, he went down to the door, where he was met by *Ancilla*, who gave him *Sylvia*'s Letter: he took it, desiring to know to whom he was indebted for that Happiness? *Ancilla* made no doubt of telling him from *Sylvia*. Bursting out into an Extasy of Joy, Oh! my Soul, my Life, (said he) all are indebted to the charming *Sylvia*, as their only Preserver. Tell her, (continu'd he) I am no longer at my own disposal, but am entirely hers. As he was naturally very generous, *Ancilla* did not miss of being well paid for her good News. He had scarcely entred his Chamber, but his Transport threw him into a Swoon, where he lay till a Servant, coming in to call him to Supper, discover'd him lying on the Floor; she scream'd out, and alarm'd the whole House, supposing him to be dead.

THEY soon, with the help of some volatile Spirits, recover'd him. *Alexis*, who was scarce come to himself, pulling out his Handkerchief, dropp'd *Sylvia*'s Letter, which they immediately gave him; not in the least mistrusting the Contents: however, no-body could prevail with him to sup, being so impatient to know the Contents of his dear *Sylvia*'s Letter, that they left him to himself; where, when he was, as he thought free from any Interruption, he read it. 'Tis impossible to express the pleasure he received from this Letter; nor did it contain any thing but what afforded him an agreeable Satisfaction.

SYLVIA waited with Impatience the return of *Ancilla*, who quickly acquainted her with what an agreeable Reception her Letter had met with, which pleas'd her to the life. The next thing that *Alexis* resolv'd upon, was to procure himself the pleasure of declaring his Satisfaction to *Sylvia* in Person; but how to accomplish it, without a little of her prudent Management, he was at a loss: but, that he might the easier effect it, he resolved to beg her Assistance, as he did in this Letter.

To SYLVIA

Madam,

I AM extremely sorry you should misinterpret my good Meaning, by thinking that those Praises, which are only due to you, were spoken by way of Ridicule: no, Madam, by Heavens, I meant no Ill, but only to declare how much I love; nay, ev'n adore your Person. You don't believe this, but it is because I am not admitted to convince you of your Error. For God's sake, alter that severe Sentence, where you tell me, I must expect to meet with the utmost Resolution of opposing my Designs: far be such obstinate Cruelty from your Heart; be more compassionate to your Lover, to rid me of that cruel Uncertainty? And what would enhance my Pleasure, would be your kind acceptance of these trifling Presents. Oh! Madam, how happy should I be, to be blest with one quarter of an hour's conversation with your dear Self. There is nothing but your Will wanting to procure me that Happiness, when I can express myself better than by writing. I wait with the greatest Impatience,

> *Dear Madam,*
> *The Favour of your Answer.*
> ALEXIS

AFTER *Alexis* had finish'd this Letter, he sought for *Simo*; and, having found him, order'd him to give it *Sylvia*. *Simo*, who knew what a bad reception he had with the former, was at a loss how to behave with this: but, having been in *France*, like other Travellers, had brought from thence a *bonne Assurance*: so watching his Opportunity, he gave it *Sylvia*; who took it with a Smile that very much astonish'd *Simo*, when he least expected it. He wonder'd to see so great a difference between the receipt of the two Letters, but imputed it to his own Cunning; which was more owing to *Sylvia*'s Conduct, who was now wholly taken up with *Alexis*'s Letter, and the Presents, which were very fine. After having well viewed them, she made her Acknowledgments in this manner.

To ALEXIS

Sir,

WITH what Retrospect must I behold the many Insinuations and Arts you young Gentlemen use to betray poor innocent credulous young Ladies, and sacrifice them afterwards to your Ambition; and then leave them the Scorn and Ridicule of the World? If you should differ from all others, 'twould be something miraculous: but how can I entertain such a Thought from such volatile inconstant Humours, as your Sex in general are addicted to? As to your Presents, I like them, because the Workmanship is excellent; and by way of Retaliation, that they may not seem the Pledges of Love, I send you a Ring, which is not of less Value. Adieu.

> SYLVIA

ANCILLA, who was made the Messenger of this Present, was received by *Alexis* with the greatest Joy imaginable. After abundance of obliging Acknowledgments for the Favour he had receiv'd, he dismiss'd her. Oh! how were his Thoughts taken up, not only with flattering himself of his being belov'd; but the Ring, which he kiss'd a thousand times, he look'd upon as an undeniable proof of it. How ardently and affectionately did he pray for his lovely *Sylvia*? sure never was Man in such Raptures. This, undoubtedly, made him more eager to see her; his Mind was now wholly employ'd, when, where, how, and which way he could effect it. But 'tis in Love as in all other things, it has its Bitters as well as Sweets; for, *Caspus*, jealous that some other was more happy than ever he was like to be in *Sylvia*, by her utter Aversion for him, did not think himself so disagreeable but that his Riches might make an Equivalent, sought all possible Means of discovering it; he thereupon, by a Sum of Money, bribed *Ancilla* to his Interest, who, for the Lucre of Gain, was so base as to betray her Mistress. *Alexis*, as I said before, imagining himself the happiest Man alive, thought proper to acknowledge his Satisfaction, and the Pleasure he had receiv'd; which he did by the following Letter.

To SYLVIA

Madam,

YOUR Billet gave me an inexpressible Pleasure, that you keep my Presents on any Terms; they will put you in mind of my Passion: 'tis true, they were but of small Value; yet do not despise the Offerings of Love. As for your Ring, it shall never go off my Finger, which, instead of you, I'll moisten with my Kisses. Assure yourself, my dearest *Sylvia*, of finding in me a Soul void of all Flattery and Dissimulation; and let my Actions justify my Merit; and then you'll find that never Breast burn'd with a more ardent Flame of pure Love, than does now that of your most faithful *Alexis*.

SIMO, as usual, executed his Commands with the utmost Zeal and Integrity. Happy had it been for our two Lovers, if *Ancilla* had not been less faithful. Joy at that time wholly employ'd the Heart of the beauteous *Sylvia*; who, now confirm'd of *Alexis*'s Love by this Letter, (so apt are we to believe what we would have so,) resolv'd to study nothing so much as their future Happiness: so that now she intended, by this Letter, to let her dear *Alexis* know some part of her Sentiments.

To ALEXIS

Sir,

I MUST own, your Conduct hitherto has been regulated with all the Caution and Respect of a Gentleman; which induces me to believe you have not been altogether romantick: but, that I may confide in your Sincerity, if you would endeavour to increase the good opinion I have already entertain'd of you, you must continue it with all imaginable Care ever to have any share in my Affections. But, should I proceed to a further declaration, you would, perhaps, think me guilty of that too common Weakness our Sex is subject to: however, blame me not for making use of your own Words;

> Weak, tho' we are, to love is no hard Task;
> And Love for Love is all that Heaven does ask.

SYLVIA

CASPUS, who was never idle to find out any thing that might disturb the Happiness of the two Lovers, was so fortunate as, by the Treachery of *Ancilla*, to intercept *Sylvia's* Letter. Oh! the Curses that he invoked to fall upon the heads of the two innocent Lovers, when he too plainly saw how strongly their Passions were united: fill'd with Rage and Madness, in having a Rival that was much his Superior in any thing but Riches, vow'd he would sacrifice *Alexis* to his Revenge; he went home almost distracted with Passion, and the next Morning sent him a Challenge. *Alexis* was surprised to receive a Challenge from a Gentleman he never knew: however, Courage being the least thing he wanted, he did not fail of the Appointment, where he found his Antagonist expecting him with the greatest Impatience. *Alexis* desired to know the cause of their Duel, and which way he had offended, having never till then laid eyes of his Adversary. To be brief, *Caspus* told him, he look'd upon him as his Rival in *Sylvia*; and except he would immediately yield up all his Pretensions to him, he must dispute it with the Sword. O Sir, said he, if that's the Motive, I am ready to give you all imaginable Satisfaction; and am proud of the Honour of drawing in her Cause. Come, come, said he, teach your Sword the dialect. They both drew, and for a long while maintained their stations with intrepid Bravery; both being dubious which should remain Victor, till *Alexis* luckily wounded his Enemy so that he fell at his feet: He begg'd his Pardon, and confessed how he had intercepted *Sylvia's* Letter, which he gave him. That so much enraged *Alexis*, that he had much ado to forbear taking what *Caspus* had justly forfeited: but Reason overcame Passion, and he freely forgave him. *Caspus's* Wounds proved not mortal, so that in a few days he was able to go abroad. In the mean time *Alexis*, proud of the opportunity of acquainting *Sylvia* with this Adventure, and the pleasure which her Letter gave him soon furnished him with a subject for this Letter.

To SYLVIA

Madam,

So vile a Treachery as *Ancilla* has been guilty of, perhaps, you never heard of: it was a perfect Providence that brought me to the knowledge of it. She deliver'd your dear Letter into the hands of *Caspus*, who the next day sent me a Challenge; when, proud of the Honour of maintaining my Pretensions to you, both Love and Fortune gave me a Victory. No Tongue but my own can express the Pleasure I received by your dear Letter. Nothing sure can equalise my Joy in having gained so sweet a declaration. Oh! now my dear, my lovely charming *Sylvia*! might I have Crowns of Gold, I'd part with all to be possessed of thee: never distrust my Love, but always think to what a height it is still aspiring.

> Belov'd of thee, what Horror can appear
> Worthy my Anger, Sorrow, or my Fear?

ALEXIS

ALEXIS with this Letter sent a very fine Ring of great Value, the Gold interwoven with a burning Heart and a Device, which was,

Pour Toi Seule;

which pleased *Sylvia* extremely, who was almost at a *Nonplus* what Measures to take with *Ancilla*: she consider'd that, if she kept her, she would be a Spy upon her Actions; if she turned her away, she would expose all their Amour to *Bracchus*; so that she could not tell what they might have cause to fear from that; the reason was, that *Alexis* was not endowed with the Gifts of Fortune in so pleantiful a manner as *Bracchus*; but was in nothing else inferior to him. In short, she thought it best to conform her Conduct to the *French* Phrase,

De deux Maux il faut eviter le pire;

that was to keep *Ancilla*, but never trust her again. If I am bit once, it may be another's Fault; but if twice, my own. It was not difficult to imagine what Surprise *Alexis*'s Letter caused in *Sylvia*, when she saw how nearly it concerned them both to be cautious of their Proceedings. In short, this Adventure did no hurt at all, as it was so luckily order'd, but put them both upon their guard, and discovered the Treachery both of *Caspus* in corrupting of *Ancilla*, and she in betraying of *Sylvia*.

SYLVIA, by the loss of her treacherous Confident, was now deprived of a Bearer, and was obliged to act with a great deal of Caution and Circumspection. After a few days had passed, *Simo* told her, that *Bracchus* was determined to visit his Country-Seat for a Fortnight, which was no disagreeable News to *Sylvia*; thinking that in his Absence she might give *Alexis* a Meeting: she long'd to let him know what hopes she had of seeing him. At last she thought, as *Simo* was faithful to *Alexis*, he would not be otherwise to her; so intrusted him with this Letter.

To ALEXIS

Sir,

THE Fidelity you repose in *Simo* makes me follow your Example. Think how great my Surprise must be at the Contents of your Letter, when you told me the Danger you had been expos'd to. Ah! *Alexis*, how could you so easily hazard your Life for a Woman you hardly knew? tho' my Weakness has compelled me to let you know part of my Sentiments, you must certainly set but little Value upon it, to be so fond of exposing it to such imminent Dangers: did you but know how much I prize it, you would be more cautious. 'Tis probable a little time may furnish us with an opportunity of discoursing other ways than by Letters in my Father's Absence, who, as *Simo* informs me, intends to leave *London* for a Fortnight. I like your Ring, of all things, except the Device; which seems to imply that you burn for me alone. Ah! *Alexis*, don't let me tax you with Infidelity.

SYLVIA

SIMO was quickly dispatched with this Letter to *Alexis*, who, overjoy'd at the sight of him, *Simo*, (says he) my Friend, how fares the lovely *Sylvia*? Oh! Sir, (said he) she is well; and I believe, wants nothing to compleat her Happiness but your Company. Really, *Simo* had much better grounds for what he said then, than before. After that *Alexis* dismiss'd him, and retired to read her Letter. Every Minute seemed an Age till the time of *Bracchus*'s Departure was come, when *Sylvia* found no other obstacle of seeing him but her Aunt; all her Thoughts were employ'd to remove that, but Fortune favoured her with a means the next day: for, a Relation of hers came to make her Aunt a Visit, who very much sollicited *Sylvia* to accompany her there the next day; which she promised to do. The appointed hour being come, *Sylvia* pretended to be taken very ill on a sudden, and counterfeited a Swoon: but recovering herself, which she had no great Trouble to do, she begg'd her Aunt to go; and, if she was better, (which she made no great doubt of, being conscious how bad she was) she would follow her: which she, not in the least suspecting the Policy, did. She was no sooner gone, but *Sylvia* dispatch'd away a Messenger to *Alexis* to let him know of the favourable opportunity. I must say they were both very fortunate; for, had the Messenger staid two minutes longer, she had certainly miss'd of *Alexis*, who was just then going to visit a particular Friend of his. I need not say how long he was before he arrived at *Sylvia*'s House; only assure you, that the Grass did not grow under his feet: no, no, Love gave him Wings; he was conducted to the Garden-Gate by the Messenger, where he was no sooner arrived, but *Sylvia*, who had waited with the greatest Impatience, flew down to receive him. 'Tis impossible to express the Satisfaction our two Lovers receiv'd at the sight of each other. Ah! my

Sylvia, my Life, my Soul, (said *Alexis*) now I have found thee alone; now all my Wishes are accomplished, that I embrace you without a Witness of our Actions. Oh! my *Sylvia*, (continued he) for you alone I live, and to you alone I owe this Happiness. *Sylvia* thinking herself thoroughly convinc'd of the Truth, answer'd him in the following manner; Alas! said she, to what Dangers have you exposed yourself! what need of more Words? It is now evident that I am most dear to your Heart; and I have now made trial of your Love, and am convinced, by many certain proofs, of the Sincerity of your Affections. You shall not find me backward in my Acknowledgments; let but the Gods give us a prosperous Fate, and a happy event to our Amour, as long as Life animates these Limbs, none shall have any power in *Sylvia* but my *Alexis*. In these and such like Endearments did they pass the Evening, giving the most faithful Assurances of an eternal Fidelity to each other, till the time they thought would be most proper for *Alexis* to depart; which cruel Separation they were forced to admit of, tho' much against their Inclinations: *Alexis*, Fortune's Favourite, was hardly gone an hundred Paces from the House, but the Coach returned with her Aunt; when she, to give her pretended Indisposition a better Look, ran up-stairs, and threw herself upon her Bed, pretending to have been there ever since, and that she was just as she left her. The old Lady little thinking how happy she had been, began to pity her, and administer all the Comfort that was requisite for one in her Condition; she immediately, by the Advice of her Aunt, went to Bed, where she was at full Leisure to reflect upon the pleasing Fallacy, and her past Happiness.

ALEXIS, on the other hand, was transported beyond himself; he set no Bounds to his unlimited Fancy. Oh! the sweet Ideas that that Night filled the Minds of our two Lovers! no prospect of any thing but their future Happiness; all their Thoughts were now employ'd upon another Assignation; they were both at a great loss what to do for *Simo*, *Bracchus* having taken him with him: but, as they were both very fortunate, they were not long without their wished-for Felicity; for, *Sylvia*'s Aunt being taken very ill, so that she was obliged to keep her Chamber, furnished them with Opportunities almost every day.

By this time *Bracchus* was upon his Return, of which the faithful *Simo* took care to advertise *Alexis* time enough to prepare *Sylvia* to be in a readiness to receive him. *Bracchus*, being arrived at his Habitation, was received by *Sylvia* with all the Joy imaginable; but was concerned to find his Sister ill, who in a few days recover'd. *Sylvia*, who had no Mother alive, look'd upon her Aunt as such; who had as much care of all her Actions as a Mother could have. In short, she was too circumspect; notwithstanding which, she was sometimes deceived, as will appear by the Sequel: for, *Caspus*, who was now very well recover'd of his Wounds, was resolved, notwithstanding his late Disaster with *Alexis*, by any means to compass his desire with *Sylvia*; so that he thought it the best way to address himself to *Bracchus*, knowing him to be a rich Man, and one that would not marry his Daughter to any one inferior to her, either in Birth or Fortune; which he had in abundance: so, trusting to his Riches for his chief Introduction; which now-a-days is a very prevailing one, he finds out *Bracchus*, proposes a Match for his Daughter, offering to make her any Settlement he should require. Gold opened the Eyes and Ears of *Bracchus*, so that they agreed but too well; for *Bracchus*, from that time, gave him free access to his house, and ordered *Sylvia* to entertain him. This was certainly a great shock to *Sylvia*, to see a Man she hated so nigh her; especially, to be introduced by her Father, with his Commands to receive him. You may imagine what a reception he had from *Sylvia*, who told him, all his Endeavours would be in vain; and that, like *Sysiphus*, his stone would end where they began: so begg'd to be free from his Importunities. In short, she told him she hated him; and that nothing but her Duty to her Father should have compell'd her to speak to him; and further assured him, that after that time she would never see him: in short, told him, she was engaged to *Alexis*. *Caspus* was very much enraged to be so received, who before had thought himself sure of Success; he endeavoured by all the Speeches he was able, to prevail with *Sylvia* to permit him only the Happiness of seeing her sometimes; which she utterly denied: so that, finding all his Rhetorick in vain, he took his leave; which gave *Sylvia* an opportunity of writing the following Letter.

To ALEXIS

Sir,

My Surprise is so great that I hardly know what I write. *Caspus* that Villain has prevailed with my Father to introduce him to me, with his Commands to entertain him, when he had the Boldness to tell me, he only wanted my Consent to make him happy. No, no, my Dear, my Resolutions are too firmly fix'd ever to be removed: none but *Alexis* shall ever share my Heart. Oh! how seasonable a little of your Advice would be to me for the managing of this Affair! I beg you won't fail of the first opportunity of letting me hear from you; which will be an inexpressible pleasure to

My Dear,
Your SYLVIA

This Letter caused no little Surprise in *Alexis* at the Temerity of *Caspus*; however, *Sylvia*'s Letter was a sufficient Satisfaction to *Alexis* of the Reception he had met with, which did not a little please him: so, according to *Sylvia*'s desire, he wrote the following Letter.

To SYLVIA

Madam,

I MUST confess I am not a little surprised at *Caspus*'s Proceedings, but more pleased with yours. I beg, my Dear, nothing may make you uneasy. As to ourselves, we must proceed with all the Caution and Secrecy imaginable, for fear your Father should, by his Vigilance over all your Actions, perceive that which I fear *Caspus* will, if he has not already discover'd to him; I mean our Amour. I must confess, my Life, I am in some Anxiety about it; therefore, as you are discreet in all your Actions, I am not dubious of your being the same in this, both for my Ease, and your own; the Inequality of our present Fortunes being the motives that may probably urge him to an Enquiry, which, when known, will undoubtedly be the immediate means of our Separation. Consult your Heart, my Dear, and see if you have Fortitude enough to face an angry Father: far be it that ever you should on my account. Our Cause, 'tis true, is just, we have Honour and Innocence on our side; and now, if we meet with any opposition to impede our Love, it must be Avarice or Ambition; so, my *Sylvia*, I rely wholly on your Discretion for the management of this Affair, which will either end in the utter Ruin, or entire Happiness of

My Life,
Your uneasy, but ever constant
ALEXIS

CASPUS, in the mean time, enraged at *Sylvia's* Denial, thought to revenge himself on *Alexis* would be but Folly, having had such bad Success before; so that he thought his only Revenge would be to raise up new Inquietudes for the two Lovers, by acquainting *Bracchus* with their Amour. In short, he divined but too well; for, having found him, he told him after what manner *Sylvia* had treated him, which a little vexed *Bracchus*, who promised *Caspus* to use the Authority of a Father, if she refused to admit of his Addresses. To strengthen his Cause the more, he told him he was well assured of the reason why she did it. *Bracchus* began to smell a Rat, guessing that he had a Rival; and desired, if he valued his Friendship, he would hide nothing from him, but declare what he knew; that he might, for the future, know how to regulate his Proceedings. To be brief, he told him of *Alexis*'s making his Addresses to *Sylvia*, and what return he had; neither did he forget to tell him how he intercepted *Sylvia*'s Letter, by the means of *Ancilla*: all which things seem'd a Mystery to *Bracchus*, who promised *Caspus* to inspect into what he had told him. *Caspus* thank'd him, saying, he hoped the Will of the Father would be obey'd, so departed very well satisfied at what he had done. *Sylvia*, in the mean time, was wholly taken up with *Alexis*'s Letter; which strengthened the Resolution she before had taken of being none but his, let what would happen. *Caspus* was no sooner gone, but *Bracchus* called *Sylvia* into his Study; who trembled at the mere apprehension of what he was going to say, being but too good a diviner of his sentiments.

SYLVIA was no sooner come to her Father but he began thus; Madam, said he, pray, what is the reason that you refuse to obey my Commands in entertaining *Caspus*? Sir, said she, I always made it my study to be obedient to your Will; and think myself happy in so good a Father. I am sensible, continued she, of the Duty that is due to you as a Parent; and will never be guilty of the least Disobedience, when under no unreasonable Command. Are then my Commands unreasonable? said he. Pardon me, Sir, said *Sylvia*, if I say, in this Case I cannot comply with them but with the greatest reluctancy. Pray, said he, your reason? You have, Sir, continued the charming *Sylvia*, commanded me to receive a Man, whose Person I can never like; and is every way disagreeable to me: his Riches might make him agreeable to some other Woman less difficult; but, at present, I have no inclination to Marriage. I beg you would not force me to do any thing involuntary. Suppose, says the cunning *Bracchus*, the Person changed; and, instead of *Caspus*, it was *Alexis*, would it then be any unreasonable Command? *Sylvia* was sensibly touch'd at that question; but, looking on the ground, said, she hardly knew him. Well enough, continued he, to send Letters to him. She desired to know who had done her that piece of service? He told her *Caspus*. Who, she said, was a vile Fellow. Have a care, said he, I don't prove it all true; and so ordered her to retire. This Lecture caused a great deal of uneasiness in her, who, the first opportunity, sent the following Letter to *Alexis*.

To ALEXIS

Sir,

MY Expectations have not failed in the least; for, yesterday my Father sent for me into his Study, where he told me that I had an Intrigue with you; and of the Letter that *Caspus* intercepted: to both which I answered in the negative. You see, my Dear, how I was catechis'd. In your last you ask'd me, if I had Courage enough to face an angry Father? do you think that I have not enough to support your Claim and my Choice, but must yield to an Interview with every Coxcomb my Father has a mind to for his Son. At what rate should I esteem the Universe without the lovely *Alexis*? even as nothing. Can I ever prove false to one so deserving as yourself? no, my Dear, assure yourself of the reverse; and think, that never any Woman loved with more Vehemency and Resolution than your

SYLVIA

With this Letter *Sylvia* sent the following *extempore* Acrostick.

A ll that I love, and all that I esteem,
M eets in *Alexis*, sure no Youth's like him;
I , in his Features, and in his Mind, can see
N othing but Pleasure, Love, Felicity:
'T is he that's Regent of my Heart, not I,
O nly am trusted, as 'twere with the Key,
R estoring it to him that lent it me.

WHILE these things were transacting, *Bracchus*, who was resolved to know the Truth of what *Caspus* had told him, sent for *Ancilla*, and questioned her in every particular; to which she (having found she had for ever lost *Sylvia*'s Favour) made no scruple of giving him a real Account: he asked her how long it was since their first acquaintance? and how it began? To all which she answered. After *Bracchus* had well examined every Circumstance, and finding nothing that he could alledge against either of them from her Confession; but that every Action of theirs was regulated with Prudence, Modesty and Discretion; and their only Fault was the love they bore each other, he thought *Caspus* and *Ancilla* the most culpable: so, as a Reward for her good Service and Fidelity to her Mistress, sent her packing. This afforded some pleasure to *Sylvia*, to be rid of a Spy. A few days after, *Caspus* went to visit *Bracchus*, full of expectation to be entertained by *Sylvia* in a less rigorous manner than before; but was very much surprised when he saw how coldly he was received by *Bracchus*: not imagining in the least but by that time he would have compelled *Sylvia* to receive him. In short, *Bracchus* told him in a few Words, that he could not prevail with *Sylvia*; and that he would do nothing against her Inclinations: that she had a mortal Aversion for him, so desired that he would give him no farther Trouble about her: she being, as he understood, otherwise engaged. *Caspus* beg'd leave to speak to her himself, which he refused, making use of *Caspus*'s own Words, when he thought *Bracchus* would have compelled her to marry him; that the Will of the Father must be obey'd. *Caspus* abruptly took his leave with the utmost Indignation, to see how he was balked.

SIMO took special care, in the mean time, to deliver *Sylvia*'s Letter to *Alexis*, who was extremely pleased with the immutable Constancy of his dear *Sylvia*: he thought every minute an Age till he had declared his Satisfaction of being so happy; which he did by this Letter.

To SYLVIA

Madam,

I WANT Words to express the Pleasure I am now involved in, caused by your dear Letter. Have a care, my Soul, lest you form a Resolution that may not be only undutiful, but prejudicial also: consider, that if you disoblige your Father, to what a Disadvantage he may turn your Dis-obedience; you ought rather to act the Fox's Part, since both our Happiness entirely depends on his Pleasure. Use him with all the Humility and Obedience imaginable; be conformable to all his Humours, entertain whoever he commands you, and use them with Respect, till at last you will, by your wise Conduct, so far insinuate yourself into his Favour, that he'll think you have no more need of his paternal Care to direct your Choice; but think you discreet enough to make yourself happy. Adieu! my Soul.

ALEXIS

SIMO, who waited while *Alexis* wrote this Letter, was the Bearer thereof, together with these *extempore* Verses.

To SYLVIA

LIKE to an Angel come from Heaven, you,
At the first sight appeared to my view;
Struck with surprize, on so much Beauty gaz'd,
'Till you had in my Soul a Passion rais'd:
Encreasing ev'ry moment, till it came
Into a painful, but a pleasing Flame.
My Thoughts, my Words, and all my Actions too,
Both day and night, were all employ'd on you:
My Mind thus tortur'd, all my hopes were this,
That you'd consent to love, and crown my Bliss.
A Thought, you'll say, so dubious for a Lover,
Who did not dare my Passion to discover:
By Love embolden'd, I resolv'd to see
Whether my Person, Love, or Fate's Decree,
Could gain admittance unto one so fair;
That I my love-sick Passion might declare:
Encourag'd thus, to my dear Object came;
Who soon with equal ardour met my flame:
Bless'd with so sweet returns, as Love and Ease,
What is there equal to my Happiness?

BRACCHUS was not long finding out who *Alexis* was: for, happening to meet with one that knew him, he gave him an exact and impartial Account of him, his Family and Fortune. In short, nothing would have pleased *Bracchus* so well as he, had he been so fortunate to have had an Estate answerable to his Merit: but, as *Bracchus* was naturally covetous, he did not think him, by reason of that defect, a fit Match for *Sylvia*; so that he resolved to prevent all future Correspondence between them. To be the more secure in the Enterprise, he took into the House an elderly Person named *Strega*, in the room of *Ancilla*; one that he was sure he could confide in, to be an *Argus* over *Sylvia*. In the mean time, a Misfortune happened that was cause of Uneasiness to both our Lovers: for *Simo*, their only Ambassador, being intoxicated with too much Liquor, fell from his Horse, and broke his Arm. During the time of his Illness, *Alexis*, very impatient to hear from *Sylvia*, often sought him, but to no purpose; wondering he never saw him, nor heard from *Sylvia*; who at the same time was as uneasy as possible to let him know of the Accident, but could trust no-body. As a Woman's Invention is never long upon the rack, she soon thought of a pretty way of doing it, which was thus: She pretended a great concern for poor *Simo*'s Misfortune, as indeed she had; so that she ordered it to be printed in the *Gazette*, that *Simo*, one of the Servants of *Bracchus*, had the Misfortune to fall from a Horse, and break his Arm; being well assured that, by that means, *Alexis* would certainly know the cause of his not hearing from her. In short, her Policy had the desired effect; for *Alexis*, the next day, to his great Concern, read it: but yet it afforded him some Satisfaction, in freeing him from a thousand doubts, which had before filled his mind; he immediately attributed it to the Cunning of his dear *Sylvia*. O my Soul! said he, how wittily have you eased your Lover of a thousand Uncertainties by this Stratagem! In short, their only Remedy was Patience till *Simo* was recovered, and able to go abroad; which he could no sooner do, than *Sylvia* sent him with a Letter, and her Picture in Miniature to *Alexis*.

To ALEXIS

Sir,

I MUST beg the continuance of your Patience to read my long Epistle; I much fear it will put it to the trial: I have so many things to say, that I don't know where to begin. 'Tis a composition of Joy, Concern and Sorrow. My Joy consists in being freed from two of the greatest Troubles of our Repose, *Caspus* and *Ancilla*, who my Father has discarded, in recompence of her good service; and *Caspus*, whom he has forbid ever troubling me again: next, my concern is for poor *Simo*, who had been so unfortunate as to break his Arm: and lastly, my Sorrow consisted in being, by that means, deprived of the pleasure of hearing from my dear *Alexis*. I here send you my Picture, which perhaps, you may esteem as well as the Original. I intend to make use of your Advice, and have already put it in execution: if your really love me, as you pretend you do, convince me of whatever Suspicion I may have on that head, by your immediate Answer. I remain,

Dear ALEXIS,

Yours, SYLVIA

SIMO's Arm not healing so fast as was expected, wrought abundances of Fears, Doubts, Jealousies and Suspicions, which alternately filled the mind of *Alexis*, and flung him into a violent Fever, so that the Physicians almost despaired of his Recovery. This was the Condition he was in, when he was told that *Simo* would speak with him; who, starting up in Bed, order'd him to come to him, desiring those who attended to retire; for he had something of moment to impart to him. *Simo*, says he, your Presence never was more agreeable than at this time; do you bring me Life or Death? how does me *Sylvia*? Oh! Sir, said he, she's well; so giving him the Letter and Picture, which he kissed a thousand times, saying, then he would not despair of living, since she had wrought a Cure. After expressing his Concern for *Simo*, he dismiss'd him, ordering him to tell *Sylvia*, she might assure herself of his Obedience to her Commands as soon as his Health would permit him. These things had so great an effect on *Alexis*, that it very much conduced to his speedy Recovery, which in a few days he enjoy'd, so as to be able to walk about; when he wrote the following Letter.

To SYLVIA

Madam,

I SHOULD send Health to the fair *Sylvia* in this Billet, but that I have not Stock enough left to make my Wishes effectual. Oh! my Dear, what Inquietudes did I undergo, by not hearing from you in so long a time: Hope and Fear alternately took place in my breast, till at last I was undeceived of the Cause; a generous Pity seiz'd my Heart: but Time seemed to halt so, that the many Passions attending a dubious Cause in Love o'ercame me; a sudden Illness seiz'd me, attended with a violent Fever, which reduced me almost to the point of death; but your dear Letter came, and snatch'd me from the jaws of that King of Terror. Oh! my Soul, how am I indebted to you for your Generosity. Your Picture I kiss'd a hundred times. Oh! best of Women! how miserable had I been without your Love; but, being bless'd with it, your Virtues can never be extoll'd enough, by,

My dearest SYLVIA,
Your happy ALEXIS

AFTER *Alexis* had finished this Letter, he was so fortunate as to light of *Simo*, to whose charge he committed it; who was no sooner come home, but he deliver'd it to *Sylvia*; who, a few days after, sent the following one to *Alexis*.

To ALEXIS

Sir,

How shall I express my Concern for the loss of your Health: I know no way but by assuring you, that the loss of my own would have been a less

Trouble to me. Could but my Endeavours have contributed to the preserving of it, how willingly would I have offer'd them? My Prayers, nevertheless, were not idle for the saving of a Life that's as dear to me as my own; which, considering those things that interrupt our sight, are the only aid I had power to afford you. I can only with my Life Joy of your happy Recovery; and give you fresh Assurances, that, whilst I live, I will never own any Stile but that of

Your unchangeable SYLVIA

THIS Letter created in *Alexis* an uncommon pleasure; how often did he bless his Fate, in being so happy as to be beloved by one of the best and most beautiful Ladies in the World. In short, many envied his Happiness; but none better deserved it. *Alexis* never missed seeing *Sylvia* once a day, at least; but it was always at a distance, never nigh enough to speak to each other; their only Conversation consisted in Letters. Thus did they live, and enjoy a perfect Tranquility for a long while, without any thing occurring that gave them the least Uneasiness, till *Bracchus*, who feared lest *Alexis* should become his Son, thought it the best way to procure one of his own chusing; that he might erase all Thoughts of *Alexis* in *Sylvia*.

(Here pages 138–150 of the original text are omitted, describing how Sylvia is banished by her father to a country seat in Surrey, almost kidnapped by Caspus, saved by Alexis (who has assumed the name of Antonio), and confronted with a new prospective husband: Furfante.)

A FEW Days after *Furfante* went to wait on *Sylvia*, who was ready to faint as soon as she saw him: but common Civility obliged her to see him, being at a Relation's, who was advertis'd of his Coming by *Bracchus*; but not without great restraint on her Inclinations. *Arabella* and her Aunt, who knew the cause of his coming, after some Discourse of indifferent things, retired, and left them together; when *Furfante* began to address *Sylvia* in the following manner.

MADAM, says he, you are sensible that I am now past the Age of being ignorant how to form a right Judgment, and to esteem so incomparable a Lady as you are, equal to your Merit; which I believe to be inferior to none. There is nothing, Madam, added he, that this World affords, which shall be wanting to make you compleatly happy; if you will condescend to admit of the sincere Affection of your humble Servant. That, Sir, answered she, is not in my power. Oh! Madam, says he, be not so severe, but yield a Cure where those Eyes have made a Wound. There is nothing, added he, that I would not do to oblige you. Swear then, said the cunning *Sylvia*, or I can't believe you. *Furfante*, who thought he was going to Heaven in a String, thundred out whole Legions of Oaths to confirm what he had just before said. *Sylvia*, who was fully bent upon getting rid of this Lover by Policy, had her End; for, *Furfante* having invok'd all the heavenly Powers to witness what he had said, that there was nothing he would not do to oblige her; I take you at your Word, said she, and from this time I enjoyn you never to see me more. *Furfante* was very much vex'd to be so outwitted, he would have used a multitude of Arguments to have defended himself, but it was then too late. *Sylvia* would then give no ear to what he said; but, leaving the Room, left him by himself like an arrogant Coxcomb.

(Pages 151–152 are omitted.)

SOME Men less resolute than *Bracchus* would, after so many Disappointments in endeavouring to procure a Husband for their Daughter, have given over all Thoughts of Success: but he, being a Gentleman of great Resolution, resolv'd every thing should accede to it; and that he would send for her up to Town, to prevail with her to marry *Furfante* by fair means, as being a Gentleman whose Estate he thought equal to her Fortune; if not, to force her to a Compliance. Poor *Sylvia*, now is the beginning of thy Miseries! for, Time and Absence he thought might by this time have effected a Cure, and effac'd all Thoughts of *Alexis*; (for so we may now call him again.) So ordering all things for his Journey, he himself resolv'd to fetch her up again to *London*. When he arriv'd, he was receiv'd by *Arabella* his Sister and *Sylvia* with a great deal of Joy; he, after some Discourse, ask'd *Arabella*, if such a Gentleman (meaning *Furfante*) had been there to wait on *Sylvia*? To whom she answer'd Yes. And pray, Madam, said he, (turning to *Sylvia*,) what Reception had he? *Sylvia* (who suppos'd he was already acquainted with it,) reply'd, I receiv'd him, Sir, with all the Civility I could force upon my Inclinations, to see a Man that was in all respects disagreeable to me. I must beg your pardon, Sir, said she, if I presume to ask you, if our Duty to God enjoins our Parents to oblige their Children to unlawful Marriages? So far as this, answer'd *Bracchus*, that no Marriage is lawful where the Consent of the Parent is wanting; (intimating, that she ought not to marry *Alexis* without his.) Then, said *Sylvia*, it is apparent to any reasonable Understanding, that no Marriage can be lawful where the Consent of the Child is wanting. I suppose, Madam, answer'd he, that you intend to out-wit your Father too; do you think you have got such another Wood-cock in your Springe as *Furfante*? Look ye, continu'd 'Squire *Wrong-Head*, declare your Choice; you shall either marry *Furfante*, or be discarded my Favour. *Sylvia*, who was sensibly touch'd at that, fell on her knees, and begg'd he would not force her to any thing so averse to her Inclinations, telling him she never could love him; and that he would plunge her into eternal Unhappiness: but he was insensible both to her Tears and Intreaties, and order'd her immediately to get ready to go to *London*: when she, o'erwhelm'd with Grief, had but just Time enough to write the following Letter to her dear *Antonio*.

To ANTONIO

Sir,

I HAD but just Time enough to acquaint my Life of my sudden Departure: my Father has again forced this Separation from all that's dear to me in the World; but nothing now can make me unhappy, being assur'd of the Fidelity of my dear *Alexis*: rest satisfy'd in the same opinion of, my only Happiness,

Your SYLVIA

SYLVIA was forced to trust this Billet in the hands of one of the Servants of *Arabella* to give to *Antonio*, when they took their leaves, and returned to *London*. She was now depriv'd of discoursing with her dear Youth, but knew she should not be long without seeing him, if her Letter was not intercepted, of which she was a little dubious: for the Person to whose Care she had committed it, being one of the Servants of *Arabella*, was descended of the antient Family of the *Wrong-Heads*; and for fear she should be guilty of any Mistake, must needs ask her Mistress leave to go to such a place, naming the Yeoman's. You may be sure she ask'd her upon what account; and she, being loth to disgrace her Family with a Lye, confess'd that she had a Letter to carry there to a Gentleman. *Arabella*, surpris'd at that, had a little of that never-failing thing in her Sex call'd *Curiosity*: so, without any hesitation, open'd the Letter; when she was surpris'd to find that the pretended *Antonio* was *Alexis*. She could not help admiring how strange and uncommon an Adventure had procur'd them so long and uninterrupted a Happiness; she told the Maid she would be the Messenger herself: but thinking it the best way to acquaint *Bracchus* of what happen'd, she immediately sent it to him.

BRACCHUS no sooner saw the Contents, but flew about raving like a Mad-Man: he was in twenty minds whether he should let *Sylvia* know of it, or no; thinking, if she did, she would be more wary of him; if he did not, he might more easily surprise her: so, concluding that the best way, he order'd *Strega* to give him a particular account of *Sylvia*'s Proceedings. It was now almost a Fortnight that *Alexis* (for so we may call him again) had not seen the charming *Sylvia*; he began to think some Accident had happen'd, yet durst not go to *Arabella*'s to see, for fear it might cause Suspicion, never being so fortunate as to receive *Sylvia*'s Letter. A few Days before *Antimus* had sent to order him up to Town about an Affair that requir'd his Presence, but was unwilling to go without seeing of *Sylvia* first; but, receiving another the next Day, he with a great deal of Regret, after having made several handsome Presents to the Yeoman, his Wife, and Daughter, for their Hospitality, promising shortly to visit them again, he departed. *Sylvia*, in the Interim, was surpris'd she had not all that time seen *Alexis*, doubted not but her Letter had never reach'd his hands, began to be in the utmost Uneasiness, till one Day *Alexis* passing by *Bracchus*'s House, could not forbear looking up where he had so often seen his dear *Sylvia*; it happen'd that she was just then come to the Window, when he, to his great Surprise, saw her: at first, they were both in some doubt whether it was the strength of Imagination that represented that Sight to their Eyes; or, whether it was really one another. At last, *Alexis* bow'd to the suppos'd Phantom, when it, to his no little Surprise, return'd it with a Courtesy and Smile, that shew'd *Sylvia* was not in *Surrey*, as he suppos'd, but in London: however, there was now no room to doubt both in their minds were seemingly satisfy'd for the present. *Alexis* immediately went home, where he wrote this Letter.

To SYLVIA

Madam,

WITH the greatest Regret 'twas I left *Surrey*, because I thought I had there left the charming Sylvia; notwithstanding my Eyes seem'd bless'd with that dear Sight to-day, yet I cannot be thoroughly satisfy'd, till I am undeceiv'd by your own hands. Oh! my Soul, 'tis a whole Fortnight since I last saw you, till this Day; how can I support so long an Absence from all that I love in the World, no way but by the Assurance you gave me of your Fidelity. Adieu, my Soul, continue faithful.

ALEXIS

ALEXIS was not long finding his faithful Servant, to whom he gave this Letter; who the first Opportunity afterwards gave it to *Sylvia*, who was extremely satisfy'd with it: she was in no doubt whose hands her Letter had fallen into by that time; so she, to undeceive *Alexis*, immediately sent this Answer.

To ALEXIS

Sir,

THE Day I left *Surrey*, I gave a Letter to a Person, who promis'd faithfully to deliver it safe into your own hands, unknown to any one but ourselves: but I find she has not kept her Word; I suppose it has fell into my Father's by this time, as I find by a small smatch of his Oratory, when he told me I must, and shall marry *Furfante*; so order'd me to fix my Resolution, and give him my final Answer: which, in obedience to him, and my own Inclination, I will do; but it shall be to live and die intirely my dear *Alexis*'s.

> Since Fate first join'd, 'tis Death alone must part;
> (No weaker Hand) *Alexis* from my Heart.

SYLVIA

Some time pass'd before *Furfante* could reassume his Courage to visit *Sylvia*, after his first Retreat; but now had hopes again, since *Bracchus* had promis'd her to him: so that he often visited *Bracchus*, and would have done *Sylvia* as often, had she not had continual Excuses for her not seeing him. At length, *Bracchus*, quite tir'd with Perseverence, one Day, sent for her to come and keep *Furfante* and him Company, which she durst not but obey. After they had talk'd some time, their subject became that of Marriage, when *Bracchus* told *Sylvia* he intended that Gentleman for her Husband, and desir'd her to entertain him as such; that he had given him his Consent, and that the Day for their Nuptials was appointed, when *Furfante* return'd him Thanks for the Honour he intended him; at which *Sylvia* could not refrain from crying. And will you, Sir, said she, force me to be miserable? Will you marry me to a Man that I hate? No, continu'd she, it shall never be; I'll sooner die than ever be any other's but *Alexis*'s. We'll try that, (said the hard-hearted *Bracchus*,) which shall have the Pre-eminence, your Will, or mine. I suppose, continu'd he, you have some knowledge of the Person who wrote that Letter, (giving it her, which *Arabella* sent him,) you have engaged yourself to *Antonio*, have you? said he, I hope you had a merry Time on't, to have a Lover with you, when I, poor mistaken Fool, thought he had been the furthest from you. Oh! said he, you have verify'd the *French* Phrase.

> Bonnes Paroles, & mauvais Jeu
> Trompent les Jeunes & les Vieux.

You have done it to a Tittle: but, for the future, I'll try if I can't root this *Alexis* out of your heart. I'll warrant you, continu'd he, I'll spoil your sending of Letters, or receiving any of his: fetch me, said he, all that ever you had from him instantly; or, by all that's good, you shall never see my Face more. In short, all that she could say to excuse herself on that head was in vain; so, seeing no remedy, was obliged to fetch them to him. I find, said he, Madam, that you are deeply engaged to this Gentleman; and, as a Reward for all his witty Contrivances to out-wit me, I'll now save you the Trouble of re-placing them, by doing it in this manner, when he cast them all into the Fire, and burnt them. This Sight affected *Sylvia* so sensibly, that it threw her into a Swoon, but they soon recover'd her. Poor *Sylvia*, what a Series of Crosses and Troubles did she suffer! Sure, such things as these, joined with the Resolution she had taken to remain inviolably *Alexis*'s, would have shook that impenetrable Heart of *Bracchus*, but it had not the least Effect on it. *Furfante* departed, and *Sylvia* retir'd to her Chamber to unburthen her troubled Mind. Oh! cursed Avarice, said she, 'tis you that are the cause of all my Inquietudes. Oh! unkind Fortune, continu'd she, why was you not favourable to my dear *Alexis*? then had two Persons been happy for ever.

In these and such like Expressions did she pass the Day; and at Night wrote this Letter to *Alexis*, which she sent by *Simo*, with the other, when he was not so fortunate as to light on *Alexis* before.

To ALEXIS

Sir,

This Day has been the most unhappy that ever I knew; I can't express what I have suffer'd, but 'tis all nothing, so long as you remain faithful: nothing, dear *Alexis*, can ever separate us; I'd sooner die than admit of a Thought of any other. I must beg your extensive Goodness to excuse all that is amiss, I being in Bed writing whilst my *Argus* sleeps; and am dubious whether my time will permit me to read it over. Adieu, my Life.

SYLVIA

ALEXIS, at the receipt of these two Letters, was not so much surpris'd as concern'd: Oh! base Villain, said he, to use a poor defenceless Woman in this manner; the greater the Brutality, in being his Daughter: Oh! unhappy me, to be the cause of so many Sufferings to my dearest *Sylvia*. Then he sent this Answer.

To SYLVIA

Madam,

What can I do? what Course can I take? what Remedy can I find for all thy Sufferings? every thing seems now to be utterly averse to our Repose. Fortune, which has often favour'd us, has now abandon'd us. O Love! O Happiness! help me to invent and find a Remedy for the growing Evil; O my *Sylvia*! I have now no other Consolation upon Earth but your dear (ah! most dear to me,) Self. May Heaven's Guardian-Angels always wait, and crown our Loves with prosperous Success; may their Endeavours always fail who strive, whenever employ'd, to force our Separation. I'll sooner die than ever suffer it. Oh! my Soul, could all our Joys but center in this Verse, then should we be happy.

> Marriage, the blest Estate of Life would be,
> If Hands were join'd, when Hearts, like ours, agree.

ALEXIS

(Pages 162–168 omitted: Bracchus and Antimus agree to send Alexis to Mexico for a while to make his fortune as a merchant. Bracchus promises Antimus not to marry Sylvia off until Alexis has returned, a promise which he does not keep. However, he fails to get rid of Alexis, since his friend Marius is carried aboard the ship by mistake and taken to Mexico.)

To ALEXIS

Sir,

NOTHING can express the Perplexity I am in, caus'd by the fear I have of my dear *Alexis* being snatch'd from me. What! my Soul, have they still new Stratagems to separate us? Oh! my Dear, for Heaven's sake, secure yourself from their Hands; if you value either my Repose, or your own: for, if we are once parted, my Grief will certainly overcome me, and Death will be the Reward of your Absence. How can you suffer yourself to be torn from me, and leave a poor disconsolate and unhappy Object the Scorn of Parents, and the Scoff of Fools? Oh! if you go, I have no Protector; but must abandon myself to despair. I conjure you, by all the Love you ever profess'd, to hide yourself from them; go, go any-where, but where they would have you; and my only Consolation in my Solitude shall be the Belief and Confidence I have of your eternal Love to your unhappy

SYLVIA

ALEXIS, after receiving this Letter, thought it the best way to follow *Sylvia*'s Advice, for fear they should force him to act contrary to his Sentiments. He accordingly made some Preparations to retire into the Country to a Relation's, for fear of a Surprize; which he did the next day, after having given the following Letter to *Simo*.

To SYLVIA

Madam,

SINCE my Stay is not disagreeable to my dearest *Sylvia*, with the greatest Joy will I endeavour it. No, my Soul, don't think Absence would sit lighter on me than you; nothing can ever separate us now: I will instantly repair into the Country, where the dear Remembrance of our former happy Hours shall be my Contemplation. Oh! my Soul, for you only do I breathe; for you only do I live: without you every thing is insipid, and disagreeable to me. Rest satisfy'd, my Dear, of my Welfare, as I will of yours, till some happy Opportunity offers. Do not regard any Stories that may be invented purely to vex you; but be well assur'd, that none but you shall have any Share in the immutable Affections of,

My dearest SYLVIA,

Your most happy ALEXIS

(Page 171 is omitted.)

ALEXIS, who was now safe in the Country, was thought both by *Bracchus* and *Antimus* to be on his Voyage to *Mexico*, instead of the lucky *Marius*, who was extremely pleas'd with the Oddness of his Fortune. *Bracchus* hugg'd himself to think how he had trick'd *Sylvia* by his Policy; as yet not thinking it proper to discover it to her: so that not hearing in a long time any thing of *Alexis*, she began to fear the worst; and concluded him certainly trapp'd, and sent away by force. In short, she enquir'd of *Simo*, whether he had seen, or heard, any thing of him since his departure: but, answering in the Negative, it caus'd a great Uneasiness in *Sylvia*. To be brief, she was immediately seiz'd with a violent Illness, which, by a long continuance, reduc'd her to a perfect Skeleton; no-body that had seen her before her Indisposition would have known her, she look'd so pale and wan, that had she not mov'd and spoke, one might easily have taken her for a *Spectre*.

SHE often blamed herself for thinking that Absence might have any Effect on *Alexis*, so as to make him waver in his Amour; who, she really believ'd, could not be guilty of such a Neglect, or of the least Ingratitude towards her: yet, when she consider'd him as one endu'd with all the Perfections that render a Man acceptable to the Ladies, she thought she had but too much reason to fear his Fidelity: but we may rather impute the cause of her Suspicion to Love, than any real Cause. Whilst she was involv'd in these Uncertainties she was made sensible of her Mistake, and freed from all her Suspicions.

ALEXIS, who had lain *perdüe* all this while in the Country, had now thought of an Expedient to undeceive *Sylvia* of any Mistrusts or Apprehensions whatsoever; which he effected in the following manner.

DURING the Time that he resided at *London*, he got acquainted with a *Grecian*, whom he thought, if he could prevail with him to lend him one of his Habits, he might find out a means of seeing his dear *Sylvia*: so that, disguising himself *a la mode de Campagne*, he went to *London*; when, going to his House, he acquainted him who he was, and with his Design; which he had no sooner done, but he readily granted him his Assistance. You may imagine he was sufficiently alter'd by his long Coat, Furr-Cap, and long Whiskers; so that, admiring himself after his Metamorphosis, he concluded it convenient to buy some little Curiosities, in order, by that means, to gain his Admittance. Being thus equipp'd, he soon gain'd the House, when, knocking at the Door, he was let in by a Servant, whom he told he had some fine Curiosities for his Lady. The Servant desir'd he would stay, while he acquainted his Lady of his being there. *Sylvia*, whose coming our counterfeit Merchant expected with the greatest Impatience, soon came down with her *Argus*: but, O Heavens! how was he astonish'd when he saw how she was alter'd; he had much ado to refrain breaking out into Expressions, which he knew would not suit with his present Employment: so that, altering his Voice as much as possible, he told her he had some fine Curiosities to shew her, and was recommended to her by a young Lady of her particular Acquaintance.

AFTER he had shew'd her several, she pitch'd upon a fine Seal only, which represented a flying *Cupid* descending with two Hearts crown'd; which another endeavour'd to part, over which was this Motto,

La Mort seule peut le faire.

Whilst *Strega* was occupy'd in viewing some others, *Alexis* took an Opportunity of slipping a Ring, that *Sylvia* had given him, on her Finger. After having paid him what he ask'd for the Seal, she dismiss'd him. It was no little Joy to him, to think he had succeeded so well in his Enterprize; nor was it, indeed, a less Pleasure to *Sylvia*, when she found the very Ring that she gave *Alexis* on her Finger. She was agreeably surpris'd, but could not imagine by what means it came there; she knew she had seen no-body that Day but the *Grecian*: so that she was involv'd in an entire Mystery; yet, upon Reflection, she imagin'd she perceiv'd some Change in his Face at her entering the Room, which might have induc'd her to believe it was *Alexis* in Disguise, had not her Father assur'd her he was really on his Voyage; that too, join'd with her not having heard from him since his departure, but too much confirm'd her in a belief of what *Bracchus* thought, and had told her: however, some peculiar motive, that is only incident to Lovers, seem'd to assure her that it was *Alexis*; so she gave immediate Orders, that she might see the *Grecian* whenever he came again, by reason she thought his Trifles very entertaining, intending to observe him with more Attention the next time he came, to see if she could discover the least glimmering of Hopes that he was her dear *Alexis*. It was not many Days before our counterfeit Merchant undertook another Negotiation, in which he was more happy than in his first, and was receiv'd by *Simo*; but, not daring to discover himself to him, he told him his Business. *Simo* was not long before he acquainted *Sylvia*, who waited her Commands, nor she before she went down. He receiv'd her with a Bow and a Smile, that shew'd her Presence created some pleasure in him, telling her, he had once more done himself the Honour to wait on her, at which she seem'd very well pleas'd; so shewing her his *Baggatelles*, took an Opportunity to give her the following Letter, which she took with a seeming pleasure, having now perceiv'd a great Similitude, notwithstanding his Disguise between him and her dear *Alexis*. Among other Things, he shew'd her her own Picture, which strenuously confirm'd her that she was no longer mistaken, but that he really was *Alexis*: so only buying a small *India* Box, order'd him to wait on her three days after. Her Joy was inexpressible, and he retir'd the most pleas'd Man in the world; he was no sooner gone, but she read the Contents of her Letter, which was in these Terms.

To SYLVIA

Madam,

I DON'T at all doubt but my turning *Greek* will a little surprize you; but, as you are conscious, Love has many Shapes, your Admiration will a little diminish, when you consider that no Inventions should escape me, no Stratagems but I would use, nor no Difficulties but I would surmount to see you, whose Life's as dear to me as my own. Oh! my Soul! my dearest *Sylvia*! there's nothing now can ever part us. I no sooner receiv'd your dear Letter, where you warn'd me of the Consequence my Stay might be of, both for your Repose and my own, but I departed, and went to a Relation's in the Country, where I changed my Name, and have now taken this Habit upon me, that I may sometimes enjoy the Pleasure of seeing all that is dear, and in whom alone centers the eternal Happiness of

ALEXIS

SYLVIA, who once more thought herself happy in being assur'd of *Alexis*'s Safety, began to look pretty well again; and the Joy, which this Letter caus'd in her, added a *bonne Eclat* to her Beauty: so that it was very easy for our *Grecian* to perceive, at his next coming, what an Alteration the Discovery of himself had made in *Sylvia*. In short, she took the Opportunity of giving him this Letter.

To ALEXIS

Sir,

I MUST own I could never have thought to have found your dear Image in Masquerade, when I least expected so great a Blessing. My Father had told me you was certainly carry'd on board by force, and banish'd, perhaps, for ever from me. This, my Soul, was the State you left me in; and since your Departure, not having heard, or seen any thing of you, I concluded it even as he said: but just Heaven, my Dear, has heard my Prayers, and kept you safe at home. Oh! what Troubles and Anxieties did I undergo, to think of the many Dangers you would be expos'd to, and the Uncertainty there was that you would ever return: but now I will return my Thanks to Heaven, my Doubts are at an end, and you are safe. Adieu, my soul, be well assur'd that none but you shall ever share my Heart.

SYLVIA

AFTER she had view'd his Merchandize over and over, he told her he had a fresh Cargo, which he expected in a few days; that then he believ'd he might have some things would please her better; and she should be sure to see them the first: so order'd him to be sure not to fail coming, and dismiss'd him.

ALEXIS impatient to know the Contents of her Letter, departed. He was no sooner accommodated with a convenient Place, but he found the above-mentioned Words, to his great Pleasure and Satisfaction.

THE happy *Grecian*, resolv'd not to make the Time seem tedious both to his dear *Sylvia* and himself, in a few days made her another Visit; when she receiv'd him with more Joy than she dared to shew: however, both she, her Aunt, and *Strega*, who never left her, were highly delighted with his *Baggatelles*. Amongst others, he shew'd *Sylvia* a fine Japan'd Box, in which he had inclos'd a Letter, which opening, she perceiv'd; so demanding the Price of it, she pretended to go fetch some Money, when she took an Opportunity of reading it, which was in these Terms.

To SYLVIA

Madam,

How shall I acknowledge your Generosity for the continual Obligations you are loading me with. Indeed, my Dear, my Debts of Love will be so much enlarged, that I must turn Bankrupt, and give up my All to you, my Soul, my only Creditor. I really believe your Father and mine have been both impos'd on; and that the Captain has made a much better use of the Effects, than I, perhaps, might have done. No, my Dear, our Destinies are all the same, and one Fate governs us both; nothing can ever part our Souls, whatever does our Bodies. Adieu, my Life, and continue in the same Belief, that does

Your unchangeable ALEXIS

HAVING read it with a great deal of Satisfaction, she return'd with the Money; so paying the suppos'd *Grecian*, who shew'd an extreme Pleasure; after which he took his leave, and retir'd the best satisfy'd Man upon Earth.

THUS did they live a good while in a great deal of Satisfaction, till *Bracchus*, who perceiving that *Sylvia* seem'd to appear every day more lively and brisk than she had been since he acquainted her of *Alexis*'s Departure, began to think that the Thoughts of *Alexis* were entirely eraz'd out of her Mind, when he forgetting his Promise to *Antimus*, thought once more of procuring her a Husband. It happen'd one day as *Alexis* was shewing his Toys, that *Sylvia* had mingled with his a little Glass-Box, wherein was a Letter, when she, through Fear or Hastiness, in giving it him, let it fall, which breaking, discover'd the Letter: when *Strega*, being over-officious, took it up, and perceiv'd this Inscription, *To my dear Greek*; but, not thinking it proper to take any notice of it then, immediately gave it *Sylvia*. *Alexis* easily perceiv'd the Emotions it caus'd in *Sylvia*, who changing colour two or three times, put it in her Pocket. A-while after our Merchant was obliged to depart without the pleasure of *Sylvia*'s Letter, and much vex'd at the Uneasiness which he thought that Accident had caus'd in her.

STREGA, who till then never had an Opportunity of gaining her Master's Favour by any Discoveries, thought this a sufficient motive; so going to him, she gave him a particular account of the Letter, and every little passage she had ever perceiv'd concerning the Familiarity of the supposed *Grecian* and *Sylvia*. It is easy to imagine that this caus'd some Suspicion in *Bracchus*; yet it was check'd by his being sure, as he thought, that *Alexis* was certainly by that Time at *Mexico*; yet he desir'd to see him the next time he came, which was in a few days.

ONE might reasonably think that his Dress would have sufficiently alter'd him; so that no one could easily have known him again: but it was not secure against the penetrating Eyes of *Bracchus*, who, after a small Examination, discover'd the Fallacy. I think, (said he to *Sylvia* in an insulting manner,) this *Grecian* has something the Resemblance of *Alexis*; and, if I am not mistaken, 'tis he too. Well, continued he in a Passion, I find I have hitherto been impos'd on; but now I'll have my Pennyworths out of him: I'll have him imprison'd for a Cheat, and one that would have stole my Daughter: so went out to call his Servants to hurry him before a Justice of Peace. *Alexis* knowing he could alledge no unjust thing against him, was resolv'd to go; but *Sylvia*, who valu'd his Safety above her own, prevail'd with him by her Tears and Intreaties to make his Escape, which he did by throwing up a Sash, that open'd into a Yard behind the House, and leaping out, soon gain'd the Street, where they sought diligently for him, but to no purpose; for he had hid himself, where he stay'd till the Darkness of the Night favour'd his Retreat, when he went to the *Grecians*'s, and gave him an account of what had happened.

(Pages 183–190: Alexis makes another attempt to see Sylvia, this time during a masquerade at which he appears disguised as a Turk. Bracchus procures a new suitor for his daughter: Flavillus.)

To ALEXIS

Sir,

I MAY justly compare myself to a Ship in a Storm continually agitated by the dashing of the Waves, with only the Hopes of a Calm to free it from so imminent a Danger: so I, by my Father's Severities, have been continually harrass'd and perplex'd; but have now (Thanks to my propitious Fate,) some Hopes of Redress: He has, since I had the pleasure of seeing your dear Self, endeavour'd to force me, both by my Duty, and Compulsion, to marry a Gentleman named *Flavillus*, whose Offers I strenuously oppos'd, and have now conquer'd all future Advances from him: I have also gained so much of my Father's Favour, as to say he'll favour you, since he perceived my Wishes ended in you alone. You may, perhaps, my Life, think this only a Stratagem he might use to find you; but I can well assure you of the contrary: so, if you value my Repose, I conjure you, by all our dearest

Ties, to come to *London* as soon as possible; whose Presence will create an inexpressible Pleasure in the dearest part of myself.

Your Unchangeable
SYLVIA

HE had no sooner read this Letter but he immediately went to *London* to one of his particular Friends, as not thinking it convenient to go directly to his Father's House, being wary lest *Sylvia* should have been impos'd upon, and that they had, as yet, some Design upon him.

(Pages 191–193 are omitted.)

He now thought of nothing more than seeing *Sylvia*, which he did the day after, as he passed by the House; this produced an agreeable Satisfaction to them both: so that *Alexis* seeking for his faithful *Simo*, was not long before he found him, to whom he gave this Letter, to deliver to his dear Idol.

To SYLVIA

Madam,

I CAN'T say but your Commands were a great motive; yet I must confess, my own Inclinations were a much greater to come to *London*, where I might once more with pleasure behold my dearest *Sylvia*. Your long Silence, my Soul, made my *Exile*; for so I may call it, when I am banish'd from you, almost insupportable. Oh! how was my mind continually tortur'd with new Distrusts, and Jealousies; Fears, Troubles, Suspicions, and Anxieties, alternately took their places in my Soul: my Time was wholly devoted to my dearest *Sylvia*. By Day you was my Meditation; by Night my Dreams; on you alone were all my Thoughts employ'd; in the greatest Solitude I found a Happiness. I must, my Dear, intrude on your Goodness, for prolonging my Letter, by giving you an account of my Dream, which I interpreted as a happy Omen, though not without some Trouble, before it can be accomplished.

The DREAM

METHOUGHT I, walking in a pleasant Shade,
O'erheard the Cries of some unhappy Maid;
Whether by Fortune, or by Chance, it were,
That did conduct me to th' oppressed Fair,
I cannot tell; but sure I am that I,
Stretch'd on the ground, a beauteous Form did 'spy.
She sigh'd and cry'd, and then she tore her Hair;
The surest Emblems of a deep Despair:
Then rais'd her drooping Head, and sighing said,
Oh! cruel Parents! Oh! unhappy Maid!

136

I, by your Scorn, have lost my dearest Swain,
The sweetest Youth! the Thoughts augment my Pain:
How could you from me banish all my Bliss,
My Joy, my Peace, my Soul, my Happiness?
Did but my dear *Alexis* know my Grief,
And what I suffer, 'twould be some Relief
To my poor drooping Soul; but oh! alas!
My Spirits fail, I sink, I die apace.
Startled at that, I could no longer bear
To be conceal'd, but straitways did appear
Armed with Pity, with the greatest speed
Flew to the succour of that charming Maid.
But, O my God! how great was my surprize?
When all that Scene presented to my Eyes,
Soon as I saw her lovely Face, did know
That 'twas my *Sylvia* that had suffer'd so,
I gently strove to raise my charming Fair,
And sighing, whisper'd softly in her ear;
Cease now, my Dearest, and no more complain,
Your happy Lover is return'd again;
Led here by Instinct, to relieve you came.
With that you rose, and faintly thus you said,
Is it *Alexis* that's come to my aid?
Ah! lovely Boy, how kind is Heaven now,
That in my great Afflictions sent me you!
I'll now embrace you with a greater Joy
Than ever *Hellen* did the *Trojan* Boy.
Clasp'd in each other's Arms we then did lie
Involv'd in Raptures, and sweet Extasy:
But, oh! I wak'd with the excess of Joy.
O strange Illusion! thus for to have seen
So much Despair and Pleasure in a Dream.

I SHOULD, my Dear, make an Apology for the Badness of my Verse; but, knowing that all Lovers are naturally Friends to the Muses, I rely on your extensive Goodness to pardon all that is amiss; and to overlook all Imperfections, which you meet with in,

My Dearest SYLVIA,
Your Eternal Admirer,
ALEXIS

THIS Letter was very acceptable to *Sylvia*, who waited impatiently in expectation of one: now she began to think that all her Troubles and

Inquietudes were at an end; and that every day would produce some new Felicity. She thought herself doubly happy in having vanquish'd her Father's Importunities, by his promise to favour their Inclinations, and *Alexis* being near her; so that they thought themselves sure of their former Pleasure of seeing, and writing to each other, tho' not of discoursing. *Sylvia* soon after sent the following Answer.

To ALEXIS

Sir,

YOUR Letter created in me a great deal of pleasure, and I must confess, it very much heightned my Admiration, to find how great a Partaker you was with me in my Sorrow, as appears in the first part of your Dream. Really, you might have concluded it ominous, and the Fore-runner of some Evil: but now, my Soul, I hope all our Fears and Anxieties are over; my Father seems to me the most alter'd Man upon the earth: he now, instead of inventing me new Vexations, makes it his whole study to please me. This, my Dear, is the state I am now in, and want nothing upon earth to compleat my Happiness but your dear Self.

> The Heavens above are pleas'd to see that we
> In Friendship, Love, and Unity, agree;
> As if our Souls were in each other's clos'd
> So fast, that they could never more be loos'd:
> But always to continue still the same,
> A bright, most lovely, and a virtuous Flame.

Adieu, my Soul! the best of Lovers.

SYLVIA

(Pages 198–207 report how Bracchus again tries to separate Sylvia from Alexis by sending her to the country. Sylvia falls seriously ill and is transferred to Bath, where her father plans to force another husband on her.)

SYLVIA's Uneasiness and Inquietudes had almost thrown her into Despair; which caused her to write the following Letter, though she knew not which way to convey it to the unhappy *Alexis*: yet, as a sort of Ease to her perplexed Mind, she wrote, as follows.

To ALEXIS

Sir,

PERMIT, thrice beloved, and most lovely *Alexis*, to the wretched *Sylvia*, but in no other manner than being detain'd from the Sight of your dear

Self, to open her Heart unto thee, which has been entirely always, and invariably thine; that, in taking my last Leave of you and the World, I may present before you, as my last Farewell, these dying Words: Since, after so many sweet Testimonies of Friendship, we must part; the remembrance of which is death itself in the most cruel manner. Alas! why has my cruel Father deprived us of that happy Time, in which, not having other Care but to please you, you seem'd to study nothing but to content me, in yielding me Love for Love, in which consisted the Feast of our Felicities. Whither are those fair days gone, when I lived but for you, nor breathed but to please you? Oh! then was I happy beyond my Merit; and should have still continued so, had my Father's Severities been more moderate: now am I, like a Prisoner, confined, because I won't submit to break, either by my Duty, or Compulsion, those dear Tyes between us. That which is my only Comfort, is, if I should survive those dear Promises you made me of your Fidelity; to which, if I compare my present Miseries, I find them all but a mean Comparison. Oh! my dear *Alexis*, 'tis impossible to express how strongly your Idea is graven in my Heart; too deep ever to be erased but by Death. In short, we must comply with an old Poet, in Imitation of our Sufferings;

> We must with Patience, more or less,
> Sustain those Ills we can't redress;
> Impatience is Affliction's Son,
> And breeds a thousand Plagues in one.

ADIEU! my Life, and assure yourself, that living, or dying, I shall never be any other than

Your most faithful
SYLVIA

WHILST these things were in agitation, as an addition to their Misery, *Furfante*, enraged at being disappointed both by *Sylvia* and *Bracchus*, resolved to make an attempt on *Alexis*'s Life, rather than he should enjoy *Sylvia*. He had discovered his Mind to one of his Retinue, (whom we shall call *Harrol*) which he had no sooner done, than he resolved on a base and unworthy Act; which was to shoot a Pistol at the Head of the innocent *Alexis*. He accordingly takes his opportunity, and when Day was shut in, (for these shameful Actions require Darkness) having learn'd he was in Company, where he passed his time in hearing a pleasant Concert of Musick, which he thought might, in some measure, abate his Melancholy; he sent for him by a Lacquey, pretending, a Gentleman under a borrow'd Name waited for him at the Door: of which he was no sooner acquainted, but went to the Door; when he no sooner appeared, but the traitorous Murtherer, who attended him *à Pied fermé*, without saying a word, presents

139

the Pistol to his Head. *Alexis* (turning of one side) happily evaded the Blow, which missing him, burst the Door like Thunder, at which all the House and Neighbourhood were alarm'd, the Concert ceased, and all ran to know the Cause: when the Villain would have drawn a Dagger, which he had purposely by his side, had not *Alexis* immediately seiz'd him, and threw him down stairs; then drawing his Sword, he thrust it twice or thrice into him. The Murtherer cry'd out fearfully. *Alexis* would have ended him, but desirous to know who was the Person that employ'd him, and for what End, left him with some remains of Life.

ALEXIS's Friends came to his assistance with their Swords drawn, thinking he was not alone, ran up and down, supposing to find more of his Accomplices; but meeting none, the Justice was sent for, into whose hands the Traytor is put; who confessed he was incited to this base Act by *Furfante*, because of a secret Revenge he ow'd *Alexis*.

(Pages 211–212 are omitted.)

ALEXIS was no longer able to be separated from the Centre of his Affections, and resolved to see her by some means or other. He accordingly sets out for *Bath*, where being arriv'd, he soon discover'd what part of the Place was so happy as to hold his dear *Sylvia*; the only Impediment that now remained, was to deceive her Guards.

BRACCHUS's Affairs happily at that Juncture required his Attendance at *London*; so that it was much easier to be effected in his Absence than otherwise. *Alexis* sends a Maid-Servant, as from a Lady, to *Sylvia*, acquainting her with his being there, and begging her Assistance to let him see her; which was deliver'd in the presence of her Aunt and *Strega*. She made no hesitation to open it, thinking it really came from some new Acquaintance, having disguised the Superscription: but when, to her great Amazement, she had open'd it, she immediately knew it came from that dear Partner of her Soul, *Alexis*; she was almost transported beyond herself, she order'd the Servant to present her Service to the Lady, and tell her, she would have the pleasure of waiting on her that Afternoon; so dismiss'd her. She accordingly went to the Lady's from whence the Letter, but *Alexis* was not there: so making a Confidante of the Lady, (whom we shall call *Alicia*) that she might aid and assist her in their Interviews, she impatiently waited *Alexis*'s Return. It was not long before the happy Minute came that both our Lovers enjoy'd the pleasure of a Rencounter, which afforded them a greater Felicity than ever they yet enjoy'd. Of such a nature is the meeting of absent Lovers, that whatever Troubles they have endured, their present Pleasure is Superintendant, and buries all past Things in Oblivion. *Alicia* could but admire the Sympathy between that charming Couple, the Beauty of the adorable *Sylvia*; nor was she less pleased with the charming *Alexis*. Oh! how did she behold him, not as a Friend, but as the Phoenix of his Sex. Love had already made a passage to her Heart, and all her Happiness consisted in beholding him; her Affection prompted her to contribute all that in her lay to procure the Happiness of the two Lovers: but, to speak more *à propos*, her own. She valued her Honour and her Friendship at so high a rate, that she thought it the highest Ingratitude to endeavour a Rivalship with *Sylvia*, if she had been sure of a Return; which she had the least Hopes to expect, if she consider'd how inseparable their Affections were: yet her Love for him increased to such a degree, that, let her use what Arguments she pleas'd against it, her Passion always was Superintendant. This is her miserable Case, she endeavours by all means to divert it; but finds that, like a Bird taken with Bird-lime, the more it flutters the more 'tis entangled; so the more she checks it, the more it rages. In short, 'tis irresistible.

(Pages 214–216 are omitted.)

IT was not difficult for him to perceive, before he had been there long, the Conquest he had made on *Alicia*; yet would never take any Liberties exceeding the bounds of Modesty, in justice to his betrothed *Sylvia*. *Alicia*, perceiving he took no notice of her Kindness, thought he degenerated from the rest of his Sex; which was but too visible to the Eyes of *Alexis*: as none are so blind as those who won't see, he would not perceive it. She was every day inventing new ways to discover it, but in vain. At last, being no longer able to contain herself, she spoke in the following manner to him.

'TIS impossible, says she, that so fine and accomplish'd a Gentleman as *Alexis* should not create Love and Admiration in every one; how then can you wonder if I should feel the same Effects. Too happy *Sylvia*! (continued she) to be sole Mistress of so many Perfections, none can see you enjoy them without Envy. Cannot you admit of a Partner in those dear Embraces? Oh! no; who can pretend to a Rivalship with the charming *Sylvia*, who is Mistress of so many Perfections and Virtues; and to whom even *Venus* must yield the Honour of superiour Beauty. At these Words she counterfeited a Swoon, from which *Alexis* soon recover'd her. Oh! how was he amazed to hear a Lady express herself in that manner. When she was come to herself, she proceeded, as before.

O *Alexis*! said she, what may be the End of my Desires, who die for you? Can you not receive a Passion, that knows no other Object than yourself? Will you suffer me to languish, and not afford a Remedy to a Wound that none but your Eyes could ever have made?

THIS she deliver'd with a Sigh and a Look, that would have charm'd any other but *Alexis*: but to him it appeared all Deformity, and nauseous.

From that time he conceived an utter Aversion for her; so that, dissembling his real Sentiments, he answer'd her in this manner.

I AM sorry, Madam, (said he) that, of all Men, you should be so unhappy as to make choice of me: had I never seen the beauteous *Sylvia*, I should have thought myself happy in so fine a Lady as the lovely *Alicia*; but, as you know how inseparable our Affections are, you'll pardon me, if I say, that I cannot, but with the greatest Injustice, at this Time, accept of any other; how can I do less than yield myself up entirely to her that has suffer'd so much for me? what Troubles, what Anxieties, what Inquietudes has she undergone, for one unworthy of so much Goodness? The least of my Acknowledgments shall be an eternal Love. Oh! Madam, continued he, rather strive to stifle a Passion in its Infancy, which may otherwise, one day, bring Desolation upon us all.

So, going out of the Room, he left her in the greatest Agonies, which her Despair could bring upon her. What is that too frequent Thing which accompanies a Disappointment in Love but Revenge, which was now uppermost in the Thoughts of *Alicia*. She thought, if he should discover her Weakness, (which he had too much Honour to do, unless to *Sylvia*,) she could become the Scoff of him, the Scorn of Fops, and Ridicule of Fools. In short, she was now, tho' late, but too sensible of her Frailty. But, unfortunate *Alicia*, thou flatterest thy Misfortunes; hadst thou not better

> Prevent those Shelves[1], and fly that fatal Shore,
> Where nought hath less of Life, and of Death more?

BUT she, like a Lion roaring, and watching to devour us; that Dragon which seduces us by these artificial Ideas, fills our Thoughts with malicious Illusions: so that her Love is now inverted into a secret Honour, and her Mind incessantly bent upon Revenge; which she endeavour'd to effect by this method.

POOR Lovers! how short and transitory are your Felicities? the next time they met, she received them with all the pleasure she could borrow of her Pride and Revenge; yet her Eyes darted flames of fire at her innocent Rival. As she knew her Absence would be more acceptable than her Presence, as with all Lovers, who never covet any Witnesses to their Amours, but especially to *Alexis*: she retired, not out of Kindness to let them have free liberty of their discourse, but to execute her own hellish Design; to cause, if possible, an eternal Separation between them.

SHE accordingly dispatch'd a Messenger away to *Bracchus*, to desire the favour of his Company; having something to tell him that required his immediate Attention. As ill News flies apace, it was not long before *Sylvia* saw her Father alight out of his Coach at the Door; at which she cry'd out, being very much surprised, Dear *Alexis*, procure your Safety; for we are betray'd. He immediately, without knowing where he was going, seeing a

Door open backwards, went out there, which fortunately led into a Garden; between which and the Fields there was nothing that could hinder his Escape, save a little Wall, which, with small difficulty, he ascended, and got clear of.

ALICIA, who waited in an inner Parlour to receive *Bracchus*, immediately conducted him in; where she failed not of giving him an impartial account of all within her knowledge: to which he could hardly give credit. But she, persisting in her Relation, cry'd, If you won't believe me, give credit to your own Eyes; (opening the Door where she discover'd *Sylvia* alone.) However, she being positive that *Alexis* was there, sought every-where to find him, but to no purpose. *Sylvia* seemed surpris'd at her Proceedings, and ask'd her what she look'd for. I seek (answer'd she) *Alexis*, who was here with you but this Minute; whom I would find, that your Father may be an Eye-Witness of what I have related. *Sylvia* would have persuaded *Bracchus*, that she certainly raved, *Alexis* not being there: which she had almost effected, when *Alicia* called in two Servants; who both affirmed, they had seen him, and that he was there but just before. *Bracchus* stood like a Man enchanted at what he heard; it being but a few days before that he heard of his being assassinated; and at that time, above all others, thought him safe at *London*: however, he thought himself *pars cautior*, since he was advertis'd of it, he resolv'd more circumspectly to watch her. *Sylvia* was in some fear for *Alexis*, lest *Bracchus* should by some means discover him, while he is lamenting her Sufferings; which he suppos'd she might by that time be under, through her Father's accustom'd Cruelty. The only Way to be freed from his Suspicion, and to let *Sylvia* know the reason why they were betray'd, was to procure once more a Disguise, which could no way be done but by a Confidante: he was not long declaring his Mind to a Gentleman, whom he esteemed his Friend, and promis'd him his utmost Endeavours. After some Consultation, the Gentleman propos'd a Miller, as knowing the Person that served *Bracchus*; who, as he said, might easily be prevailed with to let him one day go in his stead to *Bracchus*'s House, where he might have an opportunity of delivering a Letter either to *Sylvia* or *Simo*. *Alexis* returned *Antigonus* (for so was the Gentleman called) his Acknowledgments for his Proposition, which he liked extremely: whereas, being well powder'd, if he should by chance see *Bracchus*, it would be more difficult to discover him than in his *Grecian* Habit. So that the next day they put their Design in Execution; for going to the Miller, who was glad to assist them in their Design, he furnish'd *Alexis* with a Suit: so that, from a fine Gentleman he was in an instant metamorphos'd into a Buff-Coat. In short, he look'd as terrible as a Captain at the Head of his Trained-Bands storming a Dung-hill in *Bunhill-fields*. Their Project had its designed Effect; for, following the Miller's Instruction, he came to the House, took up his Sack, and in he carry'd it. The first Object he beheld was his dear *Sylvia*, to whom he beckoned; which she, being all Goodness, attributed such a Liberty taken by her Inferior to his Simplicity, went to him smiling, when he gave her the following Letter; which much surpris'd her: which she no sooner saw, than she knew it to be *Alexis*'s, by the Hands of a Miller. The Thoughts of her *Grecian* came in her head, yet was he so alter'd by his Dress, that she did not know him. Pleas'd with his Success, he returned to the Miller, when *Antigonus* impatiently waited his Return; where, after having satisfy'd the Miller for his Clothes, they departed well-pleas'd. *Sylvia*, in the mean time, was reading *Alexis*'s Letter, which contained these Words.

To SYLVIA

Madam,

THE wicked and base *Alicia* has been the Contriver of this our Separation. She, envious of the little Happiness you may expect in me, used all her Endeavours to bring me to her hateful Embraces: but finding my Love so firmly attach'd to your dear Person, from whom nothing but Death can ever separate me, that all her Effects were in vain to attract it to herself, has sought her Revenge in this manner. My Fears, my Soul, are numberless for your Sufferings; and never will cease till undeceived by your Answer; which I with the greatest pleasure will receive from your own Hands, as you received this from your

ALEXIS's

JUST Heavens! cry'd she, how false a Thing is Woman! what Vows, what Promises, did *Alicia* make, that she'd assist me, and be ever faithful? Unhappy I have hitherto been doom'd to suffer by my own perfidious Sex. Oh! dear *Alexis*, what's my Debt to thee? how great a Share of Virtue must you have, that you resisted her bewitching Charms, and would not listen to that Syren's Song? But what increas'd her Admiration was, that she had received this Letter from *Alexis*: she immediately concluded he must be the Miller; so resolved to be satisfy'd the next time he came. A few days after he made her another Visit, when, notwithstanding all her Endeavours to know him again, his Disguise so disfigured him, that she confessed afterwards she thought herself mistaken: but having, by that means, given *Alexis* an Opportunity of discovering himself, *Sylvia* promis'd to meet him a few nights after at a Ball. Now both our Lovers are easy again, whilst *Alicia* is almost distracted with Rage at what she had done; she endeavours to find out *Alexis*, but in vain: so that we may apply some Lines of an Old Poet to her Case.

> Where Conscience doth accuse our Crimes, there do
> Appear both Judge, and Executioner too.

The Constant Lovers

(Pages 225–242: Sylvia is now placed in the custody of Caesar, one of Bracchus' servants. He falls in love with her, producing a situation which she diligently exploits. With his help she manages to escape the tyranny of her father but nevertheless is in the power of a ruffian. At that point Sylvia finds an opportunity to send a letter to Alexis.)

To ALEXIS

Sir,

My Separation from all that's dear to me in the World would certainly have vanquish'd me, had I not been assured from your own Mouth of the Fidelity I might repose in your Constancy. O my Soul! I can but with Horror relate my Sufferings, and the Insolence I have been forced to bear with, from a mean servile Fellow, who is set as a Guard over me by my cruel Father's Order. In short, after all, I could perceive no way of working my Deliverance from that hateful Prison, but the soothing him, which has now brought me to this Place: if ever your Love exciteth you to any Revenge, it will now, when I tell you of this base Villain, in whose hands I now am; and can no way be deliver'd but by your dear Self: He has even dared to lift up his eyes, and behold me as a Lover, expecting with the greatest Presumption a Return. Haste then, my Life, to punish his Insolence, and free me from his Power;

Then shall my Sufferings by your Presence end,
Alexis be my Lover, Husband, and my Friend.

SYLVIA

This Letter was no sooner read by *Alexis* but he was affected with all the Passions, (*tour a tour.*) So that he immediately went with the Messenger to *Andronicus*:[2] and, having arm'd themselves, (lest this Villain should have his Guards over so rich a Prize,) they went directly to the House, conducted by the Messenger: where, being come, they found her imprison'd with Locks, Bolts and Bars; but *Caesar* happen'd (luckily for him,) to be out of the way, or *Alexis* had certainly sacrificed him to his Revenge. Oh! with what Extasies of Joy did they embrace each other, resolving now to be happy in spite of all Misfortunes; and to partake of nothing but immediate Death or Liberty.

BRACCHUS, in the mean time, was wholly employ'd what course to take to find out his Daughter, too well knowing that his cruel Usage had been the cause of her Escape; which he knew she could no way have effected without the assistance of *Caesar*; who, at his return, to his great grief, and no small disappointment, found the Nest without the Bird. Different were the Thoughts that fill'd the Mind of this Fellow. At last, consulting his Safety, he resolv'd to go and acknowledge his Fault to *Bracchus*; and, as a sort of Revenge, to declare her Escape with *Alexis*, which he immediately did. Think what reception he met with from *Bracchus*, who, at first sight of him, had drawn his Sword, and was going to serve him as he deserv'd, for his Perfidy to him, and Insolence to a poor distressed innocent Lady under his Government, had not his Sister interpos'd, and begg'd he would hear what he could say in his Defence; when, with-holding his Hand, *Caesar* upon his knee declared every Circumstance; and promising to find her, and restore her again into his hands, if he would grant his Pardon; which he agreed to do upon these Conditions. Now they are making diligent search for the two Lovers, while they are wholly employ'd in consulting their future Happiness. *Andronicus*, at whose House they were, promis'd them all the assistance imaginable; when, considering the Merit of *Alexis*, the Troubles they had both suffer'd, and the inseparable Love of their united Affections, he went to seek out *Bracchus*; whom he found swell'd with Choler at the loss of his Daughter; supposing, as he had reason to believe, she was gone with no other than *Alexis*. *Andonicus* try'd to pacify him with these Words; You'll pardon, Sir, said he, this Visit, when you are once acquainted with the Cause: I have heard, you have a Daughter, who is the Wonder and Admiration of her Sex, as well for her exterior as interior Beauties. I understand likewise, that a young Gentleman of uncommon Merit, *Alexis* by Name, has so far insinuated himself into her Favour, as to be entirely Master of her Affections, against whom you have conceived a very great Antipathy: Pray, Sir, said he, condescend to acquaint me with the Cause. Sir, answer'd *Bracchus*, as to his Person and Merit, I must confess I in every respect approve of them: but my Daughter being my sole Heiress, and whose Fortune is not inconsiderable, I could no way approve of, or consent to the Match, by reason of his defect in that Particular. You have hitherto, answer'd *Andronicus*, with *Sysiphian* Toil labour'd to separate their Affections, which the Gods, their Fates, and sympathetick Inclinations have decreed impossible: How could you inflict such Cruelty upon two Innocents, whose greatest Crime is Love? How many assured Instances have you had of it, that has reduced your Daughter almost to death's door? What greater proof could any Man give than the hazarding his Life, which the young *Alexis* has several times done? Now they, after all their Fatigues, ought to enjoy without any Molestation their so much desired Union, as a Recompence for their Constancy, Virtue and Courage, in surmounting so many Difficulties: and that their Happiness may be no longer delay'd, what *Alexis* wants in Merit to deserve the incomparable *Sylvia*, I'll make up in Fortune, constituting him my sole Heir.

BRACCHUS could no longer withstand so powerful a Temptation, when he consider'd the Worth of *Andronicus* to be little inferior to him; and immediately gave him his Consent for compleating the Happiness of the two Lovers, which he immediately acquainted them with. Their Transport was inexpressible, to see their Love, after so many seeming Impossibilities, crown'd at last: So that I may venture to apply these Lines of Mr. *Waller* to their present Felicity.

> *Thrice happy Pair, of whom we do not know*
> *Which first began to love, or loves most now.*

THEY were immediately conducted by *Andronicus* to *Bracchus*'s House, where he receiv'd them with open arms. I need not say what passed between them, in respect to his Cruelty, or their Disobedience; but only assure you, that all past things were obliterated, and their present Felicity drowned all in Oblivion.

ANTIMUS is advertised of the Happiness of his Son: thus we see what is the Recompence of Honour, Justice, Virtue, and a faithful continuance of the Affections of true Lovers to the end, in spite of all Misfortunes. Now the Hymeneal Rites were happily perform'd, with a great deal of Solemnity and Grandeur; all seem'd to participate of Joy and Pleasure at this time. *Bracchus* brings his Son and Daughter to *London*, so full of Contentment, that there was not any one that visited him to whom he did not discover in his Face and Discourse the Excess of his Joy.

HE was so carefully served, so religiously honour'd by his Son-in-law, that he thought his Life crown'd with the greatest Happiness imaginable: he thought of nothing but making good Cheer, (verifying the old Proverb, That the Miser's Feast is the most plentiful,) and of running smoothly all the rest of his days. Whilst our new Couple were involv'd in a Series of continual Happiness, there was every thing in abundance, every one pleas'd, and all the World blessed them. What doth not a virtuous and pious Person perform? *Sylvia* inspires the whole House with Devotion; she is *Mary* in her *Oraisons*, and *Martha* in her Solitude: she is all Sweetness outwardly, and all Fervour inwardly. The continual Visits of Acquaintance did no way divert her from the Service of God; whilst the happy *Alexis*, on the other side, is humble, gracious, temperate, wise, modest, pleasing, merry, the Honour and Glory of his Race.

THUS was the Happiness of these two Lovers united, after so many Obstacles that so often seem'd to oppose it: but, according to that wise Pagan, *Seneca*, an intrepid Resolution, join'd to a virtuous Inclination, will make a Man happy, in spite of all Misfortunes.

FINIS

NOTES

[1] *Shelves:* 'A sandbank in the sea or river rendering the water shallow and dangerous . . . very common till *c.* 1750' also fig. (cf. OED). *Prevent :* here 'to get in anticipation of'.

[2] *Andronicus* is here introduced as a *deus ex machina*, with no further explanation: obviously he is a friend of Alexis and could be identical with Antigonus.

The Polite Correspondence:
or Rational Amusement

Being A Series of Letters, Philosophical, Poetical, Historical, Critical, Amorous, Moral and Satyrical. (London, 1740?, Book I, pp. 1-81)

The Polite Correspondence:
or Rational Amusement

During the early part of *The Polite Correspondence* we do not quite know what is going on, what Florimond is talking about, who the correspondents are, and why they are writing to each other. Many epistolary novels which start off in the middle of a correspondence present us with similar problems, applying the old *in medias res* technique to a new form of narrative particularly suited to it. There is no omniscient narrator introducing the characters to the reader in the way Fielding does; gradually we become acquainted with Florimond, Emelia, and Eliza, later with Hypolytus, gradually we come to know their circumstances and relationships. Florimond we quickly recognise as the ideal lover, melancholy at times, full of pathos, still very much the romantic hero. It is Emelia with her good humour and her common sense who makes us realise that he is taking himself a bit too seriously. Sometimes she is mildly ironical with him, sometimes, when he is in despair, she appeals to his reason or tries to raise his spirits with a humorous tale; in her slightly detached way she displays both love and understanding for him. Eliza, her cousin, is a similarly resolute girl who, however, lacks Emelia's sense of humour. Florimond adores Eliza even more than his Emelia. Hypolytus, who figures in the dènouement, plays the rôle of the loyal and helpful friend.

The story itself is in no way original: two couples, Florimond and Emelia, Phaon and Eliza, are frustrated in their love by parental opposition. Emelia's parents fancy a son-in-law of greater fortune and nobler descent, and Eliza's father actually manages to banish the unwanted suitor from his daughter's presence. The two girls stand firmly by their lovers, though they are kept in confinement and can correspond only with the greatest difficulty. In the end, however, all misunderstandings and conflicts are happily resolved and marriage puts an end to the lovers' trials. What makes the first book of *The Polite Correspondence* one of the best epistolary novels before Richardson is the way it is written: differentiation in style is used to characterise the correspondents; an occasional witty and lively conversation takes place between them; the tone is humorous and detached, and slight touches of domestic background are included. All these are movements towards a greater realism, foreshadowing Fanny Burney and Jane Austen.

This novel, attributed to John Campbell, has already moved some distance beyond the romantic tale such as *The Constant Lovers* or even *The Love Letters Between a Nobleman and his Sister* (though it uses much the same material). Interestingly enough, the author takes a critical view of heroic and scandalous novels. Florimond refers to them as monstrous exaggerations. Emelia's story of Elvira and the faithless Alonzo who had imagined themselves to be ideal lovers illustrates the unreality of such prefabricated ideas of love. This piece of literary theorising within the novel is symptomatic of a trend at the beginning of the eighteenth century when the novel was passing through a stage of experimentation. The author, who was widely read in contemporary fiction – as indicated by his reference to the Countess D'Anois and Mme du Noyer, both authors of epistolary fiction – does however not quite succeed in avoiding the pitfalls he so clearly discerned in the works of others.

Only the first book of *The Polite Correspondence* is interesting as a novel. The five other books which followed suffer from the fact that after the two couples have been married off nothing exciting happens; moreover, the novel begins to fall to pieces as the circle of correspondents is enlarged. The letters become no more than a framework for all sorts of digressions, travel stories, short tales, and reflections on various topics. The author is unable to sustain his narrative technique throughout the correspondence.

BOOK I

LETTER I
FLORIMOND *to* EMELIA

Fair One,

If you meant last Night to be extremely malicious, you certainly succeeded; you distinguished yourself by severe Reflections on our Sex, and you distinguished me by pointing all those Reflections against a very trivial Expression, which drop'd from me by Chance. Well, Madam, you railed at Men, but I don't believe Mankind are much affected with it; you have mortified your Admirer, meerly because he is so, is not this playing the Tyrant? They say the late Emperor of *Morocco* used to threaten all the Princes of *Europe*, but they did not much regard it, because they were out of his Reach; but when he threatened his Slaves they trembled like me, because they were at the Tyrant's Mercy.

You twice mention'd *Alonzo* to that most humane Lady, who put you upon declaiming; shall I ask you who that *Alonzo* was? Perhaps some Tale hangs by it, not unlike that which the Spectator tells us of *Yarico* and *Inkle*;[1] but grant it so, or worse, it only proves that there are Monsters among Men, and not that Men are Monsters. You may doubtless, if you will ransack all your Novels and Romances, pick up a hundred Instances of Falshood, Treachery, and Baseness; but of what Use they will be to you when they are pick'd up I cannot say, unless it should be to encourage you in the laudable Project of either turning Nun Abroad, or living an old Maid at Home.

Believe me, Madam, Men of Honour think as contemptibly of bad Men, as any of you can do; they scorn to undertake their Defence, and therefore it is Cruelty to upbraid them with Stories of their Misdeeds; their Faults regard not them, why then should their Punishment? That they are Men as well as we, is true; but that we are as bad as they, for that very Reason, would be an odd Inference.

> Tho' Man to Man must ever be ally'd,
> As of one Mass alike in Birth and Death;
> Still, in their Worth, Men differ much from Men.
> So of one Matter Stones are all compos'd,
> Yet on the Gravel with Contempt we tread;
> While Diamonds glitter on the Brows of Kings.
> Be it your Pride still to distinguish Worth,
> And mine, to aim at Worth, that you may prize.

Your faithful
FLORIMOND

St. *Edmonds-Bury*,
  Tuesday Evening

LETTER II

To FLORIMOND

Good Grave Sir,

I Have read your Epistle, which is indeed a very moral and a very rational Discourse; only methinks it is a little too solemn, considering the Subject was a Woman's Wit. I grant you that I was a little malicious, and that it is fit you should know something of the Story of *Alonzo*; I wou'd fain put you in good Humour, if I could; and therefore I will first tell you the Tale, and then say a Word or two of the Occasion of it.

Last Summer, there was a fine Gentleman from *London* lodg'd in our Neighbourhood; by Degrees he became known to several Families here-abouts, and among the rest to a Clergyman's of my Acquaintance. The Doctor's eldest Daughter was a Wit, she had read whole Shelves full of Romances, spelt better than most of her Sex, and ventur'd now and then to make Verses; our *Londoner*, whose Taste turn'd the same Way, was mightily smitten with her. To cut my Story short, an Amour was com-menc'd, Billets passed between them, which were sign'd by him *Alonzo*, and by her *Elvira*; one of them fell into her Father's Hands, who show'd it to my Mother, and as Women are communicative, myself and that humane Lady, as you call her, got a Sight of it; it's ending I shall never forget, thus it ran:

Our Fondness, sweet One, shall at length become
Love's Standard; so that future Folks shall say,
When they wou'd paint a Passion pure and bright,
They're faithful as *Alonzo* and *Elvira*.

The Doctor, who, it seems, did not understand this sort of Preaching,
sent his Daughter into *Oxfordshire*, upon which *Alonzo* fell so ill, that his
Relations thought proper to send for him up to *London*; but my Brother
who is come from thence last Week informs me, that by the Help of the
Town Air, and the Town Diversions, he recover'd so effectually in six
Weeks, that he compleated a Match his Mother had made for him, with a
rich *Haberdasher's* Daughter he had never seen till he came to Town; and
this without the least Enquiry after *Elvira*, or his Mother's Handmaid
Susanna, with whom he wou'd certainly have contracted Matrimony, if he
had not been happily banished into our Part of *Suffolk*.

This, *Florimond*, is the Story of *Alonzo*, in which I believe you will see
nothing shining or uncommon; nothing of the Wonderful that *Eliza* tells
me was in the Story of the *North British* Lady, who died so strangely on her
Wedding Night; which with a sober Face, and a Train of curious Circumstances, you were pleased to tell at our Tea-Table, the Day I went with my
Aunt to *Cambridge*. Indeed, Sir, it had a mighty happy Effect, the whole
Family was full of it when I came Home, and old Nurse began to tell it with
Tears, when she went to conduct us to Bed; what View you had in frighting
so many innocent Females I know not, but supposing myself some way
concern'd, I confess my Intention to mortify, t'other Night. I wou'd not
hear your Story from Nurse or *Harriot*, so write it as you dread the Frown

Of your Tyrant,
EMELIA

P.S.   How well your Lines describe a Woman's Life,
      Unwed a Gem, a Pebble when a Wife!

LETTER III

FLORIMOND *to* EMELIA

Fair One,

IN Love and in Loyalty, Obedience is always the best Expression of
Duty; I shall therefore send you the Story you are pleased to treat me so
severely upon, and, in spite of your Raillery, am very well pleased you
would not receive it from another Hand. Your hopeful Cousin, who is
always doing me one good Turn or other, introduced a Discourse of the
unlucky Consequences which sometimes attended Breaches of Faith in
Love; I am now persuaded she did it maliciously, but at that Time look'd

upon it as an innocent and casual Topick, on which it is very possible I might talk with more than usual Warmth.

> Words of themselves with easy Current flow,
> When we discourse of Things that well we know.
> But when the Heart impels 'tis then they run,
> Like Torrents over Mountains rolling down,
> Where much of Haste and Little Judgment's shown.

After this short Excuse, perhaps you will think my Tale not so absurd; and as to its being incredible, all I can say of it is, that I had it from the Mouth of a Gentleman of great Worth and Honour, who would not have uttered a Falsehood knowingly, as he must have done if this had been so. A Lady in *Scotland*, of a great Family, had, with the Consent of her Relations, promised Marriage to a Gentleman of equal Birth, and afterwards for Reasons best known to herself broke her Promise, which I conceive was not much for her Reputation, and thereby broke his Heart; such is the Force of manly Passion! Some Years afterwards, the Lady made a second Promise, which, to shew she would not be true even to Inconstancy, she kept; the Wedding was celebrated at her Father's House, who entertained his own and the Bridegroom's Relations, in a Dining Room under the Nuptial Bed-chamber; when Night was come, and the married Pair were put to Bed, the Company returned to this Dining Room, disposed to continue their Mirth for some Hours; long they had not been there, before a great Noise was heard above; for some Time the Lady's Father would not suffer any Body to go up, but it encreasing, himself and another Gentleman went to the Chamber Door, and receiving no Answer on repeated Calls to the Bridegroom, they broke open the Door; then it was they discover'd the most dismal Spectacle that can be imagin'd, the young Gentleman in strong Convulsions on the Floor, the Lady sitting up in her Bed with her Head leaning on her Arm, but without Life, and almost without Heat. This, Madam, is the Story as I heard it without Exaggeration, and leave you to judge how applicable it was to the Subject talk'd of, and what Right I had to bring it in.

You will forgive me, Madam, if, after so melancholly a Relation, I conclude this Letter somewhat more gravely than usual. Marriage is a very serious Thing, and I never knew any Body trifle with it, without finding Cause to repent such a Conduct: This is the true Reason why I cannot be so gay as perhaps some other of your Admirers; but this I hope will not draw either my Sincerity, or my good Nature into Question; the former is seldom pointed out by laughing, and the latter, when attended with Levity, is not so much a good Quality as a Weakness. This I know, that in all Tempers I am, and always shall be, *Your devoted Servant,*
FLORIMOND

LETTER IV

EMELIA *to* FLORIMOND

My sober Lover,

I HAVE receiv'd and read with great Edification your last Epistle; but as you are a Man of Verse, I wonder you did not digest it into a Ballad, under the Title of, *The broken Vow, or the false Lady's Fall*,[2] To the Tune of *Aim not too high, Grim King of the Ghost*,[3] or, *The Children in the Wood*.[4] But now I think on't, Mr. *Dryden* has a Tale to this Purpose, and a very moving one it is;[5] so you chose to write in Prose, to avoid contending with so great a Master. Indeed you are very modest, for had you gone about it, I am verily persuaded you wou'd have out-done him, at least in Moral Reflections.

> For when the Heart the Tongue doth teach,
> Then we with mighty Success preach;
> Conjure up good old Womens Fears,
> Till out they burst in Sighs and Tears.

I protest I am so affected with your Story, that I think I could attempt something myself in the same Taste, if *William* and *Margaret*[6] did not stand in my Way. Besides, there's the old Ballad of *The wand'ring Prince of* Troy,[7] and *Patient Grizzel*,[8] tho' as to any Thing in Prose, as solemn and as well attested as your Relation, I confess I know not where to meet with it; but assure you I will most industriously enquire for such a one among all the ancient Ladies of my own and my Mother's Acquaintance; I did but mention my Mother, and here she is.

You Lovers are a sort of Fools, always unlucky in your Prophecies; here is some Mischief brewing in the Family, but I know not what; Mamma has made me a tedious Sermon on Decorum, Quality, and what she calls laudable Ambition. What she aims at I cannot with all my Penetration discover; but this I am convinced of, that it bodes us no Good; for she told me she would persuade my Father not to go to your Uncle's in the Holidays as he promised, but I believe that will be a hard Task; for as our old Gentleman seldom gives his Word, so I never knew him break it.

It is very possible I may not have an Opportunity of writing to you again in haste, I mean directly; for I shall always find a Method of corresponding, by a Way you little thought of, that is, by the Means of my hopeful Cousin as you call her; she is so far from being your Enemy, that she is the only Person I can trust in this Affair, and never rallied you with any other View than to make your Sincerity more apparent. See, Sir, another Stroke of Female Politics, and rest satisfied that Women are inscrutable. As to that, you may think it as long as you please; but as to Female Sincerity, I don't know what to say, methinks I would not have you entertain any Doubt about it; if I were in better Temper, perhaps I should give you some Reasons; as it is, believe it for the Sake of,   EMELIA

LETTER V

FLORIMOND *to* EMELIA

Mistress of my Heart,

I HAVE always admired, however charming your Person, the Perfections of your Mind, rather than that Bloom of Beauty which may be in the Power of Accident, and must feel that of Age; but your Conduct and that of your Cousin's, have, as you judiciously remark, given me such an Idea of Female Policy, that to speak ingeniously, sets it above another kind of Policy that I am acquainted with; for if to be always successful, if always to surprize, if to penetrate all Things, and to remain undiscovered by all Persons, constitute true Policy, then to me it would not seem strange, if all the Empires of the Earth were govern'd by Women; and perhaps, if the Curtains of all Cabinets were drawn, it might not prove more strange than true.

The Steadiness you express, and the Assurances given me by your Cousin, leave me nothing to fear, but that ill Fortune may oppress so many good Qualities; and that, while I admire their Beauty, I may be driven to deplore the Occasion of seeing them display'd. I am led to these grave Reflections by an Accident that has happen'd, not only within the Compass of my Knowledge, but almost under my Eye. There lives in this Neighbourhood a Lady almost as accomplish'd as yourself, and not above three Years older; she is the Wife of a Gentleman of Distinction, and the Daughter of a Man, who, when living, was of still greater Distinction. Her Husband, who is not less sensible, or less good natur'd than young Gentlemen usually are, hath lately taken it into his Head to keep a Mistress, and to keep her with *Eclat*, a Woman inferior to his Wife in Person, in Temper, and in good Sense; but she abounds with that sort of intemperate Wit which becomes Ladies of her Profession, and which has captivated this unhappy young Man, in a Manner which differs little from what the common People call Witchcraft.

Under this Misfortune, and sure a greater could not well happen, *Sophronia*, so I chuse to call his Wife, behaves with a Discretion which charms all the World, and surprizes even her nearest Relations; perhaps I cannot paint her Conduct better than by repeating what a Libertine, who is one of her Husband's Companions, said of her, *The Woman is so very good, that she may place the Man in the worse Light.* It is impossible for me to tell you what a Noise this Affair makes, or how great a Reputation *Sophronia* has obtain'd, by what would have lessen'd a Woman's Character who had fallen short of her in Prudence. At another Time perhaps I should have been cautious of telling you such a Story; but I fancy we have done with Raillery, and my Heart is so full of my own Affairs, that I should have wrote you a very dull Epistle, if this Episode had not fallen in my Way. May that Providence which delights in Innocence, and is never deficient in protecting Virtue, watch over you in all your Actions, and prevent you from suffering by the ill Qualities of others, as I am confident you will never be in Danger from any Errors of your own. Forgive this Solemnity, which is the Effect of that Sincerity wherewith I am, and shall be,

Ever yours,
FLORIMOND

LETTER VI
EMELIA *to* FLORIMOND

My sober Lover,

THE great Mystery is at length come out, and I can write you now a full and true Account of Mamma's prudent Circumspection, and of her saucy Daughter's Folly and Obstinacy. You must know, that in the next Street there lodges a Baronet, and his eldest Son and Heir, the young Gentlemen every Body agrees hath a good Person, and better Sense; but the Father is said to be deficient in all kind of Knowledge, except what relates to the Respect due to his Title, which no Body in the *Heralds-Office* knows so well. To support the Grandeur of his Family, he has lessen'd very considerably his paternal Estate; and it is proposed that my Father shall Mortgage his, in order to increase my Fortune, so as to render me a proper Match for his Son: This is the Scheme form'd by my Mother, in Concert with the Knight's House-keeper. Don't fall into your Raptures again about Female Policy, nor into Despair, least this Scheme, silly as it is, should take Effect; but have the Goodness to appear indifferent, and for once to disguise your Temper, hereafter I will assign you my Reasons; at present I have a Right to Obedience, and therefore I say dissemble, because it is my Will.

I am oblig'd to you for your News, because among other Precautions, Mamma has interdicted going abroad, for how long a Time I know not; I have since heard the same Tale from another Hand. Well, *Sophronia* is a wiser Woman than I, and bears with Patience what I am persuaded would go near to deprive me of mine; shall I tell you my Sentiments freely, *Florimond*? Perhaps *Sophronia* was too Prudent. I fancy that Men are not always charm'd with these regular Ladies, who move like the Spheres harmoniously indeed, but by Rules incomprehensible to common Understandings; who are so long in their Closets, so long at their Toilet, sit so long after Dinner, and, in short, are at every Thing so long and no longer. Variety is always pleasing, and for my Part I the less wonder at the Giddiness of *Sophronia*'s Husband, when I consider how tedious the Motions of my regular Aunt have seemed to myself. If you will trust me, *Florimond*, this Sameness in Conduct is meer Affectation, or else springs from a Deficiency of good Sense, which puts a Woman on supplying that by Habit which she wants in Abilities, if the Furniture of a Female Mind may be honour'd with that Name.

The Character, you give the Enchantress, makes my Conjecture the more probable; for what besides the Inclination of seeing something more than the same Thing over again could induce a Man to leave a Woman of Virtue, for a Woman void even of its Appearance. It was certainly a wrong and a precipitate Choice; but, *Florimond*, let us avoid the Rock upon which others strike, and rather bear with the Frailties incident even to the best Natures, than attempt by a studied Disguise, to appear Persons without Failings, *a faultless Monster which the World ne'er saw*, as one of your favourite Writers expresses it; at least this is the Sentiment of

EMELIA

P.S. To divert you a little (for you must know I have the Vanity to think you are melancholy) I send you the following Verses written on my Cousin's Birth-Day, by her Admirer *Phaon*, who is said to have a good Vein in Poetry.

To ELIZA *on her* BIRTH-DAY

An ODE

I

Hear, Heaven, on this propitious Day!
O hear! and on the Nymph bestow
Whate'er may make her bless'd and gay,
For whom my Verse and Wishes flow.

II

Let ev'ry Morn of her dear Life
Be mild and fair, and bright as she;
Free from all Clouds of Care or Strife,
And sweet to her as she to me.

III

Long let Mankind her Charms admire,
And longer still her Virtues prize;
Late may her Seraph Soul retire,
To join its kindred in the Skies.

IV

For me, whose only boast is Love.
O grant me leisure to adore!
Let Time, our mutual Flames improve,
Compleatly bless'd, I ask no more.

V

Be Wealth, on Citizens bestow'd,
To Soldiers, grant a deathless Name,
Let *STATESMEN*, shake of Envy's Load,
And rise in Power, and rise in Fame.

VI

Unmov'd, in their superior Spheres,
I shall, these mighty great Ones see;
Nor warm'd with Hopes, nor chill'd with Fears,
Who *LOVES*, from other Cares is free.

LETTER VIII

FLORIMOND *to* EMELIA

Charming Woman,

THE Desire I have, rather to amuse your Melancholy than to increase it, engages me to be more assiduous in picking up little Stories to divert you, than would otherwise become me. A spreader of Scandal is a detestable Character; yet to moralize on the Incidents in private Life, is just and reasonable. But to put off Reflections and come to my Tale.

Torquatus, is a Man of Title, Family and Fortune, he is said, to have a solid Understanding, and therewith a great deal of good Nature. He married lately *Melissa*, the Sister of a Man of Quality, a Woman of Sense, Spirit and obliging Behaviour. Their might not be much Love in their coming together; but it was a matrimonial Bargain of the best Sort. *Torquatus* was ambitious of being ally'd to a Peer; *Melissa* found no Fault with his Person; her Brother, and his Lawyers, were satisfied with his Rent Roll, and Settlements. All this took up Time; but at last they were join'd in Wedlock.

The Honey-Moon is not yet over, or to speak more properly, ought not to be over, even according to common Forms; and yet *Torquatus* is out of the Kingdom, and *Melissa* a kind of a single Woman again. Would you know the Cause? Then you must be wiser than the Parties themselves, for they know it not. *Torquatus* took it into his Head to Marry, and he did it. *Torquatus* had a fancy to leave his Wife, and so he did. But *Torquatus* married and unmarried, like a Man of Honour. His Settlement was fair, his seperate Allowance generous. *Melissa* is not very uneasy; she lives like a Woman of Quality, at ease and at large; and while her Honour is unstained, and her Fortune unabridged, hath no Notion of being unhappy.

I was going to make some of my grave Observations, when I received yours. But alas! those Observations are no more, I have no Will, no Understanding but for our own Affairs, and am so effectually puzzled by them, that I have not the least Leisure to judge of other Peoples. Hitherto I approve your Conduct, and am sorry that you would put me upon such a Conduct as I can never approve. You bid me dissemble; I do not question but you have Reasons, but whatever Dissimulation may produce in female Politics, I never knew it do any Thing but Mischief amongst us Men. I could tell you that there is nothing in its own Nature more hateful than this Quality; I could prove to you, that there is nothing more delusive than the hopes raised therefrom. I could shew you from various Instances, that in public and private Life, it is equally scandalous and pernicious. Yet I am afraid I shall obey.

But remember, Madam, you bid me dissemble; it was well you did not bid me Murder, or Fire a House; either would have been as just and reasonable, and I might do either with as safe a Conscience; but to what purpose do I torment myself and you: When did any Thing but Experience convince a Lady that she was in the Wrong. Shield me Providence from being in the Right when I say this.

> O Woman, Woman! how extreme thy Power!
> How weak our Reason in the Love-sick Hour!
> In vain we think, in vain we strive to act,
> What Reason dictates, Passion will retract:
> Against our Wills, we own our lawless sway,
> Distrust your Sense, but dare not disobey.

In what I shall ever remain,
Your faithful
FLORIMOND

LETTER VIII

ELIZA *to* FLORIMOND

Constant Lover,

MY dear Cousin *Emelia* being abridged of her Freedom, affords me this Opportunity of entring into a Correspondence with a Man whom I infinitely esteem. You will wonder at this Declaration, considering the Plague I have formerly given you. But know good *Florimond*, that nothing pleases a Woman so well as to see a Man of Sense play the Fool for her Sake. We know that you are superior to us in Sense, and we are glad of shewing that there is something in us, which can more than Ballance that Superiority. By this Time, I dare say, you forgive my Raillery, and since it has been a Means of fixing the Affection of *Emelia*, I flatter myself, I have merited your Friendship, as well as extinguish'd your Spleen.

Emelia tells me, that she sent you some Verses upon my Birth-day. The Verses have Merit, tho' I have none; I will make you acquainted with their Author, and with my own Story, which 'till this Time, I dare say, you have never heard. I am unfortunate, because my Father is not so. He was once in Trade, and having got wherewith to purchase a good Estate, hath Insured his Felicity in spite of the fickle Goddess, and is now for Life, a Gentleman of *Suffolk*. My Lover's Father was a Merchant, and once much richer than my Father. In those Days it was thought a Condescention in him to propose a Marriage between *Phaon* and Me. It was purely the Effect of that Friendship for my Parent, and of which he gave another extraordinary Instance, in making him his Executor, and Guardian to his Son. He was thought to die worth half a Plumb; but his Banker going off the Week after, and his Correspondent in *Italy* proving Insolvent, the Affairs of the Family are in much Confusion. When they are settled, *Phaon* and I shall know our Destinies. For my Father is too much a Man of this Age, to think that Merit can subsist without Money. To prevent his Daughter's Fondness from getting the better of his Prudence, he has sent *Phaon* to *Leghorn*, under Pretence of looking after his Father's Concerns; but in Truth, that he may be out of my Sight.

The young Man inherits the Candor and noble Spirit of his Father; he has too much Discernment not to penetrate my old Man's Projects, and yet he always defends his Proceedings, that he may not seem to suspect his Father's Friend. For me, knowing well, that I am to be disposed of according to the Ballance of the Account, I put on a false Gaiety in my Lover's Absence, that the old Gentleman may be in no haste to rid himself of me, before his Return. You see *Florimond*, a naked Description of our Circumstances; judge you, whether they are worse or better than your own. You see the Foibles of our Parents, are the Source of our Misfortunes; but alas! that do's not dissolve the Ties of Duty: Nature, in having made us their Children, hath left us no other Weapons, than innocent Precautions, fervent Prayers, and honourable Resolution. They cannot sure, have a right to make us miserable, any more than we have a right to make ourselves happy, without their Consent.

See, *Florimond*! how little in this World, must be trusted to Out-side; *Eliza*, to all who converse with her, is the gayest of giddy Girls, and this, with a Load of Care at her Heart; her Wildness screens her from the Addresses of the Men, and from the Jealouses of the Women, and all the World esteems her Happy in an Inconstancy of Temper, which nothing but Constancy could produce. *Emelia* has just sent me a Letter which I inclose, and a Message which I must immediately obey. Excuse the Abruptness of my Conclusion, and believe that you have a sincere Friend, in,

ELIZA

LETTER IX

EMELIA *to* FLORIMOND

Disconsolate Lover,

OUR Affairs go worse and worse. My Father is a better Husband, and at the same Time not so good a Friend as I thought him. This Morning he has written to your Uncle to excuse his coming for the Holidays to your House in *Suffolk*. The Pretence, is a bad State of Health; but if I had written the Letter, I should have ascribed it to weakness of Mind. Bless me! can a Man who spends all the Morning in his Study, who can read *Greek*, has travelled over the greatest Part of *Europe*, and had a Seat in Parliament these twenty Years, be worded out of his Promise by a Woman? But hold! I forgot, this Man is my Father, and this Woman my Mother. Well! we are apt to forget all Things when the Mind is occupy'd by any darling Passion. But to be Wise a little, since our Concerns need it. By this Specimen, I guess, that my Papa will discover Justice and Reason, in whatever his Wife shall propose to him. He has hitherto indeed, highly approved the Proposals made by your Uncle; and it was on that, I chiefly depended. All I now hope is, that if upon this breach of Promise you appear cool, he may apprehend the Danger of losing what he once thought a good Match, for the meer View of One which he cannot be sure will prove a good one. – I have another Project in my Head; but I hear my Mother coming up Stairs.

We have had but a short Conversation; she has seen the young Gentleman she would have me Marry, and is so charm'd with him, that if she were a young Woman, I dare say, we should be out of our Pain. But to deal freely with you, she is not more pleased with his Person, than I am with his Behaviour. He talk'd to her very cooly of the Affair, said, that Marriage was a Matter of great Importance, that Concerns of another Nature, took up his Thoughts at present, and that it would be sometime before she should have leisure to think of settling in the World. Well! my Mother's hopes are now centred in me. My Beauty forsooth! is to thaw this frozen Spark, and the better to enable me to make this Conquest, O' my Conscience, I believe the good old Lady would dispense with a little Paint, and take the Trouble of laying it on her self. Mr. *Tinkle* is to come in the Morning and put the Spinnet in order; the Servants are cleaning the Plate, three Dozen of Wine have been taken out of her Ladyship's private Cellar, and all the other necessary Precautions have been used to catch the 'Squire, who is to Sup here to-morrow Night.

Tell me, *Florimond*! do's not your Heart ache? have you no Suspicions of my turning Coquette? Do you really think there can be such a Thing as Constancy with a Cap on? – But if I should prove false, you know the *Scotch* Story gives you hope of Revenge. In Truth this is barbarous; but this Gaiety of mine, like Oil mix'd with Vinegar, will every now and then be getting uppermost. Be satisfied, however, I have sent for *Eliza*, we will consult together, what is best to be done, and be assured, that nothing shall give you any lasting Uneasiness, which can be prevented by,

EMELIA

LETTER X
FLORIMOND *to* ELIZA

Excellent Woman,

IT is impossible for me to express how well pleased I am at the Detection of my own Mistake, in looking upon you as a downright Hoyden,[9] full of Mirth and Gaiety, and altogether a Stranger to that steadiness of Temper, for which now I know you better; I do, and must ever Admire you. How happy is *Phaon*, in having fix'd his Affections on so amiable, so worthy an Object! and how well do's his Virtue deserve, so great, so invaluable a Reward.

I am extremely obliged to you for sending me your own Story. It puts me in Mind of one that I heard some Years ago from the Mouth of a *Turkey* Merchant, who knew every Incident of it to be true. There was a Merchant, who for Distinction Sake, we will call *Honorius*, who before the Restoration, had acquired a very considerable Estate in Trade. This by an unaccountable Fatality, he vested for the most part in Houses, which brought him in a very considerable Revenue, and thereby establish'd his Reputation for Wealth, higher than it ought to have been. He was Guardian to a young Gentleman, the Son of a Person who had been once his Partner; and this young Man whom we will stile *Myrtillo*, was bred up in the full Expectation of marrying *Honoria*, the Merchant's only Daughter. But in process of Time, the Father affecting rather to match her with a Peer, sent *Myrtillo* to his Uncle in the *Indies*. The Year after, came the Fire of *London*, which swept away the Merchant's Houses, and his Hopes, and left him in such Circumstances, that he was obliged to take up a *Coffee-House*, to avoid going to an *Almshouse*: Three Years past in this Way; and *Honoria*, now about eighteen, had the chief Management of her Papa's little Concerns. It happen'd one Day, that a Stranger call'd twice for Coffee: *Honoria*, who was making it, trembled at the Voice, she knew not why. Going to present it to the Gentleman, she fell backwards on the Floor, at the same Instant that he tumbled from his Chair. The Father came running at the Noise, and with great Amazement, saw *Myrtillo* and *Honoria*, pale and breathless. Proper Application soon brought them to themselves. Time and Absence had made no Impression on the Lover's Constancy, and his Flame was rather heightned, than abated by *Honorius*'s Reverse of Fortune. His Uncle had left him an immense Estate, which yet he thought too small a Present for the fair *Honoria*. They lived many Years happily together, and there are still some Gentlemen living, who remember both the Gentleman and the Lady.

You will certainly think me an odd Fellow when you perceive my first Letter fill'd with a melancholy Story; but alass! our Memories are generally subservient to our Inclinations, when we are full of Mirth and in high Spirits, we call to Mind a number of gay and pleasant Stories, which have slumber'd perhaps for many Years. When again the Spirits flag, and the Soul finds herself diseased, the Memory sympathizing with the troubled Imagination, sooths our Melancholy with Tales like this. Indeed *Eliza*, I begin to feel so strong, so irresistable a Gloominess o'er spread my Thoughts, that I think I cannot make you a greater Compliment, than to bid you adieu. I have inclosed however a little Poem, to make amends for the dulness of my Prose, which will not, I hope, lessen your Regard for him who is with Zeal and Esteem

Yours,

FLORIMOND

SONG *to* EMELIA

To See! See! my *Seraphina* comes

You bid me Fair, conceal my Love,
Ah! Think how hard the Task;
Think of the mighty Pains I prove,
Then think of what you ask.

Go bid the fev'rish Wretch forbear,
'Midst Burnings to complain;
Go bid the Slaves who fetter'd are,
Forget the galling Chain.

Shou'd they obey, yet greater far
The Torments which I feel;
Love's Fires than Fevers fiercer are,
Love pierces more than Steel.

Pain but the Body can controul,
The Toughts no Cord can bind;
Love is a Fever in the Soul
A Chain which holds the Mind.

LETTER XI

FLORIMOND *to* EMELIA

Sole Object of my Thoughts,

I HAVE read over and over your last Favour, sometimes with the Passion of a Lover, and sometimes with a Portion of that Discretion which I possessed before I was honour'd with that Name. You must therefore expect a Mixture of Passion and Prudence in this Epistle, the Intent of which is to tell you, that I am not more charm'd with your Kindness and Constancy, than I am amazed and confounded at the Nature of your Projects.

Your Mother must certainly desire to see you happy, and your Father, tho' he may suffer his good Sense to give Way sometimes to his Fondness, can never sacrifice his Paternal Affections, either to his Tenderness or Respect for his Wife. Would it not then be the most natural Method to try to reclaim the old Lady, and if we prove unsuccessful there, to endeavour the undeceiving your Papa? Is not your Happiness theirs? Or rather, is it not their own Happiness they seek in disposing of you? Are not mine, and my Uncle's Intentions fix'd on the same End, and after a little Altercation, is it reasonable to suppose, that People who agree so well in the main Design, should be irreconcileable about the Means?

Thus far I have follow'd the Dictates of my Understanding; and tho' that tells me I can never err, more than in offering to sacrifice it; yet after all, I yield entirely to your Pleasure, tho' I shou'd be glad when you honour me with your Commands, you wou'd favour me also with their Reasons. Even absolute Princes, who do not affect to be thought Tyrants, condescend sometimes to acquaint their Subjects with the Motives whereon they act, especially when those Subjects give them the strongest Proofs of Loyalty, and receive those Things as Acts of Grace, which among a freer People would pass for meer Matter of Right.

I had almost forgot to tell you, that I have written a strange Letter to *Eliza*, wherein I have absolutely forgot to thank her for the good Advice, which I dare say, she gave you at your last Consultation. Let me intreat you to supply this Omission, and to assure her, that when I write next, there shall be less of Distraction, and more of Amusement in my Epistle; but then you must let me hear good News from you. I say, this alass! as if Events were in your Power, which however from one, who knows nothing without it, is an excusable Error. A Coach has just stopt at the Door, and therefore I can only add what I have told you a thousand Times already, that I am,

Yours without Reserve,
FLORIMOND

P.S. I open my Letter again to tell you, that the Person who call'd just now was my Friend *Hypolytus*, who is intimately acquainted with my new Rival. He says, that as the Gentleman is descended of a very ancient and honourable Family, so he has receiv'd from Nature an agreeable Person, and from an excellent Education, all the Advantages which Art can bestow. You see *Emelia*, how well placed your Raillery was in your last; you see how ready I am to be jealous, and how troublesome I am like to be to you on that Head.

See Madam, a Sketch of my Politics. From the Character I have receiv'd of my Rival from *Hypolytus*, I depend no less upon him than upon you. It is impossible that a Man of Birth, of Honour, and of good Sense, can be capable of doing a base Thing; I know that I wou'd not do it to another, how then shall I justify suspecting it from a Man better than my self? No, *Emelia*, I will never be persuaded that a Gentleman of his Distinction, will in a Point of the greatest Importance, lay aside all Sense of Reputation, and in an Affair which so nearly concerns his own Peace, begin with breaking the Peace of those who never wish'd him ill.

LETTER XII

ELIZA *to* FLORIMOND

Much esteem'd Friend,

YOU will think when you have read this, that some ill Spirits have been lately abroad in *Suffolk*, and breath'd into its Inhabitants a Spirit of Discord and Confusion. I am at the writing of this a Prisoner in a Chamber three Story high, where my Father has confin'd me for fear I should run away – with his Footboy. You must know *Florimond*, that this Lad is my Nurse's Son, and she the Daughter of the Curate of the next Parish; on this Account I had a great Kindness for him, and used to intrust him to fetch and carry my Letters to and from the Post-House; on this Account I spoke to him oftner perhaps than I should otherwise have done, tho' I dare say, not in kinder Language; for having always had a kind Affection, or rather a Duty for his Mother, I could not but have a proportionable Concern for him.

In our Family you must understand, the supreme Person is a *French* Lady, who, for her eminent preciseness, was recommended to my Papa to be a kind of upper House-keeper; she has been with us now a Twelvemonth, and in that Time has discarded every Servant, except my Father's Man, and this Footboy. This good old Woman having seen me give the Boy two or three Times Money, and not perfectly understanding some Questions he ask'd my Maid, went to my Father with a circumstantial Account of my intending to dishonour his Family. The old Gentleman therupon went directly to my Chamber, and breaking open a little travelling Desk, found therein a Letter, which I had begun to my poor *Phaon*; happily for me there was no mention of his Name; however, it confirm'd my Father in his Suspicion, or rather gave Credit to *Madamoiselle*'s, whereupon my Maid was remov'd, and I conducted to her Room, where I am guarded like a State Prisoner; but having the Happiness to be upon good Terms with the Servants, I have procured Pen, Ink and Paper, that I might write to *Emelia*, and to you, knowing you might otherwise be very uneasy.

What the Issue of this Affair will be I know not, at present I am very easy; my Room is large and pleasant, I have some Books, no ill Company, and which is sufficient to make me happy any where, Innocence and a contented Mind. When my Father has considered my Conduct and his own attentively, I persuade my self he will see nothing amiss in the former, and nothing well founded in the latter, should it prove otherwise I am prepared. I have practised for several Years a Thoughtlessness, which I always despise, and am determin'd from this Moment to resume my natural Temper; so that whatever I lose any other Way, I shall certainly be a Gainer in point of Ease, since a continued Dissimulation is a kind of Rack, which an ingenious Mind can scarce bear with Patience.

This will be deliver'd to you by one of my Father's Servants, with whom you may safely trust an Answer. I should be glad to have a Letter in a more composed Stile than your last, not for my Sake, who am really sooth'd with melancholy Things, but for your own. I thank you for your Song, which pleased me extremely; in Return, I send you a little Piece written by *Phaon*; it was well I had it by Heart, for at present I have not the Possession of my Papers, tho' I have the Satisfaction too of knowing, that my Father can never be possessed of them, since they are out of the Sight, Reach, and Knowledge, of every Body but myself. Adieu *Florimond*, believe you will never want a sincere Friend while there lives,

ELIZA

The BRACELET

THIS Bracelet tho' no gaudy Thing,
Did from a Parent's Labour spring.
She wove it irksome Thoughts to charm,
And thenceforth wore it on her Arm.

Dying, to me, this Gift she gave,
That I might a Remembrance have,
Of her, – when I it saw, – and take,
A pleasing Sorrow, – for her Sake.

My Son, said she with falt'ring Breath.
You see me yielding unto Death,
This, my last Present, take and keep,
'Till thus like me – in Peace you sleep.

This Favour shall I give away?
Let filial Piety say – Nay.
But 'tis no Gift, when sent to thee,
Who art the noblest part of me.
Yet as a Gift, my fair One view,
It most I prize – and give it you.

LETTER XIII

EMELIA *to* FLORIMOND

Despairing Swain,

I Fancy you will now be of Opinion, that Women best understand Women. My Father sent for me last Night, and said with his wonted good Nature, What is the Reason *Emelia*, that we hear nothing of *Florimond*? I protest I had a very high Opinion of that young Man, as well as a great Esteem for his Uncle. It is true, I did not go to their House as I promised, but that was purely on Account of my ill Health; if the old Man took it amiss in me, why should the Nephew all of a sudden forget you? Methinks this is not very agreeable to the Passion he formerly expressed for you. What say you my Child? – It is enough Sir, said I, that I can account for my own Actions, I shall not pretend to render Reasons for other Peoples. He talk'd pretty much to me all the Evening, but I perceiv'd, that he was thoughtful and uneasy, tho' he did not care to express it; from whence I gather, that he is chagrin'd at the Apprehension of losing your Match. By and by this Storm will burst upon my Mother, and then to give Ease to the Family. I dare say, she will find some Way to make Overtures to you; I who am aquainted with her Temper, am sensible that Force only can work upon it, and that slighting what comes easily, she naturally pursues what seems hard to attain. But now finding her Councils altogether embarrassed, she must first make a full Stop – and then – turn into the old Road. This she would never have thought off had not Necessity jogged her by the Elbow.

I am sensible you will melt at the Account of my Father's uneasiness; but consider *Florimond*, he is not justly punished for unsteadiness, had he been punctual in his Engagements with your Uncle, my Mamma's Megrims might have plagu'd her, but never us. Besides, your Coldness has brought him round again, which a contrary Conduct never could have effected. Had it been an easy Matter to take up the Thread of Negotiation with you and your Uncle just where they dropp'd, my Parents would have spun this new Treaty out first; but being caught in their own Contrivances, bewildred in Mazes of their own raising, they must take the shortest Way out of the Wood; and if they find themselves wearing with wand'ring, they have no Guides to throw the Blame on; such *Florimond* is my Way of thinking.

Do not mope yourself with groundless Jealousies, and endless Surmises, depend for once on the Constancy of a Woman. Believe me, *Florimond*, it will increase my Value, and hereafter you will think my Virtue of more Worth than my Beauty, (if I had any) so that however these cross Accidents perplex you at present, you may be sure they are the Seeds of succeeding Pleasures. After all, Why are you dejected? You cannot lose me if I do not throw away myself, therefore set your Mind at rest, and be satisfied I am, and will be

Yours,

EMELIA

LETTER XIV

EMELIA *to* ELIZA

Dearest Friend!

MY own Distresses have for some Time past disturb'd my Thoughts not a little, and now the News you send me of your unexpected Disgrace, has quite stupified me. There is a certain Measure of Misfortune which every Disposition can bear, and good Sense and a proper Education may increase natural Fortitude, so far as to enable it to sustain a much greater Weight of Evil; but Disposition, Education, Reflection, nay, and even Piety itself will not free us from the Frailties of Nature. When therefore the Mind is over-laden, it will of course bend a little, and at some times the highest Spirits will seem humble enough in spite both of Resolution and Caution. As I thought my own none of the weakest: I confess to you I was well enough pleased sometimes to fish in troubled Waters; because I imagin'd my Conduct appear'd to Advantage, when some Difficulty was to be overcome; but I dare say, I am for ever cured of this foolish Notion, and if once I recover Quiet, I shall know at what Rate to esteem it.

> O Peace! what Price can purchase thee too dear?
> Blessings are useless if thou art not there.
> Fools fancy, Fortune's Favours, happy make,
> Alas! we take them only for thy Sake.
>
> Ev'n a low State, a Purse however poor,
> Accompanied by Thee, we can endure.
> But absent Thou! Wealth is a sordid Thing,
> And Man is wretched – e'en if he's a King.

The last Letter I wrote *Florimond*, is in quite a different Stile from this. I pique myself therein upon my Policy, and promise to defeat all the Plots of my Mother, tho' supported by the Condescension of my Father, the Cunning of an intriguing House-keeper, and the Vanity of a doating Baronet. Seriously I have promised too much; to make head with a little Virtue against such a grand Alliance of Vices, is a sort of heroical Madness! Poor *Florimond*, had I trusted to thy plain plodding Integrity, it had been better – but then my Character of a Wit had been lost for ever. Thus it comes to pass, our Passions, and our Humours drive, whereas Reason can hardly draw us; but when in the Hurry we fall, or run ourselves out of Breath, then our Understandings have Leisure to be informed, and we at last find Time to be sensible of our own Follies. – Yet what Sign of this when I write at such a Rate to you ? My fullness of my own Affairs makes me forget yours. The Maid who stays for my Answer bewails them with Tears, while I tattle to you as if nothing had happen'd.

Above all Things *Eliza*, be careful in keeping up your Spirits; that Gaiety you were wont to wear, will make any Change very remarkable. Innocence is an Armour not to be pierc'd, and being secure, Why should you not smile ? The imputation is so very improbable, that I cannot help flatt'ring myself, your Father cannot long avoid seeing he is imposed on. The Girl you sent to me is very angry with the *French* Woman at your House, I cannot tell with what Reason; we ought certainly as Christians, and as a polite Nation, to treat Strangers kindly, but in Truth I see no Cause for making them Privy Counsellors. Domestick Politics differ in all Countries, as much as those of the State, and methinks, a *French* House-keeper in the Dwelling of a Country 'Squire, is as absurd as a *French* Prime Minister would be at St. *James's*. All the World therefore will take your Part, the Ladies will make it a common Cause, the Gentlemen must follow them, and your solemn Papa will quickly be brought to Reason. I don't know how it is, my Heart's light on the sudden, and tho' I know nothing of the second Sight, I have a kind of first feeling which rarely deceives me. I hope all Things will go well with us both, that *Phaon* and *Florimond* will deliver us, and that we shall pass many a happy Hour in reflecting on these Times. Adieu, for to this I can add nothing, but that I am your sincere Sister in Sorrow and Solitude

EMELIA

P.S. Your Maid by an Accident, has informed me of something which may perhaps concern you. She tells me, that after you had given her your Message, and she was just coming out of Doors, she heard your Father take leave of a Gentleman just setting out for *London*, and at parting, used these Words. *Assure him, the Lady is unmarried, and unengaged, and that he may entirely depend on my Friendship and Interest.*

LETTER XV
ELIZA *to* FLORIMOND
Faithful Friend!

I WROTE you very lately the News of my Captivity, receive now those of my Inlargement, as unexpected, and as unaccountable as the other. Yesterday Morning, Papa sent for me to Breakfast. I drank Tea as usual, without betraying any uneasiness at my Restraint, and when the Things were taken away, my Father told me I might walk in the Garden if I pleased, and after Dinner he would have me go and take the Air in the Chariot. I thank'd him, made use of his kind Offers, and seem to stand now in as high Favour, as if I had never been suspected of liking sweet *William*, and forming dangerous Designs against the Honour of our late gentilized Family. Amazing Revolution, but now to unriddle it.

You must know our Coachman is married to a very honest Woman, to whom I have been occasionally as kind as I could. She is pretty much about the House, because she is a favourite of my Fathers, who, before our *French* Lady came, made all the uses of her which he could of a House-keeper, at a fifth Part of the Expence. To her I owe all I know of my own Affairs. She says, the young Lad own'd the Business I employ'd him in, upon which my Father appear'd very well pleased, resolved upon my Enlargement, and has recommended the Boy to a very good Place in the City. What discovery the poor Thing has made, I cannot tell, much was not in his Power, and I forgive him if he has discovered all. One Thing I did, which I flatter myself you will think prudent; I said not a Word in answer to the Coachman's Wife. One of my Maxims is to trust no Dependants on other People.

I would fain say somewhat after all this grave Stuff, to amuse you. But alas! I fancy neither your Condition, nor mine, will allow it. I have quite lost my flow of Spirits, and if I had not, you would think a sprightly Stroke on such perplex'd Affairs impertinent. But, to speak Truth *Florimond*, shall we not twenty Years hence laugh at our present Cares. I see such Changes in the World, that I am tempted to suspect myself. Yet there are noble Instances of Constancy in the present Age too. Justice *Swallow*, likes at Three-score and Ten, *October*, which was his darling Liquor at Sixteen. My Father dotes as much on a Guinea, as when he could tell whose Coin it was, without using Spectacles. Nay, the Parsons Wife, Mrs. *Tythely*, is as fond of being in the Fashion now, as when she captivated the Doctor's Heart in her Flowred Sattin Gown, which cost but – Half her Fortune. Well, if Scandal, and on the Clergy too, won't make you smile, you must be a disconsolate Creature!

As I am just got again into my old Man's good Graces, I intend to ask his Leave to visit *Emelia* To-morrow, after which, no doubt you'll expect a Letter. Let me have no melancholly Answer to this, I have Occasion for my former Giddiness, and I pray, if I can possible put it on again, do nothing to make me drop the Masque, for to deal freely, I shall have enough to do to keep the Bead in my Mouth. The World is now a Masquerade in the strictest Sense, and to appear bare-faced, is not either consistent with one's own Safety, or with good Manners. You cannot approve this Doctrine I know, but can you deny the Facts on which it is founded? Can you affirm that in a whole Day you hear three Words on which you can depend? Or see three Faces you can possitively call bare?

It is really madness in particular Persons, to fancy by their Behaviour, they can contribute to a Reformation. The contagion of Vice, spreads always from Persons of high Rank, and like a muddy Spring, grows fouler and dirtier in its Passage. All therefore that private People can do, is to go innocently along with the Fashion. These *Florimond*, are my present Sentiments, perhaps they have some Tincture of my Condition; I am condemned to perpetual Dissimulation, and that is enough to put me upon thinking, how to extenuate as much as I may the Iniquity of the Practice. But I forget that I am not talking, but writing. My Pen I find, can out-run my Tongue, to avoid therefore being tedious, I will run the hazard of Abruptness. Adieu! and when you have nothing more material in your Mind, give Place therein, to, ELIZA

LETTER XVI

FLORIMOND *to* ELIZA

Excellent Woman!

WHEN I consider thy Virtues, I adore Providence; when I contemplate they Misfortunes, I am struck with Despair. How happy ought Prudence and Integrity to make you, and yet how wretched are you made through other Peoples Wickedness and Folly. But this is the Fruits of Mortality. These Trials shall purify even thy angelick Spirit, so that hereafter, thou shalt shine with truly celestial Lustre. Yet we are not to suppose that Suff'rings even here, will be the Lot of your whole Life. Heaven lays no such heavy Burthens. It tries, and then rewards us, we benefit by Afflictions, and still Providence vouchsafes to pay our Patience with some unlook'd for good. These are discoveries Meditation will always manifest, and it is exceedingly remarkable, that we remember with more Satisfaction the Difficulties we have overcome, than our Pleasures are past.

I call to mind an Instance of this in a Lady you inquired after the last Time I was happy in your Conversation. *Belinda*, whom you commended for the best bred, and best natur'd Woman you ever saw, is that Instance. Her Brother and she were Orphans, and all their Hopes lay in an Uncle worth forty Thousand Pounds. He was kind to the young Gentleman, and after affording him University Education at Home, sent him with a Tutor to Travel. *Belinda* was not so much in his good Graces. He took some Care of her, 'tis true; he allow'd her thirty Pounds a Year, and her Discretion taught her to live on it genteely. But this gave her no prospect in the World, it depended not only on the Life, but on the Humour of an old Man, which alas, we all know to be but a very incertain Tenure!

How narrow soever her Circumstances were, her Birth and Breeding introduced her to the best Company. Amongst the rest, to the Mother of *Adolphus*, and his Sisters, who were so charm'd with her Conversation, that they invited her to pass a Summer with them in *Berkshire*. *Belinda* readily consented, and for some small Time, they were perfectly happy: But the eldest Sister of *Adolphus* being a very penetrating Woman, quickly perceived her Brother was fallen desperately in Love with her Friend. This threw the whole Family into Convulsions, the Sisters grew perfect Furies, and forgetting Decency, were for hurrying away *Belinda* to *London*. *Adolphus* appeared resolved to marry her, and *Belinda* modestly, and for the Peace of the Family, refused him. The old Lady behaved with great Prudence, she went to Town with *Belinda* in the Chariot, and when she set her down at her own Lodgings, told her, she was sorry for her Daughters Folly, and that she did not disapprove her Sons Choice.

A Week aftei, *Belinda*'s Uncle died, and left her to the Curtesy of her Brother, to whom he left his whole Estate. About two Months from her leaving *Berkshire*, *Adolphus* just of Age, follow'd her to Town, and immediately purchasing Jewels to a considerable Value, went to present them to *Belinda*, and to engage her consent to marry him immediately. When he entred her Apartment, he found her in Tears; but by Degrees she recollected herself, and the young Man, as he was full of it, told her what he came to propose. *Belinda* heard him with Attention, and after a short Silence: *Adolphus*, said she, I accept the Jewels, and agree to your Proposal, but there must be no hurry, and your Sisters must be at the Wedding. My Sisters! said *Adolphus*, sighing. Yes, returned *Belinda*, and they will be extremely well pleased; my poor Brother is dead, and I am worth forty thousand Pounds. I was going according to Custom, to add somewhat by way of Application when your second Epistle came to my Hands, and verified my Conjectures. I most heartily and most sincerly congratulate your Deliverance, and am glad your Captivity hath not left such a splenetic Smack behind it, as to hinder your resuming your former Gaiety.

I persuade myself, nothing in my Letter can contribute to your letting fall the Masque, and to deal freely with you, I desire to contribute nothing to the keeping it on, which is in my Judgment unworthy of you. The Misfortune you met with lately, proceeded from your Masquing, and Heaven avert all future Evils, which may threaten you from the same Cause. I intended in order to have amused your Melancholly, to have sent you a little Piece of Poetry, which I take to be of antient Date. I was at some stand whether I should add it now, but at last determined I would. When you next pen an Epistle to *Phaon*, communicate it, for as it was never printed, I may stile it a Curiosity. I should have waited with Impatience enough for an Explanation of your last, if you had not mentioned your going to visit *Emelia*, as it is, you may be sure I shall not taste quiet till your Billet comes. O *Eliza*! my Heart presages Storms and Tempests! May my Predictions prove no truer than those in the Almanack: May you be happy as you deserve, easy as you can wish, and in one of your gay Humours, may you rally this timerous Diffidence of,

Your sincere Friend,
FLORIMOND

LIFE
An ELEGIACK POEM

WHILE thro' *Life's* thorny Road I go,
I will not want *Companions* too:
A *dreary Journey*, and alone,
Would be alas! too troublesome.
But *Company* that's *choice* and *good*,
Makes *Trouble* hardly understood:
For *Toil* divided, seems to be,
No *Toil*, but a *Felicity*.
Therefore will I *Companions* take,
As well for *ease*, as *safeties* Sake:

Fair *TRUTH*, shall serve me for a *Guide*,
JUSTICE, shall never *leave* my *Side*.
INTEGRITY my *trusty Guard*,
Nor will I *CAUTION*, quite *discard*:
EXPERIENCE shall my *Tutor* be,
Nor will I *wiser* seem than He:
DISCRETION all my *Thoughts* shall *weigh*,
And *MODESTY* my *Words* convey.
Soft *INNOCENCE* protect my *sleep*,
And *CHARITY* my *Purse* shall *keep*.

Thus, thro' this *Wilderness*, I'll stray,
Nor ever fear to lose my Way.
The *SAGES*, I sometimes will *see*,
Be sometimes with the *MUSES free*.
With *guiltless MIRTH* an *Hour* beguile,
Or with *free-spoken SATYR* smile.
With *MEDITATION* often *walk*,
Or with *sweet MELANCHOLY talk*.
With these *Companions* dear I'll *sport*,
Nor heed the *Journey* long or short.
So *HEALTH* supply the *DOCTORS* Place,
And for a *CHAPLAIN*, I've *GOD'S GRACE*.

LETTER XVII
ELIZA *to* FLORIMOND

Constant Lover!

THE impatience with which you expect this Letter, will be but ill repaid
by its Contents. I know that you have not any sanguine Expectations; but
the News I have to tell you, will even surpass your Fears. I was Yesterday to

visit *Emelia*, and found her disconsolate beyond Description. Her new Lover was there last Night, and disappointed her very much. He seems to have fallen into her Mother's Notions, and talk'd to her very warmly; this disconcerted my Cousin so much, that I am afraid she did not behave with proper Caution, for I find she is debarr'd the Liberty of writing, and her Maid is not suffer'd to go out of Doors. Under these Distractions she keeps a resolved Silence, and as if she had taken her final determination, sees the Measures pursued by her Parents, without giving any Signs of Approbation of Dislike.

The good old Lady shows all the Marks of high Satisfaction, she talks as knowingly of her design'd Son-in-Law's Country Seat, as if she had resided in it last Summer. She is determin'd to sit in her Daughter's Pew at Church, that she may take Place of Mr. *Hardy*'s Family, who are no more than Gentlemen; tho' the Estate was in their Family before the Conquest; she had collected likewise with infinite Labour a List of all the great Families to which she is to be related, and if I guess right, the Expence of entertaining them for one Winter, would stand my Uncle in some three Years purchase of his Estate. It will be no difficult Thing for you to imagine how well this sort of Conversation pleased me; but what could I do? The old Lady cou'd not say a Word on another Subject; nay, so full was she of her own Scheme, that she gave me to understand whenever it took Effect, my Cousin would become my Betters. No doubt you think this griev'd me, considering my Notions of Family not a little, and yet I must own I was not altogether insensible. It pain'd me that this Woman was my Aunt; but what surprizes me most is, that her Husband is yet more violent than she, and this, not so much out of liking to the new Match, as from Prejudice to you, who I dare say, never offended him.

Poor *Emelia* when I came away, charg'd me to tell you, that she is in a good Measure at her Wit's End, that all her Plots are abortive, and which is worse, have turn'd upon herself; yet she flatters her Melancholy with Hopes of finding out new Recourses when she shall have recollected herself a little; but she bids me assure you, that her Constancy shall remain unshaken in spight of all the Efforts of her Parents. She has likewise directed me to inform you, that some body has told her Father, your Uncle is in a Treaty with Alderman *Scrape*, who once bubbled him of 1000 *l.* to marry you to his Niece, and this she apprehends to be the great Cause of her Father's Wrath. I assur'd her on the Credit rather of my Hopes than of my Knowledge, that the Story was an absolute Falshood, in which I hope you will stand by me, and prove it one. I have promised to visit her again after To-morrow, and shall shew her whatever Answer you write to this. If it was at all in my Power I would advise you; but as it is not, accept the most ardent Wishes of your ever affectionate Friend,

ELIZA

P.S. I forgot to thank you for the Poem you sent me, I like it extreamly, and if you were not at present so much embarrass'd, I would be glad to see something of your own in the same Taste, for that this is of an antient Date I make no Scruple to believe; tho' I know that old Poems may be counterfeited, as well as old Medals, once more good *Florimond* adieu.

LETTER XVIII

FLORIMOND *to* ELIZA

Charming Woman!

I AM infinitely oblig'd to you for the Pains you have taken in our Affairs, and for your so readily detecting the Falsehood of that Tale which had been told *Emelia*'s Father. So far is my Uncle from having entered into any such Treaty, that he has written me a very moving Letter, on the Account he has heard of what passes in that Family. I begin now to hope when *Emelia* despairs; if Plots are no more, Sincerity may restore our almost lost Game. In a Day or two my Uncle will visit there, and I hope will find an Opportunity of showing the good old Gentleman, how much he has been misled, and how desirous we both are, that he would resume his former Way of thinking.

I am not at all amazed at the old Gentlewoman's being in such Raptures, it is natural enough for wiser People than she to be extreamly fond of their own Projects, tho' they may not be over laudable. I am pretty much of your Mind with respect to Families, and yet I must confess, that I am not much displeased at having it in my Power to convince this Lady, who is so fond of Honour, that my Family is not worse than that of which she is so fond; nay, and if Title pleases her so much, my Uncle has a Nephew who is a Baronet. But these are poor Things, and enter so little into prudential Notions of Happiness, that I have often observ'd there are Women, nay, and Men too, who where their Children's Happiness is at Stake, can be weak enough to fancy, that the Phrase in speaking or writing to them will ever have a Share in it; but the managing Part of the World have so many Maxims repugnant to Reason, and the Wits abound with Notions so irreconcileable to the Nature and Course of Things, that for my own Part, I am never surpriz'd when I hear of a Family ruin'd by Oeconomy, or of a Person of prodigious Parts playing the Fool.

Now, charming *Emelia*, let me address myself to you, and let me beseech you to do your utmost to recover your Spirits. I am sorry your new Lover did not answer your Expectations, but I am so confident that he is a Man of Honour, as not to be under any great Uneasiness at what *Eliza* told me in her last; when I say this, I shall own to you freely, that I would not willingly be in his Place. I think I have as much Resolution as another, but I know that your Charms are capable of vanquishing all my Resolution.

Be so good as to lay aside plotting, and let Things go in their natural Channel. I rely so much on your Fidelity, that tho' I foresee a great deal of Trouble, yet I have pretty confident Hopes still; I am no Dissembler, and therefore you may trust this Declaration; it happen'd unluckily that my Friend who is acquainted with your Lover is out of Town, but he is expected To-morrow, and then I shall be able to form some Judgment of his Intentions and manner of proceeding. When I am next favour'd with a Letter from *Eliza*, I doubt not but I shall gain some other Lights in the mean Time perhaps, I can give her some. A Lad was at my Lodgings this Morning while I was Abroad, who left Word that he had liv'd with her Father, and is, I presume, the same who was lately turn'd away. He promis'd to call in the Evening, and I would gladly, had it been possible, delay'd writing till To-morrow Morning, but knowing that this would come too late, if I delay'd so long, I make it my Choice to send what he communicates in my next, which will be deliver'd by a Person in whom I can confide, and who is well known to both your Families. I am, tho' disconsolate enough,

Your ever faithful,
FLORIMOND

LETTER XIX

EMELIA *to* FLORIMOND

Unhappy Lover!

I Find that in private, as well as public Affairs, a little Corruption is sometimes necessary. All our Servants had Orders not to enter into any Conversation with me, or to go near your House. I found means however, to engage the *Gardiner* to admit a Maid of mine who is married in the Town, into one of the Arbors, where I write this, which the *Butler*, one of my Mother's Favourite's, will deliver you. The Reason why I took this Method is, because I doubt whether they will allow *Eliza* to visit me again. I would not throw you into Despair, and yet I must inform you, that your Schemes, I dare not call them Plots, have had no better Success than mine. My Father [is] going three Miles off next *Tuesday*, to avoid seeing your Uncle. Such, Sir, is the Fidelity, the Wisdom, and Resolution of some Men.

My new Lover, of whom you are pleas'd to have a better Opinion than I have, seems to have still a higher of himself, since at his last Meeting with my Mother, he was pleas'd to fix this Day Fortnight for our Wedding, reckoning it seems as a thing of Course on my Consent, which, if I am not very much out in my Reckoning, he will never have. Tho' I cannot help thinking this a little strange, it gives me a Week longer before we come to Extremities. My assiduous Mamma having made Choice of this Day se'ennight for that purpose, and had actually begun her Preparations for the Solemnity, though without taking any Notice of it to me, which surely was no act of Tenderness. I cannot say she was ever unkind to me before, and I see with Surprize, that Ambition, and the foolish love of Title, hath in so short a Time over-run that maternal Affection, which I had experienced from my Cradle.

The sole Thing now to be thought of *Florimond*, is, what Measures we are to take. If I marry without my Father's Consent, I have nothing. In such a Case, all my Hopes would rest on my only Brother, who is at *Cambridge*, and hath always shewn a sincere Friendship for you. Yet alas! Hopes are a bad Provision to set out with in the World. We may indeed feed on them ourselves, but alas! no body will take them in Payment. You are in like Manner dependent on your Uncle, and without doubt, he will retain a just Resentment of the Usage he has met with here, which may make your marrying me the most disagreeable Thing to him in the World. A dreadful Prospect this, and yet as it is all we have; it would be Folly not to look upon it, or to frame in its stead, some entertaining Landskip in our Imaginations. It is much easier to deceive than to deliver ourselves; but if I can do nothing towards the latter, you shall never be able to reproach me with contributing to the former.

In this sad situation, it is my Comfort however, that no part of our Misfortunes flow from ourselves. The Regard I have for you, took Birth from my Father's Recommendation, and therefore he can only blame himself for its Consequences. I have often wondred how Parents expect Duty from Children; whom they dispose off, with as little Ceremony as they do their Horses, and in the same way of Purchase too. It reflects Shame upon a Father, and more upon a Mother, if a Daughter makes a bad Wife; and yet to be thought a good Daughter, she must have such Notions as will probably, if not necessarily, render her a very bad Wife. Her Affections must be as mutable as a Weather-Cock. They must sit, now this Way, now That, just as the Breath of her Parents blows. Can there be any Thing more preposterous? Or can Parents take any Steps more likely to put their Children upon throwing of all Duty?

The result of all, *Florimond*, is this. I must be unhappy, chuse which Way I will; to marry a Man I do not Love, and desert a Man I Do, is the Way to be miserable for ever. To refuse my Consent, and to give my Hand to you, will be attended with many cross Circumstances, out of which we may be delivered, by those who threw us into them. On this reasoning, I build my Resolution, consider you, whether there be not more of Fondness and Folly, than of Firmness or Fortitude in such a Determination, and on these Considerations, ground your Choice. May it be productive of Peace and Prosperity to you, even tho' it should procure endless Sorrow to,

EMELIA

179

LETTER XX

FLORIMOND *to* ELIZA

Unfortunate Fair-one!

MY Conjecture was right, as to the Boy who called at my Lodgings. He is your Nurses Son, and deserves, and I hope will find a better Fate than he has hitherto met with. Your *French* Lady had I fancy an *Italian* Education, for she is a matchless Politician. The Intelligence she gave your Father was false indeed, but withal a Fiction so neatly contriv'd, that he must have been a Conjurer to have detected it. The Lads Mother had the Tale from his own Mouth, and it was in few Words this. That your habitual Tenderness for the Lad, though in the beginning equally innocent and laudable, might possibly alter by degrees, especially considering the Zeal and Fidelity which the Boy show'd in your Service, particularly in conveying your Letters, which tho' she suppos'd directed to Ladies of your Acquaintance; yet he was so cautious, that she could never prevail so far as to see any one Address. Upon this Information, the Lad was stop'd with a Letter of yours in his Pocket, and lock'd in the back Parlour till Notice was given to your Father. While he was there, he slipt a Key into the Foldings of the Letter, and then threw it into the Moat. On his Examination, he said only, that he carried your Letters as you directed him, and seldom or never look'd upon them himself. His Mother was sent for, to take her Son Home, but had withal a Letter of Recommendation to the Gentleman, with whom he now lives, and where he is very kindly treated.

My Friend *Hypolytus*, tells me, That he din'd lately at an *Italian* Merchant's, with a Gentleman just arrived from *Leghorn*, who, from his Description, should be *Phaon*. There is only one Circumstance which I cannot understand, and which makes me doubt that it is not he. The Gentleman at whose House he was, rally'd him on his Marriage, which is speedily to take Effect. My Friendship for you, obliges me to give you this Information, however dangerous to your Peace. The Lad tells me, his Mother sees your Maid daily, send me therefore by her, Instructions how to unriddle this Affair, and to serve you if I am able. Be pleas'd also to inform me of one Thing, which is, whether there be not at *Leghorn*, some other Gentleman of his Surname. Strange Mistakes have happened by such Accidents, and I should be glad to find mine might be added to the Number. The Person who delivers you this, will set out for *London* early the next Morning: He will sup at your House, and if you can write an Answer then, and give it him, it will be sooner with me than by any other Conveyance, and my next shall be as soon with you, as any Contrivance I am Master off, can send it.

I have receiv'd a Letter from *Emelia*, by their *Gardiner* this Moment. She seems in doubt whether you will be allow'd to see her; if she should be mistaken, tell her, that her last Epistle will be laid up both in my Heart, and in my Cabinet; that we agree exactly in Sentiments; that I know nothing shameful but Vice, and can form no Idea of the wretchedness of People who are not wicked. This is my last, though not my late Resolution; it ever was, and I dare say it ever will be, my Opinion, and if ever I should alter it, I shall be what I ought to be, miserable enough, though Power and Riches wrought the Change. My Uncle is a Man of too much good Sense, and of too nice Honour, to think my Marriage with *Emelia* a wrong Action; but if he did, I have two hundred Pounds a Year independent of him, which is sufficient to purchase Necessaries, and to secure Content to those who like each other. Forgive my writing so unentertaining a Letter, and believe that I am sincerely Yours,

FLORIMOND

LETTER XXI

ELIZA *to* FLORIMOND

Best of Friends!

IT is impossible for me to express the Pleasure your kind Epistle gives me, and yet our Affairs are in such a Situation, that I have scarce any relish for Pleasure. Yesterday Morning my Father acquainted me, that he had made Choice of a Husband for me, and that I was to prepare both to see and to marry him next Week; as to his Name I am at present a Stranger to it, my Father supposing that his Recommendation was sufficient to obtain my Consent, even in Favour of a Man I never heard off. Your Conjecture about *Phaon* is but too well founded, I know he is in *London*, but till I receiv'd your Letter, knew nothing of his intended Marriage, yet if he is so inclin'd, it dissolves all my Promises, and I might be on better Terms with my Father; however, I despise such an Expedient, I cannot change so easily, or pretend to sacrifice my own Peace, in order to procure that of my nearest Relation. I am therefore determin'd, tho' it shou'd cost me another Confinement, to express my Sentiments freely in a Letter, which I will give my old Gentleman To-morrow Morning, when I know he will expect my Answer.

I could be content you saw *Phaon*, which sure will be no difficult Thing. I suppose too, that you might easily introduce some Discourse concerning me, which of Consequence would procure a distinct Account of his Affair. What you have written me is precise and probable, and yet I know not how, I cannot think that he would deceive me, or rather I would be glad to think him faithful if it was possible; deliver me out of this Distress, which great as it is, is yet but a Part of my Distress, and I shall be grateful. Alas! I know that Intreaties are unnecessary to you, and therefore you must refer my Language not to my Notions of you, but of my own Affairs: I think you were pretty right when you foretold, that I would never resume my former Gaiety, indeed I see now no Probability of it, for if to be disturb'd at Home, slighted and betray'd Abroad, and to have no Person in the World from whom I can expect Protection, be sufficient to crush all Temper, and induce perpetual discontent, that is my Case; but still, I have done nothing to deserve it, and it is the Sense of this fills me with Satisfaction. Inclosed I send you a Copy of the Letter I wrote my Father, by which you will perceive, that on this Side at least, my Spirit is superior to my Fortune. I wish I may be able to deserve your Approbation of what I write to *Phaon*, which you will not however receive till I hear from you again.

Emelia was for once mistaken in what she wrote you of my not being admitted to see her, I was as well receiv'd by her Family as ever, nor did her Mother express the least Uneasiness at my walking near an Hour with her in the Garden alone, where all our Discourse turn'd upon our own Concerns; she expressed her Resentments in very strong Terms for the Usage she had met with, particularly from her Mamma. She told me your Uncle spoke to her in the Presence of her Mother, when he call'd there two Days ago, and that he did it with such Tenderness, as oblig'd her to go to the Window to prevent his seeing her Tears. When I came away *Emelia*'s Woman inform'd me, that her new Lover had given her Father to understand, that he had her Consent, desir'd him to make himself easy on that Head, and not disturb her with any Applications on that Subject, till he paid her another Visit, which wou'd be To-morrow. This is a new Mystery which astonishes me the more, because by an unlucky fatality, you and I are oblig'd to disturb each other, in Points of the most tender Nature; yet methinks, I could be glad you would make yourself as much answerable for *Phaon*'s Conduct, as I would venture to do for that of *Emelia*; it is improbable she should deceive you, but impossible that she should deceive us both. Suspend therefore your Judgment on what I write you, till Time the Revealer of Secrets hath written a Comment on my Text. Surely we shall not be long in the Dark, and in the bare Hopes of this I preserve my Senses; do you maintain that Reputation for good Sense and steady Virtue, which has gain'd you the Esteem of your Friends, the Affection of *Emelia*, and the most sincere Respect of,

ELIZA

LETTER XXII

ELIZA *to* PATRICIO

My Father, my Protector,

In the Years which have elaps'd since the Time of my Birth, I am not conscious of my ever having intended to offend you. While my dear Mother

was living she always told me, that when I grew a Woman, it was intended
I should marry *Phaon*; his Father in your Presence, and with your liking,
call'd me Daughter, and what Jewels I have were given me by that good
old Man. My Engagements to his Son were not so much my own Acts, as
yours and my Mother's, who had she been alive, would have prevented this
Day's Trouble. The plain Truth therefore is this, that I look upon myself
to be so much the Wife of *Phaon*, that I will never marry any other Man,
even if he should differ so far from me in Sentiments, as to think himself at
Liberty to marry another Woman. This Sir, is not a rash or a sudden
Resolution, but a Thing determin'd in my Breast from the Moment he
was torn from me to be sent to *Leghorn*, there to piece together his Father's
Accompts, till the Amount show'd whether I was to belong to him, or to a
richer Man.

The Proposal you was pleased to make me, appears so extraordinary, so
little agreeable to Reason, and so void of that paternal Tenderness you
have always shown for me, that if it had not come from yourself, I should
never have believ'd it yours. Resolve to marry a Man before I heard his
Name, or saw his Face: Sure Sir, you must have a very bad Opinion of me,
since you were too long a Husband, and had too good a Wife, not to have
a just Idea of the married State. Your Greyhound, Sir, whom you gave
away to a Stranger, ran Home again forty Miles, and do you think it more
easy to part with your Daughter? You think implicit Obedience a part of
my Duty, but sure if it be so, it was left out of the Law of God and Nature;
we are commanded to Honour our Parents, but Honour is the Service of
the Understanding, and therefore we cannot Honour those who show us no
Cause; we may fear, dread, and submit to them, and without the Grace of
God, we may secretly hate them; but Honour them we cannot. This, Sir,
is the Fruits of the Education you gave me, if you intended to treat me as a
Slave, Why did you breed me as one who was born free? Be just Sir, to
yourself, remember your Promises to your Friend, and cease to think of
calling Breach of Faith an Act of Obedience.

Your Unkindness to me is so new, that while it forces me to expostulate,
it deprives me of Abilities. The other Day I was exposed to Scandal, nay
to Infamy, if it could fall on Innocence, by locking me up, and turning
away my Footboy; it may be, you then discover'd my Correspondence
with *Phaon*, in all which there is nothing ought to make me blush or
decline your severest Scrutiny; but methinks a sudden Marriage was a
strange Punishment for this Offence, unless the Man you intend me for
was your Enemy, and you meant to plague him with a Wife, who could
have no Affection for him. Pardon, Sir, the Eagerness[10] of a Stile unbecoming a Daughter, and which I could never have brought myself to use, if from
your Conduct I had not conceiv'd you were inclin'd to forget that I was
your Daughter; had it been otherwise, you would never have conspir'd

against my Peace, by sending away *Phaon*, without the least Necessity, against my Character by confining me about a Foot-boy; and now, against any Good that Providence may have in reserve for me, by intending to marry me to a Man I neither know, nor can possibly care for. In this Distress what Remedy have I left? This only, that I appeal from your Views of Ambition, Interest, or Conveniency, to your Affection as a Father, to the Respect you owe your dead Friend, and that Tenderness you always expressed for the Memory of my Mother. I would add to these the Merits of many Years little Services in which you formerly took some Delight, when you called me your dear,

ELIZA

LETTER XXIII

FLORIMOND to ELIZA

Admirable Heroine!

I F the untoward Situation of my own Affairs, and the Perplexities in which I know you are plung'd, did not render Compliments impossible and impertinent, I would endeavour to express to you some Part at least of that Satisfaction, which your last Epistle gave me; but I think it will be a stronger Testimony of my Friendship to inform you, the Pains I have taken to be of some Use to you. *Phaon* is really in *London*, and on the Point of being married, his Wedding Cloaths and the Lady's are making, but who she is I cannot learn. I should have din'd with him to Day, but that he was oblig'd to go to *Richmond*, however I shall be introduc'd to him To-morrow, and if I can contrive how to penetrate this Mystery I will. Your Lad was with me this Morning, and tells me your Aunt in Town is buying your Wedding Cloaths. He could not sure dream this, and I always look'd upon your Father to be a Man of more Prudence, than to run the Hazard of such Disappointments. In a Word, I am so amaz'd I cannot tell what to think, only that as you say, the Darkness cannot last long, and yet methinks we have been too long in the Dark already. I hasten however to some more strange News.

The *Gardiner* who brought me my last Letter from *Emelia*, told me as a great Secret, that their young Lady was going to be married, and that it had been put off a Week, on Account of a new Chariot. This agrees exactly with the Intelligence you gave me, and yet I know not how to believe both Accounts. Chance threw me the other Day into a Place where I saw my Rival, he is certainly a very fine Gentleman, but I cannot think he is in Love with *Emelia*; because I heard him say many Things to a Lady, which I thought were too tender for Gallentry, and I am much mistaken if the Lady did not think so too. *Hypolytus* told him who I was, at which he look'd upon me and smil'd, passing by me as he went out of the Room, he said softly, *We shall be good Friends Sir, for all this;* at which I bow'd, but made no Answer. *Hypolytus* tells me he declined speaking of the Marriage, and only said, he believ'd he shou'd not disappoint *Emelia* at the Time, or she him; and that he had been in the Morning looking on Silks for her Wedding Cloaths. My Friend is no less bewilder'd than I, especially since on calling at the Gentleman's Lodgings, he was told by a Servant that he was gone down to *Suffolk*, so that he will be there three Days at least sooner than they expect him, and sooner I hope than some People desire him, tho' to tell you the Truth, my Brains begins to grow giddy, and my Faith is at its last Gasp.

My Uncle is in Town, and as much concern'd at my Misfortune as I could wish him; he offers as well as you, to be Security for *Emelia*, upon which I show'd him her last Letter, with which he seem'd transported, bid me go down to *Suffolk*, marry her, and he would settle on me his whole Estate. Yet I have no Inclination to stir, for to speak the Truth, I am so afraid of some new unexpected Turn, that I rather wait the decission of Providence, than tempt it. Besides, I incline to be at the Bottom of this Business of *Phaon*, which would not be practicable, should I go out of Town at this Juncture. The more I consider all Things, the more I am fix'd in this Resolution; for as all these Perplexities grew immediately on my coming to Town to settle my Affairs, and without my moving at all, I cannot apprehend how my making so quick a Step as going down to *Bury*, could produce any thing but new Confusions. Yet will I not be positive that I may not suddenly change my Opinion, for if I was once satisfied as to *Phaon*, I should be extreamly well pleas'd to make you a Visit, and confer with you on all our Troubles New and Old. I thought proper to say this, that my coming might not surprize you, though nothing I think could surprize you, done by a Man like me, who contradicts himself so often in so few Lines. Yet you know my Excuse, and know the force of it. I hope however this is the last Time I shall urge it, for writing in so incoherent a Manner; tho' in the midst of all my Disorder, I dare assure you I am most faithfully yours,

FLORIMOND

P.S. Just as I was about to seal this Letter, I received the inclosed from my Friend, I have read it twice, and am in no fear of forgetting the Contents; and as it concerns you no less than myself, I thought sending it would be the best Method of communicating the Intelligence it brings.

LETTER XXIV

HYPOLYTUS *to* FLORIMOND

Dearest Friend!

I AM ashamed to say that I have taken a great deal of Pains, to very little purpose, in unrevelling that perplexed Web of Misfortune, which with no small Industry your evil Genius has been for some time working. The few Discoveries I have made, I have communicated to you at several Times; but I make it my Choice to repeat them to you at once, and in Writing, that you may the better see their connection with each other, and possibly be thereby led to the discerning the Causes of those Events which have so much astonish'd you. Your Rival *Celadon*, is you know, a Man of distinguish'd Birth, with a Fortune very unequal thereto. His Father had a large Estate when he was Born, and as he set no limit to other Expences, so it must be allowed that there was no sparing in the Education of his Son. Before he travell'd, there was some talk of a Match between him and a Lord's only Daughter; but while he was in *Italy*, that Nobleman dyed, and his Widow, who was also her Daughter's Guardian, forbid *Celadon* the House, as soon as she heard of his return to *London*. This was the Lady you took Notice of the other Day, to whom *Celadon* was speaking. The Town thought there was still an Amour subsisting, and therefore the Lady's Mother heard of his Marriage with *Emelia* as a Thing very conducive to her Quiet. All this I am able to tell you of my own Knowledge, as also that *Celadon* hath lately had very large Sums of Money in his Possession, been extreamly busy with *Lawyers*, and whenever he comes to Town, is to bring out a very grand Equipage, which if he expects to support with *Emelia*'s Fortune, he will not be thought to have learn'd much of their Oeconomy, during his long Converse with the *Italians*.

What I am to tell you of *Phaon* is Matter of Hearsay. He went to *Leghorn* to settle his Father's Affairs, which he found in great Confusion, and tho' he stayed there a good while, and applied himself very industriously to Business, yet could he not bring them into any Order; his Return to *England* is sudden and unexpected, two Reasons I have heard assign'd for this in Conversation, one, That his Guardian recalled him; the other, That a Discovery has been lately made of the Effects of his Father's *Banker*, which will produce ten Shillings in the Pound, besides five Shillings which have been divided already, and as he is the principal Creditor, this must be a very considerable Thing. As to his Marriage it is kept a Secret, at the request of the Lady's Father, of whom I heard this Character, that he has a long Head, a long Purse, and a very close Fist, which Qualities belonging to many People, it can be scarce stiled any Character at all. *Phaon* since his Return to *London*, appears the most altered Man in the World, he was always of a sweet easy Temper, but a little too reserv'd, which Humour grew upon him in *Italy* more and more, insomuch that his Friends expected to have seen him a perfect Mope; they are however agreeably disappointed, for with much good Sense, and the most becoming Modesty, he has all the Frankness and Vivacity one can wish, and of these last Particulars I am myself a Witness.

I have forgot the Lady's Name, whom you mention'd to me as the Aunt of a Friend of yours; but I believe *Phaon* lodges in her House, because coming by accidentally, I saw him hand her into a Coach in his Night Gown and Slippers. You see what trivial Stories I pick up for you; but you will believe that I would have collected weightier, had they lain in my Way, and therefore you must impute the lightness of this Letter, not as a Fault, but a Misfortune, to him who in all Things, and on all Occasions will ever prove himself your true Friend, and obedient Servant,

HYPOLYTUS

P.S. If there be any Thing odd in my Letter, it is certainly out done by this Billet which I have just receiv'd.

To HYPOLYTUS

My old Friend,

THE Person who delivers you this will at the same Time bring you two Marriage Favours, one for yourself, the other for your Friend *Florimond*; be pleased to give it him, and tell him, that he shall have proper Notice of my Wedding, which in spight of Appearances, will be no unwelcome Sight to him. I should have written more, but that I am going to see *Emelia*'s Things pack'd up, and therefore I bid you both adieu,

CELADON

LETTER XXV

ELIZA *to* FLORIMOND

Most worthy Friend!

IF I have been troublesome to you by my long melancholy Letters, I will now endeavour to make you some Amends. We have had strange Things happen'd in our Family, and had I the Pen of the Countess *D'Anois*, or Madam *De Noyer*,[11] I persuade myself my true History would not make a worse Figure than their feign'd ones. To you however, a plain Detail of Facts will, I dare say, be more acceptable then any of those high finish'd Memoirs, wherein the Author's Ingenuity appears to much greater Advantage, then their Veracity. The next Day after I wrote to you, my Father after Breakfast asked me morosely enough, Whether I had thought seriously of what he had said to me? Upon which I immediately presented him the Letter, of which I sent you a Copy; he made some Difficulty of receiving it, and was pleased to tell me, that he knew well enough my Skill in writing Letters, and had seen more of them than I imagin'd. However, on my bursting into Tears, he took it up and went to the Window, I look'd upon him steadily while he was reading it, and saw with Surprize his Brow clear by Degrees, and after a second reading, was not a little amazed to see him come towards me smiling.

Eliza, said he, *Is there no Falacy in this? Are these the real Sentiments of your Heart?* Yes, Sir, return'd I, *Why then Girl*, answer'd he briskly, *they are my Sentiments too, and you may depend on being as happy as I can make you.* I threw myself at his Feet, and in the best Phrases my Passion would allow me to utter, expressed my Duty, Gratitude and Thankfulness. He quickly raised me up, embrac'd me, bid me go into the Garden and compose myself, after which he directed me to retire to my Chamber, and not stir till I was called to Dinner. I punctually obey'd him, but guess at my Amazement, when at Three o'Clock my Maid came to inform me, I was to dine in my Chamber, that my Father was gone to *London* in his Chariot, and that about two Hours before our *French* Woman was discarded, and obliged to take her Passage in the Stage-Coach. Tho' I am not absolutely free from Apprehensions, since I have no Key to my Father's Conduct, yet relying upon his Promise, I make myself easy, and hope the best. I long to hear from *Emelia*, and from you, as our Affairs have grown perplex'd together, I am in Hopes that our Misfortunes will have the same Period, and as my Happiness begins to dawn, it would afford me the most sublime Satisfaction, to have any good News from you.

My Maid informs me, that your Rival *Celadon*, passed through this Town in the Morning in his Chaise and Six, with a great deal of Baggage, and is gone to a Gentleman's House six Miles from hence, on the Road directly opposite to that which should have carried him to *Emelia*; but as his Lawyer follow'd him about Noon, I imagine Settlements are to be adjusted there, at least I know not what else to imagine. Our *French* Woman lost all Patience at my Father's Treatment, and had the Insolence to tell my Maid, that I intended to have run away with a young Fellow not worth a Groat, which she had discover'd and prevented, that my Father would marry me in a few Days; and that he had sacrificed her in this ungrateful manner, to give the lie to some Reports to my Disadvantage, but she would take Care the Truth should be known in Spight of all our Arts. I protest to you, I am unable to unriddle any Part of this strange Accusation, and as I am not willing to charge People with great Crimes on Suspicion, I am afraid the poor Gentlewoman is a little crazy, or else invented this Romance to revenge herself upon me, for the supposed Injuries I had done her. Time, my faithful Friend, will explain all these Mysteries, and I hope we shall shortly talk with Pleasure of those Things, which give us at present the greatest Pain, and in this Hope I bid you farewel.

ELIZA

P.S. I have amused myself all the Morning with *Spencer*, can you see any Sign of it in these Verses?

On HOPE

HOPE is a Charm that sooths the lab'ring Mind
   The pleasing *OPIUM* of the afflicted Soul;
In it alone the Wretched Comfort find,
   For lively *HOPE* can ev'ry Care controul.

My beating Bosom is a well wrought *CAGE*,
   Whence this sweet *GOLDFINCH* never shall elope,
Her Musick all my Sorrows can assuage,
   So soft the Songs of Heart deluding *HOPE*.

LETTER XXVI

FLORIMOND *to* EMELIA

Mistress of my Soul!

I Cannot decline this Opportunity of writing to you, tho' I have very little to say to justify my troubling you with a Letter. The Servants of your Family talk with Confidence of your Marriage. Your Mother expresses her Satisfaction in all Companies, and by my fatal Complaisance to your Commands, I have incurr'd the Indignation of your Father, on whose Integrity both you and I placed our Confidence, and had we not mismanaged it ourselves, I am persuaded very justly. *Celadon* has provided a new Equipage, and bought your Wedding Cloaths. In this Distress I have nothing to console me, but your Promise and my own Fidelity; Lovers must have Faith, and I hope I have convinc'd you, that in this Respect I was not deficient; but now to speak sincerely, Appearances are too strong not to beget Suspicions. Forgive me, *Emelia*, if I wrong you, and if it be in your Power, give me some Grounds to repent.

The Conduct of *Celadon* is so fluctuating and unintelligible, that I am weary of Conjectures, and wait with some Impatience that Event, which must necessarily end them. You will see by the inclosed what a strange Present he has sent me, yet I must own to you, that if it were not for the Sense I have of your Charms, I should still depend upon *Celadon*, who has a Frankness in his Behaviour irreconcileable with that Conduct which must destroy my Peace; but alas! if he be in my Condition, if you have the same Power over him that you have over me, his Perfidiousness will be of a Piece with my Complaisance; and to justify his Conduct, he need appeal only to mine. If it be otherwise, if as I have been told, *Celadon* was pre-ingag'd, then surely our Affairs are not desperate. But why do I trouble you with these If's and Supposes? without question you are uneasy enough already, and it ought not to be my Office to add to your Disquiets. I cannot forbear writing, and of what should I write but that of which my Heart is full. This is the Source of my Offence, and this only can excuse it. Sincerity is so acceptable a Quality in a Friend or a Lover, that it may attone for many Deficiencies, if not for all; thus like a Bankrupt I offer you what is in my Power, and you I hope will not be so rigid as to expect more.

I was just going to conclude, when *Hypolytus* came in; he has receiv'd another Billet from *Celadon*, which promises an End to all our Sorrows next Week. What the Meaning of this is I know not; but whatever it is, may Heaven render it propitious to you. *Eliza*'s Father din'd this Day at a Merchant's House with *Phaon*, they went Abroad together afterwards in the old Man's Chariot, and they have each of them an Appartment at her Aunt's; this shows they agree perfectly well, and I hope presages a happy Issue in her Affair; sure all Appearances are not delusive, or all we see and hear, Phantoms and Fictions. I have told you now *Emelia*, my Thoughts and my News, and yet I am unwilling to make an End. There is certainly in this Passion of Love, something which borders nearly upon Madness; the Series of our Actions is a String of Contradictions, our Resolutions are without force, and our Opinions change before they are well expressed. To avoid tormenting you therefore with my raving, I will only add, that however disturbed and distracted in other Things, my Heart is entirely and sincerely yours,

FLORIMOND

LETTER XXVII

HYPOLYTUS *to* FLORIMOND

Dearest Friend,

I Should think myself extreamly happy, if I could do you the same good Office in respect to your own Affairs, that I am going to perform in regard to a Lady for whom I know you have the greatest Concern. By this Time *Eliza* is the happiest Woman in the World, and by the oddest Train of Accidents that can be, it is in my Power to acquaint you how this has fallen out. In the first Place, you must know that *Eliza* corresponded with *Phaon*, by a Name different from his own. The Boy she sent with her Letters to the *Post-Office*, was very faithful, insomuch that the *French* House-keeper could not procure one of them, either by Promises or Threats. She found Means however to get the Direction copy'd at the *Post-House*, and having effected this, she procur'd a Letter to be written from *London*, to the young Lady's Father, informing him that such a Person, using the Name which *Phaon* had fix'd on for his Correspondence with *Eliza*, was on the Point of running away with his Daughter. This alarm'd him not a little, having just received Advice from *Leghorn*, that by an unforeseen Accident *Phaon* would recover all his Fathers Effects.

To prevent all ill Consequences therefore, the old Gentleman made Miss a close Prisoner, dismiss'd her Servant, and understanding that *Phaon* was about to set out for *England*, before he had put this Part of his Project in Execution, he by Letter forbad him to write any more to his Daughter, on Pain of never seeing her more. These Letters however never reached his Hands, he having left *Leghorn* on the Death of his Correspondent, who was entrusted with conveying *Eliza*'s Epistles; but upon his coming to Town, and going to *Eliza*'s Aunts, he received from her the same Caution. Upon this, he sent a Friend of his into *Suffolk*, to learn what was the Matter, who inform'd him on his Return, that the old Gentleman was resolv'd that *Phaon* should surprize his Daughter, by coming down on a sudden as a Stranger he had fix'd on for her Husband. This Scheme, when at the Point of Execution, was broke all to Pieces by a Letter the young Lady wrote her Father, which discovered that she never had a new Lover. By this, the *French* Woman was detected, and turned out of the Family. The old Man came to Town, conferr'd Notes with his Son-in-Law, and this Morning they are set out together for *Suffolk*. Without Question they will be very kindly receiv'd by *Eliza*, tho' by a Letter of hers to her Aunt, it appears she was not a little chagrin'd at *Phaon*'s being in Town so long without writing her a Line. He never saw that Epistle till Yesterday, and though he has so much Matter for his own Inspection, yet it has given him such strong Concern, that when I took my Leave of him this Morning, he was not in near so high Spirits as I expected. Surely this Love is an odd Passion, since Lovers are never easy, I should be glad to see how he behaves when a Husband. Will his Uneasinesses be then all over, or will new one's succeed? I ask this as a mere Novice in these Matters, but I hope to be well informed when you and he are become in Condition to be my Masters.

I was going to Seal my Letter when *Celadon*'s Servant call'd upon me to enquire where you liv'd. I was very urgent with him to know what was the Reason of this Enquiry, but all the Answer he would, or perhaps could give me, was that his Master had written a Letter to you, which was to be delivered by his Taylor this Afternoon. I gave him a Direction, and will not fail to call upon you in the Evening, to learn if it be possible, what this mysterious Man means. I confess the Measures he takes, astonishes me, as much as they perplex you, and I have more than once repented my Acquaintance with him, merely because of the Disquiet it gives me; yet I cannot hear that any Friend of his beside has Reason to complain, which instead of easing, adds to my inquietude, because I think it hard he should fix on me, for the first Man he deceives, and makes an Engine in deceiving Others. Perhaps I am mistaken in that; in this I am sure I am not, when I profess myself the sincerest of your Friends, and the most Faithful of your Servants,

HYPOLYTUS

191

LETTER XXVIII

EMELIA *to* ELIZA

My only Friend!

IT is with the greatest Satisfaction, that I receiv'd, though very imperfectly, the News of your Happiness. My Maid had it from the Man who brings you this, and whom your Father sent to invite all our Family to your Wedding. What Answer he will bring back I know not, for I am as closely confined as if I had been not suspected only, but convicted of a capital Offence, though I conceive it is intended that my Imprisonment shall be concluded not with Hanging, but with Marriage. My Maid is a kind of Prisoner too, for though she is allowed the Liberty of the House, and may go up and down Stairs, which is more than I have done this ten Days, yet dare she not speak to any of the Servants in private, nor dare they approach my Appartment.

Never surely was a Family in such Confusion. My Father, contrary to his usual Custom, hardly speaks a Word, and from being the best humour'd Man in the World, is become the most morose. My Mother was in top Spirits till within these three Days, when a vast Quantity of fine Cloaths and Linnen came down from *London* for me, with a Letter from *Celadon*, the Contents of which I know not. I guess however, that there is something wrong, because my Father can scarce look upon me without Tears, and my Mother talks alike harshly to us both. To add to my Distress, I hear nothing either from *Florimond*, or you. Is not this a melancholy Situation? Have I not Reason to lose my Patience, or can any one blame me for being Peevish, or even Vaporish in such a Condition? Try dear *Eliza*, try to see me, for whither our Family go to your House or not, I shall certainly remain where I am. I believe it will be best not to ask my Parents Leave. I persuade myself *Phaon* will accompany you to the Garden Gate at Nine in the Evening, my Maid shall be there, and will conduct you to an Arbor where I spend many Hours of the sleepless Night.

I know you will have the Goodness to excuse my not complementing you on your Marriage, those who are not half so much affected with it as I am, will be able to say ten Times more than I can; but as in the Course of a long tender Friendship, I never gave you any Reason to doubt either my sincerity, or my Zeal, so I hope you will not question either of them now, when the odd Posture of my Affairs renders it impossible for me to express them as I ought. I foresee some Difficulty in your Coming, and therefore if you find it impracticable, have the Goodness to write by this Servant, and send him at the same Hour to the Garden Gate. Before I conclude, I must tell you, that the Night before the Day on which I should be married, I intend to make my Escape, in which, if I should have any need of your Assistance, I shall find a Way to inform you by *Margaret*, who us'd to bring you my Letters; as yet, I have only thought of it in general, and have not settled my particular Method. It may be, Providence will prevent me, and save my taking a Step, which gives me inexpressible Pain to think on. The Usage I have received from my Mother, hath sharpened my Temper beyond any Thing I ever thought myself capable of, especially towards one for whom the Laws of God and Man require so high a Reverence. Indeed *Eliza*, I ought not to trouble you with these melancholy Things, immediately on your Marriage; but it is impossible for me to writ any Thing else, and therefore to prevent continuing in a wrong Road, I will be so rude as to make a full Stop. Adieu! Remember with Pity your unhappy Friend,

EMELIA

LETTER XXIX
FLORIMOND *to* HYPOLYTUS

Faithful Friend!

A Departure so sudden as mine, without taking Leave, without sending you a Message, or so much as excusing myself by a Letter, must appear very extravagant, nor should I be surprized if by this Time you had Thoughts of blotting both *Celadon* and myself out of the List of your Friends. You know that by an odd Accident, *Celadon*'s Taylor miss'd me in the Morning, as I miss'd your Letter the Day before, and you that Evening. The next Day the Taylor was with me before I was up, the Letter he was charged with, requested me to allow him to take my Measure, and to order him to bring the Cloaths to *Celadon*'s Lodgings as soon as they were made, whither I was also directed to go, with an Assurance that I should hear News [which] would please me. I went accordingly, when *Celadon*'s Servant told me, that his Master attended me four Miles from Town, and that I must set out immediately. I sent him to my Lodgings for Linnen and my Boots, then mounting his Master's Horses, we reach'd the Inn, where he was in an Hour. At our coming into the Yard, we found a Chaise and Six, into which I got at the Request of my Rival, and away we drove without so much as drinking a Glass of Wine.

It was the *Suffolk* Road, and *Celadon* told me that I was to lie that Night at his House, which added to my Surprize, because till then, I knew not he had one, but he did not leave me long in the Dark. I have, said he, taken a great deal of Pains to make both you and myself Happy and have succeeded in my Wish. I married a Week ago Lady *Sophia*, and have in her Right, three Thousand Pounds a Year, beside a Title to her Mother's Jointure. It was necessary for me to practice as I did upon *Emelia*'s Family, otherwise I could never have brought my own Affairs to bear. My Mother-in-Law being my implacable Enemy, tho' I hope she will not continue so. I bought all *Emelia*'s wedding Cloaths, and suffer'd her Father to be at a good deal of Expence, that a Marriage might be absolutely necessary. I then prevailed upon my Uncle to go and acquaint the Family, that I had married a Lady to whom I had been under Engagements for some Years, and that I conceived they could not take this very much amiss since their Daughter was under the like Engagements, which it would now be their Interest to fulfill. The Reception my Uncle met with was so bad a One, and the Fury of the old Lady was so great, that I was in great Fear my Plot would miscarry. Three Days past without hearing a Word, on the fourth came your Uncle, whom till then, I had never seen, though he is my Wife's near Neighbour. He acquainted me that *Emelia*'s Father had been at his House. That he told him frankly the whole Story, and that when they had compar'd Things together, he desired your Marriage might be celebrated the Day after To-morrow, being the very Day fix'd for mine. Your Uncle after dining with me, went back to their House, and I set out for the Inn where you found me, and where I had waited for you a whole Day.

That Night I lay at *Celadon*'s House, and the next Morning went in his Coach with him, his Lady, and her Aunt, to *Emelia*'s, where we were very well received by the old Man, but her Mother look'd a little coldly upon *Celadon*, who rally'd her first into a very bad, and then into a very good Humour. *Phaon* and *Eliza* were at our Wedding, and my Uncle to make *Celadon* some Amends for the rich Cloaths sent down to *Emelia*, has given him eight Bay Coach-Horses of his own Breeding. One Thing I must not forget, that my Mother-in-Law, who was so tender of her Daughter's Fortune, never thought of a Settlement till after we were married, nor had she thought of it so soon, if my Uncle had not declared that he had settled his whole Estate upon me, except a Rent Charge of two hundred Pounds a Year, which he reserved for Life, and a Power of disposing of two thousand Pounds by Will. Such my Friend, is the Conclusion of an Affair in which out of a mere benevolence of Temper you took so much Concern. If Business will permit, let us have your Company here for a Fortnight, and then you will have Leisure enough to ask *Phaon*, and myself, the Questions you formerly propos'd. *Celadon*'s new Chariot will attend you at your Lodgings, drawn by six Bays, whenever you shall appoint; but first the Taylor must wait upon you, and it is farther expected, that the Favour formerly sent you, should appear in your Hat; make what haste you can to join us, though at present our Company seem all so well pleased, that I do not see any great Sign of moving, when we do, it will be at *Celadon*'s House, where some Alterations are making, and where it is agreed we shall pass the Remainder of the Summer together. There is also a Cousin of Lady *Sophia*'s expected there, a young Lady of Nineteen, very agreeable, and has a good Fortune; suppose *Hypolytus*, you should make an experiment of the hardness, of your Heart against all these Charms. If you should be vanquish'd, it will be among your Friends, who will not deny their Assistance. A single Life has Freedom I grant you, but not much of real Felicity. More of this however, on a proper Occasion, when you have seen the Harmony in which we live, and have conversed a while with the amiable *Clarinda*. All here, present their Respects to you, and their joint Request, that you would make haste. I add no more, but that I am,

> *Your sincere Friend,*
> *As well as your most obliged,*
> *And obedient Servant,*
> FLORIMOND

NOTES

1 cf. *The Spectator* No. 11, Tuesday, March 13, 1711. It is a tale about a young merchant whose life is saved by an Indian maid, who then becomes his mistress. After his return to England he sells the girl, now pregnant with his child as a slave.

2 I have not been able to identify this ballad; it looks like a 17th century broadside.

3 Probably a mixture of two different titles, namely *Aim not too high in things above thy reach* . . ., a well-known 17th century song (cf. *Roxburghe Ballads*, ed. W. M. Chappell & J. W. Ebsworth, 1869–99, I, 326) and a ballad: *Grim King of the ghosts make haste* . . . (Th. Percy, *Reliques of Ancient poetry*, 1765, II, 350 under the title *The Lunatic Lover*) in which a disappointed lover applies to the king of the ghosts to be taken away from this world.

4 A well-known ballad of the time (cf. Percy's *Reliques*, III, 170). Two orphaned children are sent into the wood by their guardian, an uncle, where they are to be killed by two hired murderers. One of the ruffians is moved by the innocence of the children; he kills his fellow and leaves the children, who perish in the wood. Later he confesses the crime.

5 It is not quite clear what Emelia is referring to, since none of Dryden's *Fables* deal with unfaithful lovers. She may be thinking of unhappy love-stories like "Theodore and Honoria, from Boccace", where the lovers are doomed to hell in the end, or of Dryden's version of Chaucer's *Knight's Tale*, of Cinyras and Myrrha, out of the Tenth Book of Ovid's *Metamorphoses*, where Myrrha develops an unnatural passion for her father.

6 A ballad about an unfaithful lover (cf. Percy's *Reliques*, III, 12 and F. J. Child, *The English and Scottish Popular Ballads*, New York, 1882–98, No. 74: *Fair Margaret and Sweet William*). Although he loves fair Margaret William marries another girl. The very next day his former love dies, whereupon William too dies of sorrow.

7 cf. Percy's *Reliques*, III, 192: *The Wandering Prince of Troy*. A ballad well-known in the 17th century describing how Aeneas was punished for leaving Dido: her ghost carries him away from this world.

8 Boccaccio's story of *Griselda*, a lady subjected by her husband to a series of humiliations and cruelties which she bore with exemplary submissiveness, became the subject of various narratives in prose and verse, as *The Pleasant and Sweet History of patient Grissel* by Th. Deloney (1630) and *Patient Grizzel* in *A Collection of Old Ballads* (1723).

9 Miss Hoyden is a character in Vanbrugh's *The Relapse* (1696) who, involved in an intrigue laid by the younger brother of her prospective husband, gets married twice. In the end she is united with the man she loves best.

[10] *Eagerness:* bitterness, acidity, irritability.

[11] Two French novelists whose epistolary works were translated into English: *The Diverting Works of the Countess D'Anois, Author of the Ladies Travels To Spain.* (1707) – *Letters from a Lady at Paris to a Lady at Avignon, containing a particular Account of the City, the Politicks, Intrigues, Gallantry, and Secret History of Persons of the First Quality in France Written by Madame Du Noyer.* (Vol. I, 1716, vol. II, 1717).

Love-Letters
between a Noble-Man and his Sister

with the History of their Adventures.

In Three Parts. The Fifth Edition.
(Part I) London, 1718*

*For the first edition see the bibliography.

Love-Letters
between a Noble-Man and his Sister

It was Virginia Woolf who celebrated Aphra Behn as the first woman who
earned her living by her pen, one who transformed the experiences of her
own adventurous life into her writing:

> Mrs Behn was a middle-class woman with all the plebeian virtues of
> humour, vitality and courage; a woman forced by the death of her
> husband and some unfortunate adventures of her own to make her
> living by her wits. She had to work on equal terms with men. She
> made, by working hard, enough to live on. The importance of that
> fact outweighs anything that she actually wrote, . . . for here begins the
> freedom of the mind, or rather the possibility that in the course of time
> the mind will be free to write what it likes . . . Aphra Behn proved that
> money could be made by writing at the sacrifice, perhaps, of certain
> agreeable qualities.[1]

Aphra Behn wrote about fifteen plays and fifteen novels and stories.
Oroonoko: or, The Royal Slave (1688), the best known of her works, combines romance and realistic tale. The scene of the novel is Surinam; the
constant lovers are two negro slaves of royal descent who are persecuted and
tortured by their white masters. The characters still display all the virtues
of romantic heroes and the plot is activated by the usual court intrigue;
nevertheless some realistic detail is included, and the tragic ending is
quite unusual in the novel of the time. The rest of Aphra Behn's narrative
work is strongly influenced by the Italian *novella* and mostly quite conventional in character and plot.

Love-Letters between a Noble-Man and his Sister might more accurately
be labelled a "novel of passion" than any of the other epistolary stories I
have quoted, except, perhaps, for the *Portuguese Letters*. The subject of
this novel is not so much the constancy of two lovers threatened by oppres-
sive parents and adverse circumstances – in fact Philander and Sylvia
prove, after their first transports are over, quite untrue (Part II) – but
rather the rise of an unlawful passion. Philander is married to Sylvia's
elder sister. At first they try to suppress their passion, eventually they give
way to it. Love and honour are the conflicting concepts dominating their
conduct, underlying, for instance, Philander's sensuality on the one hand
and Sylvia's initial shyness on the other. Not until the second half of the
novel are the lovers happily united. The suspense of the story is achieved by
a constantly increasing passion on both sides, which finds its main outlet
in a detailed correspondence, the tone of which ranges from rage to rapture.
In her comedies Aphra Behn often displays a forced bawdiness, as though
desiring to prove herself competent in a male domain; in her epistolary

novel, however, she describes with some subtlety and persuasiveness the phenomenon of sensuality. She makes use of the conventional love soliloquy of the Euphuistic novel and the romance, and takes over stock motives from the scandal chronicle. That her novel, despite its traditional content, should so far excel those of her contemporaries is a matter of her ability to observe a little more closely than others had done the slight turns of a wavering mind, of her ability to fuse love and desire into one strong impulse that was neither pornography nor lofty romance. The touch of originality is slight but perceptible.

Love-Letters between a Noble-Man and his Sister is the first epistolary novel to tell its story without the help of a third-person narrative. A considerable amount of outward event is reported in the letters, especially towards the end of the first part, when Sylvia's family, discovering her love affair with Philander, try to force a husband on her; a duel and the separate flight of the lovers to Holland is the result. In Part II and III, however (not printed here), a complicated and at the same time repetitive plot, the introduction of a number of new characters and a decreasing interest in sentimental analysis apparently led the author to abandon her exclusively epistolary technique. Parts II and III lapse into third-person narrative with interspersed letters, a narrative of love and intrigue familiar from romance and scandalous chronicle; but in Part I we have a novel of literary merit: the story has drive and a suspense brought about by letters written in the heat of feeling so that the actual cause of Sylvia's emotion is only gradually revealed.

NOTE:
[1] V. Woolf: *A Room of One's Own*, London, 1931, pp. 95-97.

THE ARGUMENT

IN *the Time of the Rebellion of the true Protestant* Hugonots *in* Paris, *under the Conduct of the Prince of* Conde *(whom we will call* Cesario*) many illustrious Persons were drawn into the Association, amongst which there was one, whose Quality and Fortune (join'd with his Youth and Beauty) render'd him more elevated in the Esteem of the gay Part of the World than most of that Age. In his tender Years (unhappily enough) he chanc'd to fall in Love with a Lady, whom we will call* Myrtilla, *who had Charms enough to engage any Heart; she had all the Advantages of Youth and Nature; a Shape excellent; a most agreeable Stature, not too tall, and far from low, delicately proportion'd; her Face a little enclin'd round, soft, smooth and white; her Eyes were blue, a little languishing, and full of Love and Wit; a Mouth curiously made, dimpled, and full of sweetness; Lips round soft, plump and red; white Teeth, firm and even; her Nose a little* Roman, *and which gave a noble Grace to her lovely Face; her Hair light brown; a Neck and Bosom delicately turn'd, white and rising; her Arms and Hands exactly shap'd; to this a Vivacity of Youth engaging; a Wit quick and flowing; a Humour gay, and an Air unresistibly charming; and nothing was wanting to compleat the Joys of the young* Philander, *(so we call our amorous Hero) but* Myrtilla'*s Heart, which the illustrious* Cesario *had before possess'd; however, consulting her Honour and her Interest, and knowing all the Arts as Women do to feign a Tenderness; she yields to marry him: While* Philander, *who scorn'd to owe his Happiness to the Commands of Parents, or to chaffer for a Beauty, with her Consent steals her away, and marries her. But see how transitory is a violent Passion; after being satiated, he slights the Prize he had so dearly conquer'd; some say the Change was occasion'd by her too visibly continu'd Love to* Cesario; *but whatever 'twas, this was most certain,* Philander *cast his Eyes upon a young Maid, Sister to* Myrtilla, *a Beauty, whose early Bloom promis'd Wonders when come to Perfection; but I will spare her Picture here,* Philander *in the following Epistles will often enough present it to your View: He lov'd and languish'd, long before he durst discover his Pain; her being Sister to his Wife, nobly born, and of undoubted Fame, render'd his Passion too criminal to hope for a Return, while the young lovely* Sylvia *(so we shall call the noble Maid) sigh'd out her Hours in the same Pain and Languishment for* Philander, *and knew not that 'twas Love, 'till she betraying it innocently to the o'erjoy'd Lover and Brother, he soon taught her to understand 'twas Love——he pursues it, she permits it, and at last yields, when being discover'd in the criminal Intrigue, she flies with him; he absolutely quits* Myrtilla, *lives some time in a Village near* Paris, *call'd* St. Denis, *with this betray'd Unfortunate, 'till being found out, and like to be apprehended, (one for the Rape, the other for the Flight) she is forc'd to marry a* Cadet,[1] *a Creature of* Philander'*s, to bear the Name of Husband only to her, while* Philander *had the intire Possession of her Soul and Body: Still the League went forward, and all things were ready for a War in* Paris; *but 'tis* *not my Business here to mix the rough Relation of a War, with the soft Affairs of Love; let it suffice, the* Hugonots *were defeated, and the King got the Day, and every Rebel lay at the Mercy of his Sovereign.* Philander *was taken Prisoner made his Escape to a little Cottage near his own Palace, not far from* Paris, *writes to* Sylvia *to come to him, which she does, and in spight of all the Industry to re-seize him, he got away with* Sylvia.

After their Flight, these Letters were found in their Cabinets, at their House at St. Denis, *where they both liv'd together, for the space of a Year, and they are as exactly as possible plac'd in the Order they were sent, and were those suppos'd to be written towards the latter End of their Amours.*

Love-Letters

To SYLVIA

Though I parted from you resolv'd to obey your impossible Commands, yet know oh charming *Sylvia*! that after a thousand Conflicts between Love and Honour, I found the God (too mighty for the Idol) reign absolute Monarch in my Soul, and soon banish'd that Tyrant thence. That cruel Counsellor that would suggest to you a thousand fond Arguments to hinder my noble Pursuit; *Sylvia* came in view! her unresistable *Idea*! with all the Charm of blooming Youth, with all the Attractions of Heav'nly Beauty! loose, wanton, gay, all flowing her bright Hair, and languishing her lovely Eyes, her Dress all negligent as when I saw her last, discovering a thousand ravishing Graces, round white small Breasts, delicate Neck, and rising Bosom, heav'd with Sighs she would in vain conceal; and all besides, that nicest Fancy can imagine surprizing——Oh I dare not think on, lest my Desires grow mad and raving; let it suffice, oh adorable *Sylvia*! I think and know enough to justifie that Flame in me, which our weak Alliance of Brother and Sister has render'd so criminal; but he that adores *Sylvia*, should do it at an uncommon rate; 'tis not enough to sacrifice a single Heart, to give you a simple Passion, your Beauty should like it self produce wondrous Effects; it should force all Obligations, all Laws, all Ties even of Natures self: You, my lovely Maid, were not born to be obtain'd by the dull Methods of ordinary loving; and 'tis in vain to prescribe me Measures; and oh much more in vain to urge the Nearness of our Relation. What Kin, my charming *Sylvia*, are you to me? No Ties of Blood forbid my Passion? and what's a Ceremony impos'd on Man by Custom? what is it to my divine *Sylvia*, that the Priest took my Hand and gave it to your Sister? What Alliance can that create? Why should a Trick devised by the wary old, only to make Provision for Posterity, tie me to an Eternal Slavery? No, no, my charming Maid, 'tis Nonsense all; let us (born for mightier Joys) scorn the dull *beaten Road*, but let us love like the first Race of Men, nearest ally'd to God, promiscuously they lov'd, and possess'd, Father and Daughter, Brother and Sister met, and reap'd the Joys of Love without Controul, and counted it Religious Coupling, and 'twas encourag'd too by Heav'n it self: Therefore start not (too nice and lovely Maid) at Shadows of things that can but frighten Fools. Put me not off with these Delays; rather say you but dissembled Love all this while, than now 'tis born, to die again with a poor Fright of Nonsense. A Fit of

Honour! a Fantom imaginary, and no more; no, no, represent me to your Soul more favourably, think you see me languishing at your Feet, breathing out my last in Sighs and kind Reproaches, on the pitiless *Sylvia*; reflect when I am dead, which will be the more afflicting Object, the Ghost (as you are pleas'd to call it) of your murder'd Honour, or the pale and bleeding one of

The lost
PHILANDER

I have liv'd a whole Day, and yet no Letter from Sylvia.

To PHILANDER

OH why will you make me own (oh too importunate *Philander*!) with what Regret I made you promise to prefer my Honour before your Love?

I confess with Blushes, which you might then see kindling in my Face, that I was not at all pleas'd with the Vows you made me, to endeavour to obey me, and I then even wish'd you would obstinately have deny'd Obedience to my just Commands; have pursu'd your criminal Flame, and have left me raving on my Undoing: For when you were gone, and I had Leisure to look into my Heart, alas! I found whether you oblig'd or not, whether Love or Honour were preferr'd, I, unhappy I, was either way inevitably lost. Oh! what pitiless God, fond of his wondrous Power, made us the Objects of his Almighty Vanity? Oh why were we two made the first Precedents of his new found Revenge? for sure no Brother ever lov'd a Sister with so criminal a Flame before: At least my unexperienc'd Innocence ne'er met with so fatal a Story: And 'tis in vain (my too charming Brother) to make me insensible of our Alliance; to persuade me I am a Stranger to all but your Eyes and Soul.

Alas, your fatally kind Industry is all in vain. You grew up a Brother with me; the Title was fix'd in my Heart, when I was too young to understand your subtle Distinctions, and there it thriv'd and spread; and 'tis now too late to transplant it, or alter its native Property: Who can graft a Flower on a contrary Stalk? The Rose will bear no Tulips, nor the Hyacinth the Poppy, no more will the Brother the Name of Lover. Oh! spoil not the natural Sweetness and Innocence we now retain, by an Endeavour fruitless and destructive; no, no, *Philander*, dress your self in what Charms you will, be powerful as Love can make you in your soft Argument – yet, oh yet, you are my Brother still,——But why, oh cruel and eternal Powers, was not *Philander* my Lover before you destin'd him a Brother? or why, being a Brother, did you, malicious and spightful Powers, destine him a Lover!

Oh, take either Title from him, or from me a Life which can render me no Satisfaction, since your cruel Laws permit it not for *Philander*, nor his to bless the now

Unfortunate

Wednesday Morning.　　　　　　SYLVIA

To PHILANDER

After I had dismiss'd my Page this Morning with my Letter, I walk'd (fill'd with sad soft Thoughts of my Brother *Philander*) into the Grove, and commanding *Melinda* to retire, who only attended me, I threw my self down on that Bank of Grass where we last disputed the dear but fatal Business of our Souls: Where our Prints (that invited me) still remain on the press'd Greens: There with ten thousand Sighs, with Remembrance of the tender Minutes we pass'd then, I drew your last Letter from my Bosom, and often kiss'd and often read it over; but oh, who can conceive my Torment, when I came to that fatal Part of it, where you say you gave your Hand to my Sister? I found my Soul agitated with a thousand different Passions, but all insupportable, all mad and raving; sometimes I threw my self with Fury on the Ground, and press'd my panting Heart to the Earth; then rise in Rage and tear my Heart, and hardly spare that Face that taught you first to love; then fold my wretched Arms to keep down rising Sighs that almost rend my Breast, I traverse swiftly the conscious Grove; with my distracted show'ring Eyes directed in vain to pitiless Heav'n, the lovely silent Shade favouring my Complaints, I cry aloud, Oh God! *Philander's* marry'd, the lovely charming thing for whom I languish is marry'd!——— That fatal Word's enough, I need not add to whom. Marry'd's enough to make me curse my Birth, my Youth, my Beauty, and my Eyes that first betray'd me to the undoing Object: Curse on the Charms you have flatter'd, for every fancy'd Grace has help'd my Ruin on; now like Flowers that wither unseen and unpossess'd in Shades, they must die and be no more, they were to no end created, since *Philander's* marry'd: Marry'd! oh Fate, oh Hell, oh Torture and Confusion! Tell me not 'tis to my Sister, that Addition is needless and vain: To make me eternally wretched, there needs no more than that *Philander's* marry'd! than that the Priest gave your Hand away from me; to another, and not to me; tir'd out with Life I need no other Pass-port than this Repetition, *Philander's* marry'd! 'Tis that alone is sufficient to lay in her cold Tomb,

The wretched and despairing

Wednesday Night, *Bellfont*.　　　　SYLVIA

205

To SYLVIA

TWICE last Night, oh unfaithful and unloving *Sylvia*! I sent the Page to the old Place for Letters, but he returned the Object of my Rage, because without the least Remembrance from my fickle Maid: In this Torment, unable to hide my Disorder, I suffered my self to be laid in Bed; where the restless Torments of the Night exceeded those of the Day, and are not even by the Languisher himself to be express'd; but the returning Light brought a short Slumber on its Wings; which was interrupted by my atoning Boy, who brought two Letters from my adorable *Sylvia*: He wak'd me from Dreams more agreeable than all my watchful Hours could bring, for they are all tortur'd.——And even the softest mix'd with a thousand Despairs, Difficulties and Disappointments, but these were all Love, which gave a loose to Joys undeny'd by Honour! And this way my charming *Sylvia*, you shall be mine, in spight of all the Tyrannies of that cruel Hinderer; Honour appears not, my *Sylvia*, within the close drawn Curtains, in Shades and gloomy Light the Fantom frights not, but when one beholds its Blushes, when it's attended and adorn'd, and the Sun sees its false Beauties; in silent Groves and Grotto's, dark Alcoves, and lonely Recesses, all its Formalities are laid aside; it was then, and there methought my *Sylvia* yielded, with a faint Struggle and a soft Resistance; I heard her broken Sighs, her tender whispering Voice, that trembling cry'd,——Oh! Can you be so cruel.——Have you the Heart——Will you undo a Maid, because she loves you? Oh! Will you ruin me because you may?——My faithless——My unkind——then sigh'd and yielded, and made me happier than a triumphing God! But this was still a Dream, I wak'd and sigh'd, and found it vanish'd all! But oh, my *Sylvia*, your Letters were substantial Pleasure, and pardon your Adorer if he tell you, even the Disorder you express is infinitely dear to him, since he knows it all the Effects of Love; Love, my Soul! which you in vain oppose; pursue it, Dear, and call it not Undoing or else explain your Fear, and tell me what your soft, your trembling Heart gives that cruel Title to? Is it undoing to love? And love the Man you say has Youth and Beauty to justifie that Love? A Man that adores you with so submissive and perfect a Resignation; a Man that did not only love first, but is resolv'd to die in that agreeable Flame; in my Creation I was form'd for Love, and destin'd for my *Sylvia*, and she for her *Philander*: And shall we, can we disappoint our Fate? No, my soft Charmer, our Souls were touch'd with the same Shafts of Love before they had a Being in our Bodies, and can we contradict Divine Decree?

Or is it undoing, Dear, to bless *Philander* with what you must some time or other sacrifice to some hated, loath'd Object, (for *Sylvia* can never love again;) and are those Treasures for the dull conjugal Lover to rifle? Was the Beauty of Divine Shape created for the cold Matrimonial Embrace? And shall the Eternal Joys that *Sylvia* can dispense, be return'd by the clumsey Husband's careless, forc'd, insipid Duties? Oh, my *Sylvia*, shall a Husband (whose Insensibility will call those Raptures of Joy! Those heavenly blisses! The drudgery of Life) shall he I say receive 'em? While your *Philander*, with the very thought of the Excess of Pleasure the least Possession would afford, faints o'er the Paper that brings here his Eternal Vows.

Oh! where, my *Sylvia*, lies the undoing then? My Quality and Fortune are of the highest Rank amongst Men, my Youth gay and fond, my Soul all soft, all Love; and all *Sylvia*'s! I adore her, I am sick of Love and sick of Life, 'till she yields she is all mine!

You say, my *Sylvia*, I am marry'd, and there my Happiness is shipwreck'd; but *Sylvia*, I deny it, and will not have you think it: No, my Soul was marry'd to yours in its first Creation; and only *Sylvia* is the Wife of my sacred, my everlasting Vows; of my solemn considerate Thoughts, of my ripen'd Judgment, my mature Considerations. The rest are all repented and forgot, like the hasty Follies of unsteady Youth, like Vows breath'd in Anger, and die perjur'd as soon as vented, and unregarded either of Heaven or Man. Oh! why should my Soul suffer for ever, why Eternal Pain for the unheedy short-liv'd Sin of my unwilling Lips? Besides, this fatal thing call'd Wife, this unlucky Sister, this *Myrtilla*, this stop to all my Heav'n, that breeds such fatal Differences in our Affairs, this *Myrtilla*, I say, first broke her Marriage Vows to me; I blame her not, nor is it reasonable I should, she saw the young *Cesario*, and lov'd him. *Cesario*, whom the envying World in spight of Prejudice must own, has irresistible Charms, that Godlike Form, that Sweetness in his Face, that Softness in his Eyes and delicate Mouth; and every Beauty besides that Women doat on, and Men envy: That lovely Composition of Man and Angel! with the Addition of his eternal Youth and illustrious Birth, was form'd by Heaven and Nature for universal Conquest! And who can love the charming Hero at a cheaper rate than being undone? And she that would not venture Fame, Honour, and a Marriage Vow for the Glory of the young *Cesario*'s Heart, merits not the noble Victim; Oh! would I could say so much for the young *Philander*, who would run a thousand times more hazards of Life and Fortune for the adorable *Sylvia*, than that amorous Hero ever did for *Myrtilla*, though from that Prince I learn'd some of my Disguises for my Thefts of Love, for he like *Jove* courted in several Shapes; I saw 'em all, and suffer'd the Delusion to pass upon me; for I had seen the lovely *Sylvia*; yes I had seen her, and lov'd her too: But Honour kept me yet Master of my Vows; but when I knew her false, when I was once confirm'd, – when by my own Soul I found the dissembled Passion of hers, when she could no longer hide the Blushes or the Paleness that seiz'd at the Approaches of my disorder'd Rival, when I saw Love dancing in her Eyes, and her false Heart beat with nimble Motions, and soft trembling seiz'd every Limb, at the

Approach or Touch of the Royal Lover, then I thought my self no longer oblig'd to conceal my Flame for *Sylvia*; nay, e'er I broke Silence, e'er I discover'd the hidden Treasure of my Heart, I made her Falshood plainer yet: Even the Time and Place of the dear Assignations I discover'd; Certainty! happy Certainty! broke the dull heavy Chain, and I with Joy submitted to my shameful Freedom, and caress'd my generous Rival; nay, and by Heav'n I lov'd him for't, pleas'd at the resemblance of our Souls, for we were secret Lovers both, but more pleas'd that he lov'd *Myrtilla*, for that made way to my Passion for the adorable *Sylvia*!

Let the dull, hot-brain'd, jealous Fool upbraid me with cold Patience: Let the fond Coxcomb, whose Honour depends on the frail Marriage Vow, reproach me, or tell me that my Reputation depends on the feeble Constancy of a Wife, persuade me it is Honour to fight for an unretrievable and unvalu'd Prize, and that because my Rival has taken leave to Cuckold me, I shall give him leave to kill me too; unreasonable Nonsense grown to Custom. No, by Heav'n! I had rather *Myrtilla* should be false, (as she is) than with and languish for the happy Occasion; the Sin's the same, only the Act's more generous: Believe me, my *Sylvia*, we have all false Notions of Virtue and Honour, and surely this was taken up by some despairing Husband in Love with a fair Jilting Wife, and then I pardon him; I should have done as much: For only she that has my Soul can engage my Sword, she that I love and my self, only commands and keeps my Stock of Honour: For *Sylvia*! the Charming, the Distracting *Sylvia*! I could fight for a Glance or Smile, expose my Heart for her dearer Fame, and with no Recompence, but breathing out my last Gasp into her soft, white, delicate Bosom. But for a Wife! that Stranger to my Soul, and whom we wed for Interest and Necessity, – A Wife, a light, loose, unregarding Property, who for a momentary Appetite will expose her Fame, without the noble End of loving on; she that will abuse my Bed, and yet return again to the loath'd conjugal Embrace, back to the Arms so hated, that even strong Fancy of the absent Youth belov'd, cannot so much as render supportable. Curse on her, and yet she kisses, fawns and dissembles on, hangs on his Neck, and makes the Sot believe:——Damn her, Brute; I'll whistle'r off, and let her down the Wind, as *Othello* says. No, I adore the Wife, that when the Heart is gone, boldly and nobly pursues the Conqueror, and generously owns the Whore,——Not poorly adds the nauseous Sin of Jilting to't: That I could have born, at least commended; but this can never pardon; at worst then the World had said her Passion had undone her, she lov'd, and Love at worst is worthy of Pity. No, no, *Myrtilla*, I forgive your Love, but never can your poor Dissimulation. One drives you but from the Heart you value not, but t'other to my eternal Contempt. One deprives me but of thee, *Myrtilla* but t'other entitles me to a Beauty more surprizing, renders thee no Part of me; and so leaves the Lover free to *Sylvia*, without the Brother.

Thus, my excellent Maid, I have sent you the Sense and Truth of my Soul, in an Affair you have often hinted to me, and I take no Pleasure to remember: I hope you will at least think my Aversion reasonable; and that being thus undisputably freed from all Obligations to *Myrtilla* as a Husband, I may be permitted to lay Claim to *Sylvia*, as a Lover, and marry my self more effectually by my everlasting Vows, than the Priest by his common Method could do to any other Woman less belov'd, there being no other way at present left by Heav'n, to render me *Sylvia's*

Eternal happy Lover, and

PHILANDER

I die to see you.

To SYLVIA

WHEN I had sealed the inclosed, *Brilliard* told me you were this Morning come from *Bellfont*, and with infinite Impatience have expected seeing you here; which deferr'd my sending this to the old Place; and I am so vain (oh adorable *Sylvia!*) as to believe my fancy'd Silence has given you Disquiets; but sure, my *Sylvia* could not charge me with Neglect; no, she knows my Soul, and lays it all on Chance, or some strange Accident, she knows no Business could divert me. No, were the Nation sinking, the great Senate of the World confounded, our glorious Designs betray'd and ruin'd, and the vast City all in Flames; like *Nero*, unconcern'd, I would sing my everlasting Song of Love to *Sylvia*; which no Time or Fortune shall untune. I know my Soul, and all its Strength, and how it is fortify'd, the charming *Idea* of my young *Sylvia* will for ever remain there; the Original may fade, Time may render it less fair, less blooming in my Arms, but never in my Soul; I shall find thee there the same gay glorious Creature that first surprized and enslaved me, believe me, ravishing Maid, I shall. Why then, oh why, my cruel *Sylvia*! are my Joys delay'd? why am I by your rigorous Commands kept from the Sight of my Heav'n, my eternal Bliss? An Age, my fair Tormentor, 's past; four tedious live-long Days are number'd o'er, since I beheld the Object of my lasting Vows, my eternal Wishes; how can you think, oh unreasonable *Sylvia*! that I could live so long without you? and yet I am alive I find it by my Pain, by Torments of Fears and Jealousies insupportable; I languish and go downward to the Earth; where you will shortly see me laid without your recalling Mercy. 'Tis true I move about this unregarded World, appear every Day in the great Senate-House, at Clubs, Cabals, and private Consultations; (for *Sylvia* knows all the Business of my Soul, even its Politicks of State as well as Love) I say I appear indeed, and give my Voice in publick Business; but oh my Heart more kindly is employ'd, that and my Thoughts are *Sylvia's*! ten thousand times a Day

I breath that Name, my busie Fingers are eternally tracing out those six mystick Letters; a thousand Ways on every thing I touch, form Words, and make them speak a thousand Things, and all are *Sylvia* still; my melancholy Change is evident to all that see me, which they interpret many mistaken ways; our Party fancy I repent my League with them, and doubting I'll betray the Cause, grow jealous of me, till by new Oaths, new Arguments, I confirm them; then they smile all, and cry I am in Love; and this they would believe, but that they see all Women that I meet or converse with are indifferent to me, and so can fix it no where; for none can guess it *Sylvia*; thus while I dare not tell my Soul, no not even to *Cesario*, the stifled Flame burns inward, and torments me so, that (unlike the thing I was) I fear *Sylvia* will lose her Love, and Lover too; for those few Charms she said I had, will fade, and this fatal Distance will destroy both Soul and Body too; my very Reason will abandon me, and I shall rave to see thee; restore me, oh restore me then to *Bellfont*, happy *Bellfont*, still blest with *Sylvia*'s Presence! permit me, oh permit me into those sacred Shades, where I have been so often (too innocently) blest! Let me survey again the dear Character of *Sylvia* on the smooth Birch; oh when shall I sit beneath those Boughs, gazing on the young Goddess of the Grove, hearing her sigh for Love, touching her glowing small white Hands, beholding her killing Eyes languish, and her charming Bosom rise and fall with short-breath'd uncertain Breath; Breath as soft and sweet as the restoring Breeze that glides o'er the new-blown Flowers: But oh what is it? What Heav'n of Perfumes, when it inclines to the ravish'd *Philander*, and whispers Love, it dares not name aloud?

What Power with-holds me then from rushing on thee, from pressing thee with Kisses; folding thee in my transported Arms, and following all the Dictates of Love without Respect or Awe! What is it, oh my *Sylvia*, can detain a Love so violent and raving, and so wild; admit me, sacred Maid, admit me again to those soft Delights, that I may find, if possible, what Divinity (envious of my Bliss) checks my eager Joys, my raging Flame; while you too make an Experiment (worth the Trial) what 'tis makes *Sylvia* deny her

Impatient Adorer,
PHILANDER

My Page is ill, and I am oblig'd to trust Brilliard *with these to the dear Cottage of their Rendezvous; send me your Opinion of his Fidelity: And ah! remember I die to see you.*

To PHILANDER

NOT yet ?—not yet ? oh ye dull tedious Hours when will you glide away ? and bring that happy Moment on, in which I shall at least hear from my *Philander*; eight and forty tedious ones are past, and I am here forgotten still; forlorn, impatient, restless every where; not one of all your little Moments (ye undiverting Hours) can afford me Repose; I drag ye on, a heavy Load; I count ye all, and bless ye when you are gone; but tremble at the approaching ones, and with a Dread expect you; and nothing will divert me now; my Couch is tiresome, and my Glass is vain; my Books are dull, and Conversation insupportable; the Grove affords me no Relief; nor even those Birds to whom I have so often breath'd *Philander's* Name, they sing it on their perching Boughs; no nor the reviewing of his dear Letters, can bring me any Ease. Oh what Fate is reserved for me ! For thus I cannot live; nor surely thus I shall not die. Perhaps *Philander's* making a Trial of Virtue by this Silence. Pursue it, call up all your Reason, my lovely Brother, to your Aid, let us be wise and silent, let us try what that will do towards the Cure of this too infectious Flame; let us, oh let us, my Brother, sit down here, and pursue the Crime of Loving on no farther. Call me Sister— Swear I am so, and nothing but your Sister: And forbear, oh forbear, my charming Brother, to pursue me farther with your soft bewitching Passion; let me alone, let me be ruin'd with Honour, if I must be ruin'd.—For oh ! 'twere much happier I were no more, than that I should be more than *Philander's* Sister; or he than *Sylvia's* Brother: Oh let me ever call you by that cold Name, 'till that of Lover be forgotten:—Ha !—Methinks on the sudden a fit of Virtue informs my Soul, and bids me ask you for what Sin of mine, my charming Brother, you still pursue a Maid that cannot fly: Ungenerous and unkind ! why did you take advantage of those Freedoms I gave you as a Brother ? I smil'd on you, and sometimes kiss'd you too;—— But for my Sister's sake, I play'd with you, suffer'd your Hands and Lips to wander where I dare not now; all which I thought a Sister might allow a Brother, and knew not all the while the Treachery of Love: Oh none, but under that intimate Title of a Brother, could have had the Opportunity to have ruin'd me; that, that betray'd me; I play'd away my Heart at a Game I did not understand; nor knew I when 'twas lost, by degrees so subtle, and an Authority so lawful, you won me out of all. Nay then too, even when all was lost, I would not think it Love. I wonder'd what my sleepless Nights, my waking eternal Thoughts, and slumbring Visions of my lovely Brother meant: I wonder'd why my Soul was continually fill'd with Wishes and new Desires; and still concluded 'twas for my Sister all, 'till I discover'd the Cheat by Jealousie; for when my Sister hung upon your Neck, kiss'd, and caress'd that Face that I ador'd, oh how I found my Colour change, my Limbs all trembled, and my Blood inrag'd, and I could scarce forbear reproaching you; or crying out, Oh why this Fondness, Brother? Sometimes you perceiv'd my Concern, at which you'd smile; for you who had been before in Love, (a Curse upon the fatal time) could guess at my Disorder; then would you turn the wanton play on me: When sullen with my Jealousie and the Cause, I fly your soft Embrace, yet wish you would pursue and overtake me, which you ne'er fail'd to do, where after a kind Quarrel all was pardon'd, and all was well again: While the poor injur'd Innocent, my Sister, made her self sport at our delusive Wars; still I was ignorant, 'till you in a most fatal Hour inform'd me I was a Lover. Thus was it with my Heart in those blest Days of Innocence; thus it was won and lost; nor can all my Stars in Heav'n prevent, I doubt prevent my Ruin. Now you are sure of the fatal Conquest, you scorn the trifling Glory, you are silent now; oh I am inevitably lost, or with you, or without you: And I find by this little Silence and Absence of yours, that 'tis most certain I must either die, or be *Philander*'s

SYLVIA

If Dorillus *come not with a Letter, or that my Page, whom I have sent to his Cottage for one, bring it not, I cannot support my Life: for oh*, Philander, *I have a thousand wild distracting Fears, knowing how you are involv'd in the Interest you have espous'd with the young* Cesario: *How Danger surrounds you, how your Life and Glory depends on the frail Secresie of Villains and Rebels: Oh give me leave to fear eternally your Fame and Life, if not your Love; if* Sylvia *could command*, Philander *should be Loyal as he's Noble; and what generous Maid would not suspect his Vows to a Mistress, who breaks 'em with his Prince and Master! Heaven preserve you and your Glory.*

To PHILANDER

Another Night, oh Heav'ns, and yet no Letter come! Where are you, my *Philander*? What happy Place contains you! If in Heaven, why does not some posting Angel bid me haste after you? if on Earth, why does not some little God of Love bring the grateful Tidings on his painted Wings! if sick, why does not my own fond Heart by sympathy inform me? But that is all active, vigorous, wishing, impatient of delaying, silent, and busie in Imagination: If you are false, if you have forgotten your poor believing and distracted *Sylvia*, why does not that kind Tyrant Death, that meager welcome Vision of the despairing, old and wretched, approach in dead of Night, approach my restless Bed, and tole the dismal Tidings in my frighted listning Ears, and strike me for ever silent, lay me for ever quiet, lost to the World, lost to my faithless Charmer! But if a sense of Honour in you has made you resolve to prefer mine before your Love, made you take up a noble fatal Resolution never to tell me more of your Passion; this were a Trial, I fear my fond Heart wants Courage to bear; or is it a Trick, a cold Fit only assum'd to try how much I love you ? I have no Arts, Heav'n knows, no Guile or double Meaning in my Soul, 'tis all plain native Simplicity, fearful and timorous as Children in the Night, trembling as Doves pursu'd; born soft by Nature, and made tender by Love; what, oh ! what will become of me then ? Yet would I were confirm'd in all my Fears: For as I am, my Condition is yet more deplorable; for I'm in doubt, and Doubt is the worst Torment of the Mind: Oh *Philander*, be merciful, and let me know the worst; do not be cruel while you kill, do it with Pity to the wretched *Sylvia*; oh let me quickly know whether you are at all, or are the most impatient and unfortunate

SYLVIA's

I rave, I die for some Relief.

To PHILANDER

As I was going to send away this enclos'd, *Dorillus* came with two Letters; oh, you cannot think, *Philander*, with how much Reason you call me fickle Maid; for could you but imagine how I am tormentingly divided, how unresolved between violent Love, and cruel Honour, you would say 'twere impossible to fix me any where; or be the same thing for a Moment together: There is not a short Hour pass'd thro' the swift Hand of Time, since I was all despairing, raging Love, jealous, fearful and impatient; and now, now that your fond Letters have dispers'd those Demons, those tormenting Counsellors, and given a little Respite, a little Tranquillity to my Soul; like States luxurious grown with Ease, it ungratefully rebels against the Sovereign Power that made it great and happy; and now that Traitor Honour heads the Mutineers within; Honour, whom my late mighty Fears had almost famish'd and brought to nothing, warm'd and reviv'd by thy new protested Flame, makes War against Almighty Love ! and I, who but now nobly resolv'd for Love, by an Inconstancy natural to my Sex, or rather my Fears, am turn'd over to Honour's Side: So the despairing Man Stands on the River's Bank, design'd to plunge into the rapid Stream, 'till Coward-Fear seizing his timorous Soul, he views around once more the flowery Plains, and looks with wishing Eyes back to the Groves, then sighing stops, and cries, I was too rash, forsakes the dangerous Shore, and hastes away. Thus indiscreet was I, was all for Love, fond and undoing Love ! But when I saw it with full Tide flow in upon me, one Glance of glorious Honour makes me again retreat. I will——I am resolv'd——and must be brave! I cannot forget I am Daughter to the great *Beralti*, and Sister to *Myrtilla*, a yet unspotted Maid, fit to produce a Race of glorious Hero's! And can *Philander's*

213

Love set no higher Value on me than base poor Prostitution? Is that the price of his Heart?——Oh how I hate thee now! or would to Heaven I could. ——Tell me not, thou charming Beguiler, that *Myrtilla* was to blame; was it a Fault in her, and will it be Virtue in me? And can I believe the Crime that made her lose your Heart, will make me Mistress of it? No, if by any Action of hers the noble House of the *Beralti* be dishonour'd, by all the Actions of my Life it shall receive Additions of Lustre and Glory! Nor will I think *Myrtilla*'s Virtue lessen'd for your mistaken Opinion of it, and she may be as much in vain pursu'd, perhaps, by the Prince *Cesario*, as *Sylvia* shall be by the young *Philander*: The envying World talks loud, 'tis true; but oh, if all were true that busie Babbler says, what Lady has her Fame? What Husband is not a Cuckold? Nay, and a Friend to him that made him so? And it is in vain, my too subtle Brother, you think to build the Trophies of your Conquests on the Ruin of both *Myrtilla*'s Fame and mine: Oh how dear would your inglorious Passion cost the great unfortunate House of the *Beralti*, while you poorly ruin the Fame of *Myrtilla*, to make way to the Heart of *Sylvia*! Remember, oh remember once your Passion was as violent for *Myrtilla*, and all the Vows, Oaths, Protestations, Tears and Prayers you make and pay at my Feet, are but the faint Repetitions, the feeble Echo's of what you sigh'd out at hers. Nay, like young *Paris* fled with the fair Prize; your fond, your eager Passion made it a Rape. Oh perfidious!——Let me not call it back to my remembrance.——Oh let me die, rather than call to mind a Time so fatal; when the lovely false *Philander* vow'd his Heart, his faithless Heart away to any Maid but *Sylvia*: ——Oh let it not be possible for me to imagine his dear Arms ever grasping any Body with Joy but *Sylvia*! And yet they did, with Transports of Love! Yes, yes, you lov'd! by Heaven you lov'd this false, this perfidious *Myrtilla*; for false she is; you lov'd her, and I'll have it so; nor shall the Sister in me plead her Cause. She is false beyond all Pardon; for you are beautiful as Heav'n it self can render you, a Shape exactly form'd, not too low, nor too tall, but made to beget soft Desire and everlasting Wishes in all that look on you; but your Face! your lovely Face! inclining to round, large piercing languishing black Eyes, delicate proportion'd Nose, charming dimpled Mouth, plump red Lips, inviting and swelling, white Teeth, small and even, fine Complexion, and a beautiful Turn! All which you had an Art to order in so ingaging a manner that it charm'd all the Beholders, both Sexes were undone with looking on you; and I have heard a witty Man of your Party swear your Face gain'd more to the League and Association than the Cause, and has curs'd a thousand times the false *Myrtilla*, for preferring *Cesario* (less beautiful) to the adorable *Philander*; to add to this Heav'n! how you spoke, when e'er you spoke of Love! in that you far surpass'd the young *Cesario*! as young as he, almost as great and glorious; oh perfidious *Myrtilla*, oh false, oh foolish and ingrate!——That you abandon'd her was just, she was not worth retaining in your Heart, nor could be worth defending with your Sword:——But grant her false; oh *Philander*! How does her Perfidy intitle you to me? False as she is, you still are married to her; inconstant as she is, she is still your Wife; and no Breach of the Nuptial Vow can untie the fatal Knot; and that is a Mystery to common Sense; sure she was born for Mischief; and Fortune, when she gave her you, design'd the Ruin of us all; but most particularly

The Unfortunate
SYLVIA

To SYLVIA

MY Soul's eternal Joy, my *Sylvia*! what have you done, and oh how durst you, knowing my fond Heart, try it with so fatal a Stroke? What means this severe Letter? and why so eagerly at this time? Oh the Day! Is *Myrtilla's* Virtue so defended? Is it a Question now whether she is false or not? Oh poor, oh frivolous Excuse! You love me not; by all that's good, you love me not; to try your Power you have flatter'd and feign'd, oh Woman! false charming Woman! you have undone me, I rave and shall commit such Extravagance that will ruin both: I must upbraid you, fickle and inconstant, I must, and this Distance will not serve, 'tis too great; my Reproaches lose their Force; I burst with Resentment, with injur'd Love; and you are either the most faithless of your Sex, or the most malicious and tormenting: Oh I am past Tricks, my *Sylvia*, your little Arts might do well in a beginning Flame, but to a settled Fire that is arriv'd to the highest degree, it does but damp its Fierceness, and instead of drawing me on, would lessen my Esteem, if any such Deceit were capable to harbour in the Heart of *Sylvia*; but she is all Divine, and I am mistaken in the meaning of what she says. Oh my Adorable, think no more on that dull false thing a Wife; let her be banish'd thy Thoughts, as she is my Soul; let her never appear, though but in a Dream, to fright our solid Joys, or true Happiness; no, let us look forward to Pleasures vast and unconfin'd, to coming Transports, and leave all behind us that contributes not to that Heav'n of Bliss: Remember, oh *Sylvia*, that five tedious Days are past since I sigh'd at your dear Feet; and five Days, to a Man so madly in Love as your *Philander*, is a tedious Age; 'tis now six a Clock in the Morning, *Brilliard* will be with you by eight, and by ten I may have your Permission to see you, and then I need not say how soon I will present my self before you at *Bellfont*; for Heavn's sake, my eternal Blessing, if you design me this Happiness, contrive it so, that I may see no body that belongs to *Bellfont*, but the fair, the lovely *Sylvia*; for I must be more Moments with you, than will be convenient to be taken Notice of, less they suspect our Business to be Love, and that

Discovery, yet may ruin us. Oh! I will delay no longer, my Soul is impatient to see you, I cannot live another Night without it; I die, by Heav'n, I languish for the appointed Hour; you will believe, when you see my languid Face, and dying Eyes, how much and great a Sufferer in Love I am.

My Soul's Delight, you may perhaps deny me from your Fear; but oh, do not, though I ask a mighty Blessing; *Sylvia*'s Company alone, silent, and perhaps by Dark:——Oh tho' I faint with the Thought only of so bless'd an Opportunity, yet you shall secure me, by what Vows, what Imprecations or Ties you please; bind my busie Hands, blind my ravish'd Eyes, command my Tongue, do what you will; but let me hear your Angel's Voice, and have the transported Joy of throwing my self at your Feet; and if you please, give me leave (a Man condemn'd eternally to Love) to plead a little for my Life and Passion; let me remove your Fears; and tho' that mighty Task never make me intirely happy, at least it will be a great Satisfaction to me to know, that 'tis not thro' my own Fault that I am the

Most Wretched
PHILANDER

I have order'd Brilliard *to wait your Commands at* Dorillus's *Cottage, that he may not be seen at* Bellfont: *Resolve to see me to Night, or I shall come without Order, and injure both: My dear damn'd Wife is dispos'd of at a Ball* Cesario *makes to Night; the Opportunity will be lucky, not that I fear her Jealousie, but the Effects of it.*

To PHILANDER

I Tremble with the Apprehension of what you ask: How shall I comply with your fond Desires? My Soul bodes some dire Effect of this bold Enterprize, for I must own (and blush while I do own it) that my Soul yields Obedience to your soft Request, and even whilst I read your Letter, was diverted with the Contrivance of seeing you: For though, as my Brother, you have all the Freedoms imaginable at *Bellfont* to entertain and walk with me, yet it would be difficult and prejudicial to my Honour, to receive you alone any where without my Sister, and cause a Suspicion, which all about me now are very far from conceiving, except *Melinda*, my faithful Confident, and too fatal Counsellor; and but for this fear, I know, my charming Brother, three little Leagues should not five long Days separate *Philander* from his *Sylvia*: But, my lovely Brother, since you beg it so earnestly, and my Heart consents so easily, I must pronounce my own Doom, and say, Come, my *Philander*, whither Love or soft Desire invites you; and take this Direction in the Management of this mighty Affair. I would have you, as soon as this comes to your Hands, to haste to *Dorillus*'s Cottage, without your Equipage, only *Brilliard*, whom I believe you may trust both from his own Discretion, and your vast Bounties to him; wait there 'till you receive my Commands, and I will retire betimes to my Apartment, pretending not to be well; and as soon as the Evening's Obscurity will permit, *Melinda* shall let you in at the *Garden Gate*, that is next the *Grove*, unseen and unsuspected; but oh, thou powerful Charmer, have a care, I trust you with my All: My dear, dear, my precious Honour, guard it well; for oh I fear my Forces are too weak to stand your shock of Beauties; you have Charms enough to justifie my yielding; but yet, by Heav'n, I would not for an Empire: But what is dull Empire to Almighty Love? The God subdues the Monarch; 'tis to your Strength I trust, for I am a feeble Woman; a Virgin quite disarm'd by two fair Eyes, an Angel's Voice and Form; but yet I'll die before I'll yield my Honour; no, though our unhappy Family have met Reproach from the imagined Levity of my Sister, 'tis I'll redeem the bleeding Honour of our Family, and my great Parents Virtues shall shine in me; I know it, for if it passes this Test, if I can stand this Temptation, I am Proof against all the World; but I conjure you aid me if I need it: If I incline but in a languishing Look, if but a Wish appear in my Eyes, or I betray Consent but in a Sigh; take not, oh take not the Opportunity, lest when you have done I grow raging mad, and discover all in the wild Fit. Oh who would venture on an Enemy with such unequal Force? What hardy Fool would hazard all at Sea, that sees the rising Storm come rouling on? Who but fond Woman, giddy heedless Woman, would thus expose her Virtue to Temptation? I see, I know my Danger yet I must permit it: Love, soft bewitching Love will have it so, that cannot deny what my feebler Honour forbids; and though I tremble with Fear, yet Love suggests, it will be an Age to Night; I long for my Undoing; for oh I cannot stand the Batteries of your Eyes and Tongue; these Fears, these Conflicts I have a thousand times a Day; it is pitiful sometimes to see me, on one Hand a thousand *Cupids* all gay and smiling present *Philander* with all the Beauties of his Sex, with all the Softness in his Looks and Language those Gods of Love can inspire, with all the Charms of Youth adorn'd, bewitching all, and all transporting; on the other Hand, a poor lost Virgin languishing and undone, sighing her willing Rape to the deaf Shades and Fountains, filling the Woods with Cries, swelling the murmuring Rivulets with Tears, her noble Parents with a generous Rage reviling her, and her betray'd Sister loading her bow'd Head with Curses and Reproaches, and all about her looking forlorn and sad. Judge, oh judge, my adorable Brother, of the Vastness of my Courage and Passion, when even this deplorable Prospect cannot defend me from the Resolution of giving you Admittance into my Apartment this Night, nor shall ever drive you from the Soul of your

SYLVIA

To SYLVIA

I have obey'd my *Sylvia*'s dear Commands, and the Dictates of my own impatient Soul; as soon as I receiv'd them, I immediately took Horse for *Bellfont*, tho' I knew I should not see my Adorable *Sylvia* 'till Eight or Nine at Night; but oh 'tis wondrous Pleasure to be so much more near my eternal Joy; I wait at *Dorillus*'s Cottage the tedious approaching Night that must shelter me in its kind Shades, and conduct me to a Pleasure I faint but with imagining; 'tis now, my lovely Charmer, Three a Clock, and oh how many tedious Hours I am to languish here before the blessed One arrive! I know you love, my *Sylvia*, and therefore must guess at some part of my Torment, which yet is mix'd with a certain trembling Joy not to be imagin'd by any but *Sylvia*, who surely loves *Philander*; if there be Truth in Beauty, Faith in Youth, she surely loves him much; and much more above her Sex she is capable of Love, by how much more her Soul is form'd of a softer and more delicate Composition; by how much more her Wit's refin'd and elevated above her duller Sex, and by how much more she is oblig'd; if Passion can claim Passion in return, sure no Beauty was ever so much indebted to a Slave, as *Sylvia* to *Philander*; none ever lov'd like me: Judge then my Pains of Love, my Joys, my Fears, my Impatience and Desires; and call me to your sacred Presence with all the speed of Love, and as soon as it is duskish, imagine me in the Meadow behind the Grove, 'till when think me employ'd in eternal Thoughts of *Sylvia*; restless, and talking to the Trees of *Sylvia*, sighing her charming Name, circling with folded Arms my panting Heart, (that beats and trembles the more, the nearer it approaches the happy *Bellfont*) and fortifying the feeble Trembler against a Sight so ravishing and surprizing; I fear to be sustain'd with Life; but if I faint in *Sylvia*'s Arms, it will be happier far than all the Glories of Life without her.

Send, my Angel, something from you to make the Hours less tedious: consider me, love me, and be as impatient as I, that you may the sooner find at your Feet your everlasting Lover,

PHILANDER

From Dorillus's *Cottage*.

To PHILANDER

I Have at last recover'd Sense enough to tell you, I have receiv'd your Letter by *Dorillus*, and which had like to have been discover'd; for he prudently enough put it under the Strawberries he brought me in a Basket, fearing he should get no other Opportunity to have given it me; and my Mother seeing them look so fair and fresh, snatch'd the Basket with a Greediness I have not seen in her before; while she was calling to her Page for a Porcellane Dish to put them out, *Dorillus* had an Opportunity to hint to me what lay at the Bottom: Heav'ns! had you seen my Disorder and Confusion; what should I do? Love had not one Invention in store, and here it was that all the Subtilty of Women abandon'd me. Oh Heav'ns, how cold and pale I grew, lest the most important Business of my Life should be betray'd and ruin'd! but not to terrify you longer with Fears of my Danger, the Dish came, and out the Strawberries were pour'd, and the Basket thrown aside on the Bank where my Mother sate, (for we were in the Garden when we met accidentally *Dorillus* first with the Basket;) there were some Leaves of Fern put at the Bottom between the Basket and Letter, which by good Fortune came not out with the Strawberries, and after a Minute or two I took up the Basket, and walking carelessly up and down the Garden, gather'd here and there a Flower, Pinks and Jessamine, and filling my Basket, sate down again 'till my Mother had eat her Fill of the Fruit, and gave me an Opportunity to retire to my Apartment, where opening the Letter, and finding you so near, and waiting to see me, I had certainly sunk down on the Floor, had not *Melinda* supported me, who was only by; something so new, and 'till now so strange, seiz'd me at the Thought of so secret an Interview, that I lost all my Senses, and Life wholly departing, I rested on *Melinda* without Breath or Motion; the violent Effects of Love and Honour, the impetuous meeting Tides of the Extreams of Joy and Fear, rushing on too suddenly, overwhelm'd my Senses; and it was a pretty while before I recover'd Strength to get to my Cabinet, where a second time I open'd your Letter, and read it again with a thousand Changes of Countenance; my whole Mass of Blood was in that Moment so discompos'd, that I chang'd from an Ague to a Fever several times in a Minute: Oh what will all this bring me to? And where will the raging Fit end? I die with that Thought, my guilty Pen slackens in my trembling Hand, and I languish and fall over the un-employ'd Paper;——Oh help me, some Divinity,——Or if you did,——I fear I should be angry: Oh *Philander*! a thousand Passions and distracted Thoughts croud to get out, and make their soft Complaints to thee; but oh they lose themselves with mixing; they are blended in a Confusion together, and Love nor Art can divide them, to deal them out in Order; sometimes I would tell you of my Joy at your Arrival, and my unspeakable Transports at the thought of seeing you so soon, that I shall hear your charming Voice, and find you at my Feet making soft Vows anew, with all the Passion of an impatient Lover, with all the Eloquence that Sighs and Cries, and Tears from those lovely Eyes can express; and sure that is enough to conquer any where, and to which coarse vulgar Words are dull. The Rhetorick of Love is half-breath'd, interrupted Words, languishing Eyes, flattering Speeches, broken Sighs, pressing the Hand, and falling Tears: Ah how do they not persuade, how do they not charm and conquer; 'twas thus, with these soft easy Arts, that *Sylvia* first was won; for sure no Arts of speaking could have talked my Heart away, though you can speak like any God: Oh whither am I driven? What do I say? 'Twas not my Purpose, not my Business here, to give a Character of *Philander*, no nor to speak of Love; but oh! like *Cowley*'s Lute, my Soul will sound to nothing but to Love: Talk what you will, begin what Discourse you please, I end it all in Love, because my Soul is ever fix'd on *Philander*, and insensibly its Biass leads to that Subject; no, I did not, when I began to write, think of speaking one Word of my own Weakness; but to have told you with what resolv'd Courage, Honour and Virtue, I expect your coming; and sure so sacred a thing as Love was not made to ruin these, and therefore in vain, my lovely Brother, you will attempt it; and yet, oh Heav'ns! I gave a private Assignation, in my Apartment, alone and at Night; where Silence, Love and Shades, are all your Friends, where Opportunity obliges your Passion, while, Heav'n knows, not one of all these, nor any kind Power, is Friend to me; I shall be left to you and all these Tyrants expos'd, without other Guards than this boasted Virtue, which had need be wondrous to resist all these powerful Enemies of its Purity and Repose. Alas I know not its Strength, I never try'd it yet; and this will be the first time it has ever been expos'd to your Power; the first time I ever had Courage to meet you as a Lover, and let you in by stealth, and put my self unguarded into your Hands: Oh I die with the Apprehension of approaching Danger! and yet I have not Power to retreat; I must on, Love compels me, Love holds me fast; the smiling Flatterer promises a thousand Joys, a thousand ravishing Minutes of Delight; all innocent and harmless as his Mother's Doves: But oh they bill and kiss, and do a thousand things I must forbid *Philander*; for I have often heard him say with Sighs, that his Complexion render'd him less capable of the soft Play of Love, than any other Lover: I have seen him fly my very Touches, yet swear they were the greatest Joy on Earth: I tempt him even with my Looks from Virtue; and when I ask the Cause, or cry he is cold, he Vows 'tis because he dares not endure my Temptations; says his Blood runs hotter and fiercer in his Veins than any others does; nor has the oft repeated Joys reap'd in the Marriage Bed, any thing abated that which he wish'd, but he fear'd would ruin me: Thus, thus whole Days we have sate, and gaz'd, and sigh'd; but durst not trust our Virtues with fond Dalliance.

My Page is come to tell me that Madam the Dutchess of —— is come to *Bellfont*, and I am oblig'd to quit my Cabinet, but with infinite Regret, being at present much more to my Soul's Content employ'd; but Love must sometimes give place to *Devoir*, and Respect. *Dorillus* too waits, and tells *Melinda* he will not depart without something for his Lord, to entertain him till the happy Hour. The Rustick pleas'd me with the Concern he had for my *Philander*; oh my charming Brother, you have an Art to tame even Savages, a Tongue that would charm and engage Wildness it self, to Softness and Gentleness, and give the rough unthinking, Love; 'tis a tedious time to Night, how shall I pass the Hours?

To SYLVIA

SAY, fond Love, whither wilt thou lead me? Thou hast brought me from the noisie Hurries of the Town, to charming Solitude; from crouded Cabals, where mighty Things are resolving, to lonely Groves; to thy own Abodes where thou dwell'st; gay and pleas'd amongst the Rural Swains in shady homely Cottages; thou hast brought me to a Grove of Flowers, to the Brink of purling Streams, where thou hast laid me down to contemplate on *Sylvia*, to think my tedious Hours away in the softest Imagination a Soul inspir'd by Love can conceive, to increase my Passion by every thing I behold; for every Sound that meets the Sense is thy proper Musick, oh Love, and every thing inspires thy Dictates; the Winds around me blow soft, and mixing with wanton Boughs, continually play and kiss; while those, like a coy Maid in Love, resist, and comply by Turns; they, like a ravish'd vigorous Lover, rush on with a transported Violence, rudely embracing its Spring-dress'd Mistress, ruffling her Native Order; while the pretty Birds on the dancing Branches incessantly make Love; upbraiding duller Man with his defective want of Fire: Man, the Lord of all! He to be stinted in the most valuable Joy of Life; Is it not pity? Here is no troublesome Honour, amongst the pretty Inhabitants of the Woods and Streams, fondly to give Laws to Nature, but uncontroul'd they play, and sing, and love; no Parents checking their dear Delights, no slavish Matrimonial Ties to restrain their nobler Flame. No Spies to interrupt their blest Appointments; but every little Nest is free and open to receive the young fletch'd Lover; every Bough is conscious of their Passion, nor do the generous Pair languish in tedious Ceremony; but meeting look, and like, and love, imbrace with their wingy Arms, and salute with their little opening Bills; this is their Courtship, this the amorous Complement, and this only the Introduction to all their following Happiness; and thus it is with the Flocks and Herds, while scanted Man, born alone for the Fatigues of Love, with industrious Toil, and all his boasting Arts of Eloquence, his God-like Image, and his noble Form, may labour on a tedious Term of Years, with Pain, Expence, and Hazard, before he can arrive at Happiness, and then too perhaps his Vows are unregarded, and all his Sighs and Tears are vain. Tell me, oh you Fellow-Lovers, ye amorous dear Brutes, tell me, when ever you lay languish-ing beneath your Coverts, thus for your fair She, and durst not approach for fear of Honour? Tell me, by a gentle Bleat, ye little butting Rams, do you sigh thus for your soft, white Ewes? Do you lye thus conceal'd, to wait the coming Shades of Night, 'till all the cursed Spies are folded? No, no, even you are much more blest than Man, who is bound up to Rules, fetter'd by the nice Decencies of Honour.

My Divine Maid, thus were my Thoughts employ'd, when from the farthest end of the Grove, where I now remain, I saw *Dorillus* approach with thy welcome Letter; he tells you had like to have been surpriz'd in making it up; and he receiv'd it with much Difficulty: Ah *Sylvia*, should any Accident happen to prevent my seeing you to Night, I were undone for ever, and you must expect to find me stretch'd out, dead and cold under this Oak where now I lye writing on its knotty Root. Thy Letter, I confess, is dear; it contains thy Soul, and my Happiness; but this After-story of the Surprize I long to be inform'd of, for from thence I may gather part of my Fortune. I rave and die with fear of a Disappointment; not but I would undergo a thousand Torments and Deaths for *Sylvia*; but oh consider me, and let me not suffer if possible; for know, my charming Angel, my impatient Heart is almost broke, and will not contain it self without being nearer my adorable Maid, without taking in at my Eyes a little Comfort; no, I am resolv'd; put me not off with Tricks, which foolish Honour invents to jilt Mankind with; for if you do, by Heav'n I will forget all Considerations and Respect, and force my self with all the Violence of raging Love into the Presence of my cruel *Sylvia*; own her mine, and ravish my Delight; nor shall the happy Walls of *Bellfont* be of Strength sufficient to secure her; nay, persuade me not, for if you make me mad and raving, this will be the Effects on't:——Oh pardon me, my sacred Maid, pardon the Wildness of my frantick Love——I paused, took a Turn or two in the lone Path, consider'd what I had said, and found it was too much, too bold, too rude to approach my soft, my tender Maid: I am calm, my Soul, as thy bewitching Smiles; hush, as thy secret Sighs, and will resolve to die rather than offend my adorable Virgin; only send me Word what you think of my Fate, while I expect it here on this kind Mossie Bed where now I lie; which I would not quit for a Throne, since here I may hope the News may soonest arrive to make me happier than a God! which that nothing on my part may prevent, I here vow in the Face of Heav'n, I will not abuse the Freedom my *Sylvia* blesses me with; nor shall my Love go beyond the Limits of Honour. *Sylvia* shall command with a Frown, and fetter me with a Smile; prescribe Rules to my longing, ravish'd Eyes, and pinion my busie, fond, roving Hands, and lay at her Feet, like a tame Slave, her Adoring

PHILANDER

To PHILANDER

Approach, approach, you sacred Queen of Night, and bring *Philander* veil'd from all Eyes but mine; approach at a fond Lover's Call, behold how I lye panting with Expectation, tir'd out with your tedious Ceremony to the God of Day; be kind, oh lovely Night, and let the Deity descend to his beloved *Thetis*'s Arms, and I to my *Philander*'s; the Sun and I must snatch our Joys in the same happy Hours; favour'd by thee, oh sacred, silent Night!

See, see, the inamour'd Sun is hasting on apace to his expecting Mistress, while thou dull Night art slowly lingring yet. Advance, my Friend! my Goddess! and my Confident! hide all my Blushes, all my soft Confusions, my Tremblings, Transports, and Eyes all languishing.

Oh *Philander*! a thousand things I have done to divert the tedious Hours, but nothing can; all things are dull without thee. I am tir'd with every thing, impatient to end, as soon as I begin them; even the Shades and solitary Walks afford me now no Ease, no Satisfaction, and Thought but afflicts me more, that us'd to relieve. And I at last have Recourse to my kind Pen: For while I write, methinks I am talking to thee; I tell thee thus my Soul, while thou, methinks are all the while smiling and listning by; this is much easier than silent Thought, and my Soul is never weary of this Converse; and thus I would speak a thousand things, but that still, methinks, Words do not enough express my Soul; to understand that right, there requires Looks; there is a Rhetorick in Looks; in Sighs and silent Touches that surpasses all; there is an Accent in the Sound of Words too, that gives a Sense and soft Meaning to little things, which of themselves are of trivial Value, and insignificant; and by the Cadence of the Utterance may express a Tenderness which their own Meaning does not bear; by this I would insinuate, that the Story of the Heart cannot be so well told by this way, as by Presence and Conversation; sure *Philander* understands what I mean by this, which possibly is Nonsense to all but a Lover, who apprehends all the little fond Prattle of the thing belov'd, and finds an Eloquence in it, that to a Sense unconcern'd would appear even approaching to Folly: But *Philander*, who has the true Notions of Love in him, apprehends all that can be said on that dear Subject; to him I venture to say any thing, whose kind and soft Imaginations can supply all my Wants in the Description of the Soul; Will it not, *Philander*? Answer me:——But oh, where art thou? I see thee not I touch thee not; but when I haste with Transport to embrace thee, 'tis Shadow all, and my poor Arms return empty to my Bosom: Why, oh why com'st thou not? Why art thou cautious, and prudently waitest the slow-pac'd Night: Oh cold, oh unreasonable Lover, why?——But I grow wild, and know not what I say: Impatient Love betrays me to a thousand Follies, a thousand Rashnesses: I die with Shame; but I must be undone, and it is no matter how, whether by my own Weakness, *Philander*'s Charms, or both, I know not; but so it is destin'd,——Oh *Philander*, it is two tedious Hours Love has counted since you writ to me, yet are but a quarter of a Mile distant; what have you been doing all that live-long while? Are you not unkind? Does not *Sylvia* lie neglected and unregarded in your Thoughts? Huddled up confusedly with your graver Business of State, and almost lost in the ambitious Croud? Say, say, my lovely Charmer, is she not? Does not this fatal Interest you espouse, rival your *Sylvia*? Is she not too often remov'd thence to let in that haughty Tyrant Mistress? Alas, *Philander*, I more than fear she is? and oh, my adorable Lover, when I look forward on our coming Happiness, when ever I lay by the Thoughts of Honour, and give a loose to Love; I run not far in the pleasing Career, before that dreadful Thought stopp'd me on my Way; I have a fatal prophetick Fear, that gives a Check to my soft Pursuit, and tells me that thy unhappy Engagement in this League, this accursed Association, will one Day undo us both, and part for ever thee and thy unlucky *Sylvia*; Yes, yes, my dear Lord, my Soul does presage an unfortunate Event from this dire Engagement; nor can your false Reasoning, your fancy'd Advantages, reconcile it to my honest, good-natur'd Heart; and surely the Design is inconsistent with Love, for two such mighty Contradictions and Enemies, as Love and Ambition, or Revenge, can never sure abide in one Soul together, at least Love can but share *Philander*'s Heart; when Blood and Revenge (which he miscalls Glory) rivals it, and has possibly the greatest part in it: Methinks, this Notion enlarges in me, and every Word I speak, and every Minute's Thought of it, strengthens its Reason to me; and give me leave (while I am full of the Jealousie of it) to express my Sentiments, and lay before you those Reasons, that Love and I think most substantial ones; what you have hitherto desired of me, oh unreasonable *Philander*, and what I (out of Modesty and Honour) deny'd, I have Reason to fear (from the absolute Conquest you have made of my Heart) that some time or other the charming Thief may break in and rob me of; for Fame and Virtue Love begins to laugh at. My dear unfortunate Condition being thus, it is not impossible, oh *Philander*, but I may one Day, in some unlucky Hour, in some soft bewitching Moment, in some spightful, critical, ravishing Minute; yield all to the charming *Philander*; and if so, where, oh where is my Security, that I shall not be abandon'd by the lovely Victor? For it is not your Vows which you call sacred (and I alas believe so) that can secure me, tho' I, Heaven knows, believe them all, and am undone; you may keep them all too, and I believe you will; but oh, *Philander*, in these fatal Circumstances you have engag'd your self; can you secure me my Lover? Your Protestations you may, but not the dear Protestor. Is it not enough, oh *Philander*, for my eternal Unquiet, and Undoing, to know that you are marry'd, and cannot therefore be entirely mine; is not this enough, oh cruel *Philander*? But you must espouse a fatal Cause too, more pernicious than that of Matrimony, and more destructive to my Repose: Oh give me leave to reason with you, and since you have been pleas'd to trust and afflict me with the Secret, which, honest as I am, I will never betray; yet, yet give me leave to urge the Danger of it to you, and consequently to me, if you pursue it; when you are with me, we can think, and talk, and argue nothing but the mightier Business of Love; and it is fit that I, so fondly, and fatally lov'd by you, should warn you of the Danger. Consider, my Lord, you are born Noble, from Parents of untainted Loyalty; blest with a Fortune few Princes beneath Sovereignty are Masters of; blest with all gaining Youth, commanding Beauty, Wit, Courage, Bravery of Mind, and all that renders Men esteem'd and ador'd; What would you more? What is it, oh my charming Brother then, that you set up for? Is it Glory? Oh mistaken, lovely Youth, that Glory is but a glittering Light, that flashes for a Moment, and then it disappears; it is a false Bravery, that will bring an eternal Blemish upon your honest Fame and House; render your honourable Name hated, detested, and abominable in Story to after Ages; a Traytor! the worst of Titles, the most inglorious and shameful; what has the King, our good, our gracious Monarch done to *Philander*? How disoblig'd him? Or indeed, what Injury to Mankind? Who has he oppress'd? Where play'd the Tyrant, or the Ravisher? What one cruel or angry thing has he committed in all the time of his fortunate and peaceable Reign over us? Whose Ox or whose Ass has he unjustly taken? What Orphan wrong'd, or Widow's Tears neglected? But all his Life has been one continued Miracle; all good, all gracious, calm and merciful: And this good, this Godlike King is mark'd out for Slaughter, design'd a Sacrifice to the private Revenge of a few ambitious Knaves and Rebels, whose Pretence is the publick Good, and doom'd to be basely murder'd: A Murder! even on the worst of Criminals, carries with it a Cowardise so black and infamous, as the most abject Wretches, the meanest spirited Creature has an Abhorrence for: What! to murder a Man unthinking, unwarn'd, unprepar'd and undefended! oh barbarous! oh poor and most unbrave! What Villain is there lost to all Humanity, to be found upon the Face of the Earth, that, when done, dare own so hellish a Deed as the Murder of the meanest of his Fellow Subjects, much less the sacred Person of the King; the Lord's Anointed; on whose awful Face 'tis impossible to look without that Reverence wherewith one would behold a God! For 'tis most certain, that every Glance from his piercing, wondrous Eyes, begets a trembling Adoration; for my part, I swear to you, *Philander*, I never approach his sacred Person, but my Heart beats, my Blood runs cold about me, and my Eyes overflow with Tears of Joy, while an awful Confusion seizes me all over; and I am certain should the most harden'd of your bloody Rebels look him in the Face, the devilish Instrument of Death would drop from his sacrilegious Hand, and leave him confounded at the Feet of the Royal forgiving Sufferer; his Eyes have in them something so fierce, so majestick commanding, and yet so good and merciful, as would soften Rebellion itself into repenting Loyalty; and like *Caius Marius*, seem to say,——Who is it dares hurt the King?——They alone, like his Guardian Angels, defend his sacred Person; Oh? what Pity it is, unhappy young Man, thy Education was not near the King.

'Tis plain, 'tis reasonable, 'tis honest, great and glorious to believe, what thy own Sense (if thou wilt but think and consider) will instruct thee in, that Treason, Rebellion and Murder, are far from the Paths that lead to Glory, which are as distant as Hell from Heaven. What is it then to advance?

(since I say 'tis plain, Glory is never this way to be atchiev'd) Is it to add more thousands to those Fortune has already so lavishly bestow'd on you? Oh my *Philander*, that's to double the vast Crime, which reaches already to Damnation: Would your Honour, your Conscience, your Christianity, or common Humanity suffer you to inlarge your Fortunes at the Price of another's Ruin; and make the Spoils of some honest, noble, unfortunate Family, the Rewards of your Treachery? Would you build your Fame on such a Foundation? Perhaps on the Destruction of some Friend or Kinsman. Oh barbarous and mistaken Greatness; Thieves and Robbers would scorn such Outrages, that had but Souls and Sense.

Is it for Addition of Titles? What Elevation can you have much greater than where you now stand fix'd? If you do not grow giddy with your fancied false Hopes, and fall from that glorious Height you are already arriv'd to, and which, with the honest Addition of Loyalty, is of far more Value and Lustre, than to arrive at Crowns by Blood and Treason. This will last; to Ages last; in Story last: While t'other will be ridicul'd to all Posterity, short-liv'd and reproachful here, infamous and accurs'd to all Eternity.

Is it to make *Cesario* King? Oh what is *Cesario* to my *Philander*? If a Monarchy you design, then why not this King, this great, this good, this Royal Forgiver? This, who was born a King, and born your King; and holds his Crown by Right of Nature, by Right of Law, by Right of Heaven itself; Heaven who has preserv'd him, and confirm'd him ours, by a thousand miraculous Escapes and Sufferings, and indulg'd him ours by ten thousand Acts of Mercy, and endear'd him to us by his wondrous Care and Conduct, by securing of Peace, Plenty, Ease and luxurious Happiness, o'er all the fortunate Limits of his blessed Kingdoms: And will you? Would you destroy this wondrous Gift of Heav'n? this Godlike King, this real Good we now possess, for a most uncertain one; and with it the Repose of all the happy Nation? To establish a King without Law, without Right, without Consent, without Title, and indeed without even competent Parts, for so vast a Trust, or so glorious a Rule? One who never oblig'd the Nation by one single Act of Goodness or Valour, in all the Course of his Life; and who never signaliz'd himself to the Advantage of one Man of all the kingdom; A Prince unfortunate in his Principles and Morals; and whose sole, single Ingratitude to his Majesty, for so many royal Bounties, Honours, and Glories heap'd upon him, is of it self enough to set any honest generous Heart against him. What is it bewitches you so? Is it his Beauty? Then *Philander* has a greater Title than *Cesario*; and not one other Merit has he, since in Piety, Chastity, Sobriety, Charity and Honour, he as little excels, as in Gratitude, Obedience and Loyalty. What then, my dear *Philander*? Is it his Weakness? Ah, there's the Argument: You all propose, and think to govern so soft a King: But believe me, oh unhappy *Philander*! nothing is more ungovernable than a Fool; nothing more obstinate, wilful, conceited, and cunning; and for his Gratitude, let the World judge what he must prove to his Servants, who has dealt so ill with his Lord and Master; how he must reward those that present him with a Crown; who deals so ungraciously with him who gave him Life, and who set him up an happier Object than a Monarch: No, no, *Philander*; he that can cabal, and contrive to dethrone a Father, will find it easie to discard the wicked and hated Instruments, that assisted him to mount it; decline him then, oh fond and deluded *Philander*, decline him early; for you of all the rest ought to do so, and not to set a helping Hand to load him with Honours, that chose you out from all the World to load with Infamy: Remember that; remember *Myrtilla*, and then renounce him; do not you contribute to the adorning of his unfit Head with a Diadem, the most glorious of Ornaments, who unadorn'd yours with the most inglorious of all Reproaches. Think of this, oh thou unconsidering, noble Youth; lay thy Hand upon thy generous Heart, and tell it all the Fears, all the Reasonings of her that loves thee more than Life. A thousand Arguments I could bring, but these few unstudied (falling in amongst my softer Thoughts) I beg you will accept of, 'till I can more at large deliver the glorious Argument to your Soul; let this suffice to tell thee, that, like *Cassandra*, I rave and prophesie in vain; this Association will be the eternal ruin of *Philander*; for let it succeed or not, either way thou art undone; if thou pursuest it, I must infallibly fall with thee, if I resolve to follow thy good or ill Fortune; for you cannot intend Love and Ambition, *Sylvia* and *Cesario* at once: No, persuade me not; the Title to one or t'other must be laid down, *Sylvia* or *Cesario* must be abandon'd: This is my fix'd Resolve, if thy too powerful Arguments convince not in spight of Reason, for they can do't; thou hast the Tongue of an Angel, and the Eloquence of a God, and while I listen to thy Voice, I take all thou say'st for wondrous Sense. ——Farewel; about two Hours hence I shall expect you at the Gate that leads into the Garden Grove——Adieu! Remember

SYLVIA

To SYLVIA

How comes my charming *Sylvia* so skill'd in the Mysteries of State? Where learnt her tender Heart the Notions of rigid Business? Where her soft Tongue, form'd only for the dear Language of Love, to talk of the Concerns of Nations and Kingdoms? 'Tis true, when I gave my Soul away to my dear Counsellor, I reserv'd nothing to my self, not even that Secret that so concern'd my Life, but laid all at her Mercy; my generous Heart could not love at a less rate, than to lavish all, and be undone for *Sylvia*; 'tis glorious Ruin, and it pleases me, if it advance one single Joy, or add one

Demonstration of my Love to *Sylvia*; 'tis not enough that we tell those we love all they love to hear, but one ought to tell them too, every Secret that we know, and conceal no part of that Heart one has made a Present to the Person one loves; 'tis a Treason in Love not to be pardon'd: I am sensible that when my Story is told (and this happy one of my Love shall make up the greatest Part of my History) those that love not like me will be apt to blame me, and charge me with Weakness, for revealing so great a Trust to a Woman, and amongst all that I shall do to arrive at Glory, that will brand me with Feebleness; but, *Sylvia*, when Lovers shall read it, the Men will excuse me, and the Maids bless me! I shall be a fond admir'd Precedent for them to point out to their remiss reserving Lovers who will be reproach'd for not pursuing my Example. I know not what Opinion Men generally have of the Weakness of Woman; but 'tis sure a vulgar Error, for were they like my adorable *Sylvia*, had they had her Wit, her Vivacity of Spirit, her Courage, her generous Fortitude, her Command in every graceful Look and Action, they were most certainly fit to rule and reign; and Man was only born robust and strong, to secure them on those Thrones they are form'd (by Beauty, Softness, and a thousand Charms which Men want) to possess. Glorious Woman was born for Command and Dominion; and tho' Custom has usurp'd us the Name of Rule over all; we from the Beginning found our selves (in spight of all our boasted Prerogative) Slaves and Vassals to the Almighty Sex. Take then my Share of Empire, ye Gods! and give me Love! Let me toil to gain, but let *Sylvia* triumph and reign; I ask no more than the led Slave at her Chariot Wheels, to gaze on my charming Conqueress, and wear with Joy her Fetters! Oh how proud I should be to see the dear Victor of my Soul so elevated, so adorn'd with Crowns and Scepters at her Feet, which I had won; to see her smiling on the adoring Croud, distributing her Glories to young waiting Princes; there dealing Provinces, and there a Coronet. Heavn's! methinks I see the lovely Virgin in this State, her Chariot slowly driving through the Multitude that press to gaze upon her, she dress'd like *Venus*, richly, gay and loose, her Hair and Robe blown by the flying Winds, discovering a thousand Charms to View; thus the young Goddess look'd, then when she drove her Chariot down descending Clouds, to meet the Lovesick Gods in cooling Shades; and so would look my *Sylvia*! Ah, my soft, lovely Maid; such Thoughts as these fir'd me with Ambition: For me, I swear by every Power that made me love, and made thee wondrous fair, I design no more by this great Enterprize than to make thee some glorious thing, elevated above what we have seen yet on Earth; to raise thee above Fate or Fortune, beyond that Pity of thy duller Sex, who understand not thy Soul, nor can ever reach the Flights of thy generous Love! No, my Soul's Joy, I must not leave thee liable to their little natural Malice and Scorn, to the Impertinence of their Reproaches. No, my *Sylvia*, I must on, the great Design must move forward; tho' I abandon it, 'twill advance; it is already too far to put a Stop to it, and now I am enter'd, it is in vain to retreat; if we are prosperous, it will to all Ages be call'd a glorious Enterprize; but if we fail, it will be base, horrid and infamous; for the World judges of nothing but by the Success; that Cause is always good that is prosperous, that is ill which is unsuccessful. Should I now retreat, I run many Hazards; but to go on I run but one; by the first I shall alarm the whole Cabal with a Jealousie of my discovering, and those are Persons of too great Sense and Courage, not to take some private way of Revenge, to secure their own Stakes; and to make my self uncertainly safe by a Discovery indeed, were to gain a Refuge so ignoble, as a Man of Honour would scorn to purchase Life at; nor would that Baseness secure me. But in going on, oh *Sylvia*! when three Kingdoms shall lye unpossess'd, and be expos'd, as it were, amongst the raffling Croud, who knows but the Chance may be mine, as well as any other's, who has but the same Hazard, and Throw for it? If the strongest Sword must do it, (as that must do it) why not mine still? Why may not mine still? Why may not mine be that fortunate one? *Cesario* has no more Right to it than *Philander*; 'tis true, a few of the Rabble will pretend he has a better Title to it, but they are a sort of easie Fools, lavish in nothing but Noise and Nonsense; true to Change and Inconstancy, and will abandon him to their own Fury for the next that cries Haloo: Neither is there one Part of fifty (of the Fools that cry him up) for his Interest, tho' they use him for a Tool to work with, he being the only great Man that wants Sense enough to find out the Cheat which they dare impose upon. Can any body of Reason believe, if they had design'd him good, they would let him bare-fac'd have own'd a Party so opposite to all Laws of Nature, Religion, Humanity, and common Gratitude? When his Interest, if design'd, might have been carry'd on better, if he had still dissembled, and stay'd in Court: No, believe me, *Sylvia*, the Politicians shew him, to render him odious to all Men of tolerable Sense of the Party; for what Reason soever they have who are disoblig'd (or at least think themselves so) to set up for Liberty, the World knows *Cesario* renders himself the worst of Criminals by it, and has abandon'd an Interest more glorious and easy than Empire, to side with and aid People that never did, or ever can oblige him; and he is so dull as to imagine that for his Sake, who never did us Service or Good, (unless Cuckolding us be good) we should venture Life and Fame to pull down a true Monarch, to set up his Bastard over us. *Cesario* must pardon me, if I think his Politicks are shallow as his Parts, and that his own Interest has undone him; for of what Advantage soever the Design may be to us, it really shocks ones Nature to find a Son engag'd against a Father, and to him such a Father. Nor, when time comes, shall I forget the Ruin of *Myrtilla*. But let him hope on——and so will I, as do a thousand more, for ought I know; I set out as fair as they, and will start as eagerly; if I miss it now, I have Youth and Vigour sufficient for another Race;

and while I stand on Fortune's Wheel as she rolls it round, it may be my Turn to be o'th' Top; for when 'tis set in Motion, believe me, *Sylvia*, it is not easily fix'd: However let it suffice, I am now in, past a Retreat, and to urge it now to me, is but to put me into inevitable Danger; at best it can but set me where I was; that is worse than Death, when every Fool is aiming at a Kingdom; what Man of tolerable Pride and Ambition can be unconcern'd, and not put himself into a Posture of catching, when a Diadem shall be thrown among the Croud? It were Insensibility, stupid Dulness, not to lift a Hand, or make an Effort to snatch it as it flies: Though the glorious falling Weight should crush me, it is great to attempt; and if Fortune do not favour Fools, I have as fair a Grasp for it as any other Adventurer.

This, my *Sylvia*, is my Sense of a Business you so much dread; I may rise, but I cannot fall; therefore, my *Sylvia*, urge it no more; Love gave me Ambition, and do not divert the glorious Effects of your wondrous Charms, but let them grow, and spread, and see what they will produce for my lovely *Sylvia*, the Advantages will most certainly be hers:——But no more: How came my Love so dull to entertain thee so many Minutes thus with Reasons for an Affair, which one soft Hour with *Sylvia* will convince to what she would have it; believe me, it will, I will sacrifice all to her Repose, nay, to her least Command, even the Life of

(*My Eternal Pleasure*)

Your PHILANDER

I have no longer Patience, I must be coming towards the Grove, tho' it will do me no good, more than knowing I am so much nearer my adorable Creature.

I conjure you burn this, for writing in haste I have not counterfeited my Hand.

To SYLVIA

Writ in a Pair of Tablets

My Charmer, I wait your Commands in the Meadow behind the Grove, where I saw *Dorinda*, *Dorillus* his Daughter, entring with a Basket of Cowslips for *Sylvia*, unnecessarily offering Sweets to the Goddess of the Groves, from whence they (with all the rest of their gaudy Fellows of the Spring) assume their ravishing Odours. I take every Opportunity of telling my *Sylvia* what I have so often repeated, and shall be ever repeating with the same Joy while I live, that I love my *Sylvia* to Death and Madness; that my Soul is on the Wrack, till she send me the happy advancing Word. And yet believe me, lovely Maid, I could grow old with waiting here the blessed Moment, though set at any distance (within the Compass of Life, and impossible to be 'till then arriv'd to) but when I am so near approach'd it,

Love from all Parts rallies and hastens to my Heart for the mighty Encounter, 'till the poor panting overloaded Victim dies with the pressing Weight. No more,——You know it, for it is, and will be eternally *Sylvia*'s.

POSTSCRIPT

Remember, my Adorable, it is now seven a Clock : I have my Watch in my Hand, waiting and looking on the slow-pac'd Minutes. Eight will quickly arrive, I hope, and then it is dark enough to hide me : think where I am, and who I am, waiting near Sylvia, *and her* Philander.

I think, my dear Angel, you have the other Key of these Tablets, if not, they are easily broke open: You have an Hour good to write in, *Sylvia* and I shall wait unimploy'd by any Thing but Thought. Send me Word how you were like to have been surpriz'd; it may possibly be of Advantage to me in this Night's dear Adventure. I wonder'd at the Superscription of my Letter indeed, of which *Dorillus* could give me no other Account, than that you were surpriz'd, and he receiv'd it with difficulty; give me the Story now, do it in Charity, my Angel. Besides, I would employ all thy Moments, for I am jealous of every one that is not dedicated to *Sylvia*'s *Philander*.

To PHILANDER

I Have receiv'd your Tablets, of which I have the Key, and Heav'n only knows (for Lovers cannot, unless they lov'd like *Sylvia*, and her *Philander*) what Pains and Pantings my Heart sustain'd at every Thought they brought me of thy near Approach; every Moment I start, and am ready to faint with Joy, Fear, and something not to be express'd that seizes me. To add to this, I have busy'd my self with dressing my Apartment up with Flowers, so that I fancy the Ceremonious Business of the Light looks like the Preparations for the dear Joy of the Nuptial Bed; that too is so adorn'd and deck'd with all that's sweet and gay; all which possesses me with so ravishing and solemn a Confusion, that it is even approaching to the most profound Sadness it self. Oh *Philander*, I find I am fond of being undone; and unless you take a more than mortal Care of me, I know this Night some fatal Mischief will befal me; what it is I know not, either the loss of *Philander*, my Life, or my Honour, or altogether, which a Discovery only of your being alone in my Apartment, and at such an Hour will most certainly draw upon us: Death is the least we must expect, by some Surprize or other, my Father being rash, and extremely jealous, and the more so of me, by how much more he is fond of me, and nothing would enrage him like the Discovery of an Interview like this; though you have Liberty to range the House of *Bellfont* as a Son, and are indeed at home there; but when you come by stealth, when he shall find his Son and Virgin Daughter, the Brother and the Sister so retir'd, so entertain'd,——What but Death can ensue? Or what is worse, Eternal Shame? Eternal Confusion on my Honour? What Excuse, what Evasions, Vows and Protestations will convince him, or appease *Myrtilla*'s Jealousy; *Myrtilla*, my Sister, and *Philander*'s Wife? Oh God! that cruel Thought will put me into Ravings; I have a thousand Streams of killing Reflections which flow from that Original Fountain! Curse on the Alliance that gave you a Welcome to *Bellfont*. Ah *Philander*, could you not have stay'd ten short Years longer; Alas, you thought that was an Age in Youth, but it is but a Day in Love: Ah could not your eager Youth have led you to a thousand Diversions, a thousand times have baited in the long Journey of Life without hurrying on to the last Stage, to the last Retreat, but the Grave; and to me seem as irrecoverable, as impossible to retrieve thee?——Could no kind Beauty stop thee on thy Way, in Charity or Pity? *Philander* saw me then. And though *Myrtilla* was more fit for his Caresses, and I but capable to please with Childish Prattle; oh could he not have seen a promising Bloom in my Face, that might have foretold the future Conquests I was born to make? Oh! was there no prophetick Charm that could bespeak your Heart, engage it, and prevent that fatal Marriage? You say, my adorable Brother, we were destin'd from our Creation for one another; that the Decrees of Heav'n, or Fate, or both design'd us for this mutual Passion: Why then, oh why did not Heav'n, Fate, or Destiny, do the mighty Work, when first you saw my Infant Charms? But oh, *Philander*, why do I vainly rave? Why call in vain on Time that's fled and gone? Why idly wish for ten Years Retribution? That will not yield a Day, an Hour, a Minute: No, no, 'tis past, 'tis past and flown for ever, as distant as a thousand Years to me, as irrecoverable. Oh *Philander*, what hast thou thrown away? Ten glorious Years of ravishing Youth, of un-match'd heav'nly Beauty, on one that knew not half the Value of it! *Sylvia* was only born to set a Rate upon it, was only capable of Love, such Love as might deserve it: Oh why was that charming Face ever laid on any Bosom that knew not how to sigh, and pant, and heave at every Touch of so much distracting Beauty! Oh why were those dear Arms, whose soft Pressings ravish where they circle, destin'd for a Body cold and dull, that could sleep insensibly there, and not so much as dream the while what the transporting Pleasure signify'd; but unconcern'd receive the wondrous Blessings, and never knew its Price, or thanked her Stars? She has thee all the Day to gaze upon, and yet she lets thee pass her careless Sight, as if there were no Miracles in view: She does not see the little Gods of Love that play eternally in thy Eyes; and since she never receiv'd a Dart from thence, believes there's no Artillery there. She plays not with thy Hair, nor weaves her snowy Fingers in thy Curls of Jet, sets it in Order, and adores its Beauty: The Fool with Flaxen-Wigg had done as well for her; a dull, white Coxcomb had made as good a Property; a Husband is no more, at best no more. Oh thou charming Object of my eternal Wishes, why wert thou thus dispos'd? Oh save my Life, and tell me what indifferent Impulse oblig'd thee to these Nuptials: Had *Myrtilla* been recommended or forc'd by the Tyranny of a Father into thy Arms, or for base Lucre thou hadst chosen her, this had excus'd thy Youth and Crime; Obedience or Vanity I could have pardon'd, ——But oh——'twas Love; Love, my *Philander*! thy raving Love, and that which has undone thee was a Rape rather than Marriage; you fled with her. Oh Heavens, mad to possess, you stole the unloving Prize!——Yes, you lov'd her, false as you are, you did; perjur'd and faithless. Lov'd her; ——Hell and Confusion on the Word; it was so——Oh *Philander*, I am lost——

This Letter was found torn in Pieces.

To *Monsieur*, the Count of ——

My Lord,

THESE Pieces of Paper which I have put together as well as I could, were writ by my Lady to have been sent by *Dorinda*, when on a sudden she rose in Rage from her Seat, tore first the Paper, and then her Robes and Hair, and indeed nothing has escap'd the Violence of her Passion; nor could my Prayers or Tears retrieve them, or calm her: 'Tis however chang'd at last to mighty Passions of weeping, in which Employment I have left her on her Repose, being commanded away. I thought it my Duty to give your Lordship this Account, and to send the pieces of Paper, that your Lordship may guess at the Occasion of the sudden Storm which ever rises in that fatal Quarter; but in putting them in Order, I had like to have been surpriz'd by my Lady's Father; for my Lord, the Count, having long solicited me for Favours, and taking all Opportunities of entertaining me, found me alone in my Chamber, employ'd in serving your Lordship; I had only time to hide the Papers, and to get rid of him, having given him an Assignation to Night in the Garden-Grove, to give him the hearing to what he says he has to propose to me: Pray Heaven all things go right to your Lordship's Wish this Evening, for many ominous Things happen'd to Day. Madam, the Countess, had like to have taken a Letter writ for your Lordship to Day; for the Dutchess of —— coming to make her a Visit, came on a sudden with her into my Lady's Apartment, and surpriz'd her writing in her Dressing-Room, giving her only time to slip the Paper into her Comb-Box. The first Ceremonies being pass'd, as Madam, the Dutchess, uses not much, she fell to commend my Lady's Dressing-Plate, and taking up the Box, and opening it, found the Letter, and laughing cry'd, Oh, have I found you

233

making Love? At which my Lady, with an infinite Confusion, would have
retriev'd it,——But the Dutchess not quitting her hold, cry'd——Nay, I
am resolv'd to see in what manner you write to a Lover, and whether you
have a Heart tender or cruel; at which she began to read aloud, my Lady to
blush and change Colour a hundred times in a Minute; I ready to die with
Fear; Madam the Countess, in infinite Amazement, my Lady interrupting
every Word the Dutchess read, by Prayers and Intreaties, which heighten'd
her Curiosity, and being young and airy, regarded not the Indecency, to
which she preferr'd her Curiosity, who still laughing, cry'd, she was
resolv'd to read it out, and know the Constitution of her Heart; when my
Lady, whose Wit never fail'd her, cry'd, I beseech you, Madam, let us
have so much Complaisance for *Melinda* as to ask her Consent in this Affair,
and then I am pleas'd you should see what Love I can make upon Occasion:
I took the Hint, and with a real Confusion, cry'd — I implore you, Madam,
not to discover my Weakness to Madam, the Dutchess; I would not for the
World——be thought to love so passionately, as your Ladyship, in favour
of *Alexis*, has made me profess, under the Name of *Sylvia* to *Philander*.
This encourag'd my Lady, who began to say a thousand pleasant things of
Alexis, *Dorillus* his Son, and my Lover, as your Lordship knows, and who is
no inconsiderable Fortune for a Maid, enrich'd only by your Lordship's
Bounty. My Lady, after this, took the Letter, and all being resolv'd it
should be read, she her self did it, and turn'd it so prettily into Burlesque
Love by her manner of reading it, that made Madam, the Dutchess, laugh
extreamly; who, at the End of it, cry'd to my Lady——Well, Madam, I
am satisfy'd you have not a Heart wholly insensible of Love, that could so
express it for another. Thus they rally'd on, till careful of my Lover's
Repose, the Dutchess urg'd the Letter might be immediately sent away; at
which my Lady readily folding up the Letter, writ, *For the Constant* Alexis,
on the Out-side: I took it, and begg'd I might have Leave to retire to write
it over in my own Hand; they permitted me, and I carry'd it, after sealing it,
to *Dorillus*, who waited for it, and wondring to find his Son's Name on it,
cry'd——Mistress *Melinda*, I doubt you have mistook my present Business;
I wait for a Letter from my Lady to my Lord, and you give me one from
your self to my Son *Alexis*; 'twill be very welcome to *Alexis* I confess, but
at this time I had rather oblige my Lord than my Son: I laughing reply'd,
He was mistaken, that *Alexis*, at this time, meant no other than my Lord,
which pleas'd the good Man extreamly, who thought it a good Omen for
his Son, and so went his way satisfy'd; as every Body was, except the
Countess, who fancy'd something more in it than my Lady's Inditing for
me; and after Madam the Dutchess was gone, she went ruminating and
pensive to her Chamber, from whence I am confident she will not depart to
Night, and will possibly set Spies in every Corner; at least 'tis good to fear
the worst, that we may prevent all things that would hinder this Night's

Assignation: As soon as the Coast is clear, I'll wait on your Lordship, and be your Conducter, and in all things else am ready to shew my self,

My Lord,
Your Lordship's most humble
and most obedient Servant,
MELINDA

Sylvia *has given Orders to wait on your Lordship as soon as all is clear.*

To MELINDA

OH *Melinda*, what have you told me? Stay me with an immediate Account of the Recovery and Calmness of my adorable weeping *Sylvia*, or I shall enter *Bellfont* with my Sword drawn, bearing down all before me, 'till I make my Way to my charming Mourner: Oh God! *Sylvia* in a Rage! *Sylvia* in any Passion but that of Love? I cannot bear it, no, by Heav'n I cannot; I shall do some Outrage either on my self or at *Bellfont*. Oh thou dear Advocate of my tenderest Wishes, thou Confident of my never dying Flame, thou kind administring Maid, send some Relief to my breaking Heart — Haste and tell me, *Sylvia* is calm, that her bright Eyes sparkle with Smiles, or if they languish, say 'tis with Love, with expecting Joys; that her dear Hands are no more employ'd in Exercises too rough and unbecoming their Native Softness. O eternal God! tearing perhaps her Divine Hair, brighter than the Sun's reflecting Beams, injuring the heavenly Beauty of her charming Face and Bosom, the Joy and Wish of all Mankind that look upon her: Oh charm her with Prayers and Tears, stop her dear Fingers from the rude Assaults, bind her fair Hands; repeat *Philander* to her, tell her he's fainting with the News of her Unkindness and Outrage on her lovely self; but tell her too, I die adoring her; tell her I rave, I tear, I curse my self,—— for so I do; tell her I would break out into a Violence that should set all *Bellfont* in a Flame, but for my Care of her. Heaven and Earth should not restrain me,——no, they should not,——But her least Frown should still me, tame me, and make me a calm Coward: Say this, say all, say any thing to charm her Rage and Tears. Oh I am mad, stark mad, and ready to run on that frantick Business I die to think her guilty of: Tell her how it would grieve her to see me torn and mangled; to see that Hair she loves ruffled and diminish'd by Rage, violated by my insupportable Grief, my self quite bereft of all Sense but that of Love, but that of Adoration for my charming, cruel Insensible, who is possess'd with every Thought, with every Imagination that can render me unhappy, born away with every Fancy that is in disfavour of the wretched *Philander*. Oh *Melinda*, write immediately, or you will behold me enter a most deplorable Object of Pity.

When I receiv'd yours, I fell into such a Passion that I forc'd my self back to *Dorillus* his House, lest my Transports had hurry'd me to *Bellfont*, where I should have undone all: But as I can rest no where, I am now returning to the Meadow again, where I will expect your Aid, or die.

From Dorillus *his Cottage, almost Nine a Clock.*

To PHILANDER

I Must own, my charming *Philander*, that my Love is now arriv'd to that Excess, that every Thought which before but discompos'd me, now puts me into a Violence of Rage unbecoming my Sex; or anything but the mighty Occasion of it, Love, and which only had Power to calm what it had before ruffl'd into a destructive Storm: But like the anger'd Sea, which pants and heaves, and retains still an uneasie Motion long after the rude Winds are appeas'd and hush'd to Silence; my Heart beats still, and heaves with the sensible Remains of the late dangerous Tempest of my Mind, and nothing can absolutely calm me but the Approach of the all-powerful *Philander*; though that Thought possesses me with ten thousand Fears, which I know will vanish all at thy Appearance, and assume no more their dreadful Shapes 'till thou art gone again: Bring me then that kind Cessation, bring me my *Philander*, and set me above the Thoughts of Cares, Frights, or any other Thoughts but those of tender Love: Haste then, thou charming Object of my eternal Wishes, and of my new Desires; haste to my Arms, my Eyes, my Soul,——But oh, be wondrous careful there, do not betray the easie Maid that trusts thee amidst all her sacred Store.

'Tis almost dark, and my Mother is retir'd to her Chamber, my Father to his Cabinet, and has left all that Apartment next the Garden wholly without Spies. I have, by trusty *Dorillus*, sent you a Key *Melinda* got made to the Door, which leads from the Garden to the Back-stairs to my Apartment, so carefully lock'd, and the Original Key so closely guarded by my jealous Father: That Way I beg you to come; a Way but too well known to *Philander*, and by which he has made many an Escape to and from *Myrtilla*. Oh damn that Thought, what makes it torturing me, — let me change it for those of *Philander*, the Advantage will be as great as bartering Hell for Heaven; haste then, *Philander*: But what need I bid thee, Love will lend thee his Wings; thou who command'st all his Artillery, put them on, and fly to thy Languishing

SYLVIA

Oh I faint with the dear Thought of thy Approach.

To the Charming SYLVIA

WITH much ado, with many a Sigh, a panting Heart, and many a languishing Look back towards happy *Bellfont*, I have recover'd *Dorillus* his Farm, where I threw me on a Bed, and lay without Motion, and almost without Life for two Hours; 'till at last, through all my Sighs, my great Concern, my Torment, my Love and Rage broke Silence, and burst into all the different Complaints both soft and mad by turns, that ever possess'd a Soul extravagantly seiz'd with frantick Love; ah, *Sylvia*, what did not I say? How did I not curse, and who, except my charming Maid? For yet my *Sylvia* is a Maid: Yes, yes, ye envying Powers, she is, and yet the sacred and inestimable Treasure was offer'd a trembling Victim to the o'erjoy'd and fancy'd Deity, for then and there I thought my self happier than a Triumphing God; but having overcome all Difficulties, all the Fatigues and Toils of Love's long Sieges, vanquish'd the mighty Fantom of the Fair, the Giant Honour, and routed all the numerous Host of Womens little Reasonings, pass'd all the Bounds of peevish Modesty; nay, even all the loose and silken Counterscarps that fenc'd the sacred Fort, and nothing stopp'd my glorious Pursuit: Then, then, ye Gods, just then, by an Over-transport, to fall just fainting before the surrendring Gates, unable to receive the yielding Treasure! Oh *Sylvia*! what *Demon*, malicious at my Glory, seiz'd my Vigour? What God, envious of my mighty Joy, rendred me a shameful Object of his Raillery? Snatch'd my ('till then) never failing Power, and left me dying on thy charming Bosom. Heav'ns, how I lay! silent with Wonder, Rage and Extasie of Love, unable to complain, or rail, or storm, or seek for Ease, but with my Sighs alone, which made up all my Breath; my mad Desires remain'd, but all unactive, as Age or Death it self, as cold and feeble, as unfit for Joy, as if my youthful Fire had long been past, or *Sylvia* had never been blest with Charms. Tell me, thou wondrous perfect Creature, tell me, where lay the hidden Witchcraft? Was *Sylvia*'s Beauty too Divine to mix with mortal Joys? Ah no, 'twas Ravishing, but Human all. Yet sure 'twas so approaching to Divinity, as chang'd my Fire to awful Adoration, and all my wanton Heat to reverend Contemplation.——But this is Nonsense all, 'twas something more that gave me Rage, Despair and Torments insupportable: No, 'twas no dull Devotion, tame Divinity, but mortal killing Agony, unlucky Disappointment, unnatural Impotence. Oh! I am lost, enchanted by some Magick Spell: Oh, what can *Sylvia* say? What can she think of my fond Passion; she'll swear 'tis all a Cheat, I had it not. No, it could not be; such Tales I've often heard, as often laugh'd at too, of disappointed Lovers; would *Sylvia* believe (as sure she may) mine was Excess of Passion: What! my *Sylvia*! being arriv'd to all the Joy of Love, just come to reap the glorious Recompence, the full Reward, the Heav'n for all my Sufferings, do I lye gazing only, and no more? A dull, a feeble unconcern'd Admirer!

Oh my eternal Shame!——Curse on my Youth; give me, ye Powers, old Age, for that has some Excuse, but Youth has none: 'Tis Dullness, stupid Insensibility: Where shall I hide my Head when this lewd Story's told? When it shall be confirm'd, *Philander* the young, the brisk and gay *Philander*, who never fail'd the Woman he scarce wish'd for, never baulk'd the Amorous conceited Old, nor the Ill-favour'd Young; yet when he had extended in his Arms the Young, the charming Fair and longing *Sylvia*, the untouch'd, unspotted, and 'till then, unwishing lovely Maid, yielded, defenceless, and unguarded all, he wanted Power to seize the trembling Prey: Defend me, Heav'n, from Madness. Oh *Sylvia*, I have reflected on all the little Circumstances that might occasion this Disaster, and damn me to this degree of Coldness, but I can fix on none: I had, 'tis true, for *Sylvia*'s sake, some Apprehensions of Fear of being surpriz'd; for coming through the Garden, I saw at the farther end a Man, at least I fancy'd by that Light it was a Man; who perceiving the Glimps of something approach from the Grove, made softly towards me, but with such Caution, as if he fear'd to be mistaken in the Person, as much as I was to approach him: And reminding what *Melinda* told me, of an Assignation she had made to *Monsieur* the Count —— imagin'd it him; nor was I mistaken when I heard his Voice calling in low Tone——*Melinda*,——At which I mended my Pace, and e'er he got half way the Garden recover'd the Door, and softly unlocking it, got in unperceiv'd, and fasten'd it after me, well enough assur'd that he saw not which way I vanish'd: However, it fail'd not to alarm me with some Feats on your dear Account, that disturb'd my Repose, and which I thought then not necessary to impart to you, and which indeed all vanish'd at the Sight of my adorable Maid: When entering thy Apartment, I beheld thee extended on a Bed of Roses, in Garments, which, if possible, by their wanton loose Negligence and Gaiety, augmented thy natural Charms: I trembling fell on my Knees by your Bed-side, and gaz'd a while, unable to speak for Transports of Joy and Love: You too were silent, and remain'd so, so long that I ventur'd to press your Lips with mine, which all their eager Kisses could not put in Motion, so that I fear'd you fainted; a sudden Fright, that in a Moment chang'd my Fever of Love into a cold Ague Fit; but you reviv'd me with a Sigh again, and fir'd me a-new, by pressing my Hand, and from that silent soft Incouragement, I, by degrees, ravish'd a thousand Blisses; yet still between your tempting charming Kisses, you would cry——Oh, my *Philander*, do not injure me, ——be sure you press me not to the last Joys of Love;—Oh have a Care, or I am undone for ever: restrain your roving Hands,—Oh whither would they wander,——my Soul, my Joy, my everlasting Charmer, oh whither would you go?——Thus with a thousand Cautions more, which did but raise what you design'd to calm, you made me but the madder to possess: Not all the Vows you bid me call to mind, could now restrain my wild and head-strong Passion; my raving, raging (but my soft) Desire: No, *Sylvia*, no, it was not in the Power of feeble Flesh and Blood to find Resistance against so many Charms; yet still you made me swear, still I protested, but still burnt on with the same torturing Flame, 'till the vast Pleasure even became a Pain: To add to this, I saw, (yes, *Sylvia*, not all your Art and Modesty could hide it) I saw the ravishing Maid as much inflam'd as I; she burnt with equal Fire, with equal Languishment: Not all her Care could keep the Sparks conceal'd, but it broke out in every Word and Look; her trembling Tongue, her feeble fainting Voice betray'd it all; Sighs interrupting every Syllable; a Languishment I never saw till then dwelt in her charming Eyes that contradicted all her little Vows, her short and double Breathings heav'd her Breast, her swelling snowy Breast, her hands that grasp'd me trembling as they clos'd, while she permitted mine unknown, unheeded to traverse all her Beauties, 'till quite forgetting all I'd faintly promis'd, and wholly abandoning my Soul to Joy, I rush'd upon her, who all fainting lay beneath my useless Weight, for on a sudden all my Power was fled, swifter than Lightning hurry'd through my infeebled Veins, and vanish'd all: Not the dear lovely Beauty which I prest, the dying Charms of that fair Face and Eyes, the Clasps of those soft Arms, nor the bewitching Accent of her Voice, that murmur'd Love half smother'd in her Sighs, nor all my Love, my vast, my mighty Passion, could call my fugitive Vigour back again: Oh no, the more I look — the more I touch'd and saw, the more I was undone. Oh pity me, my too too lovely Maid, do not revile the Faults which you alone create. Consider all your Charms at once expos'd, consider every Sense about me ravish'd, o'ercome with Joys too mighty to be supported, no wonder if I fell a shameful Sacrifice to the fond Deity: Consider how I waited, how I strove, and still burnt on, and every tender Touch still added Fuel to the vigorous Fire, which by your Delay consum'd it self in Burning. I want Philosophy to make this out, or Faith to fix my Unhappiness on any Chance or natural Accident; but this, my charming *Sylvia*, I am sure, that had I lov'd you less, I'd been less wretched: Nor had we parted, *Sylvia*, on so ill Terms, nor had I left you with an Opinion so disadvantagious for *Philander*, but for that unhappy Noise at your Chamber-door, which alarming your Fear, occasion'd your Recovery from that dear Trance, to which Love and soft Desire had reduc'd you, and me from the most tormenting silent Agony that disappointed Joy ever possest a fond expecting Heart with. Oh Heavn's! to have my *Sylvia* in my Power, favour'd by Silence, Night and safe Retreat! then, then, to lye a tame cold Sigher only, as if my *Sylvia* gave that Assignation alone by stealth, undrest, all loose and languishing, fit for the mighty Business of the Night, only to hear me prattle, see me gaze, or tell her what a pretty Sight it was to see the Moon shine through the dancing Boughs. O Damn my harden'd Dullness, ——But no more,——I am all Fire and Madness at the Thought,——But I was saying, *Sylvia*, we both recover'd then when the Noise alarm'd us. I long to know whether you think we were betray'd, for on that Knowledge rests a mighty Part of my Destiny: I hope we are not, by an Accident that befel me at my going away, which (but for my untimely Force of leaving my lovely *Sylvia*, which gave me Pains insupportable) would have given me great Diversion. You know our Fear of being discover'd occasion'd my Disguise, for you found it necessary I should depart, your Fear had so prevail'd, and that in *Melinda*'s Night-gown and Head-dress: Thus attir'd, with much ado, I went and left my Soul behind me, and finding no Body all along the Gallery, nor in my Passage from your Apartment into the Garden, I was a thousand Times about to return to all my Joys; when in the midst of this almost ended Dispute, I saw by the Light of the Moon (which was by good Fortune under a Cloud, and could not distinctly direct the Sight) a Man making towards me with cautious Speed, which made me advance with the more haste to recover the Grove, believing to have escap'd him under the Covert of the Trees? for retreat I could not, without betraying which way I went; but just at the Entrance of the Thicket, he turning short made up to me, and I perceiv'd it *Monsieur* the Count, who taking me for *Melinda*, who it seems he expected, caught hold of my Gown as I would have pass'd him, and cry'd, Now *Melinda*, I see you are a Maid of Honour, — Come retire with me into the Grove, where I have a Present of a Heart and something else to make you, that will be of more Advantage to you than that of *Alexis*, though something younger.——I all confounded knew not what to reply, nor how, lest he should find his Mistake, at least if he discover'd not who I was: Which Silence gave him Occasion to go on, which he did in this manner: What not a Word, *Melinda*, or do you design I shall take your Silence for Consent? if so, come my pretty Creature, let us not lose the Hour Love has given us; at this he would have advanc'd, leading me by the Hand, which he press'd and kiss'd very amorously: Judge, my adorable *Sylvia*, in what a fine Condition your *Philander* then was in. What should I do? to go had disappointed him worse than I was with thee before; not to go, betray'd me: I had much ado to hold my Countenance, and unwilling to speak. While I was thus employ'd in Thought, *Monsieur* —— pulling me (eager of Joys to come,) and I holding back, he stopp'd and cry'd, Sure, *Melinda*, you came not hither to bring me a Denial. I then reply'd, whispering,——Softly, Sir, for Heav'ns sake (sweetning my Voice as much as possible) consider I'm a Maid, and would not be discover'd for the World. Who can discover us? reply'd my Lover, what I take from thee shall never be miss'd, not by *Alexis* himself upon thy Wedding Night;——Come——sweet Child, come:——With that I pull'd back and whisper'd——Heav'ns! would you make a Mistress of me?——Says he——A Mistress, what would'st thou be a Cherubin? then I reply'd as before——I am no Whore, Sir,——

No, crys he, but I can quickly make thee one, I have my Tools about me, Sweet-heart, therefore let's lose no time; but fall to work: This last Raillery from the brisk old Gentleman, had in spight of Resolution almost made me burst out into a loud Laughter, when he took more Gravity upon him, and cry'd——Come, come, *Melinda*, why all this foolish Argument at this Hour in this Place, and after so much serious Courtship; believe me, I'll be kind to thee for ever; with that he clapt fifty Guineas in a Purse into one Hand, and something else that shall be nameless into the other, Presents that had been both worth *Melinda*'s Acceptance: All this while was I studying an Evasion; at last, to shorten my pleasant Adventure, looking round, I cry'd softly, Are you sure, Sir, we are safe——for Heav'ns sake step towards the Garden Door and see, for I would not be discover'd for the World.——Nor I, cry'd he——but do not fear, all's safe:——However see (whisper'd I) that my Fear may not disturb your Joys. With that he went toward the House, and I flipping into the Grove, got immediately into the Meadow, where *Alexis* waited my coming with *Brilliard*, so I left the expecting Lover, I suppose, ranging the Grove for his fled Nymph, and I doubt will fall heavy on poor *Melinda*, who shall have the Guineas, either to restore or keep, as she and the angry Count can agree: I leave the Management of it to her Wit and Conduct.

This Account I thought necessary to give my Charmer, that she might prepare *Melinda* for the Assault, who understanding all that pass'd between us, may so dispose of Matters, that no Discovery may happen by Mistake, and I know my *Sylvia* and she can find a thousand Excuses for the suppos'd *Melinda*'s Flight. But, my adorable Maid, my Business here was not to give an Account of my Adventure only, nor of my Ravings, but to tell my *Sylvia*, on what my Life depends; which is, in a Permission to wait on her again this ensuing Night; make no Excuse, for if you do, by all I adore in Heav'n and Earth I'll end my Life here where I receiv'd it. I'll say no more, nor give your Love Instructions, but wait impatiently here the Life or Death of your

PHILANDER

'Tis Six a Clock, and yet my Eyes have not clos'd themselves to sleep: Alexis *and* Brilliard *give me hopes of a kind Return to this, and have brought their Flute and Violin to charm me into a Slumber: If* Sylvia *love, as I am sure she does, she'll wake me with a dear Consent to see me, if not, I only wake to sleep for ever.*

To my Fair CHARMER

When I had seal'd the inclos'd, my Page, whom I had order'd to come to me with an Account of any Business extraordinary, is this Morning arriv'd with a Letter from *Cesario*, which I have sent here inclos'd, that my *Sylvia* may see how little I regard the World, or the mighty Revolution in hand, when set in Competition with the least hope of beholding her adorable Face, or hearing her charming Tongue when it whispers the soft Dictates of her tender Heart into my ravish'd Soul; one Moment's Joy like that surmounts an Age of dull Empire. No, let the busie unregarded Rout perish, the Cause fall or stand alone for me: Give me but Love, Love and my *Sylvia*; I ask no more of Heav'n; to which vast Joy could you but imagine (Oh wondrous Miracle of Beauty!) how poor and little I esteem the valu'd Trifles of the World, you would in return contemn your Part of it, and live with me in silent Shades for ever. Oh! *Sylvia*, what hast thou this Night to add to the Soul of thy

PHILANDER

To the Count of——

I'll allow you my Dear, to be very fond of so much Beauty as the World must own adorns the lovely *Sylvia*: I'll permit Love too to Rival me in your Heart, but not out-rival Glory; haste then, my Dear, to the Advance of that, make no delay, but with the Morning's Dawn let me find you in my Arms, where I have something that will surprize you to relate to you: You were last Night expected at——It behoves you to give no Umbrage to Persons whose Interest renders them enough jealous. We have two new Advancers come in of Youth and Mony, teach them not Negligence; be careful, and let nothing hinder you from taking Horse immediately, as you value the Repose and Fortune of,

My dear,
Your CESARIO

I call'd last Night on you, and your Page following me to my Coach, whisper'd me——if I had any earnest Business with you, he knew where to find you; I soon imagin'd where, and bid him call within an Hour for this, and post with it immediately, though dark.

To PHILANDER

Ah! What have I done, *Philander*, and where shall I hide my guilty blushing Face? Thou hast undone my eternal Quiet: Oh, thou hast ruin'd my ever-lasting Repose, and I must never, never look abroad again: Curse on my Face that first debauch'd my Virtue, and taught thee how to love! Curse on my tempting Youth, my Shape, my Air, my Eyes, my Voice, my Hands,

and every Charm that did contribute to my fatal Love, a lasting Curse on
all——But those of the adorable *Philander*, and those——even in this
raging Minute, my furious Passion dares not approach with an indecent
Thought: No, they are sacred all, Madness it self would spare 'em, and
shouldst thou now behold me as I sit, my Hair dishevell'd, ruffled and
disorder'd, my Eyes bedewing every Word I write, when for each Letter I
let fall a Tear; then (press'd with Thought) starting, I dropp'd my Pen, and
fell to rave anew, and tear those Garments whose loose Negligence help'd to
betray me to my shameful Ruin, wounding my Breast, but want the
Resolution to wound it as I ought; which when I but propose, Love stays
the Thought, raging and wild as 'tis, the Conqueror checks it, with whispering only *Philander* to my Soul; the dear Name calms me to an Easiness, gives
me the Pen into my trembling Hand, and I pursue my silent soft Complaint:
Oh! shouldst thou see me thus, in all these sudden different changes of
Passion, thou wouldst say, *Philander*, I were mad indeed; Madness it self
can find no stranger Motions: And I would calmly ask thee, for I am calm
again, How comes it, my adorable *Philander*, that thou canst possess a
Maid with so much Madness? Who art thy self a Miracle of Softness, all
Sweet and all Serene, the most of Angel in thy Composition that ever
mingled with Humanity; the very Words fall so gently from thy Tongue,
——are utter'd with a Voice so ravishingly soft, a Tone so tender and so
full of Love, 'twould charm even Frenzy, calm rude Distraction, and
Wildness would become a silent Listner; there's such a sweet Serenity in
thy Face, such Innocence and Softness in thy Eyes, should desart Savages
but gaze on thee, sure they would forget their native Forest Wildness, and
be inspir'd with easie Gentleness: Most certainly this God-like Power thou
hast. Why then? Oh tell me in the Agony of my Soul, why must those
Charms that bring Tranquillity and Peace to all, make me alone a wild,
unseemly Raver? Why has it contrary Effects on me? Oh! all I act and say
is perfect Madness: Yet this is the least unaccountable Part of my most
wretched Story;——Oh! I must ne'er behold thy lovely Face again, for if
I should, sure I should blush my Soul away; no, no, I must not, nor ever
more believe they dear deluding Vows; never thy charming perjur'd Oaths,
after a Violation like to this. Oh Heav'n, what have I done? Yet by Heav'n
I swear, I dare not ask my Soul, lest it inform me how I was to blame,
unless that fatal Minute would instruct me how to revenge my Wrongs
upon my Heart, my fond betraying Heart,——Despair and Madness seize
me, Darkness and Horror hide me from human Sight, after an Easiness
like this;——What, to yield,——To yield my Honour! Betray the Secrets
of my Virgin Wishes.——My new Desires, my unknown shameful Flame,
——Hell and Death! Where got I so much Confidence? Where learn'd I
the harden'd and unblushing Folly? To wish was such a Fault, as is a
Crime unpardonable to own; to shew Desire is such a Sin in Virtue as must

deserve Reproach from all the World; but I, unlucky I, have not only betray'd all these, but with a Transport void of Sense and Shame, I yield to thy Arms——I'll not endure the Thought—By Heav'n! I cannot; there's something more than Rage that animates that Thought: Some Magick Spell, that in the midst of all my Sense of Shame keeps me from true Repentance; this angers me, and makes me know my Honour but a Fantom: Now I could curse again my Youth and Love; but Oh! when I have done, alas, *Philander*, I find my self as guilty as before; I cannot make one firm Resolve against thee, or if I do, when I consider thee, they weigh not all one lovely Hair of thine. 'Tis all in vain, the charming Cause remains, *Philander*'s still as lovely as before, 'tis him I must remove from my fond Eyes and Heart, him I must banish from my Touch, my Smell, and every other Sense; by Heav'n! I cannot bear the mighty Pressure, I cannot see his Eyes, and touch his Hands, smell the Perfume every Pore of his breaths forth, taste thy soft Kisses, hear thy charming Voice, but I am all on a Flame: No, 'tis these I must exclaim on, not my Youth, 'tis they debauch my Soul, no natural Propensity in me to yield, or to admit of such destructive Fires. Fain I would put it off, but 'twill not do, I am the Aggressor still; else why is not every living Maid undone, that does but touch or see thee? Tell me why? No, the Fault's in me, and thou art innocent.——Were but my Soul less delicate, were it less sensible of what it loves and likes in thee, I yet were dully happy; but oh, there is a Nicety there so charm'd, so apprehensive of thy Beauties, as has betray'd me to Unrest for ever:—— Yet something I will do to tame this lewd Betrayer of my Right, and it shall plead no more in thy Behalf; no more, no more disperse the Joys which it conceives thro' every Vein (cold and insensible by Nature) to kindle new Desires there.——No more shall fill me with unknown Curiosity; no, I will in spight of all the Perfumes that dwell about thee, in spight of all the Arts thou hast of looking, of speaking and of touching, I will, I say, assume my native Temper, I will be calm, be cold and unconcern'd, as I have been to all the World, — but to *Philander*.——The Almighty Power he has is unaccountable:——By yonder breaking Day that open in the East, opens to see my Shame — I swear — by that great Ruler of the Day, the Sun, by that Almight Power that rules them both, I swear——I swear, *Philander*, charming lovely Youth! thou art the first e'er kindled soft Desires about my Soul, thou art the first that ever did inform me that there was such a sort of Wish about me. I thought the Vanity of being belov'd made up the greatest part of the Satisfaction; 'twas Joy to see my Lovers sigh about me, adore and praise me, and increase my Pride by every Look, by every Word and Action; and him I fancy'd best I favour'd most, and he pass'd for the happy Fortune; him I have suffer'd too to kiss and press me, to tell me all his Tale of Love, and sigh, which I would listen to with Pride and Pleasure, permitted it, and smil'd him kind

Returns; nay, by my Life, then thought I lov'd him too, tho' I could have been content to have pass'd my Life at this gay rate, with this fond hoping Lover, and thought no farther than of being great, having rich Coaches, shewing Equipage, to pass my Hours in dressing, in going to the Opera's and the Tower, make Visits where I list, be seen at Balls; and having still the Vanity to think the Men would gaze and languish where I came, and all the Women envy me; I thought no farther on — But thou, *Philander*, hast made me take new Measures, I now can think of nothing but of thee, I loath the Sound of Love from any other Voice, and Conversation makes my Soul impatient, and does not only dull me into Melancholy, but perplexes me out of all Humour, out of all patient Sufferance, and I am never so well pleas'd when from *Philander*, as when I am retir'd, and curse my Character and Figure in the World, because it permits me not to prevent being visited; one Thought of thee is worth the World's Enjoyment; I hate to dress, I hate to be agreeable to any Eyes but thine; I hate the Noise of Equipage and Crouds, and would be more content to live with thee in some lone shaded Cottage, than be a Queen, and hinder'd by that Grandeur one Moment's Conversation with *Philander*: May'st thou despise and loath me, a Curse the greatest that I can invent, if this be any thing but real honest Truth. No, no, *Philander*, I find I never lov'd till now, I understood it not, nor knew what those Sighs and Pressings meant which others gave me; yet every speaking Glance thy Eyes put on, inform my Soul what 'tis they plead and languish for: If you but touch my Hand, my Breath grows faint and short, my Blood glows in my Face, and runs with an unusual Warmth thro' every Vein, and tells my Heart what 'tis *Philander* ails, when he falls sighing on my Bosom; oh then, I fear, I answer every Look, and every Sigh and Touch, in the same silent but intelligible Language, and understood, I fear, too well by thee: 'Till now I never fear'd Love as a Criminal. Oh tell me not, mistaken foolish Maids, true Love is innocent, ye cold, ye dull, ye unconsidering Lovers; tho' I have often heard it from the grave and wise, and preach'd my self that Doctrine: I now renounce it all, 'tis false, by Heav'n! 'tis false, for now I love, and know it all a Fiction; yes, and love so, as never any Woman can equal me in Love, my Soul being all compos'd (as I have often said) of softer Materials. Nor is it Fancy sets my Rates on Beauty, there's an intrinsick Value in thy Charms, which surely none but I am able to understand, and to those that view thee not with my judging Eyes, Ugliness fancy'd would appear the same, and please as well. If all could love or judge like me, why does *Philander* pass so unregarded by a thousand Women, who never sigh'd for him? What makes *Myrtilla*, who possesses all, looks on thee, feels thy Kisses, hears thee speak, and yet wants Sense to know how bless'd she is, 'tis want of Judgment all; and how, and how can she that judges ill, love well?

Granting my Passion equal to its Object, you must allow it infinite, and more in me than any other Woman, by how much more my Soul is compos'd of Tenderness; and yet I say I own, for I may own it, now Heav'n and you are Witness of my Shame, I own with all this Love, with all this Passion, so vast, so true and so unchangeable, that I have Wishes, new unwonted Wishes; at every Thought of thee, I find a strange disorder in my Blood, that pants and burns in every Vein, and makes me blush, and sigh, and grow impatient, asham'd and angry; but when I know it the effects of Love, I am reconcil'd, and wish and sigh a-new; for when I sit and gaze upon thy Eyes, thy languishing, thy lovely dying Eyes, play with thy soft white Hand, and lay my glowing Cheeks to thine——oh God! what Language can express my Transport! All that is tender, all that is soft Desire, seizes every trembling Limb, and 'tis with Pain conceal'd.——Yes, yes, *Philander*, 'tis the fatal Truth, since thou hast found it, I confess it too, and yet I love thee dearly; long, long it was that I essay'd to hide the guilty Flame, if Love be Guilt; for I confess I did dissemble a Coldness which I was not Mistress of: There lyes a Woman's Art, there all her boasted Virtue, it is but well dissembling, and no more——But mine, alas, is gone, for ever fled; this, this feeble Guard that should secure my Honour, thou hast betray'd, and left it quite defenceless. Ah what's a Woman's Honour when 'tis so poorly guarded! No wonder that you conquer with such Ease, when we are only safe by the mean Arts of base Dissimulation, an Ill as shameful as that to which we fall. Oh silly Refuge! What foolish Nonsense fond Custom can persuade! Yet so it is; and she that breaks her Laws, loses her Fame, her Honour and Esteem. Oh Heav'ns! how quickly lost it is! Give me, ye Powers, my Fame, and let me be a Fool; let me retain my Virtue and my Honour, and be a dull Insensible——But, oh! where is it? I have lost it all; 'tis irrecoverably lost: Yes, yes, ye charming perjur'd Man, 'tis gone, and thou hast quite undone me.——

What tho' I lay extended on my Bed, undrest, unapprehensive of my Fate, my Bosom loose and easy of Access, my Garments ready, thin and wantonly put on, as if they would with little Force submit to the fond straying Hand: What then, *Philander*, must you take the Advantage? Must you be perjur'd because I was tempting? 'Tis true, I let you in by Stealth by Night, whose silent Darkness favour'd your Treachery; but oh, *Philander*, were not your Vows as binding by a glimmering Taper, as if the Sun with all his awful Light had been a Looker on? I urg'd your Vows as you press'd on,—— But oh, I fear it was in such a way, so faintly and so feebly I upbraided you as did but more advance your Perjuries. Your Strength encreas'd, but mine alas declin'd; 'till I quite fainted in your Arms, left you triumphant Lord of all: No more my faint Denials do persuade, no more my trembling Hands resist your Force, unregarded lay the Treasure which you toil'd for, betray'd and yielded to the lovely Conqueror——But oh tormenting,—— when you saw the Store, and found the Prize no richer, with what Contempt, (yes, false dear Man) with what Contempt you view'd the unvalu'd Trophy: What, despis'd! Was all you call a Heav'n of Joy and Beauty expos'd to View, and then neglected? Were all your Prayers heard, your Wishes granted, and your Toils rewarded, the trembling Victim ready for the Sacrifice, and did you want Devotion to perform it? And did you thus receive the expected Blessing?——Oh——by Heav'n I'll never see thee more, and 'twill be Charity to thee, for thou hast no Excuse in store that can convince my Opinion that I am hated, loath'd,——I cannot bear that Thought——or if I do, it shall only serve to fortifie my fix'd Resolve never to see thee more.——And yet I long to hear thy false Excuse, let it be quickly then; 'tis my Disdain invites thee——To strengthen which, there needs no more than that you let me hear your poor Defence.——But 'tis a tedious time to that slow Hour wherein I dare permit thee, but hope not to incline my Soul to love; No, I am yet safe if I can stop but here, but here be wise, resolve and be my self.

SYLVIA

To PHILANDER

As my Page was coming with the inclos'd, he met *Alexis* at the Gate with yours, and who would not depart without an Answer to it;——to go or stay is the Question. Ah, *Philander*! why do you press a Heart too ready to yield to Love and you! Alas, I fear you guess too well my Answer, and your own Soul might save me the blushing Trouble of a Reply. I am plung'd in past hope of a Retreat; and since my Fate has pointed me out for Ruin, I cannot fall more gloriously. Take then, *Philander*, to your dear Arms, a Maid that can no longer resist, who is disarm'd of all defensive Power: She yields, she yields, and does confess it too; and sure she must be more than mortal, that can hold out against thy Charms and Vows. Since I must be undone, and give all away, I'll do it generously, and scorn all mean Reserves: I will be brave in Love, and lavish all; nor shall *Philander* think I love him well, unless I do. Take, charming Victor, then, what your own Merits, and what Love has given you; take, take, at last, the dear Reward of all your Sighs and Tears, your Vows and Sufferings. But since, *Philander*, 'tis an Age to Night, and till the approach of those dear silent Hours, thou know'st I dare not give thee admittance; I do conjure thee, go to *Cesario*, whom I find too pressing, not to believe the Concerns great; and so jealous I am of thy dear Safety, that every thing alarms my Fears: Oh! satisfie 'em then and go, 'tis early yet, and if you take Horse immediately, you will be there by eight this Morning; go, I conjure you; for tho' 'tis an unspeakable Satisfaction to know you are so near me, yet I prefer your Safety and Honour to all Consideration else. You may soon dispatch your Affair, and render your

247

self time enough on the Place appointed, which is where you last Night waited, and 'twill be at least eight at Night before 'tis possible to bring you to my Arms. Come in your Chariot, and do not heat your self with Riding; have a care of me and my Life in the Preservation of all I love. Be sure you go, and do not, my *Philander*, out of a Punctilio of Love, neglect your dear Safety——Go then, *Philander*, and all the Gods of Love preserve and attend thee on thy way, and bring thee safely back to

SYLVIA

To SYLVIA

OH, thou most charming of thy Sex! thou lovely dear Delight of my transported Soul! thou everlasting Treasure of my Heart! what hast thou done? given me an Over-joy, that fails but very little of performing what Grief's Excess had almost finish'd before: Eternal Blessings on thee, for a Goodness so Divine, oh, thou most excellent and dearest of thy Sex! I know not what to do, or what to say. I am not what I was, I do not speak, nor walk, nor think as I was wont to do; sure the Excess of Joy is far above dull Sense, or formal thinking, it cannot stay for Ceremonious Method. I rave with Pleasure, rage with the dear Thought of coming Extasy. Oh *Sylvia, Sylvia, Sylvia*! my Soul, my vital Blood, and without which I could as well subsist——Oh, my adorable, my *Sylvia*! methinks I press thee, kiss thee, hear thee sigh, behold thy Eyes, and all the wondrous Beauty of thy Face; a solemn Joy has spread it self through every Vein, sensibly through every Artery of my Heart, and I can think of nothing but of *Sylvia*, the lovely *Sylvia*, the blooming flowing *Sylvia*? and shall I see thee? shall I touch thy Hands, and press thy dear, thy charming Body in my Arms, and taste a thousand Joys, a thousand Ravishments? Oh God! shall I? oh *Sylvia*, say; but thou hast said enough to make me mad, and I, forgetful of thy Safety and my own, shall bring thy wild adoring Slave to *Bellfont*, and throw him at thy Feet, to pay his humble Gratitude for this great Condescension, this vast Bounty.

Ah, *Sylvia*! how shall I live 'till Night? and you impose too cruelly upon me, in conjuring me to go to *Cesario*; alas! does *Sylvia* know to what she exposes her *Philander*? whose Joy is so transporting, great, that when he comes into the grave Cabal, he must betray the Story of his Heart, and, in lieu of the mighty Business there in Hand, be raving still on *Sylvia*, telling his Joy to all the amaz'd Listeners, and answering Questions that concern our great Affair, with something of my Love; all which will pass for Madness, and undo me: No, give me leave to rave in Silence, and unseen among the Trees, they'll humour my Disease, answer my murmuring Joy, and

Echos flatter it, repeat thy Name, repeat that *Sylvia*'s mine! and never hurt her Fame; while the Cabals, Business and noisy Town will add Confusion to my present Transport, and make me mad indeed: No, let me alone, thou sacred lovely Creature, let me be calm and quiet here, and tell all the Insensibles I meet in the Woods what *Sylvia* has this happy Minute destin'd me: Oh, let me record it on every Bark, on every Oak and Beech, that all the World may wonder at my Fortune, and bless the generous Maid; let it grow up to Ages that shall come, that they may know the Story of our Loves, and how a happy Youth, they call'd *Philander*, was once so blest by Heav'n as to possess the charming, the ador'd and lov'd by all, the glorious *Sylvia*! a Maid, the most Divine that ever grac'd a Story; and when the Nymphs would look for an Example of Love and Constancy, let them point out *Philander* to their doubted Swains, and cry, Ah! love but as the young *Philander* did, and then be fortunate, and then reap all your Wishes: And when the Shepherd would upbraid his Nymph, let him but cry,——— See here what *Sylvia* did to save the young *Philander*; but oh! there never will be such another Nymph as *Sylvia*; Heav'n form'd but one to shew the World what Angels are, and she was form'd for me, yes she was———in whom I would not quit my glorious Interest to reign a Monarch here, or any boasted gilded thing above! take all, take all, ye Gods, and give me but this happy coming Night! Oh, *Sylvia*, *Sylvia*! by all thy promis'd Joys I am undone if any Accident should ravish this Night from me: This Night! No not for a Lease of Years to all Eternity would I throw thee away: Oh! I am all Flame, all joyful Fire and Softness; methinks 'tis Heaven where-ever I look around me, Air where I tread, and ravishing Musick when I speak, because 'tis all of *Sylvia*——Let me alone, oh let me cool a little, or I shall by an Excess of joyful Thought lose all my hop'd for Bliss. Remove a little from me; go, my *Sylvia*, you are so excessive sweet, so wondrous dazzling, you press my Senses even to pain——away——let me take Air——let me recover Breath: Oh let me lay me down beneath some cooling Shade, near some refreshing Crystal murmuring Spring, and fan the gentle Air about me, I suffocate, I faint with this close loving, I must allay my Joy or be undone——I'll read thy cruel Letters, or I'll think of some sad melancholy Hour wherein thou hast dismiss'd me dispairing from thy Presence: Or while you press me now to be gone with so much Earnestness, you have some Lover to receive and entertain; perhaps 'tis only for the Vanity to hear him tell his nauseous Passion to you, breath on your lovely Face, and daub your Garments with his fulsome Embrace: But oh, by Heav'n, I cannot think that Thought! and thou hast sworn thou canst not suffer it——if I should find thee false——but 'tis impossible——Oh! should I find *Foscario* visit thee, him whom thy Parents favour, I should undo you all, by Heav'n I should——but thou hast sworn, what need *Philander* more? Yes, *Sylvia*, thou hast sworn, and call'd Heav'n's Vengeance down whene'er thou gavest a Look, or a dear smile in Love to that pretending Fop: Yet from his mighty Fortune there is danger in him——What makes that Thought torment me now?——be gone, for *Sylvia* loves me, and will preserve my Life——

I am not able, my adorable Charmer, to obey your Commands in going from the Sight of happy *Bellfont*; no, let the great Wheel of the vast Design roul on——or for ever stand still, for I'll not aid its Motion to leave the mightier Business of my Love unfinish'd; no, let Fortune and the duller Fools toil on——for I'll not bate a Minute of my Joys with thee to save the World, much less so poor a parcel of it: and sure there is more solid Pleasure even in these expecting Hours I wait to snatch my Bliss, than to be Lord of all the Universe without it: Then let me wait, my *Sylvia*, in those melancholy Shades that part *Bellfont* from *Dorillus*'s Farm; perhaps my *Sylvia* may walk that Way so unattended, that we might meet and lose our selves for a few Moments in those intricate Retreats: Ah, *Sylvia*! I am dying with that Thought——Oh Heav'ns! what cruel Destiny is mine? whose fatal Circumstances do not permit me to own my Passion, and lay Claim to *Sylvia*, to take her without Controul to Shades and Palaces, to live for ever with her, to gaze for ever on her, to eat, to loll, to rise, to play, to sleep, to act over all the Pleasures and the Joys of Life with her——But 'tis in vain I rave, in vain employ my self in the Fools barren Business, wishing,——this Thought has made me sad as Death: Oh, *Sylvia*! I can ne'er be truly happy——adieu, employ thy self in writing to me, and remember my Life bears Date but only with thy Faith and Love.

PHILANDER

Try, my Adorable, what you can do to meet me in the Wood this Afternoon, for there I'll live to Day.

To PHILANDER

Obstinate *Philander*, I conjure you by all your Vows, by all your sacred Love, by those dear Hours this happy Night design'd in favour of you, to go without Delay to *Cesario*; 'twill be unsafe to disobey a Prince in his jealous Circumstances. The Fatigue of the Journey cannot be great, and you well know the Torment of my Fears! Oh! I shall never be happy, or think you safe, 'till you have quitted this fatal Interest: Go, my *Philander* ——and remember what-ever Toils you take will be rewarded at Night in the Arms of

SYLVIA

To SYLVIA

Whatever Toils you take shall be rewarded in the Arms of *Sylvia*!——By Heav'n, I am inspir'd to act Wonders: Yes, *Sylvia*, yes, my adorable Maid, I am gone, I fly as swift as Lightning, or the soft Darts of Love shot from thy charming Eyes, and I can hardly stay to say——Adieu——

To the LADY ——

Dear Child,

LONG foreseeing the Misery whereto you must arrive, by this fatal Correspondence with my unhappy Lord, I have often, with Tears and Prayers, implor'd you to decline so dangerous a Passion: I have never yet acquainted our Parents with your Misfortunes, but I fear I must at last make use of their Authority for the Prevention of your Ruin. 'Tis not, my dearest Child, that part of this unhappy Story that relates to me that grieves me, but purely that of thine.

Consider, oh young noble Maid, the Infamy of being a Prostitute! and yet the Act it self in this fatal Amour is not the greatest Sin, but the Manner which carries an unusual Horror with it; for 'tis a Brother too, my Child, as well as a Lover, one that has lain by thy unhappy Sister's Side so many tender Years, by whom he has a dear and lovely Off-spring, by which he has more fixt himself to thee by Relation and Blood: Consider this, oh fond heedless Girl! and suffer not a momentary Joy to rob thee of thy Eternal Fame, me of my Eternal Repose, and fix a Brand upon our noble House, and so undo us all.——Alas, consider, after an Action so shameful, thou must obscure thy self in some remote Corner of the World, where Honesty and Honour never are heard of: No, thou canst not shew thy Face, but 'twill be pointed at for something monstrous; for a hundred Ages may not produce a Story so leudly infamous and loose as thine. Perhaps (fond as you are) you imagine the sole Joy of being belov'd by him, will attone for those Affronts and Reproaches you will meet with in the censuring World: But, Child, remember and believe me, there is no lasting Faith in Sin; he that has broke his Vows with Heav'n and me, will be again perjur'd to Heav'n and thee, and all the World!——He once thought me as lovely, lay at my Feet, and sigh'd away his Soul, and told such pitious Stories of his Sufferings, such sad, such mournful Tales of his departed Rest, his broken Heart and everlasting Love, that sure I thought it had been a Sin not to have credited his charming Perjuries; in such a way he swore, with such a Grace he sigh'd, so artfully he mov'd, so tenderly he look'd. Alas, dear Child, then all he said was new, unusual with him, never told before; now 'tis a beaten Road, 'tis learn'd by Heart, and easily address'd to any fond believing Woman, the tatter'd, worn-out Fragments of my Trophies, the Dregs of what I long since drain'd from off his fickle Heart; then it was fine, then it was brisk and new, now pall'd and dull'd by being repeated often. Think, my Child, what your victorious Beauty merits, the Victim of a Heart unconquer'd by any but your Eyes: Alas, he has been my Captive, my humble whining Slave, disdain to put him on your Fetters now; alas, he can say no new thing of his Heart to thee, 'tis Love at second Hand, worn out, and all its gaudy Lustre tarnish'd; besides, my Child, if thou hadst no Religion binding enough, no Honour that could stay thy fatal Course, yet Nature should oblige thee, and give a Check to the unreasonable Enterprize. The Griefs and Dishonour of our noble Parents, who have been eminent for Virtue and Piety, oh suffer 'em not to be regarded in this censuring World as the most unhappy of all the Race of old Nobility; thou art the darling Child, the Joy of all, the last Hope left, the Refuge of their Sorrow; for they, alas, have had but unkind Stars to influence their unadvis'd Off-spring; no want of Virtue in their Education, but this last Blow of Fate must strike 'em dead: Think, think of this, my Child, and yet retire from Ruin; haste, fly from Destruction which pursues thee fast; haste, haste, and save thy Parents and a Sister, or what's more dear, thy Fame; mine has already receiv'd but too many desperate Wounds, and all thro' my unkind Lord's growing Passion for thee, which was most fatally founded on my Ruin, and nothing but my Ruin could advance it; and when, my Sister, thou hast run thy Race, made thy self loath'd, undone and infamous as Hell, despis'd, scorn'd and abandon'd by all, lampoon'd, perhaps diseas'd; this faithless Man, this Cause of all will leave thee too, grow weary of thee, nauseated by use; he may perhaps consider what Sins, what Evils, and what Inconveniences and Shames thou'st brought him to, and will not be the last shall loath and hate thee: For though Youth fancy it have a mighty Race to run of pleasing Vice and Vanity, the Course will end, the Goal will be arriv'd to at the last, where they will sighing stand, look back, and view the length of precious Time they've fool'd away; when travers'd o'er with Honour and Discretion, how glorious were the Journey, and with what Joy the weary'd Traveller lies down and basks beneath the Shades that end the happy Course.

Forgive, dear Child, this Advice, and pursue it; 'tis the Effect of my Pity, not Anger; nor could the Name of Rival ever yet have Power to banish that of Sister from my Soul——Farewel, remember me; pray Heav'n thou hast not this Night made a Forfeit of thy Honour, and that this which comes from a tender bleeding Heart may have the Fortune to inspire thee with Grace to avoid all Temptations for the future, since they must end in Sorrow; which is the Eternal Prayer of,

Dearest Child,
Your Affectionate Sister

To PHILANDER

ASK me not, my dearest Brother, the Reason of this sudden Change, ask me no more from whence proceeds this strange Coldness, or why this Alteration; it is enough my Destiny has not decreed me for *Philander*: Alas, I see my Error, and looking round about me, find nothing but approaching Horror and Confusion in my Pursuit of Love: Oh whither was I going, to what dark Paths, what everlasting Shades had smiling Love betray'd me, had I pursu'd him farther? but I at last have subdu'd his Force, and the fond Charmer shall no more renew his Arts and Flatteries; for I'm resolv'd as Heav'n, as fix'd as Fate and Death, and I conjure you trouble my Repose no more; for if you do (regardless of my Honour, which if you lov'd you would preserve) I'll do a Deed shall free me from your Importunities, that shall amaze and cool your vicious Flame. No more——remember you have a noble Wife, Companion of your Vows, and I have Honour, both which are worth preserving, and for which, though you want generous Love, you'll find neither that nor Courage wanting in *Sylvia*.

To SYLVIA

YES, my Adorable *Sylvia*, I will pursue you no farther; only for all my Pains, for all my Sufferings, for my tormenting sleepless Nights, and thoughtful anxious Days; for all my faithless Hopes, my Fears, my Sighs, my Prayers and my Tears, for my unequall'd and unbounded Passion, and my unweary'd Pursuits in Love, my never dying Flame, and lastly, for my Death; I only beg, in Recompence for all, this last Favour from your Pity; That you will deign to view the bleeding Wound that pierc'd the truest Heart that ever fell a Sacrifice to Love; you'll find my Body lying beneath that spreading Oak, so sacred to *Philander*, since 'twas there he first took into his greedy ravish'd Soul the dear, the soft Confession of thy Passion, tho' now forgotten and neglected all——Make what haste you can, you'll find there stretch'd out the mangled Carkass of the lost

PHILANDER

Ah *Sylvia*! was it for this that I was sent in such haste away this Morning to *Cesario*? Did I for this neglect the World, our great Affair, and all that Prince's Interest, and fly back to *Bellfont* on the Wings of Love? where in lieu of receiving a dear Blessing from thy Hand, do I find——Never see me more——good Heav'n——but, with my Life, all my Complaints are ended; only 'twould be some Ease, even in Death, to know what happy Rival 'tis has arm'd thy cruel Hand against *Philander*'s Heart.

To PHILANDER

STAY, I conjure thee stay thy Sacrilegious Hand; for the least Wound it gives the Lord of all my Wishes, I'll double on my Breast a thousand fold; stay then, by all thy Vows, thy Love, and all the Hopes, I swear thou hast this Night a full Recompence of all thy Pains from yielding *Sylvia*; I do conjure thee stay——for when the News arrives thou art no more, this poor, this lost, abandon'd Heart of mine shall fall a Victim to thy Cruelty: No, live, my *Philander*, I conjure thee, and receive all thou canst ask, and all that can be given by

SYLVIA

To PHILANDER

OH, my charming *Philander*! how very ill have you recompens'd my last soft Commands? which were that you should live; and yet at the same Moment, while you are reading of the dear Obligation, and while my Page was waiting your kind Return, you desperately expos'd your Life to the Mercy of this innocent Rival, betraying unadvisedly at the same time my Honour, and the Secret of your Love, and where to kill, or to be kill'd, had been almost equally unhappy: 'Twas well my Page told me you disarm'd him in this Rencounter; yet you, he says, are wounded, some sacred Drops of Blood are fallen to the Earth and lost, the least of which are precious enough to ransom Captive Queens: Oh! haste, *Philander*, to my Arms for Cure, I die with Fear there may be Danger,——haste, and let me bathe the dear, the wounded Part in Floods of Tears, lay to my warm Lips, and bind it with my torn Hair: Oh! *Philander*, I rave with my Concern for thee, and am ready to break all Laws of Decency and Duty, and fly, without consider-ing, to thy Succour, but that I fear to injure thee much more by the Discovery, which such an unadvis'd Absence would make. Pray Heav'n the unlucky Adventure reach not *Bellfont*; *Foscario* has no reason to proclaim it, and thou art too generous to boast the Conquest, and my Page was the only Witness, and he's as silent and as secret as the Grave: But why, *Philander*, was he sent me back without Reply? what meant that cruel Silence——say, my *Philander*, will you not obey me?——will you abandon me? can that dear Tongue be perjur'd? and can you this Night disappoint your *Sylvia*? what have I done, oh obstinately cruel, irreconcilable—— what, for my first Offence? a little poor Resentment and no more? a little faint Care of my gasping Honour, could that displease so much? besides I had a Cause, which you shall see; a Letter that would cool Love's hottest Fires, and turn it to Devotion; by Heav'n 'twas such a Check——such a Surprize——but you your self shall judge; if after that I could say less, than bid eternally farewel to Love——at least to thee——but I recanted soon; one sad dear Word, one soft resenting Line from thee, gain'd Love the Day again, and I despis'd the Censures of the duller World: Yes, yes, and I confess'd you had o'ercome, and did this merit no Reply? I ask'd the Boy a thousand times what you said, how and in what manner you received it, chid him, and laid your silent Fault on him, till he with Tears convinc'd me, and said he found you hastning to the Grove,——and when he gave you my Commands——you look'd upon him with such a stedfast, wild and fix'd Regard, surveying him all o'er while you were opening it—as argu'd some unusual Motion in you; then cry'd, Be gone——I cannot answer Flattery——Good Heav'n, what can you mean? but e'er he got to the farther End of the Grove, where still you walk'd a solemn Death-like Pace, he saw *Foscario* pass him unattended, and looking back saw your Rencounter, saw all that happen'd between you, then ran to your assistance just as you parted; still you were roughly sullen, and neither took notice of his proffer'd Service, nor that you needed it, although you bled apace; he offer'd you his Aid to tie your Wounds up——but you reply'd——Be gone, and do not trouble me——Oh, could you imagine I could live with this Neglect? could you, my *Philander*? oh, what would you have me do! If nothing but my Death or Ruin can suffice for my Attonement, I'll sacrifice either with Joy; yes, I'll proclaim my Passion aloud, proclaim it at *Bellfont*, own the dear criminal Flame, fly to my *Philander*'s Aid and be undone; for thus I cannot, no, I will not live, I rave, I languish, faint and die with Pain; say that you live, oh, say but that you live, say you are coming to the Meadow behind the Garden-grove in order to your Approach to my Arms: Oh, swear that all your Vows are true; oh, swear that you are *Sylvia*'s; and, in return, I'll swear that I am yours without Reserve, whatever Fate is destin'd for your

SYLVIA

I die with Impatience, either to see or hear from you; I fear 'tis yet too soon for the first——oh therefore save me with the last, or I shall rave, and wildly betray all by coming to Dorillus *his Farm, or seeking you where-e'er you cruelly have hid your self from*

SYLVIA

To SYLVIA

AH, *Sylvia*, how have you in one Day destroy'd that Repose I have been designing so many Years! Oh, thou false——but wondrous fair Creature! why did Heaven ordain so much Beauty and so much Perfidy, so much excellent Wit and so much Cunning, (things inconsistent in any but in

255

Sylvia) in one Divine Frame, but to undo Mankind: Yes, *Sylvia*, thou wert born to murther more believing Men than the unhappy and undone *Philander*. Tell me, thou charming Hypocrite, why hast thou thus deluded me? why, oh, why was I made the miserable Object of thy fatal Vow-breach? What have I done, thou lovely, fickle Maid, that thou shouldst be my Murtherer? And why dost thou call me from the Grave with such dear soft Commands as would awake the very quiet Dead, to torture me anew, after my Eyes (curse on their fatal Sense) were too sure Witnesses of thy Infidelity? Oh, fickle Maid, how much more kind 't had been to have sent me down to Earth, with plain heart-breaking Truth, than a mean subtle Falshood, that has undone thy Credit in my Soul: Truth, tho' 'twere cruel, had been generous in thee, tho' thou wert perjur'd, false, forsworn——thou shouldst not have added to it that yet baser Sin of Treachery: You might have been provok'd to have kill'd your Friend, but it were base to stab him unawares, defenceless and unwarn'd; smile in my Face, and strike me to the Heart; sooth me with all the tenderest Marks of Passion——nay, with an Invitation too, that would have gain'd a Credit in one that had been jilted o'er the World, flatter'd and ruin'd by all thy cozening Sex, and all to send me vain and pleas'd away, only to gain a Day to entertain another Lover in. Oh, fantastick Woman! destructive glorious Thing, what needed this Deceit? Hadst thou not with unwonted Industry persuaded me to have hasted to *Cesario*, by Heav'n, I had dully liv'd the tedious Day in traversing the flow'ry Meads and silent Groves, laid by some murmuring Spring had sigh'd away the often counted Hours, and thought on *Sylvia*, 'till the bless'd Minute of my ravishing Approach to her; had been a fond, believing and impos'd on Coxcomb, and never had dreamt the Treachery, never seen the Snake that bask'd beneath the gay, the smiling Flowers; securely thou hadst cozen'd me, reap'd thy new Joys, and made my Rival sport at the Expence of all my Happiness: Yes, yes, your hasty Importunity first gave me Jealousie, made me impatient with *Cesario*, and excuse my self to him by a hundred Inventions; neglected all to hasten back, where all my Joys, where all my killing Fears and Torments resided——But when I came—— how was I welcom'd? With your confirming Billet; yes, *Sylvia*, how! let *Dorillus* inform you, between whose Arms I fell dead, Shame on me, dead——and the first Thought my Soul conceiv'd when it return'd, was, not to die in Jest. I answer'd your Commands, and hasten'd to the Grove, where——by all that's sacred, by thy self I swear (a dearer Oath than Heav'n and Earth can furnish me with) I did resolve to die; but oh, how soon my soft, my silent Passion turn'd to loud Rage, Rage easier to be born, to dire Despair, to Fury and Revenge; for there I saw *Foscario*, my young, my fair, my rich and powerful Rival, he hasted through the Grove all warm and glowing from the fair false ones Arms; the Blushes which thy Eyes had kindled were fresh upon his Cheeks, his Looks were sparkling with the new-blown Fire, his Heart so briskly burnt with, a glad, a peaceful Smile dress'd all his Face, trick'd like a Bridegroom, while he perfum'd the Air as he pass'd thro' it——None but the Man that loves and dotes like me is able to express my Sense of Rage: I quickly turn'd the Sword from my own Heart to send it to his elevated one, giving him only time to——draw—— that was the Word, and I confess your Spark was wondrous ready, brisk with Success, vain with your new-given Favours he only cry'd——If *Sylvia* be the Quarrel——I am prepar'd——And he maintain'd your Cause with admirable Courage I confess, though Chance or Fortune luckily gave me his Sword, which I would fain have render'd back, and that way would have dy'd; but he refus'd to arm his Hand anew against the Man that had not took Advantage of him, and thus we parted: Then 'twas that Malice supported me with Life, and told me I should scorn to die for so perfidious and so ruinous a Creature; but charming and bewitching still, 'twas then I borrow'd so much Calmness of my lessening Anger to read the Billet o'er, your Page had brought me, which melted all the rough remaining Part of Rage away into tame Languishment: Ah, *Sylvia*! this Heart of mine was never form'd by Nature to hold out long in stubborn Sullenness; I am already on the excusing Part, and fain would think thee innocent and just; deceive me prettily, I know thou canst sooth my fond Heart, and ask how it could harbour a faithless Thought of *Sylvia*——do——flatter me , protest a little, swear my Rival saw thee not, say he was there by chance—— say any thing; or if thou saw'st him, say with how cold a Look he was receiv'd——Oh, *Sylvia*, calm my Soul, deceive it, flatter it, and I shall still believe and love thee on——Yet should'st thou tell me Truth, that thou art false, by Heav'n I do adore thee so, I still should love thee on; should I have seen thee clasp him in thy Arms, print Kisses on his Cheeks and Lips, and more——so fondly and so dotingly I love, I think I should forgive thee; for I swear by all the Powers that pity frail Mortality, there is no Joy, no Life, no Heav'n without thee! Be false, be cruel, perjur'd, infamous, yet still I must adore thee; my Soul was form'd of nothing but of Love, and all that Love, and all that Soul is *Sylvia*'s: But yet, since thou hast fram'd me an Excuse, be kind and carry it on;——to be deluded well, as thou can'st do't, will be the same to Innocence as loving: I shall not find the Cheat: I'll come then——and lay my self at thy Feet, and seek there that Repose, that dear Content which is not to be found in this vast World besides; though much of my Heart's Joy thou hast abated, and fix'd a Sadness in my Soul that will not easily vanish——Oh *Sylvia*, take care of me, for I am in thy Power, my Life, my Fame, my Soul are in thy Hands, be tender of the Victims, and remember if any Action of thy Life should shew a fading Love, that very Moment I perceive the Change, you shall find dead at your Feet the abandon'd

PHILANDER

Sad as Death, I am going towards the Meadow, in order to my Approach towards Sylvia, *the World affording no Repose to me, but when I am where the dear Charmer is.*

To PHILANDER *in the Meadow*

AND can you be jealous of me, *Philander*? I mean so poorly jealous as to believe me capable of Falshood, of Vow-Breach, and what's worse, of loving any thing but the adorable *Philander*? Oh, I could not once believe so cruel a Thought could have entered into the Imaginations of a Soul so entirely possess'd with *Sylvia*, and so great a Judge of Love? Abandon me, reproach me, hate me, scorn me, whenever I harbour any thing in mind so destructive to my Repose and thine. Can I, *Philander*, give you a greater Proof of my Passion, of my faithful, never-dying Passion, than being undone for you? Have I any other Prospect in all this soft Adventure, but Shame, Dishonour, Reproach, eternal Infamy, and everlasting Destruction, even of Soul and Body: I tremble with Fear of future Punishment; but oh, Love will have no Devotion (mix'd with his Ceremonies) to any other Deity; and yet, alas, I might have lov'd another, and have been sav'd, or any Maid but *Sylvia*, might have possess'd without Damnation. But 'tis a Brother I pursue, it is a Sister gives her Honour up, and none but *Cannace*, that ever I read in Story, was ever found so wretched as to love a Brother with so criminal a Flame, and possibly I may meet her Fate. I have a Father too as great as *Æolus*, as angry and revengeful where his Honour is concern'd; and you found, my dearest Brother, how near you were last Night to a Discovery in the Garden: I have some Reason too to fear this Night's Adventure, for as ill Fate would have it (loaded with other Thoughts) I told not *Melinda* of your Adventure last Night with *Monsieur* the Count, who meeting her early this Morning, had like to have made a Discovery, if he have not really so already; she strove to shun him, but he cry'd out——— *Melinda*, you cannot fly me by Light, as you did last Night in the Dark——— She turn'd and begg'd his Pardon, for neither coming nor designing to come, since she had resolv'd never to violate her Vows to *Alexis*: Not coming cry'd he, not returning again, you meant, *Melinda*; secure of my Heart and my Purse, you fled with both: *Melinda*, whose Honour was now concern'd and not reminding your Escape in her Likeness, blushing, she sharply denied the Fact, and with a Disdain that had laid aside all Respect, left him; nor can it be doubted, but he fancied (if she spoke Truth) there was some other Intrigue of Love carried on at *Bellfont*. Judge, my charming *Philander*, if I have not Reason to be fearful of thy Safety, and my Fame, and to be jealous that so wise a Man as *Monsieur* did not take that Parly to be held with a Spirit last Night, or that 'twas an Apparition he courted: But if there be no Boldness like that of Love, nor Courage like that of a Lover; sure there never was so great a *Heroine* as *Sylvia*. Undaunted, I resolve to stand the Shock of all, since 'tis impossible for me to leave *Philander* any Doubt or Jealousie that I can dissipate, and Heav'n knows how far I was from any Thought of seeing *Foscario*, when I urg'd *Philander* to depart. I have to clear my Innocence, sent thee the Letter I receiv'd two Hours after thy Absence, which falling into my Mother's Hands, whose Favourite he is, he had Permission to make his Visit, which within an Hour he did; but how received by me, be thou the Judge, whene'er it is thy Fate to be oblig'd to entertain some Woman to whom thy Soul has an entire Aversion. I forced a Complaisance against my Nature endured his racking Courtship with a Fortitude that became the great Heart that bears thy sacred Image; as Martyrs do, I suffer'd without murmuring, or the least Sign of the Pain I endur'd——'Tis below the Dignity of my mighty Passion to justifie it farther, let it plead its own Cause, it has a thousand ways to do it, and those all such as cannot be resisted, cannot be doubted, especially this last Proof of sacrificing to your Repose the never more to be doubled

SYLVIA

About an Hour hence I shall expect you to advance.

To the LADY——

Madam,
'TIS not always the Divine Graces wherewith Heav'n has adorn'd your resplendent Beauties, that can maintain the innumerable Conquests they gain, without a noble Goodness, which may make you sensibly compassionate the poor and forlorn Captives you have undone: But most fair of your Sex, 'tis I alone that have a Destiny more cruel and severe, and find my self wounded from your very Frowns, and secur'd a Slave as well as made one; the very Scorn from those triumphant Stars, your Eyes, have the same Effects as if they shin'd with the continual Splendor of ravishing Smiles; and I can no more shun their killing Influence, than their all saving Aspects: And I shall expire contentedly, since I fall by so glorious a Fate, if you will vouchsafe to pronounce my Doom from that Storehouse of Perfection, your Mouth, from Lips that open like the blushing Rose, strow'd o'er with Morning Dew, and from a Breath sweeter than holy Incense; in order to which, I approach you, most excellent Beauty, with this most humble Petition, that you will deign to permit me to throw my unworthy self before the Throne of your Mercy, there to receive the Sentence of my Life or Death; a Happiness tho' incomparably too great for so mean a Vassal, yet with that Reverence and Awe I shall receive it, as I would the Sentence of

the Gods, and which I will no more resist than I would the Thunderbolts of *Jove*, or the Revenge of angry *Juno*: For Madam, my immense Passion knows no *medium* between Life and Death, and as I never had the Presumption to aspire to the Glory of the first, I am not so abject as to fear I am wholly depriv'd of the Glory of the last: I have too long lain convicted, extend your Mercy, and put me now out of Pain: You have often wreck'd me to confess my Promethean Sin; spare the cruel Vulture of Despair, take him from my Heart in Pity, and either by killing Words, or blasting Lightning from those refulgent Eyes, pronounce the Death of,

Madam,
Your admiring Slave,
FOSCARIO

To SYLVIA

My Everlasting Charmer,

I Am convinc'd and pleas'd, my Fears are vanish'd, and a Heav'n of solid Joy is open'd to my View, and I have nothing now in Prospect but Angel-Brightness, glittering Youth, dazling Beauty, charming Sounds, and ravishing Touches, and all around me Ecstasies of Pleasure, unconceivable Transports without Conclusion; *Mahomet* never fancy'd such a Heav'n, not all his Paradise promis'd such lasting Felicity, or ever provided there the Recompence of such a Maid as *Sylvia*, such a bewitching Form, such soft, such glorious Eyes, where the Soul speaks and dances, and betray's Love's Secrets in every killing Glance, a Face, where every Motion, every Feature sweetly languishes, a Neck all tempting——and her lovely Breast inviting, presses from the eager Lips; such Hands, such clasping Arms, so white, so soft and slender! no, nor one of all his hea'vnly Enjoyments, though promis'd Years of fainting in one continu'd Ecstasie, can make one Moment's Joy with charming *Sylvia*. Oh, I am wrapt (with bare Imagination) with a much vaster Pleasure than any other dull Appointment can dispense——Oh, thou Blessing sent from Heav'n to ease my Toils of Life! Thou sacred dear Delight of my fond doting Heart, oh, whither wilt thou lead me, to what vast heights of Love? into Extremes as fatal and as dangerous as those Excesses were that render'd me so cold in your Opinion. Oh, *Sylvia*, *Sylvia*, have a care of me, manage my over-joy'd Soul, and all its eager Passions, chide my fond Heart, be angry if I faint upon thy Bosom, and do not with thy tender Voice recal me, a Voice that kills out-right, and calls my fleeting Soul out of its Habitation: Lay not such charming Lips to my cold Cheeks, but let me lye extended at thy Feet untouch'd, unsigh'd upon, unpress'd with Kisses: Oh, change those tender, trembling Words of Love into rough Sounds and Noises unconcern'd, and when you see me dying, do not call my Soul to mingle with thy Sighs; yet should'st thou bate one Word, one Look or Tear, by Heav'n, I should be mad; oh, never let me live to see Declension in thy Love! no, no, my Charmer, I cannot bear the least suppos'd Decay in those dear Fondnesses of thine; and sure none e'er became a Maid so well, nor ever were receiv'd with Adorations like to mine!

Pardon, my adorable *Sylvia*, the Rashness of my Passion in this Rancounter with *Foscario*; I am satisfy'd he is too unhappy in your Disfavour to merit the being so in mine; but 'twas sufficient I then saw a Joy in his Face, a pleas'd Gaiety in his Looks to make me think my Rage reasonable, and my Quarrel just; by the Style he writes, I dread his Sense less than his Person; but you, my lovely Maid, have said enough to quit me of my Fears for both——the Night comes on——I cannot call it envious, though it rob me of the Light that should assist me to finish this, since it will more gloriously repay me in a happier Place——Come on then, thou blest Retreat of Lovers, I forgive thy Interruptions here, since thou wilt conduct to the Arms of *Sylvia*——the adoring

PHILANDER

If you have any Commands for me, this Weeder of the Gardens, whom I met in going in thither, will bring it back; I wait in the Meadow, and date this from the dear Primrose-Bank, where I have sate with Sylvia.

To PHILANDER

After the happy Night

'Tis done; yes, *Philander*, 'tis done, and after that what will not Love and Grief oblige me to own to you? Oh, by what insensible Degrees a Maid in Love may arrive to say any thing to her Lover without Blushing! I have known the time, the blest innocent time, when but to think I lov'd *Philander*, would have cover'd my Face with Shame, and to have spoke it would have fill'd me with Confusion——have made me tremble, blush, and bend my guilty Eyes to Earth, not daring to behold my charming Conqueror, while I made that bashful Confession——though now I am grown bold in Love, yet I have known the time when being at Court, and coming from the Presence, being offer'd some officious Hand to lead me to my Coach, I have shrunk back with my Aversion to your Sex, and have conceal'd my Hands in my Pockets to prevent their being touch'd;——a Kiss would turn my Stomach, and amorous Looks (though they would make me vain) gave me a Hate to him that sent them, and never any Maid resolv'd so much as I to tread the Paths of Honour, and I had many Precedents before me to make me careful: Thus I was arm'd with Resolution, Pride and Scorn, against all Mankind; but alas, I made no Defence against a Brother, but innocently lay expos'd to all his Attacks of Love, and never thought it criminal 'till it kindled a new Desire about me, Oh, that I should not die with Shame to own it——Yet see (I say) how from one soft Degree to another, I do not only confess the shameful Truth, but act it too; what with a Brother——Oh Heav'ns! a Crime so monstrous and so new——But by all thy Love, by those surprizing Joys so lately experienced——I never will——No, no, I never can——repent it: Oh incorrigible Passion! oh harden'd Love! At least I might have some Remorse, some Sighing after my poor departed Honour; but why should I dissemble with the Powers Divine; that know the Secrets of a Soul doom'd to eternal Love? Yet I am mad, I rave and tear my self, traverse my guilty Chamber in a disorder'd, but a soft Confusion; and often opening the conscious Curtains, survey the Print where thou and I were last Night laid, surveying it with a thousand tender Sighs, and kiss and press thy dear forsaken Side, imagine over all our solemn Joys, every dear Transport, all our ravishing repeated Blisses; then almost fainting, languishing, cry——*Philander*, oh, my charming little God! then lay me down in the dear Place you press'd, still warm and fragrant with the sweet Remains that thou hast left behind thee on the Pillow. Oh, my Soul's Joy! my dear, eternal Pleasure! what Softness hast thou added to my Heart within a few Hours? But oh *Philander*——if (as I've oft been told) Possession, which makes Women fond and doting, should make thee cold, and grow indifferent——if nauseated with repeated Joy, and having made a full Discovery of all that was but once imaginary, when Fancy render'd every thing much finer than Experience, oh, how were I undone! For me, by all the Inhabitants of Heav'n I swear, by thy dear charming self, and by thy Vows——thou so transcend'st all Fancy, all dull Imagination, all wond'ring Ideas of what Man was to me, that I believe thee more than human! some Charm Divine dwells in thy Touches; besides all these, thy charming Look, thy Love, the Beauties that adorn thee, and thy Wit, I swear there is a Secret in Nature that renders thee more dear, and fits thee to my Soul; do not ask it me, let it suffice, 'tis so, and is not to be told; yes, by it I know thou art the Man created for my Soul, and he alone that has the Power to touch it; my Eyes and Fancy might have been diverted, I might have favour'd this above the other, preferr'd that Face, that Wit, or Shape, or Air——but to concern my Soul to make that capable of something more than Love, 'twas only necessary that *Philander* should be form'd, and form'd just as he is, that Shape, that Face, that Height, that dear Proportion; I would not have a Feature, not a Look, not a Hair alter'd, just as thou art, thou art an Angel to me, and I, without considering what I am, what I might be, or ought, without considering the fatal Circumstances of thy being marry'd (a Thought that shocks my Soul whene'er it enters) or whate'er other Thought that does concern my Happiness or Quiet, have fix'd my Soul to Love and my *Philander*, to love thee with all thy Disadvantages, and glory in my Ruin; these are my firm Resolves——these are my Thoughts. But thou art gone, with all the Trophies of my Love and Honour, gay with the Spoils, which now perhaps are unregarded: The Mystery's now reveal'd, the mighty Secret's known, and now will be no Wonder or Surprize: But hear my Vows, by all on which my Life depends I swear——if ever I perceive the least Decay of Love in thee, if e'er thou break'st an Oath, a Vow, a Word, if e'er I see Repentance in thy Face, or Coldness in thy Eyes (which Heav'n divert) by that bright Heav'n I'll die; you may believe me, since I had the Courage and durst love thee, and after that durst sacrifice my Fame, lose all to justifie that Love, will, when a Change so fatal shall arrive, find Courage too to die; yes, die, *Philander*, assure thy self I will, and therefore have a Care of

SYLVIA

To PHILANDER

OH, where shall I find Repose, where seek a silent Quiet, but in my last Retreat, the Grave! I say not this, my dearest *Philander*, that I do or ever can repent my Love, though the fatal Source of all: For already we are betray'd, our Race of Joys, our Course of stol'n Delight is ended e'er begun. I chid, alas, at Morning's Dawn, I chid you to be gone, and yet, Heav'n knows, I grasp'd you fast, and rather would have dy'd than parted with you; I saw the Day come on, and curs'd its busie Light, and still you cry'd one blessed Minute more, before I part with all the Joys of Life! and Hours were Minutes then, and Day grew old upon us unawares, 'twas all abroad, and had call'd up all the Houshold Spies to pry into the Secrets of our Loves, and thou, by some Tale-bearing Flatterer, wert seen in passing through the Garden; the News was carry'd to my Father, and a mighty Consult has been held in my Mother's Apartment, who now refuses to see me; while I, possess'd with Love, and full of Wonder at my new Change, lull'd with dear Contemplation, (for I am alter'd much since Yesterday, however thou hast charm'd me) imagining none knew our Theft of Love, but only Heav'n and *Melinda*. But oh, alas, I had no sooner finish'd this inclos'd, but my Father enter'd my Cabinet, but 'twas with such a Look——as soon inform'd me all was betray'd to him; a while he gaz'd on me with Fierceness in his Eyes, which so surpriz'd and frighted me, that I, all pale and trembling, threw my self at his Feet; he, seeing my Disorder, took me up, and fix'd so steadfast and so sad a Look upon me, as would have broken any Heart but mine, supported with *Philander's* Image; I sigh'd and wept ——and silently attended when the Storm should fall, which turn'd into a Shower so soft and piercing, I almost dy'd to see it; at last delivering me a Paper——Here, (cry'd he, with a Sigh and Trembling-interrupted Voice) read what I cannot tell thee. Oh, *Sylvia*, cry'd he,——thou Joy and Hope of all my aged Years, thou Object of my Dotage, how hast thou brought me to my Grave with Sorrow? so left me with the Paper in my Hand: Speechless, unmov'd a while I stood, 'till he awak'd me by new Sighs and Cries; for passing through my Chamber by Chance, or by Design, he cast his melancholy Eyes towards my Bed, and saw the dear Disorder there, unusual—— then cry'd——Oh, wretched *Sylvia*, thou art lost! and left me almost fainting. The Letter, I soon found, was one you'd sent from *Dorillus* his Farm this Morning, after you had parted from me, which has betray'd us all, but how it came into their Hands I since have understood; for, as I said, you were seen passing through the Garden, from thence (to be confirm'd) they dog'd you to the Farm, and waiting there your Motions, saw *Dorillus* come forth with a Letter in his Hand, which though he soon conceal'd, yet not so soon but it was taken notice of, when hast'ning to *Bellfont* the nearest Way, they gave an Account to *Monsieur*, my Father, who going out to *Dorillus*, commanded him to deliver him the Letter; his Vassal durst not disobey, but yielded it with such Dispute and Reluctancy as he durst maintain with a Man so great and powerful; before *Dorillus* return'd you had taken Horse, so that you are a Stranger to our Misfortune——What shall I do? where shall I seek a Refuge from the Danger that threatens us? A sad and silent Grief appears throughout *Bellfont*, and the Face of all things are chang'd, yet none knows the unhappy Cause but *Monsieur* my Father, and *Madam* my Mother, *Melinda* and my self? *Melinda* and my Page are both dismiss'd from waiting on me, as suppos'd Confidents of this dear Secret, and Strangers, Creatures of *Madam* the Countess, put about me. Oh *Philander*, what can I do? thy Advice, or I am lost: But how, alas, shall I either convey these to thee, or receive any thing from thee, unless some God of Love, in Pity of our Miseries, should offer us his Aid? I'll try to corrupt my new Boy, I see Good-nature, Pity and Generosity in his Looks, he's well born too, and may be honest.

Thus far, *Philander*, I had writ when Supper was brought me, for yet my Parents have not deign'd to let me come into their Presence; those that serve me tell me *Myrtilla* is this afternoon arriv'd at *Bellfont*; all's mighty close carry'd in the Countess's Apartment. I tremble with the Thought of what will be the Result of the great Consultation: I have been tempting of the Boy, but I perceive they have strictly charg'd him not to obey me; he says, against his Will he shall betray me, for they will have him search'd; but he has promis'd me to fee² one of the Weeders, who working in the Garden, into which my Window opens, may from thence receive what I shall let down; if it be true, I shall get this fatal Knowledge to you, that you may not only prepare for the worst, but contrive to set at Liberty

The unfortunate
SYLVIA

My Heart is ready to break, and my Eyes are drown'd in Tears: Oh Philander, *how much unlike the last will this fatal Night prove! Farewel, and think of* Sylvia.

This was writ in the Cover to both the foregoing

Letters to PHILANDER

Philander, all that I dreaded, all that I fear'd is fallen upon me: I have been arraign'd, and convicted; three Judges, severe as the three infernal ones, sate in Condemnation on me, a Father, a Mother, and a Sister; the Fact, alas, was too clearly prov'd and too many circumstantial Truths appear'd against me, for me to plead not guilty. But, oh Heav'ns! had you seen the Tears and heard the Prayers, Threats, Reproaches and Upbraidings—— these from an injur'd Sister, those my Heart-broken Parents; a tender Mother here, a railing and reviling Sister there——an angry Father, and a guilty Conscience——thou wouldst have wonder'd at my Fortitude, my Courage, and my Resolution, and all from Love! for surely I had died, had not thy Love, thy powerful Love supported me; thro' all the Accidents of Live and Fate, that can and will support me; in the midst of all their Clamours and their Railings I had from that a secret and soft Repose within, that whisper'd me, *Philander* loves me still; discarded and renounc'd by my fond Parents, Love still replies, *Philander* still will own thee; thrown from thy Mother's and thy Sister's Arms, *Philander*'s still are open to receive thee: And tho' I rave and almost die to see them grieve, to think that I am the fatal Cause who makes so sad Confusion in our Family; (for, oh, 'tis pitious to behold my Sister's Sighs and Tears, my Mother's sad Despair, my Father's raging and his weeping, by melancholy Turns;) yet even these deplorable Objects, that would move the most obdurate, stubborn Heart to Pity and Repentance, render not mine relenting; and yet I am wondrous pitiful by Nature, and I can weep and faint to see the sad Effects of my loose, wanton Love, yet cannot find Repentance for the dear, charming Sin; and yet, should'st thou behold my Mother's Languishment, no bitter Words proceeding from her Lips, no Tears fall from her down-cast Eyes, but silent and sad as Death she sits, and will not view the Light; should'st thou, I say, behold it, thou would'st, if not repent, yet grieve that thou hadst lov'd me: Sure Love has quite confounded Nature in me, I could not else behold this fatal Ruin without revenging it upon my stubborn

265

Heart; a thousand times a Day I make new Vows against the God of Love, but 'tis too late, and I'm as often perjur'd——Oh, should the Gods revenge the broken Vows of Lovers, what Love-sick Man, what Maid betray'd like me, but would be damn'd a thousand times? for every little Love-quarrel, every kind Resentment makes us swear to love no more; and every Smile, and every flattering Softness from the dear Injurer, makes us perjur'd: Let all the Force of Virtue, Honour, Interest join with my suffering Parents to persuade me to cease to love *Philander*, yet let him but appear, let him but look on me with those dear charming Eyes, let him but sigh, or press me to his fragrant Cheek, fold me——and cry——Ah, *Sylvia*, can you quit me?——nay, you must not, you shall not, nay, I know you cannot, remember you are mine——There is such Eloquence in those dear Words, when utter'd with a Voice so tender and so passionate, that I believe 'em irresistible——alas, I find 'em so——and easily break all the feebler Vows I make against thee; yes, I must be undone, perjur'd, forsworn, incorrigible, unnatural, disobedient, and any thing, rather than not *Philander's*——Turn then, my Soul, from these domestick, melancholy Objects, and look abroad, look forward for a while on charming Prospects; look on *Philander*, the dear, the young, the amorous *Philander*, whose very Looks infuse a tender Joy throughout the Soul, and chase all Cares, all Sorrows and anxious Thoughts from thence, whose wanton Play is softer than that of young fledg'd Angels, and when he looks, and sighs, and speaks, and touches, he is a very God: Where art thou, oh thou Miracle of Youth, thou charming, dear Undoer! Now thou hast gain'd the Glory of the Conquest, thou slightest the rifled Captive: What, not a Line? Two tedious Days are past, and no kind Power relieves me with a Word, or any Tidings of *Philander*——and yet thou may'st have sent——but I shall never see it, till they raise up fresh Witnesses against me——I cannot think thee wavering or forgetful; for if I did, surely thou know'st my Heart so well, thou canst not think 'twould live to think another Thought: Confirm my kind Belief, and send to me——

There is a Gate well known to thee through which thou passest to *Bellfont*, 'tis in the Road about half a League from hence, an old Man opens it, his Daughter weeds in the Garden, and will convey this to thee as I have order'd her, by the same Messenger thou may'st return thine; and early as she comes I'll let her down a String, by which way unperceiv'd I shall receive 'em from her: I'll say no more, nor instruct you how you shall preserve your

SYLVIA

To SYLVIA

That which was left in her Hands by Monsieur, *her Father, in her Cabinet*

My Adorable Sylvia.

I Can no more describe to thee the Torment with which I part from *Bellfont*, than I can that Heav'n of Joy I was rais'd to last Night by the transporting Effects of thy wondrous Love; both are to Excess, and both killing, but in different kinds. Oh, *Sylvia*, by all my unspeakable Raptures in thy Arms, by all thy Charms of Beauty, too numerous and too ravishing for Fancy to imagine——I swear——by this last Night, by this dear new Discovery, thou hast increas'd my Love to that vast Height, it has undone my Peace—— all my Repose is gone——this dear, dear Night has ruin'd me, it has con-firm'd me now I must have *Sylvia*, and cannot live without her, no, not a Day, an Hour——to save the World, unless I had the intire Possession of my lovely Maid: Ah, *Sylvia*, I am not that indifferent dull Lover that can be rais'd by one Beauty to an Appetite, and satisfie it with another, I cannot carry the dear Flame you kindle, to quench it in the Embraces of *Myrtilla*; no, by the eternal Powers, he that pretends to love, and loves at that coarse rate, needs fear no Danger from that Passion, he ne'er was born to love, or die for Love; *Sylvia*, *Myrtilla* and a thousand more were all the same to such a dull Insensible; no, *Sylvia*, when you find I can return back to the once left matrimonial Bed, despise me, scorn me: swear (as then thou justly may'st) I love not *Sylvia*: Let the hot Brute drudge on (he who is fir'd by Nature, not by Love, whom any Body's Kisses can inspire) and ease the necessary Heats of Youth; Love is a nobler Fire, which nothing can allay but the dear She that rais'd it; no, no, my purer Stream shall ne'er run back to the Fountain, whence 'tis parted, nay it cannot, it were as possible to love again, where one has ceas'd to love, as carry the Desire and Wishes back; by Heav'n, to me there's nothing so unnatural; no, *Sylvia*, it is you I must possess, you have compleated my undoing now, and I must die unless you give me all—but oh, I am going from thee——when are we like to meet——oh, how shall I support my absent Hours! Thought will destroy me, for 'twill be all on thee, and those at such a Distance will be insupportable——What shall I do without thee? If after all the Toils of dull insipid Life I could return and lay me down by thee, *Herculean* Labours would be soft and easie——the harsh Fatigues of War, the dangerous Hurries of Affairs of State, the Business and the Noise of Life, I could support with Pleasure, with wondrous Satisfaction, could treat *Myrtilla* too with that Respect, that generous Care as would become a Husband. I could be easie every where, and every one should be at Ease with me; now I shall go and find no *Sylvia* there, but sigh and wander like an unknown thing, on some strange foreign Shore; I shall grow peevish as a new wean'd Child, no Toys, no Bauble of the gaudy World will please my wayward

Fancy: I shall be out of Humour, rail at every thing, in Anger shall demand, and sullenly reply to every Question ask'd and answer'd, and when I think to ease my Soul by a Retreat, a thousand soft Desires, a thousand Wishes wreck me, pain me to raving, 'till beating the sensless Floor with my Feet ——I cry'd aloud——My *Sylvia*!——thus, thus, my charming Dear, the poor *Philander* is employ'd when banish'd from his Heav'n! If thus it us'd to be when only that bright Outside was ador'd, judge now my Pain, now thou hast made known a thousand Graces more——oh, pity me—— for 'tis not in thy Power to guess what I shall now endure in Absence of thee; for thou hast charm'd my Soul to an Excess too mighty for a patient suffering: Alas, I die already——

I am yet at *Dorillus* his Farm, lingring on from one swift Minute to the other, and have not Power to go; a thousand Looks all languishing I've cast from Eyes all drown'd in Tears towards *Bellfont*, have sigh'd a thousand Wishes to my Angel, from a sad breaking Heart——Love will not let me go——and Honour calls me——alas, I must away; when shall we meet again? ah when, my *Sylvia*?——oh charming Maid——thou'lt see me shortly dead, for thus I cannot live; thou must be mine, or I must be no more——I must away——farewel——may all the softest Joys of Heav'n attend thee——adieu——fail not to send a hundred times a Day, if possible; I've order'd *Alexis* to do nothing but wait for all that comes, and post away with what thou send'st to me——again adieu, think on me——and 'till thou call'st me to thee, imagine nothing upon Earth so wretched as *Sylvia*'s own

PHILANDER

Know, my Angel, that passing through the Garden this Morning, I met Erasto ——*I fear he saw me near enough to know me, and will give an Account of it; let me know what happens——adieu half dead, just taking Horse to go from* Sylvia.

To PHILANDER

Written in a Leaf of a Table-Book

I Have only time to say, on *Thursday* I am destin'd a Sacrifice to *Foscario*, which Day finishes the Life of

SYLVIA

To SYLVIA

From Dorillus *his Farm*

Raving and mad at the News your Billet brought me, I (without considering the Effects that would follow) am arriv'd at *Bellfont*; I have yet so much

Patience about me, to suffer my self to be conceal'd at *Dorillus* his Cottage; but if I see thee not to Night, or find no hopes of it——by Heav'n I'll set *Bellfont* all in a Flame but I will have my *Sylvia*; be sure I'll do't——What? to be marry'd——*Sylvia* to be marry'd——and giv'n from *Philander*—— Oh, never think it, thou forsworn fair Creature——What? give *Foscario* that dear charming Body? Shall he be grasp'd in those dear naked Arms? taste all thy Kisses, press thy snowy Breasts, command thy Joys, and rifle all thy Heav'n? Furies and Hell environ me if he do——Oh, *Sylvia*, faithless, perjur'd, charming *Sylvia*——and canst thou suffer it——Hear my Vows, oh fickle Angel——Hear me, thou faithless Ravisher! That fatal Moment that the daring Priest offers to join your Hands, and give thee from me, I'll sacrifice your Lover; by Heaven I will, before the Altar, stab him at your Feet; the holy Place, nor the Numbers that attend ye, nor all your Prayers nor Tears, shall save his Heart; look to't, and be not false—— yet I'll not trust thy Faith; no, she that can think but falsly, and she that can so easily be perjur'd——for, but to suffer it is such a Sin——such an undoing Sin——that thou art surely damn'd! and yet, by Heav'n, that is not all the Ruin shall attend thee; no, lovely Mischief, no——you shall not scape 'till the Damnation Day; for I will rack thee, torture thee and plague thee, those few Hours I have to live, (if spiteful Fate prevent my just Revenge upon *Foscario*) and when I'm dead——as I shall quickly be kill'd by thy Cruelty——know, thou fair Murtherer, I will haunt thy Sight, be ever with thee, and surround thy Bed, and fright thee from the Ravisher; fright all thy loose Delights, and check thy Joys——Oh, I am mad!——I cannot think that Thought, no, thou shalt never advance so far in Wicked-ness, I'll save thee, if I can——Oh, my adorable, why dost thou torture me? How hast thou sworn so often and so loud that Heav'n I'm sure has heard thee, and will punish thee? How didst thou swear that happy blessed Night, in which I saw thee last, clasp'd in my Arms, weeping with eager Love, with melting Softness on my Bosom——remember how thou swor'st ——oh, that dear Night——let me recover Strength——and then I'll tell thee more——I must repeat the Story of that Night, which thou perhaps (oh faithless!) hast forgot——that glorious Night, when all the Heav'ns were gay, and every favouring Power look'd down and smil'd upon our Thefts of Love, that gloomy Night, the first of all my Joys, the blessed'st of my Life——trembling and fainting I approach'd your Chamber, and while you met and grasp'd me at the Door, taking my trembling Body in your Arms——remember how I fainted at your Feet, and what dear Arts you us'd to call me back to Life——Remember how you kiss'd and press'd my Face——Remember what dear charming Words you spoke——and when I did recover, how I ask'd you with a feeble doubtful Voice——Ah, *Sylvia*, will you still continue thus, thus wondrous soft and fond? Will you be ever mine, and ever true?——What did you then reply, when kneeling on the Carpet where I lay, what, *Sylvia*, did you vow? how invoke Heav'n? how call its Vengeance down if e'er you lov'd another Man again, if e'er you touch'd or smil'd on any other, if e'er you suffer'd Words or Acts of Love but from *Philander*? Both Heav'n and Hell thou didst awaken with thy Oaths, one was an angry Listener to what it knew thou'dst break, the other laugh'd to know thou would'st be perjur'd, while only I, poor I, was all the while a silent fond Believer; your Vows stopp'd all my Language as your Kisses did my Lips, you swore and kiss'd, and vow'd and clasp'd my Neck——oh charming Flatterer! oh artful, dear Beguiler! Thus into Life, and Peace, and fond Security, you charm'd my willing Soul! 'Twas then, my *Sylvia*, (certain of your Heart, and that it never could be given away to any other) I press'd my eager Joys, but with such tender Caution ——such Fear and Fondness, such an awful Passion, as overcame your faint Resistance; my Reasons and my Arguments were strong, for you were mine by Love, by sacred Vows, and who could lay a better Claim to *Sylvia*? How oft I cry'd——Why this Resistance, *Sylvia*? My charming Dear, whose are you? not *Philander*'s? and shall *Philander* not command his own——you must—ah cruel——then a soft Struggle follow'd, with half-breath'd Words, with Sighs and trembling Hearts, and now and then—— Ah cruel and unreasonable——was softly said on both Sides; thus strove, thus argu'd——'till both lay panting in each others Arms, not with the Toil, but Rapture; I need not say what follow'd after this——what tender Showers of strange indearing Mixtures 'twixt Joy and Shame, 'twixt Love and new Surprize, and ever when I dry'd your Eyes with Kisses, unable to repeat any other Language than——Oh my *Sylvia*! oh my charming Angel? while Sighs of Joy, and closely grasping thee——spoke all the rest—— while every tender Word, and every Sigh, was echo'd back by thee; you press'd me——and you vowed you lov'd me more than ever yet you did; then swore anew, and in my Bosom, hid your charming blushing Face, then with Excess of Love would call on Heav'n, be Witness, oh ye Powers (a thousand times ye cry'd) if ever Maid e'er lov'd like *Sylvia*——punish me strangely, oh eternal Powers, if e'er I leave *Philander*, if e'er I cease to love him; no Force, no Art, not Interest, Honour, Wealth, Convenience, Duty, or what other necessary Cause——shall never be of force to make me leave thee——Thus hast thou sworn, oh charming, faithless Flatterer, thus 'twixt each ravishing Minute thou would'st swear – and I fast believ'd – and lov'd thee more – Hast thou forgot it all, oh fickle Charmer, hast thou? Hast thou forgot between each awful Ceremony of Love how you cry'd out, Farewel the World and mortal Cares, give me *Philander*, Heav'n, I ask no more——Hast thou forgot all this? Did all the live-long Night hear any other Sound but those our mutual Vows, of Invocations, broken Sighs, and soft and trembling Whispers? say, had we any other Business for the tender Hours? Oh, all ye Host of Heav'n, ye Stars that shone, and all ye Powers the faithless lovely Maid has sworn by, be Witness how she's perjur'd; revenge it all, ye injur'd Powers, revenge it, since by it she has undone the faithfullest Youth, and broke the tenderest Heart——that ever fell a Sacrifice to Love; and all ye little weeping Gods of Love, revenge your murther'd Victim——your

PHILANDER

To PHILANDER

In the Leaves of a Table-Book

OH, my *Philander*, how dearly welcome, and how needless were thy kind Reproaches? which I'll not endeavour to convince by Argument, but such a Deed as shall at once secure thy Fears now and for the future. I have not a Minute to write in; place, my dear *Philander*, your Chariot in St. *Vincent*'s Wood, and since I am not able to fix the Hour of my Flight, let it wait there my coming; 'tis but a little Mile from *Bellfont, Dorillus* is suspected there, remove thy self to the High-way-Gate Cottage——there I'll call on thee ——'twas lucky, that thy Fears, or Love, or Jealousie brought thee so near me, since I'd resolv'd before upon my Flight. Parents and Honour, Interest and Fame, farewel——I leave you all to follow my *Philander*—— Haste the Chariot to the thickest Part of the Wood, for I'm impatient to be gone, and shall take the first Opportunity to fly to my *Philander*——Oh, love me, love me, love me!

Under Pretence of reaching the Jessamin which shades my Window, I un-perceiv'd let down and receive what Letters you send by the honest Weeder; by her send your Sense of my Flight, or rather your Direction, for 'tis resolv'd already.

To SYLVIA

My lovely Angel,
So careful I will be of this dear mighty Secret, that I will only say, *Sylvia* shall be obey'd; no more——nay, I'll not dare to think of it, lest in my Rapture I should name my Joy aloud, and busie Winds should bear it to some officious Listner, and undo me; no more, no more, my *Sylvia*, Extremes of Joy (as Grief) are ever dumb: Let it suffice, this Blessing which you proffer I had design'd to ask, as soon as you'd convinc'd me of your Faith; yes, *Sylvia*, I had ask'd it, though 'twas a Bounty too great for any Mortal to conceive Heav'n should bestow upon him; but if it do, that very

271

Moment I'll resign the World, and barter all for Love and charming *Sylvia*. Haste, haste, my Life; my Arms, my Bosom and my Soul are open to receive the lovely Fugitive; haste, for this Moment I am going to plant my self where you directed. *Adieu*.

To PHILANDER

After her Flight

AH, *Philander*, how have you undone a harmless poor unfortunate? Alas, where are you? why would you thus abandon me? Is this the Soul, the Bosom, these the Arms that should receive me? I'll not upbraid thee with my Love, or charge thee with my Undoing; 'twas all my own, and were it yet to do, I should again be ruin'd for *Philander*, and never find Repentance, no not for a Thought, a Word or Deed of Love, to the dear false forsworn; but I can die, yes, hopeless, friendless——left by all, even by *Philander*—— all but Resolution has abandon'd me and that can lay me down, whene'er I please, in safe Repose and Peace: But oh, thou art not false, or if thou be'st, oh, let me hear it from thy Mouth, see thy repented Love, that I may know there's no such thing on Earth, as Faith, as Honesty, as Love or Truth; however be thou true, or be thou false, be bold and let me know it, for thus to doubt is Torture worse than Death. What Accident, thou dear, dear Man, has happen'd to prevent thee from pursuing my Directions, and staying for me at the Gate? Where have I miss'd thee, thou Joy of my Soul? By what dire Mistake have I lost thee? And where, oh, where art thou, my charming Lover? I sought thee every where, but like the languishing abandon'd Mistress in the *Canticles*, I sought thee, but I found thee not, no Bed of Roses would discover thee; I saw no Print of thy dear Shape, nor heard no amorous Sigh that could direct me——I ask'd the Wood and Springs, complain'd and call'd on thee through all the Groves, but they confess'd thee not; nothing but Echo's answer'd me, and when I cry'd *Philander*——cry'd——*Philander*; thus search'd I 'till the coming Night and my increasing Fears made me resolve for Flight, which soon we did, and soon arriv'd at *Paris*, but whither then to go, Heav'n knows, I could not tell, for I was almost naked, friendless and forlorn; at last, consulting *Brilliard* what to do, after a thousand Revolutions, he concluded to trust me with a Sister he had, who was marry'd to a *Guidon* of the *Guard de Corps*, he chang'd my Name, and made me pass for a Fortune[3] he had stol'n; but oh, no Welcomes, nor my safe Retreat were sufficient to repose me all the ensuing Night, for I had no News of *Philander*; no, not a Dream inform'd me; a thousand Fears and Jealousies have kept me waking, and *Brilliard*, who has been all Night in Pursuit of thee, is now return'd successless and distracted as thy *Sylvia*, for Duty and Generosity have almost the same Effects in him, with Love and Tenderness and Jealousie in me; and since *Paris* affords no News of thee, (which sure it would if thou wert in it, for oh, the Sun might hide himself with as much Ease as great *Philander*) he is resolved to search St. *Vincent*'s Wood, and all the adjacent Cottages and Groves; he thinks that you, not knowing of my Escape, may yet be waiting thereabouts; since quitting the Chariot for fear of being seen, you might be so far advanc'd into the Wood, as not to find the way back to the Thicket where the Chariot waited: 'Tis thus he feeds my Hope, and flatters my poor Heart, that fain would think thee true——or if thou be'st not——but curs'd be all such Thoughts, and far from *Sylvia*'s Soul; no, no, thou art not false, it cannot be, thou art a God, and art unchangeable: I know, by some Mistake, thou art attending me, as wild and impatient as I; perhaps thou think'st me false, and think'st I have not Courage to pursue my Love, and fly; and, thou perhaps art waiting for the Hour wherein thou think'st I'll give my self away to *Foscario*: Oh cruel and unkind! to think I loved so lightly, to think I would attend that fatal Hour; no, *Philander*, no, faithless, dear Enchanter: Last Night, the Eve to my intended Wedding-Day, having repos'd my Soul by my Resolves for Flight, and only waiting the lucky Minute for Escape, I set a willing Hand to every thing that was preparing for the Ceremony of the ensuing Morning; with that Pretence I got me early to my Chamber, try'd on a thousand Dresses, and ask'd a thousand Questions, all impertinent, which would do best, which look'd most gay and rich, then drest my Gown with Jewels, deck'd my Apartment up, and left nothing undone that might secure 'em both of my being pleas'd, and of my Stay; nay, and to give the less Suspicion, I undress'd my self even to my Under-Petticoat and Night-gown; I would not take a Jewel, not a Pistole, but left my Women finishing my Work, and carelesly, and thus undress'd, walk'd towards the Garden, and while every one was busie in their Office, getting my self out of Sight, I posted o'er the Meadow to the Wood as swift as *Daphne* from the God of Day, 'till I arriv'd most luckily where I found the Chariot waiting, attended by *Brilliard*; of whom when I (all fainting and breathless with my swift Flight) demanded his Lord, he lifted me into the Chariot, and cry'd, A little farther, *Madam*, you will find him; for he, for fear of making a Discovery, took yonder shaded Path—— towards which we went, but no dear Vision of my Love appear'd——And thus, my charming Lover, you have my kind Adventure; send me some Tidings back that you are found, that you are well, and lastly that you are mine, or this that should have been my Wedding-Day, will see it self that of the Death of

SYLVIA

Paris, Thursday, from my Bed, for want of Cloaths, or rather News from Philander.

To SYLVIA

My Life, my *Sylvia*, my eternal Joy, art thou then safe! and art thou reserv'd for *Philander*? am I so blest by Heav'n, by Love, and my dear charming Maid? Then let me die in Peace, since I have liv'd to see all that my Soul desires in *Sylvia*'s being mine; perplex not thy soft Heart with Fears or Jealousies, nor think so basely, so poorely of my Love, to need more Oaths or Vows; yet to confirm thee, I would swear my Breath away; but oh, it needs not here;——take then no Care, my lovely Dear, turn not thy charming Eyes or Thoughts on afflicting Objects; oh think not on what thou hast abandon'd, but what thou art arriv'd to; look forward on the Joys of Love and Youth, for I will dedicate all my remaining Life to render thine serene and glad; and yet my *Sylvia*, thou art so dear to me, so wondrous precious to my Soul, that in my Extravagance of Love, I fear I shall grow a troublesome and wearying Coxcomb, shall dread every Look thou giv'st away from me——a Smile will make me rave, a Sigh or touch make me commit a Murther on the happy Slave, or my own jealous Heart, but all the World besides is *Sylvia*'s, all but another Lover; but I rave and run too fast away; Ages must pass a tedious Term of Years before I can be jealous, or conceive thou can'st be weary of *Philander*——I'll be so fond, so doting and so playing, thou shalt not have an idle Minute to throw away a Look in, or a Thought or any other; no, no, I have thee now, and will maintain my Right by dint and force of Love——Oh, I am wild to see thee——but, *Sylvia*, I am wounded——do not be frighted though, for 'tis not much or dangerous, but very troublesome, since it permits me not to fly to *Sylvia*, but she must come to me in order to it. *Brilliard* has a Bill on my Goldsmith in *Paris* for a thousand Pistoles to buy thee something to put on; any thing that's ready, and he will conduct thee to me, for I shall rave my self into a Feaver if I see thee not to Day——I cannot live without thee now, for thou art my Life, my everlasting Charmer: I have order'd *Brilliard* to get a Chariot and some unknown Livery for thee, and I think the Continuance of passing for what he has already render'd thee will do very well, 'till I have taken farther care of thy dear Safety, which will be as soon as I am able to rise; for most unfortunately, my dear *Sylvia*, quitting the Chariot in the Thicket for fear of being seen with it, and walking down a shaded Path that suited with the Melancholy and Fears of Unsuccess in thy Adventure; I went so far, as e'er I could return to the Place where I left the Chariot, 'twas gone——it seems with thee; I know not how you miss'd me——but possess'd my self with a thousand false Fears, sometimes that in thy Flight thou might'st be pursu'd and overtaken, seiz'd in the Chariot and return'd back to *Bellfont*; or that the Chariot was found and seiz'd on upon Suspicion, though the Coachman and *Brilliard* were disguis'd past Knowledge——or if thou wert gone, alas, I knew not whither; but that was a Thought my Doubts and Fears would not suffer me to ease my Soul with; no, I (as jealous Lovers do) imagin'd the most tormenting things for my own Repose, I imagin'd the Chariot taken, or at least so discover'd as to be forc'd away without thee: I imagin'd that thou wert false——Heav'n forgive me, false, my *Sylvia*, and hadst chang'd thy Mind; mad with this Thought (which I fancy'd most reasonable, and fixt it in my Soul) I rav'd about the Wood, making a thousand Vows to be reveng'd on all; in order to it I left the Thicket, and betook my self to the high Road of the Wood, where I laid me down amongst the Fern, close hid, with Sword ready, waiting for the happy Bridegroom, whom I knew (it being the Wedding Eve) would that Way pass that Evening; pleas'd with Revenge, which now had got even the Place of Love, I waited there not above a little hour but heard the trampling of a Horse, and looking up with mighty Joy, I found it *Foscario*'s; alone he was, and unattended, for he'd outstripp'd his Equipage, and with a Lover's Haste, and full of Joy, was making towards *Bellfont*; but I (now fir'd with Rage) leap'd from my Cover, cry'd, Stay, *Foscario*, e'er you arrive to *Sylvia*, we must adjust an odd Account between us——at which he stopping, as nimbly alighted;——in fine, we fought, and many Wounds were given and received on both Sides, till his People coming up, parted us just as we were fainting with Loss of Blood in each others Arms; his Coach and Chariot were amongst his Equipage; into the first his Servants lifted him, when he cry'd out with a feeble Voice, to have me, who now lay bleeding on the Ground, put into the Chariot, and to be safely convey'd where-ever I commanded, and so in haste they drove him towards *Bellfont*, and me, who was resolved not to stir far from it, to a Village within a Mile of it; from whence I sent to *Paris* for a Surgeon, and dismiss'd the Chariot, ordering, in the hearing of the Coachman, a Litter to be brought me immediately, to convey me that Night to *Paris*; but the Surgeon coming, found it not safe for me to be removed, and I am now willing to live, since *Sylvia* is mine; haste to me then, my lovely Maid, and fear not being discover'd, for I have given Order here in the Cabaret where I am, if any Enquiry is made after me, to say, I went last Night for *Paris*: Haste, my Love, haste to my Arms, as feeble as they are, they'll grasp thee a dear Welcome: I'll say no more, nor prescribe Rules to thy Love, that can inform thee best what thou must do to save the Life of thy most passionate Adorer,

PHILANDER

To PHILANDER

I Have sent *Brilliard* to see if the Coast be clear, that we may come with Safety; he brings you, instead of *Sylvia*, a young Cavalier that will be alto-

275

gether as welcome to *Philander*, and who impatiently waits his Return at a little Cottage at the end of the Village.

To SYLVIA

From the Bastill

I Know my *Sylvia* expected me at home with her at Dinner to Day, and wonders how I could live so long as since Morning without the eternal Joy of my Soul; but know, my *Sylvia*, that a trivial Misfortune is now fallen upon me, which in the midst of all our Heav'n of Joys, our softest Hours of Life, has so often chang'd thy Smiles into Fears and Sighings, and ruffled thy calm Soul with Cares: Nor let it now seem strange or afflicting, since every Day for these three Months we have been alarm'd with new Fears that have made thee uneasie even in *Philander*'s Arms; we knew some time or other the Storm would fall on us, though we had for three happy Months shelter'd our selves from its threatning Rage; but Love, I hope, has arm'd us both; for me——let me be depriv'd of all Joys, (but those my Charmer can dispense) all the false World's Respect, the dull Esteem of Fools and formal Coxcombs, the grave Advice of the censorious Wife, the kind Opinion of ill judging Women, no matter, so my *Sylvia* remain but mine.

I am, my *Sylvia*, arrested at the Suit of *Monsieur* the Count your Father for a Rape on my lovely Maid: I desire, my Soul, you will immediately take Coach and go to the Prince *Cesario*, and he will bail me out. I fear not a fair Trial; and, *Sylvia*, Thefts of mutual Love were never counted Felony; I may die for Love, my *Sylvia*, but not for Loving——go, haste, my *Sylvia*, that I may be no longer detain'd from the solid Pleasure and Business of my Soul——haste, my lov'd Dear——haste and relieve

PHILANDER

Come not to me, lest there should be an Order to detain my Dear.

To PHILANDER

I Am not at all surpriz'd, my *Philander*, at the Accident that has befallen thee, because so long expected, and Love that has so well fortify'd my Heart, that I support our Misfortune with a Courage worthy of her that loves and is belov'd by the glorious *Philander*; I am arm'd for the worst that can befal me, and that is my being render'd a publick Shame, who have been so in the private Whispers of all the Court for near these happy three Months, in which I have had the wondrous Satisfaction of being retir'd from the World with the charming *Philander*; my Father too knew it long since, at least he could not hinder himself from guessing it, though his fond Indulgence suffer'd his Justice and his Anger to sleep, and possibly had still slept had not *Myrtilla*'s Spight and Rage (I should say just Resentment, but I cannot) rouz'd up his drowsie Vengeance: I know she has ply'd him with her softning Eloquence, her Prayers and Tears, to win him to consent to make a publick Business of it; but I am enter'd, Love has arm'd my Soul, and I'll pursue my Fortune with that height of Fortitude as shall surprize the World; yes, *Philander*, since I have lost my Honour, Fame and Friends, my Interest and my Parents, and all for mightier Love, I'll stop at nothing now; if there be any Hazards more to run, I'll thank the spireful Fates that bring 'em on, and will even tire them out with my unweary'd Passion. Love on, *Philander*, if thou darst, like me; let 'em pursue me with their Hate and Vengeance, let Prisons, Poverty and Tortures seize me, it shall not take one Grain of Love away from my resolved Heart, nor make me shed a Tear of Penitence for loving thee; no, *Philander*, since I know what a ravishing Pleasure 'tis to live thine, I will never quit the Glory of dying also thy

SYLVIA

Cesario, *my Dear, is coming to be your Bail* (*with* Monsieur *the Count of*——
I die to see you after your suffering for Sylvia.

To SYLVIA

Believe me, charming *Sylvia*, I live not those Hours I am absent from thee, thou art my Life, my Soul, and my Eternal Felicity; while you believe this Truth, my *Sylvia*, you will not entertain a thousand Fears, if I but stay a Moment beyond my appointed Hour; especially when *Philander*, who is not able to support the Thought that any thing should afflict his lovely Baby, takes care from Hour to Hour to satisfie her tender doubting Heart. My dearest, I am gone into the City to my Advocate's, my Trial with *Monsieur* the Count, your Father, coming on to Morrow, and 'twill be at least two tedious Hours e'er I can bring my Adorable her

PHILANDER

To SYLVIA

I Was call'd on, my dearest Child, at my Advocate's by *Cesario*; there is some great Business this Evening debated in the Cabal which is at *Monsieur*

—— in the City; *Cesario* tells me there is a very diligent Search made by *Monsieur* the Count, your Father, for my *Sylvia*; I die if you are taken, lest the Fright should hurt thee; if possible, I would have thee remove this Evening from those Lodgings, lest the People, who are of the Royal Party, should be induc'd thro' Malice or Gain to discover thee; I dare not come my self to wait on thee, lest my being seen should betray thee, but I have sent *Brilliard* (whose Zeal for thee shall be rewarded) to conduct thee to a little House in the *Fauxburgh S. Germans*, where lives a pretty Woman, and Mistress to *Chevalier Tomaso*, call'd *Belinda*, a Woman of Wit, and discreet enough to understand what ought to be paid to a Maid of the Quality and Character of *Sylvia*; she already knows the Stories of our Loves; thither I'll come to thee, and bring *Cesario* to Supper, as soon as the Cabal breaks up. Oh, my *Sylvia*, I shall one Day recompense all thy Goodness, all thy Bravery, thy Love and thy Suffering for thy Eternal Lover and Slave,

PHILANDER

To PHILANDER

So hasty I was to obey *Philander*'s Commands, that by the unweary'd Care and Industry of the faithful *Brilliard*, I went before three a Clock disguis'd away to the Place whither you order'd us, and was well receiv'd by the very pretty young Woman of the House, who has Sense and Breeding as well as Beauty: But oh, *Philander*, this Flight pleases me not; alas, what have I done? my Fault is only Love, and that sure I should boast, as the most Divine Passion of the Soul; no, no *Philander*, 'tis not my Love's the Criminal, no, not the placing it on *Philander* the Crime, but 'tis thy most unhappy Circumstances, thy being marry'd, and that was no Crime to Heav'n 'till Man made Laws, and can Laws reach to Damnation? if so, curse on the fatal Hour that thou wert marry'd, curse on the Priest that join'd ye, and curst be all that did contribute to the undoing Ceremony—— except *Philander*'s Tongue, that answer'd Yes——Oh, Heav'ns! was there but one dear Man of all your whole Creation that could charm the Soul of *Sylvia*? and could ye——oh, ye wise all-seeing Powers that knew my Soul, could ye give him away? How had my Innocence offended ye? Our Hearts you did create for mutual Love, how came the dire Mistake? Another would have pleas'd the indifferent *Myrtilla*'s Soul as well, but mine was fitted for no other Man; only *Philander*, the ador'd *Philander*, with that dear Form, that Shape, that charming Face, that Hair, those lovely speaking Eyes, that wounding Softness in his tender Voice, had Pow'r to conquer *Sylvia*; and can this be a Sin? oh, Heav'ns, can it? must Laws, which Man contriv'd for mere Conveniency, have Power to alter the divine

278

Decrees at our Creation——Perhaps they argue to morrow at the Bar, that *Myrtilla* was ordain'd by Heaven for *Philander*; no, no, he mistook the Sister, 'twas pretty near he came, but by a fatal Error was mistaken; his hasty Youth made him too negligently stop before his time at the wrong Woman, he should have gaz'd a little farther on——and then it had been *Sylvia*'s Lot——'Tis fine Divinity they teach, that cry Marriages are made in Heav'n——Folly and Madness grown into grave Custom; should an unheedy Youth in heat of Blood take up with the first convenient She that offers, though he be an Heir to some grave Politician, great and rich, and She the Outcast of the common Stews, coupled in Height of Wine, and sudden Lust, which once allay'd, and that the sober Morning wakes him to see his Error, he quits with Shame the Jilt, and owns no more the Folly; shall this be called a heav'nly Conjunction? Were I in Height of Youth, as now I am, forc'd by my Parents, oblig'd by Interest and Honour, to marry the old, deform'd, diseas'd, decrepid Count *Anthonio*, whose Person, Qualities and Principles I loath, and rather than suffer him to consummate his Nuptials, suppose I should (as sure I should) kill my self, 'twere Blasphemy to lay this fatal Marriage to Heav'ns Charge——Curse on your Nonsense, ye imposing Gownmen, curse on your holy Cant; you may as well call Rapes and Murthers, Treason and Robbery, the Acts of Heav'n; because Heav'n suffers 'em to be committed, is it Heav'n's Pleasure therefore, Heav'ns Decree? A Trick, a wise Device of Priests, no more——to make the nauseated, tir'd out Pair drag on the careful Business of Life, drudge for the dull got Family with greater Satisfaction, because they're taught to think Marriage was made in Heav'n; a mighty Comfort that, when all the Joys of Life are lost by it: Were it not nobler far that Honour kept him just, and that Good-nature made him reasonable Provision? Daily Experience proves to us, no Couple live with less Content, less Ease, than those who cry Heav'n joins? who is't loves less than those that marry? and where Love is not, there is Hate and Loathing at best, Disgust, Disquiet, Noise and Repentance: No, *Philander*, that's a heav'nly Match when two Souls touch'd with equal Passion meet, (which is but rarely seen) ——when willing Vows, with serious Consideration, are weigh'd and made, when a true View is taken of the Soul, when no base Interest makes the hasty Bargain, when no Conveniency or Design or Drudge, or Slave, shall find it necessary, when equal Judgments meet that can esteem the Blessings they possess, and distinguish the good of either's Love, and set a Value on each other's Merits, and where both understand to take and pay; who find the Beauty of each other's Minds, and rate 'em as they ought; whom not a formal Ceremony binds, (with which I've nought to do, but dully give a cold consenting Affirmative) but well consider'd Vows from soft inclining Hearts, utter'd with Love, with Joy, with dear Delight, when Heav'n is call'd to witness; she is thy Wife, *Philander* he is my Husband;

this is the Match, this Heav'n designs and means; how then, oh how came I to miss *Philander*? or he his

SYLVIA

Since I writ this, which I design'd not an Invective against Marriage, when I began, but to inform thee of my being where you directed; but since I writ this, I say, the House where I am is broken open with Warrants and Officers for me, but being all undress'd and ill, the officer has taken my Word for my Appearance to Morrow; it seems they saw me when I went from my Lodgings, and pursu'd me; haste to me, for I shall need your Counsel.

To SYLVIA

MY Eternal Joy, my Affliction is inexpressible at the News you send me of your being surpriz'd; I am not able to wait on thee yet——not being suffer'd to leave the Cabal, I only borrow this Minute to tell thee the Sense of my Advocate in this case; which was, if thou shouldst be taken there was no way, no Law to save thee from being ravish'd from my Arms, but that of marrying thee to some Body whom I can trust; this we have often discours'd, and thou hast often vow'd thou'lt do any thing rather than kill me with a Separation; resolve then, oh thou Charmer of my Soul, to do a Deed, that though the Name would fright thee, only can preserve both thee and me; it is——and tho' it have no other Terror in it than the Name, I faint to speak it——to marry, *Sylvia*; yes, thou must marry; tho' thou art mine as fast as Heav'n can make us, yet thou must marry; I've pitch'd upon the Property, 'tis *Brilliard*, him I can only trust in this Affair; it is but joining Hands——no more, my *Sylvia*,——*Brilliard's* a Gentleman, tho' a *Cadet*, and may be suppos'd to pretend to so great a Happiness, and whose only Crime is want of Fortune; he's handsome too, well made, well bred, and so much real Esteem he has for me, and I've so oblig'd him, that I am confident he'll pretend no farther than to the Honour of owning thee in Court; I'll time him from it, nay, he dares not do't, I'll trust him with my Life——but oh, *Sylvia* is more——think of it, and this Night we will perform it, there being no other way to keep *Sylvia* eternally

PHILANDER'S

To SYLVIA

Now, my adorable *Sylvia*, you have truly need of all that heroick Bravery of Mind I ever thought thee Mistress of; for, *Sylvia*, coming from thee this

Morning, and riding full speed for *Paris*, I was met, stopt and seiz'd for High-Treason by the King's Messengers, and possibly may fall a Sacrifice to the Anger of an incens'd Monarch. My *Sylvia*, bear this last Shock of Fate with a Courage worthy thy great and glorious Soul; 'tis but a little Separation, *Sylvia*, and we shall one Day meet again; by Heav'n I find no other Sting in Death but parting with my *Sylvia*, and every Parting would have been the same; I might have dy'd by thy Disdain, thou might'st have grown weary of thy *Philander*, have lov'd another, and have broke thy Vows, and tortur'd me to Death these crueller ways; but Fate is kinder to me, and I go blest with my *Sylvia*'s Love, for which Heav'n may do much, for her dear sake, to recompense her Faith, a Maid so innocent and true to sacred Love; expect the best, my lovely Dear, the worst has this Comfort in't, that I shall die my charming *Sylvia*'s

PHILANDER

To PHILANDER

I'LL only say, thou dear Supporter of my Soul, that if *Philander* dies, he shall not go to Heav'n without his *Sylvia*——by Heav'n and Earth I swear it, I cannot live without thee, nor shalt thou die without thy

SYLVIA

To SYLVIA

SEE, see my adorable Angel, what Cares the Powers above take of Divine Innocence, true Love and Beauty; oh, see what they have done for their darling *Sylvia*; could they do less?

Know, my dear Maid, that after being examined before the King, I was found guilty enough to be committed to the *Bastile*, (from whence, if I had gone, I had never return'd, but to my Death;) but the Messenger, into whose Hands I was committed, refusing other Guards, being alone with me in my own Coach, I resolv'd to kill if I could no other way oblige him to favour my Escape; I try'd with Gold before I shew'd my Dagger, and that prevail'd, a way less Criminal, and I have taken Sanctuary in a small Cottage near the Sea-shore, where I wait for *Sylvia*; and tho' my Life depend upon my Flight, nay, more, the Life of *Sylvia*, I cannot go without her; dress yourself then, my dearest, in your Boy's Cloaths, and haste with *Brilliard*, whither this Seaman will conduct thee, whom I have hir'd to set us on some Shore of Safety; bring what News you can learn of *Cesario*; I would not have him die poorly after all his mighty Hopes, nor be conducted to a Scaffold with Shouts of Joy, by that uncertain Beast the Rabble, who us'd to stop his Chariot-wheels with fickle Adorations whene'er he look'd abroad——by Heav'n, I pity him; but *Sylvia*'s Presence will chase away all Thoughts, but those of Love, from

PHILANDER

I need not bid thee haste.

The End of the first Part

NOTES

[1] *Cadet:* a gentleman who entered the army without a commission to find a carrier for himself; it was regularly done by younger sons of a family.

[2] *to fee:* obsolete word for 'to bribe'.

[3] *Fortune:* short for: a woman of fortune; an heiress.

Select Bibliography

TEXTS[1]

anon.: *The Academy of Complements, or A New Way of Wooing*. London, 1685.
The Athenian Gazette: or Casuistical Mercury, Resolving all the most Nice and Curious Questions proposed by the Ingenious. London, 1690–1697.

Beaumont, Robert: *Loves Missives to Virtue*. London, 1660.

[Behn, Aphra]: *Love-Letters between a Noble–Man and his Sister*. London, 1694. (Part I 1689, Part II, III 1693).

Boyer, Abel: *Letters of Wit, Politicks and Morality . . . Also Select Letters of Gallantry . . . To which is added a large Collection of Original Letters of Love and Friendship. Written, by several Gentlemen and Ladies, particularly . . . Capt. Ayloffe; . . .* London, 1701.

Breton, Nicholas: *The Good and the Badde, or Descriptions of the Worthies and Unworthies of his Age*. London, 1616.

Breton, Nicholas: *A Poste with a Packet of Mad Letters*. London, 1609.

Brown, Thomas: *Letters from the Dead to the Living. By Mr. Tho. Brown, Capt. Ayloffe, Mr. Hen. Barker, etc. . . . And several others with their Answers*. London, 1702.

Brown, Thomas (Ed.): *The Works of Monsieur Voiture . . . Containing His Familiar Letters To Gentlemen and Ladies. Made English by John Dryden Esq., Thomas Cheek, Esq., . . . With Three Collections of Letters on Friendship and several other Occasions: Written by John Dryden, Esq., William Wycherley, Esq., William Congreve, Esq., Mr. Dennis, Mr. –, Mr. Tho. Brown, Mr. Edward Ward. And Facetious Letters out of Greek, Latin and French. By the late Ingenious Mr. Tho. Brown*. London, 1705.

anon.: *The Double Captive, or Chains upon Chains: Containing the Amorous Poems and Letters of A Young Gentleman, one of the Preston Prisoners in Newgate . . .* London, 1718.

Cavendish, Margaret Duchess of Newcastle: *CCXI Sociable Letters*. London, 1664.

anon. (Campbell, John?): *The Polite Correspondence: or, Rational Amusement; Being A Series of Letters Philosophical, Poetical, Historical, Critical, Amorous, Moral and Satyrical*. London (1740?).

Costeker, John Littleton: *The Constant Lovers: Being an Entertaining History of the Amours and Adventures of . . . Alexis and Sylvia . . .* London, 1731.

Davys, Mary: *Familiar Letters Betwixt a Gentleman and a Lady*. (1725). Ed. A. Day. Publications of the Augustan Reprint Society, No. 54, Los Angeles, 1955.

Defoe, Daniel: *The Little Review; or, an Inquisition of Scandal; Consisting in Answers of Questions and Doubts, Remarks, Observation and Reflection*. (6 June – 22 Aug., London, 1705, 23 nos.).

[Dunton, John]: *The Challenge, Sent by a Young Lady to Sir Thomas – etc., or the Female War . . . The Whole Encounter consists of Six Hundred Letters, Pro and Con, on all the Disputable Points relating to Women . . .* London, 1697.

Earle, John: *Micro-cosmographie, or a Peece of the World Discovered. In Essayes and Characters*. London, 1628.

Farquhar, George: *Love and Business in a Collection of Occasionary Verse and Epistolary Prose*. London, 1702. (Ed. Charles Stonehill, *The Complete Works of George Farquhar* ..., London, 1930, Vol. II, pp. 271–343).

The Free-Thinker (London, 24 March 1718 – 28 July 1721, 350 nos.).

G., D.: *A Sunday's Adventure, or, Walk to Hackney. Being A Description of an Amorous Intrigue Acted there*. London, 1683.

Gildon, Charles: *The Post-boy rob'd of his Mail: or, the Pacquet broke open. Consisting of Five hundred Letters, to Persons of several Qualities and Conditions. With Observations upon each Letter. Publish'd by a Gentleman concern'd in the Frolick*. London, 1692.

H., M.: *The Lover's Week: or, the Six Days Adventures of Philander and Amaryllis. Written by a Young Lady*. London, 1718 (by Mrs. Mary Hearne?).

Hall, Joseph: *Characters of Vertues and Vices*. London, 1608.

Haywood, Eliza: *Love-Letters on All Occasions Lately passed between Persons of Distinction. Collected by Mrs. Eliza Haywood*. London, 1730.

[Haywood, Eliza]: *The Female Spectator*. (London, April 1744 – March 1746, 24 nos.).

Hill, John: *The Young Secretary's Guide. Or a Speedy Help to Learning*. London, 1687.

anon.: *A Letter from Mrs. Jane Jones, alias Jenny Diver, In Drury-Lane, to Mrs. Arabella B——wl——s, Near Wine-Office Court, Fleetstreet* ... London, 1737.

anon.: *Letters of Love and Gallantry and several other Subjects. All Written by Ladies*. Vol. I., London, 1963, vol. II., London, 1694.

anon.: *Familiar Letters of Love, Gallantry, And Several Occasions, By the Wits of the last and present Age, From their Originals. Together with Mr. T. Brown's Remains* ..., 2 vols. London, 1718.

anon.: *Letters upon several Occasions; written by and between Mr. Dryden, Mr. Wycherley, Mr.——, Mr. Congreve and Mr. Dennis. With a new Translation of Select Letters of Monsieur Voiture* ... London, 1696. (appeared in 1700 under the title of *Letters of Friendship and several other occasions*).

Lillie, Charles: *Original and Genuine Letters sent to the Tatler and Spectator, During the Time those Works were publishing. None of which have been before Printed*. 2 vols. London, 1725.

anon.: *The Adventures of Lindamira, A Lady of Quality. Written by her Own Hand to her Friend in the Country. In IV Parts Revised and Corrected by Mr. Tho. Brown*. London, 1702. Ed. Benjamin Boyce. Minneapolis, 1949.

The Lover. (25 Febr. 1714 – 27 May 1714, 40 nos.). Ed. R. Steele, reprinted in book form: *The Lover and the Reader*, London, 1715.

anon.: *Love's Poesie, or a Collection of Seven and Twenty Love-Letters, Both in Verse and Prose; That lately pass'd betwixt a Gentleman and a Very Young Lady in France*. London, 1686.

(anon. translation of *Le commerce galant, ou Lettres tendres et galants de la jeune Iris & de Timandre*, Paris, 1682).

[Manley, Mary de la Rivière]: *Court Intrigues, in a Collection of Original Letters, from the Island of the New Atlantis, etc. By the Author of those Memoirs*. London, 1711.

[Manley, Mary de la Rivière]: *The Unknown Lady's Pacquet of Letters Taken from her By a French Privateer in a Holland* ... London, 1707.

Manley, Mary de la Rivière: *A Stage-Coach Journey to Exeter. Describing The Humours on The Road, with the Characters and Adventures of the Company. In Eight Letters to a Friend.* London, 1725.

Overbury, Sir Thomas: *A Wife Now the Widdow of Sir Thomas Overburye. Being A most exquisite and singular Poem of the choice of a Wife. Whereunto are added many witty characters* ... London, 1614.

P., W., Gent.: *The Wit's Academy: or the Muse's Delight, Consisting of Merry Dialogues* ... *As Also Divers sorts of Letters upon Several occasions* ... London, 1677.

anon.: *Love Letters Between Polydorus The Gothick King, and Messalina, Late Queen of Albion.* Paris, 1689.

'Portuguese Letters': *Five Love-Letters from a Nun to a Cavalier Done out of French into English by Roger L.Estrange.* London, 1678 (Ed. E. Prestage, *The Letters of a Portuguese Nun.* Portland Maine, 1900).

Letters from a Portuguese Nun written in the year 1667 by Marina Alcoforado. Translated by Lucy Norton, with an introduction by Raymond Mortimer. London, 1956.

anon.: *Seven Portuguese Letters; Being a Second Part to the Five Love-Letters from a Nun to a Cavalier.* London, 1681.

anon.: *Five Love-Letters Written by a Cavalier, in Answer to the Five Love-Letters Written to him by a Nun.* 1683. (anon. transl. of anon., *Réponse aux lettres portugaises,* 1669).

anon.: *Post-Office Intelligence: or Universal Gallantry. Being a Collection of Love-Letters, Written by Persons, in all Stations, from most Parts of the Kingdom* ... London, 1736.

Richardson, Samuel: *Clarissa, Or, The History of a Young Lady Comprehending the most Important Concerns of her Private Life. And particularly shewing, The Distress that may attend the Misconduct Both of Parents and Children, In Relating to Marriage.* 7 vols., London, 1748.

Richardson, Samuel: *The History of Sir Charles Grandison. In a Series of Letters Published from the Originals By the Editor of Pamela and Clarissa.* 7 vols., London 1754.

[Richardson, Samuel]: *Letters Written To and For Particular Friends* . . . London, 1741.

[Richardson, Samuel]: *Pamela: or, Virtue Rewarded. In a Series of Familiar Letters from a Beautiful young Damsel, To her Parents. Now first Published In order to cultivate the Principles of Virtue and Religion in the Minds of the Youth of Both Sexes.* 4 vols., London, 1741–1742.

Rowe, Elizabeth: *Friendship in Death, in Twenty Letters from the Dead to the Living.* London, 1728.

Rowe, Elizabeth: *Letters Moral and Entertaining, in Prose and Verse.* London, 1728.

The Spectator. (London, 1 March – 6 Dec. 1712, 555 nos.). Ed. George A. Aitken, 6 vols., n.d. (The New Universal Library).

The Tatler. By Isaac Bickerstaff. Esq. (London, 12 April 1709 – 2–4 January 1711, 271 nos.).

Wilmot, John; Second Earl of Rochester: *Familiar Letters: Written by the Right Honourable John late Earl of Rochester, And several other Persons of Honour and Quality* ... London, 1697.

anon.: *Wit's Cabinet: A Companion For Gentleman and Ladies.* London, 1684.

REFERENCE BOOKS

Baker, Ernest A.: *The History of the English Novel*. 10 vols., London, 1924-1939.

Bechstein, Julius: *Richardsons 'Pamela', nach ihrem Gedankengehalt betrachtet. Mit einem Anhang: Die Quellenfrage bei der 'Pamela'*. Bremen, 1929.

Black, Frank Gee: 'The Technique of Letter Fiction in English from 1740 to 1800'. In: *Harvard Studies and Notes in Philology and Literature* XV, 1933, pp. 291-312.

Bond, Richmond Pugh (ed.): *New Letters to the 'Tatler' and 'Spectator'*. Austin, 1959.

Bond, Richmond Pugh: *Studies in the Early English Periodical*. Chapel Hill, 1957.

Booth, Wayne C.: 'The Self-Conscious Narrator in Comic Fiction before *Tristram Shandy*'. In: *PMLA* LXVII, 1952, pp. 163-185.

Bryant, Sir Arthur Wynne Morgan (ed.): *Postman's Horn. An Anthology of Letters of the Latter Seventeenth Century England*. London, 1936.

Crawford, Batholow V.: 'The Use of Formal Dialogue in Narrative'. In: *Philological Quarterly* I, 1922, pp. 179-191.

Danielowski, Emma: *Die Journale der frühen Quäker*. Berlin, 1921.

Danielowski, Emma: *Richardsons erster Roman. Entstehungsgeschichte*. Diss. Tubingen, 1917.

Day, Robert A.: *The Epistolary Technique in English Prose Fiction. 1660-1740*, (Unpubl. Harvard Diss. 1952).

Day, Robert A. (ed.): *Mary Davy's Familiar Letters Betwixt a Gentleman and a Lady* (1725). With an Introduction and a Bibliography of Epistolary Fiction 1660-1740. Publ. of The Augustan Reprint Society, 54, Los Angeles, 1955.

Day, Robert A.: *Told in Letters. Epistolary Fiction Before Richardson*, Ann Arbor, 1966.

Dottin, Paul: 'Samuel Richardson et le roman epistolaire'. In: *Revue anglo-americaine* XIII, 1936, pp. 481-99.

Forster, E. M.: *Aspects of the Novel*. London, 1927.

Green, F. C.: 'Who was the Author of the "Lettres portugaises" ' In: *Modern Language Review* XXI, 1926, pp. 159-167.

Hamburger, Käte: *Die Logik der Dichtung*. Stuttgart, 1957.

Hornbeak, Katherine Gee: *The Complete Letter Writer in English*. Smith College Studies in Modern Languages, vol. XI, no. 3, Northampton, Mass., 1934.

Hudson, Derek: *British Journalists and Newspapers*, London, 1945.

Hughes, Helen Sard: 'English Epistolary Fiction before Pamela'. In: *The Manly Anniversary Studies in Language and Literature*, Chicago, 1923, pp. 156-69.

Irving, William Henry: *The Providence of Wit in the English Letter Writers*. Durham, N.C., 1955.

Kany, Charles E.: *The Beginnings of the Epistolary Novel in France, Italy and Spain*. Berkeley, Cal., 1937.

Lämmert, Eberhard: *Bauformen des Erzählens*. Stuttgart, 1955.

McKillop, Alan D.: 'Epistolary Technique in Richardson's Novels'. In: *Rice Institute Pamphlet* XXXVIII, 1951, no. 1, pp. 36-54.

Merrill, Elizabeth: *The Dialogue in English Literature*. New York, 1911.

Morgan, Charlotte E.: *The Rise of the Novel of Manners. A Study of English Prose Fiction Between 1600 and 1740*. New York, 1911.

Pascal, Roy: *Design and Truth in Autobiography*. London, 1966.

Petsch, Robert: 'Der epische Dialog'. In: *Euphorion* XXXII, 1931, pp. 187-205.

Purpus, Eugene R.: 'The "Plain, Easy, and Familiar Way"; The Dialogue in English Literature, 1660–1725'. In: *A Journal of English Literary History* XVII, 1950, pp. 47–58.

Robertson, Jean: *The Art of Letter Writing. An Essay on the Handbooks Published in England During the Sixteenth and Seventeenth Centuries*, London & Liverpool, 1942.

Romberg, Bertil: *Studies in the Narrative Technique of the First-Person Novel*, Stockholm, 1962.

Singer, Godfrey Frank: *The Epistolary Novel. Its Origin Development, Decline, and Residuary Influence*, Philadelphia, 1933.

Spearman, Diana: *The Novel and Society.* London, 1966.

Stanzel, Franz K.: *Die typischen Erzählsituationen im Roman. Dargestellt an Tom Jones, Moby-Dick, The Ambassadors, Ulysses.* Wien, 1955.

Voss, Ernst Theodor: *Erzählprobleme des Briefromans dargestellt an vier Beispielen des 18. Jahrhunderts. Sophie La Roche, 'Geschichte des Fräulein von Stern-heim'. Joh. Wolfg. Goethe, 'Die Leiden des jungen Werther'. Joh. Timoth. Hermes. 'Sophiens Reise von Memel nach Sachsen'. Christoph Martin Wieland, 'Aristipp und einige seiner Zeitgenossen'*, Diss. Bonn, 1960.

Watt, Ian: *The Rise of the Novel. Studies in Defoe, Richardson and Fielding.* London, 1957.

Whicher, George Frisbie: *The Life and Romances of Mrs. Eliza Haywood.* New York, 1912.

Würzbach, Natascha: *Die Struktur des Briefromans und seine Entstehung in England.* Diss. München, 1964.

NOTE
[1] In listing titles in both the bibliography and the notes, I have retained capitals in prepositions, articles, and conjunctions wherever they can be identified as capitals. The problem arises because words which are not nouns are often capitalised.

Corrections to the Text

Obvious misprints in the original texts have been silently corrected. For the interested reader, these corrections are listed below, with the original reading first, followed by the corrected version.

page	line	
16	36	very well) Unfortunate,: very well). Unfortunate
21	30	Necesity: Necessity
34	15	his Maidenhead: her Maidenhead
35	13	could never a Love a Woman: could never Love a Woman
36	5	foolshly: foolishly
41	17	ungreatful: ungrateful
42	3	perserving: persevering
42	7	Powder: Power
42	41	Lanlady's: Landlady's
43	10	a very honest a Gentleman: a very honest Gentleman
43	29	Phanton: Phantom
43	36	Business call'd her: Business [that] call'd her
43	41	shoul: should
44	29	the the finest: the finest
44	30	leasst: least
44	43	Gaiety;: Gaiety
45	1	by me: by me;
47	18	She ask me: She ask'd me
48	7	Maids: Maid
48	16	to: so
49	14	as I as was kneeling: as I was kneeling
49	36–7	and in the Chamber: and [I was] in the Chamber
51	16	did but laught: did but laugh
52	16	Fondess: Fondness
58	33	must to be a Woman: must be to a Woman
60	26–7	worthy and better Fate: worthy a better Fate
60	27	by guarding me: by guarding you
97	6	Lay: Way
129	3	light of: light on
163	41	ach: ache
178	31	My Father going: My Father [is] going
183	40	Eagness: Eagerness
193	23	News please me: News [which] please me
208	9	*Silvia*: *Sylvia*
209	30	Tormentor's past: Tormentor, 's past
222	33	PHYLANDER: PHILANDER